Thinking Small

··· Ballantine Books ··· New York

Andrea Hiott

Thinking Small

○ ○

The Long, Strange Trip of
the Volkswagen Beetle

Published in the United States by Ballantine Books, an imprint
of The Random House Publishing Group, a division of Random
House, Inc., New York.

BALLANTINE and colophon are registered trademarks of
Random House, Inc.

LIBRARY OF CONGRESS CATALOGING-IN-PUBLICATION DATA

Hiott, Andrea.
Thinking small : the long, strange trip of the Volkswagen Beetle /
Andrea Hiott.
p.   cm.
Includes bibliographical references and index.
ISBN 978-0-345-52142-2 (hardcover)—ISBN 978-0-345-52144-6 (eBook)
1. Volkswagen Beetle automobile—History. I. Title.
TL215.V618H56 2012
629.222'2—dc23   2011041090

Printed in the United States of America on acid-free paper

www.ballantinebooks.com

2 4 6 8 9 7 5 3 1

FIRST EDITION

Book design by Simon M. Sullivan

For all those driven
by hunger and love

Contents

○ ○

Photo Credits

∘ ∘

What is love? After all, it is quite simple. Love is everything which enhances, widens, and enriches our life, in its height and in its depths. Love has as few problems as a motor-car. The only problems are the drivers, the passengers, and the road.

—Franz Kafka

Introduction

∘ ∘

In 1949, a ship called the MS *Westerdam* departed from the coast of Europe, its hundreds of passengers headed toward U.S. shores. Nestled deep in the ship's cargo compartment, a pair of headlights peeped out of a dark tarp; two wide, open circles leading to the soft curves of what would soon be known as the world's most recognizable car. Protesters, rebels, dissidents, politicians, businessmen, the world's corporate elite—all would eventually become entwined in its story. By the end of the 1960s, it would do what no other car had done before: transcend age, class, and country to become a symbol adopted by them all. Americans would call the car the Beetle. In other places it would become the Flea, the Turtle, the Vocho, the Foxi, the Buba, the Fusca, the Poncho, and the Mouse.

Over the years, the car developed a cult following as well as a more public persona. It had fan club after fan club created on its behalf; it showed up in the films of Woody Allen and Stanley Kubrick; Disney endearingly dubbed it "The Love Bug"; it was even driven—briefly—by James Bond. For decades, the car filled college towns and campuses, the choice of students and faculty alike. It appeared on the cover of *Abbey Road.* John Lennon had a white one in his driveway. Packs of them dotted the beaches of California, surfboards strapped to their roofs. A children's game even spontaneously developed around the car as kids scanned the roads in search of it: *Punch Bug red! No punch back!* The car became so ubiquitous that pop artist Andy Warhol included it in his iconic series of silk screens, placing it in the company of personalities such as Elvis and Marilyn Monroe.

Today the original Volkswagen is still known as the longest-running and best-selling single car design in history, and it is the only car to have been brought back by popular demand . . . *twice.* Sometimes referred to as the world's most huggable car, perhaps no other automobile has ever been lavished with such attention and affection. But onboard the MS *Westerdam* on that cold winter day in 1949, none of that had yet come to pass. In those days, very few thought the car had potential. Reaching U.S. shores for the first time, the car had much more in common with the millions of immigrants coming over on similar ships, men and women who had been through dark times and were now seeking refuge or hoping to reinvent themselves, eager to find out if what they'd heard about the American dream was real.

It had been a long road. In fact, after nearly two decades of work and planning, the Volkswagen had only barely made it into existence at all. During the Second World War, the car's country and factory were all but destroyed. Caught in the ugliness of the Nazi machine, it became a symbol of the hated party. By 1949, one of the men responsible for it had committed suicide and another had been kidnapped and placed in prison, where he languished, imagining he'd failed to fulfill one of his lifelong dreams.

Needless to say, when the car was unloaded on the docks of New York City that first time, it was not greeted warmly. Not only because of the dark stain of war that washed over with it, but also because of the undeniable fact that the round little car just didn't fit in. America had been through a long Depression and a long war, but now unprecedented prosperity was finally leaking into the land and the country was on the verge of an automotive boom. The United States of the 1950s would be marked by wide elegant cars—the bigger the better—with flamboyant tail fins, extra comforts, and plenty of chrome. In contrast, the Volkswagen was oddly shaped and excruciatingly austere. People found it comical, awkward, and strange.

And yet on those very same New York shores, in pockets

throughout the city, there were men and women—people considered just as out of place as the car itself was in those days—who were feeling a new kind of energy, readying themselves to take the risk of dissenting, of going against the common way of doing things, of *thinking strange*. Likewise, back in Germany, a similar change was happening as the country struggled to come to terms with its dark history. On both shores, there was a desire to evolve from within, a need for individual freedom and economic responsibility, for less empty extravagance and for more meaning and truth. It would take a while to mature, but a revolution was rising, and the Beetle would be at the center of the wave. After so many years of obstacles and near misses, the car would finally be in just the right place at just the right time, merging with the larger flow of modernizing governments and evolving markets to revive a sense of joy and wonder in the world.

Beetle owners have a saying: They don't find their cars, their cars find them. To some degree, that's how this book came to be. My first real encounter with the original Beetle happened only after I'd graduated from college and moved to Germany. Riding back to Berlin after an artist residency in the countryside, lulled and drowsy in the backseat of an SUV, I was shaken from my daze when we came upon one particular town. That evening, the landscape had been empty and dark until suddenly there was the bright illumination of towering glass structures and fiery smokestacks: I was overwhelmed at the way this alien-like city suddenly sprang up out of the somber, empty terrain. One of the German friends I was with saw the effect it had on me: *That's Wolfsburg,* she said, *Isn't it strange?* She went on to explain that this town was originally built by the Nazis; Adolf Hitler had built it for his car. *What car?* I asked. *You don't know it?* she wondered aloud. *I thought everyone in America knows the Bug.*

In German, "Volkswagen" means "People's Car." At first, it seemed impossible to me that the same car that was once a child of Nazi Germany could grow up to become a symbol of freedom,

The Volkswagen factory at Wolfsburg, 2011.

democracy, and love. But as I would soon discover in my research, the car had always been meant for *the people,* and it
lived up to that dream in ways no one expected and no one
could have planned.

Through all the years of its development, the basic look and
feel of the car did not change, but the world around it did. Like
a still point through the storm, it survived the chaos of so much
contradiction and turmoil, and—thanks to the persistence of the
men who championed it—eventually proved that an idea created in darkness can indeed become a vessel for light.

Part One

○ ○

Wobbly First Steps

"Myths are public dreams, dreams are private myths."

—Joseph Campbell

William Bernbach did not look like a revolutionary. His sober meticulous suits and conservative ties did not catch the eye or distinguish him from any of the other advertising men walking New York City's bustling streets in the 1950s. Thin and compact, with short dark hair neatly combed to one side, Bill had a small physique that was almost childlike. True, he was the creative head of his own advertising agency—Doyle Dane Bernbach, soon to be familiarly known as DDB—but he didn't come off as a typical executive of the time: his evenings were rarely full of expensive dinner parties or multiple martinis, he wasn't embroiled in a string of heated affairs, he didn't own a pristine country home, or live in a fancy penthouse uptown. Instead, for much of his life, Bill lived in an anonymous neighborhood in the Bay Ridge area of Brooklyn, he took the subway into work each day, and he left on time every night to go home and have dinner with his kids and his wife.

Bill may not have looked like the kind of man who could catch the world's attention, but he was, and by the late 1950s, people were beginning to notice him. Unlike the rest of the cookie-cutter ad agencies on Madison Avenue, DDB had a fresh sense of purpose filling its rooms, drawing people in. Walking into their offices in those days, through the haze of cigarette smoke, past the ringing phones and the interactive rush of talented young men and women, one always found Bill Bernbach at the center of the buzz, his Brooklyn-tinged voice—simultaneously gentle and disarming—leaking out of his office and into the halls, his door always open. There was something alluring about his clear, blue-eyed gaze, and as the years passed, Bill rose to be known as the creative center of his agency, the person all the art directors and copywriters wanted to speak to about their work, the man who could get that work into print, or make it disappear without a trace. Bill was confident, and his confidence became DDB's backbone. It's what made so many want to be near him—his approval was a good luck charm of sorts—but it was also what made people hide from him at times, unsure or unready to face his clear and veracious eye. There were no rules with Bill; only vigilance.

Bill Bernbach, the unexpected revolutionary.

The crew at DDB was a motley and roughish bunch, in no way typical of most advertising agencies in New York. In certain younger circles, DDB was considered one of the only ad agencies where a person could work on something different, something exciting, something "meaningful," if you dared to use that term. Whereas other successful agencies at the time were full of serious-faced men in expensive suits, DDB was more like an experimental powwow. Art and writing were respected as crafts within themselves rather than as the means to a financial end. DDB employees worked in teams; they communicated and sparred. Those who witnessed this process called it *creative,* in a way that the advertising world had never really seen before.

DDB was different, and different was exciting. But that didn't mean the agency was going to leave its mark. In the larger scheme of things, DDB was more likely to be beaten by the establishment than it was to change it. After all, in 1959, the majority of Americans had never encountered a DDB ad. When it came to the heavyweights of economics and industries, DDB was small: They didn't have any of the accounts that mattered—no car company from Detroit, no major tobacco brand, no national retail chain.

And there was something else, too. In business terms, DDB was often dismissed as a quirky place that did "ethnic" advertising, a crude way of saying that most people considered DDB a Jewish company that did "unabashedly, recognizably Jewish" ads. Most of their clients were Jewish. Bill Bernbach was Jewish. And many on the staff were Jewish as well. Thus DDB's success was a local success: advertisements for El Al airlines or Ohrbach's department store caught the eye but had a limited scope, catering strictly to Manhattan and its boroughs. Bernbach's shop was no more a threat to the established giants than were the strange beatniks and folk singers who had started congregating downtown.

Advertising was incredibly lucrative in those days though, and the big agencies were prospering. Their ads showed beautiful and successful people enjoying a product, and upon seeing such stimulation, customers were supposed to be stimulated too. This underlying equation of "consumption equals happiness" had proven appeal: America's culture of materialism was thriving, fed on eye-popping advertisements for big houses, big cars, big smiles, and big words. It was the decade of dazzle, and yet as that decade entered its final year, some began to wonder if any of it had been real. The country's foundations no longer seemed so solid. A recession eventually set in, and it wasn't solely economic. The spirit of the country began to change; there was a sense of disquiet. As poet Allen Ginsberg wrote in the *Village Voice* in 1959: "No one in America knows what will happen. No one is in real control." The country was begging for a shift in perspective, and that would mean taking risks and thinking strange.

And DDB epitomized thinking strange. Take Bill's newest

choice of projects, for instance: a German car that, for more than one reason, looked like an impossible sale. Manhattan's major agencies were making millions advertising the cars of Detroit: Buick, Lincoln, Chrysler, Mercury, Oldsmobile, Ford—these were the brand names Americans craved and bought. One such advertisement for Pontiac depicted a large crowd chanting, "We're everybody . . . and we want a Big Car . . ." Even the sound of the door closing had to be big. As the general manager of Chevrolet boasted in 1957, "We've got the finest door slam this year we've ever had—a big car slam. . . ."

The Volkswagen, a car Americans would later nickname the "The Beetle," seemed to represent the opposite of such a desire. Though it had been trying to enter the market ever since that first transatlantic trip in 1949, its overall sales compared to the numbers coming out of Detroit were laughable, barely a blip on America's automotive map. Some at DDB couldn't help but wonder if perhaps Bill wasn't wasting his time with Volkswagen's little car. Foreign companies just weren't a market that big advertising agencies in the United States were courting in those days, and, lack of monetary gain aside, a Jewish advertising agency representing a German car just wasn't the most likely combination. Nevertheless, Bill wanted Volkswagen's business: He had a thing or two he wanted to say about the concept of bigness he saw many American corporations and advertising firms touting, and he had no qualms about flying overseas to Wolfsburg and visiting a German car factory in order to have that chance. He soon found out, however, that few others at DDB felt the same way. More than ten years had passed since the end of the war, but some wounds had not healed and the anger it had fostered still simmered. Feelings had been held in, papered over. After all, this was the car that *The New York Times* had referred to as the "Baby Hitler" in 1938, and while it's been said that no baby is ugly, this one certainly had a unique face.

Trekking to a country that Americans had once hated about as much as anyone could hate a place, meeting with former enemies who had fought on the side of the Nazis during the Second World War, having to find the good points about a car that, when people were being generous, was described as "a motorized tortoise" or a "pregnant roller skate"—needless to say, it wasn't the most attractive account that Bill could have offered his staff. Nevertheless, the men Bill eventually convinced to work on the account—a beatnik Jewish boy (Julian Koenig), a loudmouthed Greek who always seemed to be getting himself into hot water (George Lois), and a German American who had very unresolved feelings about his parents' German past (Helmut Krone)—would come together and, in a moment of seemingly fated timing, set a fire under Madison Avenue, and the entire nation beyond.

2

Adolf Hitler's eyes were reportedly "bright blue—bordering on the violet." In the psychological reports done on him in the 1940s by the OSS (a precursor to the CIA), there is mention of his "hypnotic glance" and the ability of his eyes to "bore through people." One policeman describes Hitler's gaze as "fatal," with an "irresistible glare." But by other accounts, his eyes are "dead" and "lacking in brilliance and the sparkle of genuine animation." Perhaps all of these descriptions are true. When I look at his portrait today, however, I have to admit that I don't see an incomprehensible monster: I see a man who sensed the power available to us all, and then violently abused it, brutalizing and destroying millions of lives, including his own. It's hard to imagine living in a city that was founded by such a man, but every citizen in Wolfsburg lives with that legacy. Without Adolf Hitler, their town would never have been born.

The town's original name wasn't even Wolfsburg. At the time of its official creation, the town was being made to house the factory for a car, and the entire project was being funded by a division of the Nazi German Labor Front (the DAF) called Strength through Joy. Thus, in May of 1938, Adolf Hitler christened Wolfsburg "The Town of the Strength through Joy Car," the town of the *Volkswagen*. Volkswagen was a generic term being used in technical and automotive circles at the time to mean a car for the common man, something still thought impractical and impossible in Germany by most. The idea of a Volkswagen carried a lot of power: To speak of motorizing the population was to speak of giving people more control over their lives, an idea that evoked both awe and desire. As one German automotive writer named Wilfried Bade proclaimed in 1938: "Until now the automobile has conquered the world. Now begins the true possession of the automobile by the people." The dream of the car, and the dream of the city being built for it, went hand in hand. Each spoke to the masses, each served as a symbol of unification, and each was directly linked to strengthening the nation through industry—all major aspects of the Nazi conception of power that was taking hold of the country then.

Hitler's Town of the Strength through Joy Car was originally created to be a "model German workers' city," an urban and residential center that incorporated the Third Reich's emphasis on unified work. Just as the People's Car was supposed to be a car that *all* Germans would drive, Hitler wanted its city to be a model on which all industrial towns could be built. It was to be a place of common purpose, where men and women worked together toward the realization of a singular goal, the ultimate point being the strengthening of Germany. Industry, alongside loyalty and labor, would structure the nation, make the Fatherland strong.

The hope for a People's Car had been rising in Europe for over twenty years. It was a kind of leitmotif, in fact, recurring regularly though never resolved; automobiles were driven only by the rich and elite. Hitler was the first person to come to power in Europe who saw the mass production of automobiles as an essential industrial and national aim. He envisioned a great motorized nation, a nation that could expand and expand and expand. Germany needed more *Lebensraum,* more living space, he told the citizens. The motor car was a natural part of that plan.

Hitler came to power in 1933 with cars on his mind and his agenda, but the process was full of twists and turns and it was only five years later, in the spring of 1938, that it began to look as if his goal might be achieved. The first steps toward *Volksmotorisierung,* motorizing the people, were being made, and the erection of the new auto city was proof. Land for the enormous car factory had been found, and Albert Speer, the Inspector General for Building in Berlin at that time, had approved the location. Plans had been drawn up, an engineer had been hard at work on prototypes of the car. It was time for the cornerstone of the factory to be laid, time to celebrate the coming wave of vehicles with pride, and on May 26, 1938, the Nazis planned an elaborate fête in The Town of the Strength through Joy Car.

The German Labor Front sent invitations to over 50,000 people, though they were not invited so much as ordered to attend. Trumpets blared. Long bloodred banners were unfurled. Twenty-eight special Town of the Strength through Joy Car–bound trains left from all parts of the country and carried the citizens to the grounds where they were promised the new industrial town was soon to rise. This place, the propaganda promised, would be better than any American city, and Germany's new car factory would be better than anything yet built by America's automotive hero Henry Ford. Members of the Hitler Youth and the SS marched. The workers were on show: Bricklayers were given pristine white outfits and black top hats to wear; carpenters were decked out in black velvet and corduroy. Everyone raised his arm as Hitler appeared, arriving in the front seat of one of the prototypes of his Strength through Joy Car. People pointed at the new automobile, and discussed it; perhaps they imagined owning one, too. For those who couldn't make it to the opening ceremony, a radio show was broadcast, one of the first of its kind, detailing Hitler's every move. It was supposed to be a day of triumph, but spectators who were there would later report there was a strange tension in the air, a kind of growing apprehension.

Perhaps it was the chancellor's aloofness that sent such an impression reverberating through the crowd. He certainly wasn't himself that day. In previous automotive events, Hitler had al-

The ceremony to inaugurate the new factory in The Town of the Strength through Joy Car. Adolf Hitler prepares to speak.

ways been fervent, even joyful, as he talked passionately about this project's potential. On the day of the ceremony, however, the car was no longer at the forefront, or even close to the forefront of Hitler's mind: By the spring of 1938, a new reality was setting in and other parts of his grand scheme were now in motion as well. Hitler's focus was not on the People's Car that day because he was preoccupied with the war that he knew was imminent. His desired moment had arrived. Already Austria had been annexed, had come too willingly, some would say. And the pogrom of the Crystal Night (*Kristallnacht*) was only six months away— that horrific and incendiary evening in which hundreds of synagogues were set on fire, Jewish shops and homes were destroyed and plundered, the shattered glass of their windows littering the streets, and around 30,000 Jews were sent to concentration camps or killed. The political air in Germany was toxic, but few were aware of the noxious fumes that surrounded them. The celebration for the car was in many ways a perfect metaphor for the mood of the country: lush decoration slathered onto a deepening

The crowd gathered in The Town of Strength through Joy Car for the cornerstone-laying ceremony. Three prototypes of the People's Car face them, guarded by the Nazi authorities.

sense of unrest. People looked at the spectacle and tried not to notice the anxiety swelling underneath.

Watching the black-and-white footage from the ceremony, I notice Hitler is sitting up front with the driver when his car enters the grounds. It was well known that Hitler's preferred place in any car was next to the driver. (On long trips, he liked to wear a leather driving cap and study the road atlas, planning the route.) But in the footage of him leaving the celebration that day, the führer is sitting in the backseat of the open-roofed car and looks much happier than he did while giving his speech. That old automotive joy flashes in his face again, perhaps because he is no longer alone: An older man in an oversized tweed coat, his belly a bit large, his face creased from age and perpetual squinting, has joined him. Hitler is obviously content to be in this man's company. He is turned toward him, conversing in a casual sort of way as the crowds lining either side of the road wave and cheer when the little Volkswagen chugs past. It's a striking moment, I realize, for in that brief instant the car is carrying both its fathers, two men whose legacies will follow it forever, for better and for worse. Cushioned in its backseat is Adolf Hitler, and in that same backseat is the Bug's engineer and designer, Ferdinand Porsche.

It's no wonder Adolf Hitler was so concerned with the idea of motorizing Germany, or that the high rollers on Madison Avenue have historically received some of their biggest accounts from automobile firms. Mobility, as both a word and an idea, cuts to the heart of the connection between creativity and change, and it is through that connection that humans have found a way of satisfying certain primary desires: the desires for freedom and prosperity, and the desires to join together and commune. To put it another way, the history of our progress as humans, both socially and politically, is inextricably linked to the ways we've found to move. For better or worse, humans have always been curious about what lies beyond the horizon, about what else is out there to be experienced and seen, and in order to explore those new worlds, we've had to find new ways of getting there. Whether it is by horseback, carriage, bicycle, motorcycle, ship, car, plane, spacecraft—or through more virtual means such as reading a book, listening to music, or going online—we have put a great deal of time, energy, and money into finding ways to transcend ever greater distances at ever greater speeds. But just as no political or economic revolution has come easily, so no revolution in transportation has come without resistance to change.

Take the introduction of passenger trains, for example. Today, the idea of *being transported* has a somewhat mystical connotation. But when passenger trains were first being introduced, the word *transport* roused disdain, if not outright anger, when it was applied to people. *Transport* was a word for the movement of animals, objects, and food. Mass transportation of people felt sacrilegious, as though humans were being turned into a commodity. "Freedom has been sacrificed to speed," wrote one German journalist in 1902. "The train ticket is purchased not only with money but also with forfeiture of one's right of self-determination. . . ."

Like all technological advances, however, convenience and curiosity eventually won out and the train was accepted and embraced. First-class cabins and onboard dining made those with money feel as though they were something more than eggs or lumber or livestock. People developed a taste for travel, for seeing new parts of the world, and for the rush of movement. And, once motor cars appeared on the scene, those who could afford the new vehicles found them liberating; they were able to achieve the effects of train travel, but individually, without restriction. It's one underlying reason why motor cars in Europe—and in the United States, before Henry Ford—came into the world as items of luxury. Automobiles were symbols of prestige from their very inception; it is only the details signifying that prestige that have changed.

There have always been different needs and different levels of liberation involved in travel, and because of this wide spectrum, rarely do the old methods disappear with the introduction of the new. Today, for example, there are ways in which trains continue to be the most convenient means of travel. Stepping onto a train requires little stress; there are no long lines, security checks, or traffic-clogged streets to endure. Yet the lure of driving remains clear. The rush of having a physical connection to one's speed and direction—pressing the pedal, turning the wheel—is surely more exciting than simply stepping aboard and taking a seat.

One thing Adolf Hitler understood well in his call for a People's Car was the desire everyone experiences at some point for two things: power and control. Automobiles, like most technologies, are tools we use to extend our natural capabilities and increase what we can accomplish. They allow humans to go faster and farther; they give us more speed and a wider reach than we could ever have with our bodies alone. And the automobile is an easy metaphor for class mobility; it's less about where we're coming from, and more about where we want to go.

But there has always been another side to automobiles as well, a less political or Darwinian one, a side closer to the heart. Automobiles conjure feelings of freedom and possibility, of fantasy and escape. To some extent, all new technologies are as much about this poetic side of life as they are about anything practical or productive. It's the spirit of adventure that motivates inventors: Their innovations require a great deal of risk and courage to be brought to life. Innovators test limits, dealing with tools that have the potential of bringing great good to the world, or great destruction. Think of the men who were out on the cliffs of North Carolina experimenting with the first human flight, or of those who worked on splitting the atom during the Second World War. And, more recently, there are those curious groups of people dreaming up new ways of connecting the world via a vast, virtual web.

Technology is about broadening our ideas of what is possible. And often the men and women who find or discover the scientific principles that change our world are men and women who are moved—in the same way any writer or artist is moved—by a deep curiosity about the unknown. They are not only intellectually but also emotionally stirred by the work they produce. People like Albert Einstein or the Wright brothers, Jane Goodall or

Mary Walton, Michael Faraday or Steve Jobs, are often instinctively drawn to their occupations. The engineer Ferdinand Porsche was like that as well, so much so that his lifelong obsession hardly seems to have sprung from a conscious choice.

It started when he was just a boy. There were people in his village, people in his own family in fact, who whispered about him and wondered if he might be possessed. They found it hard to explain the boy's knowledge and understanding of something as incomprehensible as electricity still was back then. *How does he even know it is there?* Born in a small Bohemian village called Maffersdorf in 1875, Porsche entered a world where familiarity with an electric spark went about as far as rubbing amber against a cat's fur, then standing back to watch the ensuing flash of light.

Things were changing rapidly, however, and by the time Porsche was thirteen years old, there was one building in a neighboring town that did indeed have electric light: the local carpet factory. One day, while running an errand for his father, who was the area's best tinsmith, Porsche happened upon the factory and could not drag himself away. He was fascinated, awed, and fearlessly began inspecting the gadgets and burning bulbs. The owner of the factory noticed the big-eyed boy and, rather than running him off, brought him in and explained the way the system worked. Porsche began taking mental notes about the batteries and chemicals and charges he saw. He wanted to build an electrical system for himself.

But Ferdinand's father, Anton, had other plans for his son. Having already lost one of his boys in an accident (a loss that cast an unacknowledged shadow over their home), he now looked to Ferdinand to learn and inherit the business from him. Ferdinand could feel the importance and weight of his father's wishes, but there was something about electricity that just simply would not leave him alone. Often, even after working all day for his father in the tinsmith shop, he would stay up half the night to experiment with the batteries and other tools and chemicals he'd managed to acquire. His father found such preoccupations unhealthy and distracting and eventually forbade Ferdinand from tinkering with what did not relate directly to the tinsmith trade, fearing that his son's hobby was getting out of hand. Ferdinand's adolescent struggles eventually grew into serious quarrels. He tried to explain his passion to his father, but the unfamiliar words and terms he used only frustrated Anton further. He didn't want to hear about it. He just wanted it to end.

Ferdinand appealed to his mother. He *couldn't* stop; perhaps he could just set up a place in the attic, out of the way, which his father would never see. He'd only work up there when his father wasn't at home, and he'd keep up with all his tinsmith work. Thus, his mother, sensitive to her son's talent, turned a blind eye to the little laboratory Ferdinand established in the topmost room of the house. Because Anton was such a gifted tinsmith, and also a politically involved man, he was often traveling or away overnight, and Ferdinand found ample time to continue his experiments. But there was one night when he misjudged his father's time of return. Anton, in search of his son, discovered Ferdinand's secret laboratory and flew into a rage. His orders had clearly been disobeyed. He was stunned and angered by the recalcitrance and oddity in what his son was doing, and not understanding the acids that went into the batteries and chemicals Ferdinand had assembled, his father began stomping on them with his large, heavy work boots, pushing Ferdinand away when he tried to intervene. The acids ate through the soles of Anton's shoes, burning his skin as it splashed up from the floor. It took Ferdinand's mother's interference to calm him down again. Ferdinand watched in a sad daze, but he didn't apologize for what he had done.

4

Electricity was still something to be wondered at in America, too. In 1939 at the New York World's Fair held at Flushing Meadows in Queens, an advertisement for the Commonwealth and Southern utility company showed a long candle beside a squat but brilliant lightbulb, telling its readers: "It now costs the average American household only $1.71 to light its house or apartment by electricity for a month . . . If this home had to use candles, it would have to pay $346.65 a month for an equivalent amount of light . . ." The text goes on to say that it would require over half a ton of candles, some 5,778 of them in fact. In suggesting that it will be innovations in electric lighting that will, literally and metaphorically, "make the future bright," the ad implicitly asks Americans to trust the new market that is emerging. Private enterprise, the ad explains, "rewards individual initiative," "encourages inventive genius," and "induces investors to supply capital."

By the time of the World's Fair, the United States was pulling itself out of the Depression, and it already had quite a history of trying to bring electricity to its population. It had been nearly 200 years since Ben Franklin had flown his kites and made his notes about charges and sparks. And Thomas Edison, having demonstrated the first incandescent lightbulb only three years after Ferdinand Porsche was born, had since developed the first electrical lighting system with a common generator that allowed lines to be connected to various homes. By 1882, Edison had acquired his first 50 customers toward what, just over half a century later, was one of the main staples of the growing free market: the business of energy and light. It was a slow process: In 1935, nine out of ten farms still did not have electricity in many American states, but the market for it, alongside a desire for it, were taking off. A new technological world was arriving, and it would bring with it a seemingly endless amount of bewildering new choices: Old problems were being solved, but new ones were being created.

For Americans emerging from the 1930s, this change in economic and social perspective, the idea of looking toward the future, was not yet understood so much as felt: it had an emotional resonance. For the first time, 44 million people from all over the globe could travel to Flushing Meadows to intermingle at the biggest World's Fair in American history. They could hear a speech on cosmic rays given by Albert Einstein, listen to President Roosevelt talk about new technologies, stand in front of a Vermeer painting that had been shipped all the way from Amsterdam, see a streamlined pencil sharpener, or touch a new fabric called nylon. They could gaze at color photography—the first splashes of reds and greens ever reproduced—or be introduced to the possibility of controlling temperature through something called "air-conditioning." Each evening, crowds could also bask in the glow of fluorescent lights, as, for the first time, the exhibits and buildings were draped in them. People called it "otherworldly" and "magical." They let themselves get carried away; many were hungry to feel optimistic again, to come together and share the warm expectation that tomorrow would be better than today.

In the swarmed Transportation Zone of the fair, people could enter the General Motors Futurama exhibit, a 36,000-square-foot miniworld complete with thousands of tiny cars, highways, and homes that presented itself as a visualization of what the country was soon to become, like looking at the world through the window of a time machine. This was truly an original vision at the time, as much of America was still rural and blanketed in farms and fields. According to Dan Howland, the editor of the *Journal of Ride Theory,* "the audience had never even considered a future like this. . . . There wasn't an interstate freeway system in 1939. Not many people owned a car."

In some ways, the 1939 World's Fair echoed the ceremony that had taken place just a year earlier in The Town of the Strength through Joy Car, when Adolf Hitler had christened his

*A poster for the "World of Tomorrow," the
1939 New York World's Fair. An unprecedented
poster campaign accompanied the fair, and
many of the city's best designers (such as
Paul Rand) contributed to it.*

"modern workers' city" and spoke of motorizing the population; Futurama reflected that same vision Hitler had of providing Germany with its first network of autobahns. In other words, the powerful elite of both Germany and America now believed that the future would be built around the automobile, and they were working toward that future in a very significant way. The difference in Hitler's vision and the version presented by General Motors, however, was bound up in the very idea vaunted by the lightbulb ad: the importance of free enterprise. The push and pull between markets and governments around the world was entering a new phase, and the question of which economic and political path was best was still a matter of debate. In America, President Roosevelt's New Deal had momentarily shifted economic power toward governmental control in an attempt to alleviate the Depression, beginning public projects to employ people and bring back a spirit of enterprise. It was working, but it had come with a great deal of controversy and debate. New Deal projects that supplied electricity or infrastructures made private companies feel as if the government was imposing on their domain, but in the eyes of Roosevelt and his administration, those projects were a way of providing work and money to the people, and of lifting them out of the Depression. American businessmen were quick to challenge governmental interference in the market, however, engaging in a frustrating deliberation that would nevertheless ultimately prove to be for the country's good. Hitler's People's Car and People's City was an answer to those same dire economic times, after all, but rather than deal with the inherent tensions of a democratic system, his party blamed democracy itself: Business and the economy could not be trusted to the masses, Hitler said, but needed to be funneled through one ultimate point of control.

Taken together, these two urges—one toward centralization of power, the other toward a responsible diffusion of power—were to shape the events of the next two decades in profound and deeply transformative ways: Along with their new political and economic realities, the United States and Europe would enter into a race to develop new technology, a debate about free and managed markets, and a search for the balance between two seemingly contradictory human desires: to have both freedom and control at once. "The eyes of the Fair are on the future," the official pamphlet for the World's Fair read, promising that the best preparation for tomorrow is "familiarity with today." And it was true: If one looked closely, the next five years were already implicit. The Second World War, less than a year away for most of the countries participating in the Fair, would soon prove the importance of technology and communication in an increasingly interconnected world. The United Nations would be created. International borders would be redrawn. Great amounts of money and research would be placed into weaponry and transportation. Mass production would arrive on a scale as yet unseen. Ballistics and code breaking would jump-start the development of electronic computer technology. And most unforgettable of all, endeavors like the Manhattan Project would put the peril of nuclear weapons into worldwide collective consciousness, contributing to the iron curtain that was soon to fall. By the close of the 1940s, technological innovation would be associated with a new urgency, one that demanded a new kind of clarity and care.

In 1933, in London's *Daily Mail,* the 3rd Viscount Rothermere of Britain had written that it was "Germany's great good fortune to have found a leader who can combine for the public good all the most vigorous elements in the country," and by "vigorous elements," he'd meant German spirit, ingenuity, and a reverence for authority and work. There had been words of praise for Adolf Hitler from many other countries as well. But by 1939, all were trying to take those words back. The same people who had earlier sung the praises of the German chancellor and the remarkable growth he was bringing to his country were now walking along the Futurama's moving sidewalks wondering how much longer it would be before their countries were at war. And, as evidenced by Albert Einstein's presence in America (he had fled Germany earlier that year) and his speech on the Fair's opening day, a new kind of refugee was becoming part of America's cultural and intellectual elite, men and women coming over in an attempt to escape Hitler and his racism and vitriol. The World's Fair and its emphasis on an international future was a harbinger of the mixed social and economic world that would soon emerge. And so was Germany's conspicuous absence from the party. Hitler had refused to allow Germans to attend.

$$5$$

After that tense episode of Anton Porsche finding out about his son's secret lab in 1889, Ferdinand had not abandoned his electrical experiments. But something had shifted between them: Both father and son seemed to have realized that the situation was not going to change; they had to accept it, like it or not. Another son had been born to the Porsches, and was coming of age by then, and the younger boy was more excited about following his father's path than was the teenage Ferdinand, so his father began looking toward him to take up the family trade. Ferdinand's mother, Anna, continued to speak to Anton in quiet moments, wondering if perhaps Ferdinand really did have some kind of gift, wondering if perhaps they needed to allow him to explore it. Eventually Anton stopped bothering his son so much about what he did in his free time, just as long as he kept up with his work.

One night, walking back from a political meeting in town that had followed a long day in the shop, Anton received an enormous shock. Perhaps he even stopped and shook his head, wondering if he'd already walked home, if he'd fallen asleep and was stumbling through a dream. The trees and grass stretched out in front of him along the path to the house had a strange glow, a reflected brightness that grew stronger with each step. The house itself seemed to have been filled with some kind of luminous liquid that was now dripping out of the windows and doors. Anton could see the profiles of his wife and children, shadows on the wall. His son had succeeded in his experiments: Anton was now the only man in the entire town whose house and workshop were lit with electric light.

It had not been easy to keep the surprise from his father, but Ferdinand had waited until everything was working properly before he'd taken it downstairs and put it in place, unveiling it that night for his brother and sisters and mother, knowing his

*Ferdinand Porsche as a boy in the early 1890s,
with the electrical system he built from scratch
for his family's home.*

father was on his way home. He'd built the entire system, including the generator, from scratch, with the help of nothing more than a curious mind, the knowledge that comes from trial and error, and whatever intuition had been gifted to him from who knows where. It was astounding, not only to his family but also to the town. Anton told his son that he could attend night classes at the local technical school, if he wished. Ferdinand was thrilled.

As Ferdinand got older, however, he began to wonder about bigger things, about Vienna and the innovations being undertaken there. His classes at the village school were not quite able to satisfy his curiosity. In fact, sometimes he learned just as much by studying the work being done at Ginzkey's carpet factory, the place where he'd had his first encounter with electric light. Ginzkey's business had become an impressive and thriving industry by then, and his influence in the area around Maffersdorf was considerable. Anton Porsche respected Mr. Ginzkey immensely and listened to him when he spoke about the prospects he saw for Ferdinand. It was perhaps time to send him to Vienna, Ginzkey said. Anton agreed, and thus when Ferdinand Porsche turned eighteen, he was allowed to leave Maffersdorf and go to the Austro-Hungarian Empire's thriving capital.

Mr. Ginzkey, having full confidence in Ferdinand, set up a job for him with a company that manufactured electrical equipment and machinery. Ferdinand fell into step immediately upon starting his new job, working long hours, sometimes sneaking into classes at the Vienna Technical University at night. Ferdinand knew he had none of the usual engineering degrees expected of someone in his position at the time, but he was so good at what he did that he advanced quickly nonetheless; people often talked of his "sixth sense." By the time he was twenty-two, the obsessive young man had already worked his way up to becoming a company manager. He'd also started thinking more and more about the newest invention in transportation: the motor car.

Ferdinand Porsche (far rigiht) during a learning session on his first job in Vienna at Bella Egger. He is the only one taking notes.

Around the same time that Ferdinand Porsche had been born in 1875, Europe had experienced a turn toward industrialization, and automotive pioneers had begun developing internal combustion engines and connecting them to vehicles that were not cars so much as carts, but that were nevertheless a large step forward from the usual horse-and-carriage method of mobility. By the time Ferdinand Porsche was an adult, automobiles had come a long way: Those early gasoline-powered carts had grown, widened, and attached themselves to four large wooden wheels. Now people could ride in seats on the carts and steer; they could also control their speed. Still, the majority of the population detested the motor car's noise and its rude way of taking up the entire street. Few people took them very seriously in those early decades; few considered them much more than an upper-class toy. The horse and carriage still ruled the roads.

But then, as the twentieth century began, the automobile began to generate more excitement and mystique, even among those who were not wealthy enough to own one. One reason for this was the establishment of the auto race in 1894: The very first one ran in France from Paris to Rouen and then from Rouen to Bordeaux. People heard about it and came out to the streets to watch and cheer. The newspapers reported on it extensively. Such races gradually became frequent, much-anticipated events. And the motor car became a source of amusement rather than a nuisance that disturbed horses and made the streets unsafe: Particular cars or drivers took on the quality of a favorite sports team or sports figure, and the race thus became something one could participate in without having to experience firsthand.

Auto racing was exciting, but the transportation option that was having the most success in finding new customers in the 1880s was the motorcycle. In many ways, the idea of individual transportation for the masses had started not with the car, but with a two-wheeler, the bicycle. The bicycle had been popularized in Paris in the mid-1800s, and it was a natural step for many of Europe's bicycle manufacturers to find a way for a two-wheeler to propel itself. So began the motorcycle business.

Though auto races slowly increased people's appreciation of the automobile, it was nevertheless the motorcycle that seemed the logical mode of transportation for everyday life, and they caught on much more quickly than cars. From 1921 to 1931 the number of motorcycles in Germany rose from 26,700 to just under 800,000. For that reason, at least in big cities like Vienna, the traditional horse-and-carriage manufacturers started making motorcycles as well. One such place was Jacob Lohner & Co., a company that would play a big role in Ferdinand Porsche's development. It was one of the oldest and most respected luxury coach–building establishments in the world, and the official supplier for the Imperial Majesty himself, Archduke Franz Ferdinand.

Motorcycles brought new business for carriage maker Jacob Lohner, and he was glad to have taken the risk of getting into the new venture. In 1896, however, seeing the demand for two-wheelers beginning to taper off, Lohner decided it was time to take an even bigger risk. He wanted to try his hand at developing the new technology of motor cars. To do so, he'd need to expand his staff. He wanted someone young, someone curious, someone who knew his way around an electronics shop. Being friends with some of Ferdinand Porsche's coworkers, Lohner soon heard about their unusually talented colleague from the country. Ferdinand was the perfect candidate: young, curious, and longing to try his hand at building a car. Lohner asked him if he might like to come around the shop sometime. What Lohner wanted, he told Ferdinand, was to build an electric car. Luckily, electricity was already something Ferdinand understood well.

Energy and its relation to mobility has long been a mysterious connection that innovators are hungry to explore. Engines are basically controlled explosions of energy; building an engine is a way of directing energy to achieve maximum force, and it comes with a compelling rush of adrenaline. Leonardo da Vinci started making drawings of self-propelled vehicles as far back as the fifteenth century, but it was only at the turn of the twentieth century that something modestly resembling the modern automobile was designed. In those years, men like Karl Benz, the highly respected German engineer who acquired the first patent for a gasoline-powered car in 1886, worked mainly with automobiles that used internal-combustion engines. But Lohner wanted to try using electricity. Many of the first auto races had actually been won by using either steam or electric power, so it was still a toss-up as to which way the future would go: by no means did it look certain that the world would become oil-dependent (the petroleum industry was only just getting started, and that industry was certainly not dependent on cars). Lohner chose electric power because he had the Imperial Majesty to consider. Being the official supplier for the Austro-Hungarian Empire's transportation, if he was going to make a car, it had better be regal. That meant something quiet and clean, something worthy of being taken to a theater premiere or a state dinner. The messy, noisy, internal-combustion engine simply would not do. He discussed all this with the young man from Maffersdorf, who had never built a car, but was anxious to try. Lohner hired him, and they set to work. From that moment on, Ferdinand Porsche's main obsession would be the automobile. It was the first step on the path that would eventually lead to the creation of the Bug.

Adolf Hitler, a man that history will forever link to Germany, was not a German citizen by birth. Like Ferdinand Porsche, he was born in a small village in the Austro-Hungarian Empire, the eldest son of a well-respected Austrian customs official. By the time he arrived in the world, born in Braunau am Inn in 1889, fourteen years after Ferdinand Porsche's birth, the industrial-age Eiffel Tower was being built and industrialization was slightly less alien to most Europeans than it had been a decade before; the automobile was slowly gaining ground. The first official auto race would occur when Hitler was five years old, and though his family would have been familiar with the idea of automobiles, they would nevertheless have been a very unlikely sight in their town.

From early on, Adolf was a troubled boy. When he was still a child, his younger brother and playmate Edmund died, causing a noticeable change in the family and further heartbreak for his mother Klara, who had already lost three children. Adolf, now her only son, wasn't a "mother's boy" in the traditional sense, but by all reports the two were sincerely close. "I never witnessed a closer attachment," the family doctor, a Jewish man named Eduard Bloch, would later write.

As Adolf grew, he would seem at first to be a meek boy, yelled at and beaten often by his father, coddled by his mother, neither popular nor unpopular at school. Once the family moved to Linz, considered by some to be the most German city in the empire, Hitler was attracted to the popularized Pan-German ideas, ideas that discriminated against Czechs and others who did not speak German as their first tongue. He also identified with the Schönerer lifestyle, a movement that advised boys to restrain from sexual relations until at least the age of twenty-five, and warned them away from drinking alcohol, smoking, or eating red meat. In these same years, Adolf became rather obsessed with the Native American tales of the German author Karl May. Likewise, he was entranced by stories his history teacher told him of a mythologized German past, and men such as Frederick the Great. The stories impacted him deeply; he would talk of May and of Frederick the Great for the rest of his life. As he grew into an adolescent, this fantasy life would only expand. By the time he reached his teenage years, he had decided that he was destined to become a great artist and would consider doing nothing else. He and his father quarreled violently over this, and in rebellion, Adolf no longer tried hard at his studies and his grades suffered. This only caused more beatings from his father. His mother demurred and did not stand in her husband's way.

. . .

As Hitler struggled through his adolescence, Ferdinand Porsche was in Jacob Lohner's workshop designing his first car. Around Hitler's eleventh birthday, Ferdinand Porsche presented his creation at the Paris Exhibition of 1900. It would be Ferdinand's inaugural visit to the French capital, his first time mingling with people from all over Europe. The event drew in millions, one of the first large-scale shows about technology ever held. Engineers and scientists were ecstatic about it, coming from many European countries to attend, showing off not only cars but also inventions such as escalators and talking films. Excitement was in the air, and so was controversy. The Eiffel Tower seemed the perfect metaphor for the age of industry breaking upon the world: While some loved the structure, others protested that it was an ugly monument to all that was wrong with industrialization. And yet technical progress was a fever that could not be cooled; its seductiveness was evident in the way even the most anti-industry of voices could not help but be awed when standing outside the Paris Exhibition at night: It was the first of its kind to be electrically lit.

At Lohner & Co., the past few years had been exciting but difficult. Ferdinand Porsche's trial-and-error method had cost Jacob quite a lot of money: Each time one idea of Porsche's failed, he was quick to adjust and come up with a new idea that he just *had* to test. Lohner somehow found a way to grit his teeth and stick with the young man, and by the time of the Paris Exhibition, his patience was indeed paying off. The Lohner-Porsche car was the automotive star of the show; European newspapers wrote that it was the most outstanding innovation there.

It's easy to see why people made such a fuss. The car really is beautiful—primitive-looking by contemporary standards, with its big wooden wheels, its uncovered seating, and its tall, thin steering wheel—but the design is elegant and neat, streamlined with a little wave of steel at its front. The car was perfectly balanced and poised, exactly the kind of thing to be taken to the theater by an emperor or a queen: It was quiet because it had no transmission or layshafts, working instead with little electrical engines that were connected directly to the wheels. And it could travel 50 miles at 9 mph before its batteries needed to be recharged. Even today, such a construction would seem a unique and splendid thing. It was awarded a grand prize for its design. Ferdinand had been only twenty-three years old at the time he'd created the car's design. "He is very young," Jacob Lohner told the crowd in Paris, "but he's a man with quite a career ahead of him. You'll certainly hear of him again." And indeed, that was just the beginning. Over the next two years, Porsche would build the world's first hybrid as well as a car called "Mixt," which used a mix of electric and internal-combustion engines. Both these cars were extraordinary and unprecedented. In the following years, Porsche would also design the first front-wheel- and the first four-wheel-drive automobile. In 1902, Porsche won the most prestigious medal in Austrian engineering, the Pöttinger, for his work. He had truly left the Austrian countryside

An advertisement showing the award-winning electric Lohner-Porsche car that Ferdinand designed when he was twenty-three years old. This car was powered by the hub-mounted motors on the front wheels.

Ferdinand Porsche at the wheel of the world's first functional hybrid automobile, the Semper Vivus. The front of this car represents one of the first attempts at an aerodynamic design.

and was now moving toward fame. In contrast, Hitler's move to Vienna did not go nearly so well.

In 1903, when Hitler was fourteen years old, his father died suddenly. Hitler showed little remorse over his father's death, but his health temporarily declined and he used his persistent flu-like sickness, alongside his new position as the only male in the house, to convince his mother that he should drop out of high school. For the following two years, he stayed home, doted on by his mother, sister, and aunt, spending his days reading and drawing. In the evenings, he attended Wagner operas with his friend August Kubizek, fantasizing and pontificating about architecture and music and art. Eventually, Hitler set off to Vienna with the expectation that he would study at the prestigious art academy there, and convinced Kubizek to follow him. But Hitler did not have the help of any well-connected friends. Nor did he have the "sixth sense" or the talent for his subject that Porsche had. While Hitler's drawings were better than average, they were not extraordinary or even skilled; he was not good at drawing the human figure, and there was nothing particularly unique or eye-catching about his buildings or landscapes. But Hitler was not aware of such things. He was convinced he was a genius, buoyed by his thoughts of fame. He didn't try to find a job, living instead off some money his aunt had given him. He looked into *everything,* but casually, usually skimming the surface rather than going too deep. He liked to read only the first and last chapters of books, for instance, thinking he could grasp their entire meaning that way. But Vienna impressed him with its architecture and music and voluminous museums, and he spent his days surrounding himself with the city's music and art.

There was another passion that began in earnest during these years for Hitler though: his love for automobiles. It was the first time that he had been exposed to cars to any real extent, and the first time he could attend an auto race. In Vienna, Adolf began reading motoring publications and keeping up with the latest races and news. It was the beginning of a lifelong self-education in automobiles. In later years, he would spend hours and hours personally interviewing potential drivers for his own car, asking them detailed, technical questions that astonished and sometimes even upended the most experienced of them. This was one subject in which Hitler apparently did not skim.

In different ways, both Adolph Hitler and Ferdinand Porsche had been infected by the spirit of their times, a moment when progress was the name of the game, and when an individual was believed to have some great upward rise connected with fate. Since the eighteenth century, with the onset of the Enlightenment, thought and the power of using one's thinking to solve great social and individual problems had become increasingly paramount, and in turn, both the cult of the individual and the strength of "the masses" were rising. Whereas industry had started in England and come fully of age and power only recently in the German-speaking world, the idea of progress and of using one's reason to achieve such progress was already well installed in big cities like Vienna. Tied up in that idea was mankind's "war" against space and time; identification with a group was one way of fighting this war (because it made a person feel part of something larger and "timeless") and, so it seemed, was celebrity or fame (because it gave one the sense of having a lasting presence in the world, of immortality). This desire for dominance can be traced back in history, to conquerors such as Alexander the Great and Napoleon, but in the 1900s it was becoming characteristic not only of the political world but of the commercial world as well. There was a new emphasis on buying and selling, on mass appeal: New forms of media connected more people, increasing audience size and proximity, thus intensifying a product's, or a person's, ability to be known and also raising the social desire "to belong." The automobile was a natural part of this wave: It was for the individual, but it was a way of showing off one's individuality in a crowd; it was an engine of both economic and social expansion, a way to simultaneously "stand apart," *and* belong to a particular class. Motion itself was a sign of power. As early as 1906, one European newspaper talked of the automobile as the tool that would finally "grant humans their conquest over time and space."

Hitler came to Vienna with big plans, boasting of all the great things he would do at school. Unfortunately, real life was beginning to fall short of his expectations. As the months passed, his money ran thin, as did his prospects of becoming an artist. His application to the Academy of Fine Arts was rejected. When he later tried applying a second time, he was not even allowed to sit for the exam. He tried the architecture school too, but was told he didn't have the proper credentials because he had not finished high school. The success that had come naturally to Porsche was what Hitler now strove to patch together after skimming everything he encountered or found. And whereas Porsche never cared much for fame, and certainly had never gone in search of it, it was the attention itself, the very quality of *being known,* for which Hitler longed. He would later write in his autobiography that Vienna was the first time in his life that he felt "at odds with himself." He no longer felt he was in control.

Adolf lied to his mother about getting into art school. He told her the city was embracing him with open arms, that he'd been accepted into the prestigious university and all was well. It's hard to imagine she believed him. Perhaps, as mothers often do, she was able to see through his ruse. These were difficult years for her too; the loss of her husband and the absence of her son weighed heavily on her. Adolf had known his mother was sick before he'd left for Vienna, but he'd gone ahead with his plans. When word came that Klara's condition had dramatically deteriorated, however, Adolf went back to Linz to take care of her, showing more care and responsibility than he ever had in his life, and perhaps ever would again. When his mother died, he sobbed uncontrollably, "prostrate with grief" as Klara's doctor would later attest. Hitler was eighteen at the time. He grieved for weeks before resolving himself and leaving for the anonymous big city again. Back in Vienna, he was alone in a new way. He had little money, no job and no motivation to find one. After his second rejection from art school, he cut off contact with his childhood friend Kubizek, failing to return to the apartment they shared. Aside from his sister, whom he sometimes went to for financial help, Hitler no longer had any ties to his former life.

Meanwhile, Ferdinand Porsche had grown used to the big city of Vienna and his new status there. He had fallen in love with a girl named Aloisia Kaes; electricity sparked between them, but of a whole different kind. The daughter of Bohemian artisans, Aloisia was independent and smart; a bookkeeper in the shop where Porsche worked, she was a workingwoman at a time when many women would not consider such a thing. She was also tough, a fortunate characteristic for someone who would share life with a man as obsessed (and sometimes, simply selfish) as Ferdinand Porsche, and she too enjoyed cars. Later, Aloisia would unabashedly ride with Ferdinand during the Prince Henry trials, a famous motor race where it was certainly an unusual sight to see a woman in one of the competing cars! She also liked taking his vehicles into the country with him to visit his family, all of whom were still living in Maffersdorf. The first such trip they took was right after Ferdinand's success at the Paris Exhibition; they drove his winning car home to his village. When Aloisia met his mother and father, Ferdinand introduced her as his fiancée. The two were married in 1903, and a year later, they welcomed their first child, a daughter they named Louise, a little girl who wouldn't take long to get behind the wheel; in childhood, she was sometimes seen sitting at the wheel on their way to school!

In the same year Ferdinand Porsche and Aloisia were married, a Viennese paper did an article about Ferdinand, who was now becoming simply known as "Porsche," calling him "a tireless creator and worker." "To dream and to act," the journalist said, "that is the essence of people like Porsche." He was not even thirty, and already he had changed the automotive landscape of his country. It all seemed to arrive at once—marriage, family, and then, in 1906, a job as chief designer at Austria-Hungary's primary car company, Austro-Daimler. Porsche was an elite automotive man now, his name well known. Versions of

As a young man in Vienna, Ferdinand Porsche fell in love with Aloisia Kaes.

"the Porsche system" were being used all over the city: Even the Vienna fire brigade decided to become motorized by using hub-mounted electric motors he had designed.

Ferdinand Porsche had just the kind of talent that the future would need. In these early years of the 1900s—a time when Germany and Austria were still empires, and when Europe and America had no concept of what it would be like to fight a world war—all the main car companies we know of today were taking their first steps. Thanks to new inventions such as the telephone, ideas were spreading more quickly, and that meant the race to advance technologically was speeding up too. Automakers were constantly observing one another, and a sense of competition had set in. Individual, motorized mobility was getting closer. But there was still so far to go.

Around the same time Porsche was starting his new job and his new family, Henry Ford, with the help of two Hungarian immigrant designers, was beginning to design a car called the Model T. This vehicle would later be known as the world's first car for the masses. But the gap of time between the invention of that car and the motorization of the United States was a matter of decades. Horses and carriages still felt inevitable, and most people still died in the very same towns where they'd been born, rarely traveling farther than a radius of twelve miles. The primary reason was an economic one: In the early 1900s, the average American made about five hundred dollars a year. That meant automobiles, which ranged in price from $650 to $6,000, were beyond most people's budget. (Later, car companies would invent credit systems, and the sales of cars would soar.) While in retrospect we can talk about 1908 as the birth of Ford's Model T, the time when "the people" got a car, in fact, all Ford had that year was "a wonderful car—one, single, wonderful car." As author and historian Douglas Brinkley points out: "At the time, Ford himself wondered aloud whether his company would ever build even a tenth Model T."

. . .

In 1909, the same year that the United States laid down its first mile of paved road, Porsche and his wife welcomed their second child into the world, a boy they named Ferdinand, after his father, but who would come to be known simply as Ferry. Now working for Austro-Daimler, a place that made cars for the elite as well as top-of-the-line racing cars, Porsche was at the Semmering hill climb racing one of his new designs on the nineteenth of September when word came that his son had been born. It is a potent image—to imagine Porsche at the racetrack at the very moment his son enters the world—and not only because Porsche's main connection to his children would always be tied up with the automobile, but also because his son's birth occurred on the verge of a dramatic new decade of technological progress.

Between the years 1910 and 1920, the United States and Europe would experience a breathtaking degree of change. Change in transportation, economics, and political systems would go hand in hand. Technology was now, more than ever, beginning to be seen as a tool, indeed an engine, of political and economic influence, and Porsche himself was an example of how intimately these paths were being intertwined. Porsche was never interested in politics, and yet because he worked in the field of transportation, which was becoming an integral part of political and social development, politics would always be a part of his life. At times, this was because government subsidies were a means of getting money for his cars, but there was also a more simple reason: cars were for the elite, and who was more elite than royalty? Before 1914, Europe was still a place of empires, of kings and queens and archdukes—and they were among the first to buy cars. Jacob Lohner & Co., Porsche's first employer, had built cars for royalty, and Porsche had eventually been asked to build a car for Archduke Franz Ferdinand. When serving mandatory military service in 1904, Porsche was called on to drive the archduke on various occasions as well.

And so the dramatic turn of events that occurred in 1914 hit

Porsche and his family close to home. That year, all that speed and dynamic change being generated by the Western world produced a loud and violent crash: the First World War. As a result, the structures of government and country that Porsche had known would soon be dismantled and rearranged. It would be the world's first mechanized war—replete with machine guns, airplanes, and tanks—and so it seems fitting that its opening shot involved one of the world's first car bombs: Archduke Franz Ferdinand himself was the target, and though he survived the explosion, he and his wife were shot and killed later that same night while riding in their open-roofed automobile. With their murders, the First World War began. By the end of it, two empires would fall and a new balance would descend upon the political and economic world. The war would be ugly, as all wars are, and yet somehow, out of all the pain and chaos, a new symbiosis would develop between the United States and Europe, paving the way for the automobile to become the twentieth century's most intoxicating adventure.

Young Bill Bernbach got a job working at the 1939 New York World's Fair. The past decade had not been easy for him, and now well into his twenties, he was still unsure exactly what he wanted to do with his life. Bill had graduated from New York University with a Bachelor of Commercial Science in 1933, just as the Depression was in full swing and jobs were hard to find, especially for a slight and shy young man, whose brilliant blue eyes were nearly always glued to a book.

Through family connections, he'd found his first job in the mailroom of Schenley Distributors, working for sixteen dollars a week, stuffing envelopes with promotional brochures. Working in an idyllic brownstone in midtown New York City, Bill read fiction and philosophy in the lulls between his mailroom responsibilities. Though he loved literature, he was not someone who thought of himself as a writer or an artist, or someone who had any conscious inspirations toward the creative life. He had studied business in school, but he had a contemplative streak that made it difficult for him to fit in with typical corporate manners and moods. Aside from his close relationship to his large family, he was a bit of a loner in those years. Lucky for him, there was another person working in the mailroom who also liked books. Her name was Evelyn Carbone, the daughter of Italian immigrants, fluent in French, with a recent degree from Hunter College and plans to go back. She liked to watch Bill drift away into the paperbacks he smuggled into work, and she liked the intelligent way he could talk about what he read. The feelings Bill had for Evelyn were nearly bursting to be voiced by the time Evelyn took the initiative and invited him to one of her family's elaborate Sunday lunches. On the day she asked, Bill said "yes" even before she could get the question out.

But Catholic girls were not supposed to ask Jewish boys to meals at their home, or so certain members of Bill's family thought. When he told his mother about the invitation, she literally threw herself on the floor and wailed. Bill's parents had experienced persecution in their home countries and had come to America looking for a new life: It was their faith and their religion they credited with having saved and strengthened them, and they clung to it passionately, or at least his mother Rebecca did. She was very strict about the Jewish orthodoxies she'd practiced all her life, and she demanded her family respect them as well. She told Bill, her beloved youngest son, that it would kill her if he married a non-Jewish girl. *It's just a Sunday lunch,* Bill said.

At that point, Bill was still shy about forcibly stating his own wants and opinions, even to his family. Thanks to some unexpected relationships, however, that was beginning to change. Bill was always drawing attention and protection from powerful strangers, though it was hard to say exactly why. Even though his father was a clothing designer who dressed with flair, Bill inherited none of that love for ornamentation. He wore simple clothing and in those early years at least was not afraid to repeat the same few outfits every week. He was five foot seven, and thin to the point of looking a bit malnourished. But there was something else about him, a kinetic curiosity, an energy and presence that imbued all his gestures with a charismatic appeal. Bill's own initial innocence about this charisma is perhaps what made others want to take him under their wing. One of the first men to do so was one of the most powerful men in New York City at the time: Grover Whalen, who, in 1935, was elected to preside over the coming World's Fair.

Whalen was a former commissioner of the New York Police Department, a gregarious and experienced man of business who was the chairman of Schenley's for most of the 1930s. He was also the "official greeter" of New York City, which meant he met and schmoozed with all the big personalities who came in and out of town. Whalen noticed something about Bill, the boy in the mailroom, and brought him up to work as his personal assistant. The job was not glamorous—Bill ran errands and did clerical tasks—but the atmosphere often was: Whalen once took Bill with him on a business trip to Washington, D.C., for instance, just so the young man could experience his first plane ride. Bill would remember Whalen giving him five one-dollar bills when they walked into the Carlton Hotel, telling him, "Now Bill, what you do is get quarters for these, because we're going to need quarters for tips." It was a whole new environment for Bill. "I didn't have that kind of experience," he would later admit. "I learned the ways." Whalen liked Bill's innocence, and would often invite Bill and Evelyn to attend star-studded events with him around New York. Bill confided in Whalen about the troubles he was experiencing at home thanks to his controversial relationship with Evelyn, which, in the parlance of the day, would be a "mixed marriage," if they decided to take that step. Whalen's only piece of advice was this: *Follow your heart.*

Once the World's Fair got closer and required more time and

energy, Whalen brought Bill on board to help. At Schenley, Bill surprised everyone by writing an ad for one of their products, American Cream Whiskey, and sending it in to their ad agency, Lord & Thomas. A version of Bill's concept was printed in *The New York Times* soon after (or so Bill thought). He showed the ad to those around him and told them it had been his idea. Bill was becoming more and more eager to impress and move up the corporate ladder, and that only endeared him all the more to his boss at Schenley, and to Whalen. Here was a kid who was hungry to learn. The perfect audience for someone who is hungry to teach.

Bill started taking the train all the way out to Flushing Meadows nearly every day. Soon, there would be millions doing the same. At the World's Fair offices, Whalen put him to work writing short speeches and press statements. Bill was fascinated by the futuristic exhibits at the Fair, and by one of its main speakers in particular, Albert Einstein. He would soon memorize many of Einstein's quotes, and his own speeches would later be littered with them. "A problem cannot be solved on the same level on which it was created," Einstein once said.

What Bill picked up from Einstein was the realization that a release from categorical thinking could lead one to new levels of creativity. Reading men like Einstein and the philosopher Bertrand Russell, Bill came to understand science in a new way. He realized that the epiphanies of the writers he admired, and the epiphanies of the men and women who were creating the technological and scientific structures of the world, had been possible due to the same combination of social freedom and individual discipline. He saw that scientific work could also be creative work, that the two were not as distinct as they seemed. In fact, traces of both could even be found in the time capsule of the Fair, which included, among other things, a new invention called the wristwatch, a fountain pen, a sampling of alloys, various pieces of industrial machinery, articles on philosophy and economics, and the books of Thomas Mann.

During the evenings at the Fair in 1939, there were often fireworks exploding into the sultry night sky. Perhaps Bill stayed around after work to watch them sometimes, or to gaze at the glowing fountains of water that were also a popular attraction. And maybe Evelyn, who was now his wife, joined him there some nights. Bill had followed his heart and asked Evelyn to marry him, and she'd said yes. They found the pull between them too strong to deny, but getting married had not been an easy decision. Relations with Bill's family had been very tense. They'd hoped the situation would sort itself out with time. It didn't. In fact, it got worse. Upon hearing of Bill's marriage, his mother exercised her immense sway over Bill's father and demanded the ultimate: Her husband had to follow the traditional Orthodox rules and declare their youngest son dead.

It was the beginning of some hard years for Bill. Leaving his job at the distiller's to work with Whalen, Bill probably imagined great things would soon follow, but nothing materialized. Once Whalen's work at the World's Fair was over, Bill found himself thirty years old, disowned by his parents, newly married, and without a job. Evelyn was still working at Schenley and hers would be their only income for nearly a year. Watching months and months pass, in his desperation (and naïveté) Bill finally took a job with a mobster organization that was not very safe. When his boss at Schenley heard about this from Evelyn, he realized how strapped Bill must have been. He told Evelyn that the two of them should have spoken up about their situation. Shortly after, he arranged for Bill to go and talk with a man named William H. Weintraub. Mr. Weintraub was in the advertising business. And soon, so was Bill.

8

Hitler: Our last hope. That's the message of one earnest German poster from 1932, its drawings purposely dim, chalk-rendered, sorrowful: Half a dozen faces, the People, stare out in desperation, their skin and bodies yellow, smudged, thin. How did so many Germans come to think of Adolf Hitler as their last hope? And how did Adolf Hitler get so many people to believe in him?

Julius Caesar was apparently the first person to refer to the area of Europe beyond the Danube and the Rhine as Germania. Today the word *Germania* can have a distinctively Nazi flair—having been the name of Albert Speer's architectural model of the projected "World Capital" of Berlin, as well as of an SS regiment during the Second World War—but in 1900, it was a reference to a time when indigenous German-speaking people lived in small communities and had a strong connection to the land, an era that would become mythologized as the pure-blooded foundation of the German nation, though no "pure-blooded" foundation actually exists.

In large part, this idea had grown out of the writings of the Roman orator Tacitus: His work, *Germania,* was the first study of the natives of what is now Germany, and while it was brief and often used rather exalted terms to describe the characteristics of the native population, its overall conclusions would be passed down through the generations, still prevalent many hundreds of years later when German-speaking kingdoms finally did indeed become a legal nation in 1871. In that year, the German chancellor Otto von Bismarck, in a power move that blatantly excluded Austria, employed his "blood and iron" philosophy of politics and market unification to bring the formerly separate kingdoms, duchies, principalities, and free cities (*freie städte*) together, establishing the German Empire under Emperor Wilhelm II. It was a time when many nations, or countries, as we now know them, were just struggling to form. In response to Bismarck's unification of so many German-speaking areas, for example, the dualism of "Austria-Hungary" was formed, a troubled vestige of the original Habsburg monarchy and an empire mixed with diverse peoples and languages that would themselves eventually form separate nation-states. Bismarck's unification of Germany ushered in the creation of new national models, and that meant new models of trade and commerce. Soon after unification, the German industrial revolution began in full.

All of this was coming to pass around the time Ferdinand Porsche and Adolf Hitler were born, and in the years of their childhood, years moving up to the turn of the century, the German Empire became a place that garnered envy and respect. It was, in fact, second only to the United States in its economy and industry, even though the Empire's entire area could have fit easily into just a few American states. It was during these crucial years that Germans began to emerge as exceptionally innovative engineers with a deep concern for quality and precision. In fact, "German Quality Work," *Deutsche Qualitätsarbeit,* is a term and a principle rooted deep in the German idea of labor, stemming from the times of the farmer and the artisan, the days of the tinsmiths, blacksmiths, tanners, weavers, and others who worked directly with their hands.

Even though Bismarck had excluded them from the German Empire, it was not uncommon for German-speaking people born in Austria-Hungary to think of themselves as German. Thus Hitler, from a young age, rebelling against his father who was an Austrian civil servant, felt it was only the German side of his heritage he wished to adopt; it was a spirit easily accelerated by the Pan-German influences in his childhood town of Linz. And though it was the myths of Wagner's operas and romanticized ideas of Germanic heroes like Frederick the Great that quickened Hitler's pulse, tied up in that was the widespread desire to be part of a continuous story, a *nation.* It was something many in Austria-Hungary were searching for at the time, and it was an easy intoxication for some German-speaking young men.

Whatever the reasons for Adolf Hitler's identification with Germany, however, in the years leading up to the First World War, he was still alone, destitute, and wandering Vienna's streets, with no easy way of getting to Germany. For money he offered to carry people's bags for them at the train station, or drew and painted postcards and sold them wherever he could. Once his funds for rent ran out, he found himself sleeping in the streets. Eventually, with lice in his hair and his clothes tattered, he got himself into a homeless shelter and off the streets. He would eventually step up to staying in a Men's Home, something along the lines of a modern European youth hostel, a place where he had his own bed and locker and was in the company of men down on their luck or passing through town instead of the drug addicts and tramps of previous shelters. The Men's Home had a library and a room where "the intellectuals" often met. It was here Hitler spent most of the day, reading books, drawing his postcards, and giving impromptu speeches about his hatred for Vienna and the city's liberal tendencies.

Vienna was a city rife with anti-Semitism in those years. Hitler had a friend who was Jewish at the time, and in selling his postcards he often did business with Jewish men, but somewhere inside his animosity was beginning to grow, even if his rants at the time were not against Jewish people but against Bolsheviks, capitalists, and trade unions—words that were jumbled together and misused in both the city and his head. He began to hate all things associated with the fin de siècle artistic vibe of men like Egon Schiele and Gustav Klimt (whose art he would later try to destroy), and he told the men in the home that he planned to go to Germany soon and study *real* art.

When Hitler turned twenty-four on April 20, 1913, the money that had been left for him in his father's will finally became available and he was able to buy a train ticket to Munich, where he found a dingy apartment and continued making and selling postcards to pay the bills. Then, the unexpected happened. The archduke of Austria-Hungary, Franz Ferdinand, was shot, and the continent began to whip itself up into the violent frenzy of war.

Hitler snuck into the German army in the chaos, no one questioning his citizenship in the rush of recruitment then taking place. The First World War was a kind of miracle for Hitler. Not only did he get to serve for his "real country," but he also got to experience all the qualities he associated with that place. Suddenly he had a uniform; he had orders; he had a purpose, a place for all his manic energy to flow. Now there were rules, and a clear goal. He had never been very patient or able to study or concentrate for long, and the immediate action of war, the lack of choice in circumstances, and the regimented lifestyle taught him how to control himself, even as it further romanticized Germany and Hitler's idea of the classical German hero. Hitler gave his all during the war, working as a messenger, a dangerous job that meant he was often making his way to the front line. He was wounded and given a medal for his deeds. The men in his division said what others had also said: He was a strange fellow with odd ideas and unexpected determination, a manic sense of loyalty, clearly intoxicated by war's rush; he never got letters and rarely took leave; he often sat in a corner alone. But he was exceedingly loyal to his regiment, even deferring possible promotions just so he could stay with this new group he'd found. Stories would later be told of his close calls with death—stepping out of a command post a moment before it was blown to pieces, or moving from a trench just before it was attacked—and true or not, these stories would stir and exemplify his sincere and eventually horrific belief that he had been selected by Providence to fulfill a great task on Germany's behalf.

Those years of fighting were among the best he'd known. But then the very thing that Hitler feared most came to pass: Germany lost, and the war came to an end. All his grand ideas of Germania were defeated. Hitler was shocked. Germany's defeat infuriated him and made him, literally, very sick. He later wrote that he had not cried since his mother's death, but he cried when he heard the war had been lost. Lying in a hospital bed, temporarily blind and recovering from wounds he'd suffered, he thought of killing himself as he absorbed the news.

Hitler was not the only person shocked by the defeat. At the time of surrender, German industry was still pumping along normally. The entire country was untouched; there was not a single occupying foreign force in its midst. Having not witnessed the fighting from the lines, it is understandable that some German people came out of the war feeling shocked and betrayed, not knowing how many Germans had been killed in the past few months, having no experience of how weakened the German forces actually were. Because the defeat was not obvious to ordinary Germans, it was easy for conspiracy theories to spread: *it was the fault of the Communists, it was the fault of those who wanted democracy, it was the fault of the Jews.* These feelings were only strengthened during the summit held to decide how to punish Germany at the end of the war. Precisely because Germany was so rich in industry, the Allies now wanted to cut that potency down. There were grumblings that it had been German hubris that had started the war in the first place, and this perception only added to the punitive mood in 1919 as the Allies came together in Paris to work out the Treaty of Versailles.

Throughout the war, the rallying call of the United States under President Woodrow Wilson had been the mission to "make the world safe for democracy." It was the main reason given to the American people for the eventual U.S. involvement in the war, and it was the cause that many young Americans had enlisted, fought, and died for. In that spirit, Wilson had proposed the Fourteen Points Program for the Peace of the World, and the Allies had eventually embraced his plan.

Millions in Europe saw Wilson as a man who had come to save them with his plan for unification under the League of Nations. But while he sincerely believed in his ideals, they would prove hard to live up to once the war ended; at that point, the Allies were no longer united under one goal, and each leader had to look to the well-being of his own country. The United States was still young and unsure, and all that energy that had gone into "making the world safe for democracy" suddenly felt less urgent when the war finished, especially to the American people, who were removed from the reality of Europe, and who did not truly understand what was at stake. Wilson was left in a difficult gray area where he had promises to keep but lacked the people's support, and was all but abandoned by much of the U.S. Congress.

In the negotiations in Paris, Wilson found himself compromising much more than the people of Europe had expected he
would, giving in to the demands of more determined men like
France's Clemenceau. By the end, penalty upon penalty had
been heaped upon Germany; they were charged 269 billion gold
marks (about $32 billion), an impossible sum at the time for
them to pay. Land was taken away. Poland became a nation of
its own. France got the German colonies in Africa; Japan got the
ones in the South Pacific. And in addition to claiming full moral
and emotional responsibility for the war, the Germans were ordered to cut their army down to 100,000, give up their entire air
force, and destroy all their tanks. In effect, Germany was psychologically and economically debilitated. But the Allies were
not trying to be cruel; the war had been horrendous, violence on
a scale unknown before, and every European country was now
in dire need of money and resources, scrambling and lost in a
sense of lack and fear.

As economist John Maynard Keynes later said of the postwar
conference, "Paris was a nightmare, and everyone there was
morbid." No one seemed able to think clearly. No one seemed
ready to accept responsibility for what had taken place. And no
one seemed to know how to marshal the ideals and slogans of
democracy into a workable plan. In response, the German delegation claimed their burgeoning postwar democracy was being
annihilated "by the very persons who throughout the war never
tired of maintaining that they sought to bring democracy to us."
But that too was unfair. The Germans had no alternative to offer,
and no rationale for the trouble they'd caused. Nevertheless,
Keynes would warn the Allies that their economies were
"deeply and inextricably intertwined with their victims by hidden psychic and economic bonds," saying that the only way to
avoid a worse situation in the future was to take the path of
magnanimity now, for "the perils of the future lay not in fron-
tiers or sovereignties but in food, coal, and transport." Keynes
might have been right, but it was hard to get anyone to listen to
such words at the time: In the heat of the moment, most nations

felt desperate to take as much as they could for themselves, unable to see that by hurting one another they might also be hurting themselves. Still, whatever mistakes may or may not have been made both economically and politically, the aftermath of the First World War was a turning point: The old economic, social, and political world order had been deeply disrupted. It could not return to its prewar state; something new had to be developed now.

The First World War was a turning point for Ferdinand Porsche as well. Though he was the foremost automotive designer of Austria-Hungary, it was the war that brought him to the attention of the international community on a larger scale. In Austria, Porsche had been inundated with medals and awards. The University of Vienna, for instance, had given him an honorary doctorate, of which he was very proud, happy to finally have the weighty initials attached to his name, letters that gave him equal footing with other engineers in his field. During the war, his designs for tanks were among the best any country produced, and he contributed solutions to problems such as how to make the first practical, four-wheel-drive vehicle. At the close of the war, one of the top English technical journals concluded that the aircraft motors that Porsche was designing at Austro-Daimler were heads above anything else coming from the central European powers at that time.

Because the configurations of Europe itself also changed after the war, the Austro-Hungarian Empire was broken into pieces, and Porsche found that he was now a citizen of Czechoslovakia. He was given his choice of nationality, and for both practical and professional reasons, he decided to take the nationality of his hometown: "I do not change my nationality like my shirt," he said, expressing a deep loyalty to his parents and siblings still living there. Aside from work, family and personal relationships were the center of Porsche's life. Aloisia grounded and nurtured him. His daughter, Louise, an excellent driver in her

*Ferry and Louise sitting in one of their father's cars.
Automobiles were a part of life in the Porsche home
from day one.*

own right, was developing an interest in art, but when it came
to her father's business and automotive concerns, she was proving to be as tough and shrewd as he. Ferry, his son, had become
Ferdinand's constant companion, tagging along with his father
nearly every chance he got, exploring the automotive factories
where his father worked, and unbeknownst to his father, even
driving the cars.

For Christmas in 1919, the war having finally come to an end,
ten-year-old Ferry was given his very own handmade Porsche
car to drive. It was small but solid, with an old trolley engine
powering it from behind. Ferdinand, excited to finally have the
chance to teach his young son how to drive, was shocked when
Ferry jumped into the car, shifted its gears, and pressed just the
right pedals without any instruction or help. Demanding to
know who had taught the boy such things, Ferdinand forced his
son to admit that he'd taught himself when no one was watching. His father was upset, but secretly perhaps he was also
proud. After all, Ferry's sister had started driving early too.

Family was obviously important to Porsche, but by this time
in his life, he now knew what was important to him on a professional level as well. One was his desire to build the ultimate

race car. Another was his dream to build a small and affordable car that could be mass produced. As Europe entered the 1920s, it was clear to him that the current state of the European automobile was far away from what the future would demand, and this excited him: There was a whole new kind of car yet to be built. He wanted to discover the design for that car; like a sculptor who has been given a block of marble, he could already sense what was there. He just had to cut the excess stone away so the inherent shape could be revealed.

The idea of building a small car had been on Porsche's mind since he worked for Jacob Lohner and had created a vehicle called the Voiturette, and it had continued at Austro-Daimler in an early attempt called the Maja. But the concept of a car that was not simply small, but could also do everything a larger car could do, only really began to form in his mind in 1921 when he started work on a car called the Sascha at Austro-Daimler. The executives at Austro-Daimler had not loved the idea of a Volkswagen—what "common man" can afford a car in these times, they asked—but Porsche was relentless, and eventually a compromise was found. Porsche could try out his new small car design ideas, such as an 1,100-cc engine, but he'd have to do it on a race car, not a car for civilian use. The result was the Sascha.

There was little about its design, other than its size, that showed signs of the Bug that was to come. When the Sascha debuted in 1922, people were skeptical—it was much smaller and more compact than any car to have ever entered the track—but when it won the entire race for its class, that doubt turned to respect. London's *Autocar* magazine wrote that the Sascha was a "very positive attraction indeed," and the *Viennese Motoring Paper* said if there was ever to be a design for a "car of the little man" one day, then surely it would come from something like this. Not only was the car striking to look at—like the body of a butterfly or a dragonfly with invisible wings—but it also was a spectacular achievement of design: It combined the capacity for high speeds with the durability of a four-cylinder engine that amazingly had the smallest cubic capacity of any race car of the time. Porsche had made the car smaller by also making the engine smaller, and he'd done so without losing power or thrust, using the swept volume of the engine to its absolute capacity and enlarging the valves. In a sense, such use of the four-cylinder engine was a precursor to the more fuel-efficient cars of today.

The Sascha was also the first car on which Porsche experimented with materials for the body that were of lighter weight but of higher quality than those found on other cars. These things alongside more technical shifts and changes with carburetion and ignition allowed him to get the tiny car up to nearly 50 bhp (brake horsepower). Even though he'd promised not to make a version of the car to be mass-produced, Porsche did make a version of the Sascha called "a touring car" that could have been produced and sold to the public if Austro-Daimler had chosen to do so. But they didn't. No one was interested. As Porsche's dream to build the People's Car became ever more im-

The Sascha, a small, 4-cylinder racing car designed by Porsche. Porsche is standing to the right of the car, the little boy at his side is Ferry. To the left of the car stands its patron, and the man after whom Porsche gave the car its name.

portant to him, he began to realize that following through on it was going to require a fight. He welcomed that struggle, though at the time he could never have imagined just how tough it was going to be for him, or how political.

Hitler decided not to kill himself. Instead, he channeled all that despair and anger into blaming the Weimar Republic, the new liberal democracy of Germany, a parliamentary republic established to replace the imperial government that had fallen at the end of the war. Unfortunately, with all the reparations and punishment inflicted upon the country by the Treaty of Versailles, the Weimar Republic had little chance of making the country happy or of winning its full trust. With more than thirty parties fighting among themselves, the new democracy was an astounding burst of improbability, diversity, creativity, and intelligence; certainly, it appeared extremely chaotic at times. With so many parties, it sometimes felt impossible that any decision could be made. All of this fed perfectly into Hitler's new way of seeing the world: He decided that Germany was being diluted by too many kinds of people and too many liberal ideas, and the new government was just another force weakening Germany. In Vienna, he'd seen pamphlets saying something similar about racial dilution—a popular topic in both Europe and the United States at the time—and he now adopted an extreme version of this idea as his own, blending it into his political ideology.

Hitler was not the only one getting caught up in such ideas at the time. Democracy had been so built up during the time of the First World War, but when reality set in afterward, it did not live up to expectations, and many felt it was not going to last. As historian Richard Overy has pointed out, during the 1920s and '30s, a significant number of people in Britain, the country that had been the pinnacle of democracy in Europe up till then, felt that there was a crisis of civilization at hand and that they would soon experience the end of capitalism, and perhaps the end of democracy as well. "The obituaries were, as it turned out, written in indecent haste," Overy writes, "but at the time a great deal of British opinion, across the class divides, believed on the basis of the evidence all around them that capitalism's days were numbered." At the time, there was also a surging interest in issues such as eugenics—a biological argument that set levels of desirability on particular genetic traits. Hitler's promotion of this perceived importance of blood and race would be an extreme manifestation of such concerns, but many respected and distinguished people considered themselves eugenicists in those days, including the economist J. M. Keynes and the Irish playwright George Bernard Shaw. One eugenicist in Britain named Marie Stopes, for example, cut off all contact with her son simply because he'd married a woman who had to wear eyeglasses: She said her son had "willfully ruined a fine genetic inheritance." As Overy writes, "the power of the popular biological argument was evident in its most extreme form in Hitler's Germany, but the phenomenon was international."

Hitler went a step further, however, combining the biological argument with a political and economic one. He was against capitalism, which made him antidemocratic, and being against democracy eventually became the same (in his mind) as being against the Jews, and being against the Jews was the same as being against the Communists (because, again, in his mind all Communists were also Jews). Somehow, with this warped logic, he believed that the same people who were behind finance capital were also the ones trying to destroy the country with Marxist doctrines forecasting the end of capitalism. Everything he hated merged together into one.

Diversity was the main culprit in Hitler's eyes; he felt there was too much debate and compromise because there were too many diverse voices being heard, and it was this repulsive diversity that democracy and capitalism represented. He wanted a pristine, pure state. And so, even though Hitler was still not a German citizen, and even though he did not have blond hair, he decided that blond-haired German citizens were destined to become the master race. It's hard to say exactly what kinds of insecurities had gone into such thinking, but whatever might have been going on inside his head, on the surface he was finding his poise and control, schooling himself in the art of rhetoric and propaganda at every turn. He now sought and accepted offers to speak with relish, sometimes giving as many as ten speeches a day, speeches with titles like "Social and Economic Catchwords" and "Emigration," which were well-attended and which helped him begin to make a name for himself with the higher-ups in nationalistic circles. When it came to speaking to crowds of people, he discovered he had a great deal of skill.

Hitler was only the fifty-fifth member of the German Workers Party, later renamed the National Socialist Party, or NSDAP, the Nazis. When he joined, the party was small, an amalgam of other organizations that had drifted into one. Hitler became its leader and christened himself "the Führer" in 1921, and he brought with him the fire of propaganda that he had been patching together over the years. A symbol of good fortune and fecundity in many ancient cultures, the swastika had been adopted by German nationalists at the beginning of the 19th century. Now Hitler adopted and adapted the swastika to become the symbol of the NSDAP. He also began to think of colors in connection to the emotions they inspired, using red as the background to the black swastika in a white circle. And he took the Roman salute used by Benito Mussolini and copied the gesture, creating the Nazi salute that so many in the world now associate with the word "heil." None of the characteristics of the Nazi party were original ideas of Hitler: His one devasting act was to combine all these things into one.

As head of the NSDAP, Hitler traveled by car as much as he could through Germany, meeting and speaking to people about his party's goals. He studied the German people and asked himself what it was they wanted to hear, what would give them that spark of power he knew they wanted to feel. He was careful in how he timed and planned his words, gestures, and speech. "The art of propaganda lies in understanding the emotional ideas of the great masses," he would write in *Mein Kampf*, "and finding, through a psychologically correct form, the way to the intention of the broad masses, and thus also to their heart." These years of speeches were like prolonged practices before a big game. He nearly always had pictures taken of himself from all angles and sides as he spoke, then afterward he would sit and study these pictures and tally them with the responses of the crowd. He listened to his own voice. He studied his own gestures. He practiced his facial expressions. He came to know his movements very well. He did this for years, noticing and watching the reactions, learning how to control himself, learning what worked.

Even so, in 1923 Adolf Hitler still did not look like much of a threat. He was an extremely busy, almost manic, man who was cobbling together an ideology, but there was a very large gap between the reality of his life and the fantasy he had of it. Certainly he had come a long way. He was the leader of a small but dedicated party; he had some attention, he had colleagues, he had support. But in the wider picture, he was not well-respected or feared. His newfound confidence was rather shaky too. When he pulled off his big "Beer Hall Putsch," for instance—the extreme event that he imagined would change the country overnight—he was met with a disturbing wake-up call. Even with war hero General Ludendorff by his side, the whole thing resulted in a disaster and he came off looking naïve and weak.

Hitler had wanted a coup that night, a putsch. He'd planned to take over the government by force, but in the end, his brazen declarations fell flat. The coup didn't work. Embarrassed, he fled the scene. He was eventually captured and placed in jail for his stunt. Once there, he fell into a deep depression, forced to confront the fact that his fantasy had not become reality, as he'd been so sure that it would. Once again, he thought about taking his own life. In the prison where he was being held until the trial, he reportedly told the psychologist on hand, "I'm finished. If I had a revolver, I would take it."

But then, an unlikely thing happened: The court decided to try him for treason. And just that one word—"treason"—was (in his eyes) the best thing that could have happened to him. The government was taking his attempted coup seriously. He had a voice. Many in the country, alongside Hitler, would now reinterpret the putsch: With the public's help, he could rewrite the story exactly as he wished. And, in another unexpected twist, he pleaded guilty to the charges of treason, and did so with pride. He gave the court a loud and clear speech about how the real betrayal in the country had come from the government, not from him. The German people had been betrayed by the First World War, and now he was merely trying to stand up for them, to put their country into more capable hands, he said.

These words might sound dubious today, but at the time, in a country with many disillusioned people who were angry and confused, it resonated. There were those in Germany who knew this man was not to be trusted, but there were also many who were looking for someone with such boldness, someone they could believe in, someone to lift them out of their depression and spiritual doubt. The courtroom was electrified by Hitler's prolonged and passionate speeches: The place became a sensationalized stage. And thanks to modern media of the time, that stage was surrounded by men and women from the press. Hitler, a nobody before the trial began, was a known and controversial voice in Germany by the time it ended. People wanted to hear from him; and the number of Nazi sympathizers began to grow.

Hitler was learning how to whip people up into a state of frenzy. As his biographer Ian Kershaw would later write, "Crisis was Hitler's oxygen." He was developing a philosophy that everything good was based on struggle and on the feeling of struggling toward a common cause. At the time of the trial, he still thought of himself as "the drummer," the person who would use propaganda to set that struggle's mood and tone; at that point, he did not see himself as an eventual dictator of Germany, though he did feel such a figure would have to rise. "The man who is born to be a dictator is not compelled; he wills it," Hitler told the court. "He is not driven forward, but drives himself." And remarkably, such words seem to have cast a spell. Even the majority of the judges did not want to find him guilty once he had delivered his speech. They had to be persuaded to hand Hitler a sentence of five years, only conceding after being assured that he would be eligible for parole.

After the trial, upon reaching Landsberg Prison, Hitler was given a very nice room with a desk. He was allowed to receive gifts, cards, Nazi Party members, and to order and request reading materials at will. He was thirty-five years old now, and the trial had given him his first taste of fame. Hundreds of people lined up to visit him in jail. While there, Hitler read and studied endlessly: "Landsberg was a university paid for by the state," he'd later say. While there, he also wrote the first draft of his autobiography, *My Struggle,* or *Mein Kampf.* His original title for it was *Four and a Half Years of Struggle Against Lies, Stupidity and Cowardice.* He worked on it day and night, buoyed by memories of his courtroom show. He'd felt the public's admiration, and he wanted more. As he wrote and reflected on the new way he was being seen by those around him, he began to cast himself in a new light: perhaps he wasn't simply "the drummer"; perhaps *he* was the man who would save Germany, he thought, the man born to be a dictator, reliant on his own will.

Oddly, even as he was writing *Mein Kampf,* thus solidifying his politics of racism and authoritarian angst, he was also having a revelation about the power of the democratic vote. While in jail, Hitler decided that the Nazi Party would have to come to power the legal way. Whereas before the Beer Hall coup, he'd felt that force was the only way to gain control, he now decided that his power must be given to him by the people of Germany themselves, by their votes. Hitler was also very concerned with getting Germany back into a place of international respect again.

To him, that meant breaking the Treaty of Versailles and proceeding with rearmament. A prime motivating factor for Hitler's every move would be revenge for the capitulation and punishment Germany suffered at the end of the First World War. He would speak about it incessantly, with the promise that such humiliation would not happen again.

Hitler's reverence and enthusiasm for motor cars was also closely connected to his plan to return Germany to a position of international power. He would find a way to combine two things he felt very passionate about—the automobile and national power. Already, it was common knowledge around the Nazi offices that if Hitler could not be found, he was probably at one of two places: the nearby car showroom where his new friend Jakob Werlin worked or the auto racetrack. Even before the 1923 Beer Hall Putsch, before jail, before the NSDAP was much of anything at all, Hitler had forced the party to stretch their limited funds in order to acquire two cars, both from the Austrian-born Werlin.

Jakob Werlin, a stocky man with hard eyes, first met Hitler in Munich, where the Nazi offices were located. There was a printing shop where Hitler used to go each time he needed to make flyers or posters for an upcoming lecture or rally the Nazis had planned. In the very same building as that printer, there was a Daimler-Benz showroom, and Hitler could never pass by without looking at the cars. Werlin worked there, and the printer knew him well. "I've brought a new customer for you!" the printer said on the day he introduced Werlin and Hitler. The two quickly became friends, talking and negotiating over Daimler's cars. One of the cars Hitler acquired from Werlin was candy-apple red, an unusual thing at the time, but Hitler wanted to make a statement with it. When Hitler was taken to jail, this car was confiscated. From prison, he told the Party they would have to buy him another one, and he wrote to Werlin asking questions about what he currently had in the showroom, and what it might be possible to buy. He thought of perhaps acquiring a

Daimler-Benz 11/40, or a 16/50 that had a roaring engine he especially liked. He wanted the car to be gray, and he wanted "wire wheels" on it. He also asked Werlin if he could get a special deal on the car, saying that he'd have to find a loan in order to purchase it because the legal fees he now owed were "making his hair stand on end."

Hitler loved cars in ways that had nothing to do with his own ambitions, but while he was in jail, he began to think of the automobile in a political sense. He read automotive magazines and sketched out designs for possible cars. His favorite book at the time was the autobiography of Henry Ford. Ford became a hero to Hitler. He even hung a life-size picture of the American on his office wall. It was (in large part) from Ford that he got his idea for giving Germany a People's Car.

The Model T, that "single, wonderful car" that the Ford company had first produced back in 1908 had, by 1923, grown into millions of cars and thus become the world's first car for the common man, the first car to be made for, and driven by, a class of people who were not necessarily elite or rich. Ford's customers were farmers, artisans, housewives; people with essential, everyday jobs. The Model T was a car that these people could both afford and understand, and they adopted it as their own.

Ford had accomplished this feat by introducing the moving assembly line into his new Highland Plant in Michigan, an innovation that increased output while at the same time lowering production costs and making automobiles more affordable. In 1914, Ford had also introduced new conditions for workers, raising wages considerably (his revolutionary "$5 a day" policy doubled the average wage in one stroke) while at the same time shortening the workday to an average of eight hours rather than the usual ten or twelve. These policies would eventually become the manufacturing standard for factories all over the world, providing the structural template for the modern automotive company, as well as the guiding example for the size and style of an automotive factory. It was a mode of business built on efficiency and speed. As Brinkley writes of Ford's first Highland

*Henry Ford and the world's first People's Car, the Model T,
which debuted in 1909. Comparing this photo to the early
photos of Porsche's Volkswagen shows how much the design of
cars had changed between 1909 and the early 1930s.*

Park plant that opened in 1910, "No sooner did production start up than the company's executives began prowling the factory floors looking for ways to save time, money and manpower through future mechanization . . . it was corporate development through unceasing improvement—and that, in essence, constitutes what came to be called Fordism, the restless approach to management that would sweep the industrialized world. . . ."

The Model T had taken nearly a decade to steadily spread through the country, but the point was, it *had* spread. Nearly fifteen million Model T's had been sold by the time Hitler went to jail, and nothing comparable had been attempted successfully in Europe. News of the car traveled slowly to the majority of people in Europe, but even for those in the know (and there were certainly people in Europe who bought and drove Model Ts), there was not a great deal of professional desire to create a similar car. In Europe, the conditions were very different and it was thought that the American model simply would not work. The American landscape and its mass of potential consumers differed greatly from the small European countries and their comparatively limited means of making a cheap car *and* a profit: With fewer people to buy the car, there was less of a reason to make one. But Hitler began to see the potential political points he could gain by being the one to bring the German people such an automobile.

Still, Hitler certainly was not the first to think Germany's future would be in a car for the common man. Inspired and intelligent men like Josef Ganz and Hans Ledwinka had been championing and writing about the People's Car for years. In 1923, for instance, the very same year that Hitler was taken to jail, the following was written in the *Automobil-Revue*:

> *Things will develop with the automobile as they did for the horse, the railway, and the bicycle. Not the grand automobile, which for a long time, if not forever, will belong only to a small, privileged minority, but the middle-sized and especially the small car ... The day will come—more quickly than we think—when ... everyone keeps an automobile (and that means speed) at home. ...*

If Hitler didn't read this exact article, he certainly read one saying something like it. They were easy to find in automotive journals of the time. The powerful car companies might not have been interested in making a Volkswagen, but ideas of industrial progress in connection to the automobile were being talked about openly in print and even in German universities. In his inaugural speech as the rector of the University of Karlsruhe, Herr Kluge suggested the need for a new spatial design and consciousness that took the automobile into account, saying that "right of way in the literal sense must be introduced ... even the middle-size cities will sooner or later have to undertake street construction, open up thoroughfares, build over- and underpasses ..." For many academics who studied progress, it was clear that the car's next step would be in the direction of everyday use. New inventions start in small circles, usually at high prices and requiring a lot of expertise, and then slowly become more familiar, more accessible, finally ending up in everyone's home or on everyone's desk. The washer and dryer are one example; the computer is another. In the years of Hitler's rise in Germany, the car was silently going through just such a change.

Even so, on the whole, it was a small percentage of German citizens who would have read or heard such a thing, and an even smaller percentage who would have believed it. To say that the average German could have "speed" in his or her control was like a fairy tale. But Hitler knew all of this, and like the color red, the swastika, and the democratic vote, he would adopt the idea of a People's Car and twist it into something toward his own ends.

When Hitler emerged from Landsberg Prison on December 20, 1924, Jakob Werlin had come through for him. Hand-delivered, waiting by the road, Hitler feasted his eyes on a brand-new shiny Mercedes. He'd gone to jail feeling defeated and depressed but now, a little over a year later, he was riding away with an entirely new image of himself. Remarkably, however, Hitler could not actually drive his new car. He did not have a driver's license, and he never would. As much as he loved cars, Hitler never actually powered one. Perhaps even he didn't completely trust himself behind the wheel.

As luck would have it, just as Hitler was making his entry into German politics, Ferdinand Porsche was preparing to leave Austria and take up his first job in the German automotive world. He had been creating cars for Austro-Daimler—cars such as the Model 27/80, which he designed for the Prince Henry trials—for most of his adult life, over fifteen years. By 1916, he had moved up to become the company's managing director, a position in which he felt he should be able to determine what kinds of cars the company chose to make. But Porsche and the other executives at Austro-Daimler did not agree about the future of car development. Porsche may have been idealistic, dreamy, all those traits that get caricatured under the term *artistic,* but he was also simple, practical, and severe; this combination of impatience and idealism became such a volatile combination for him that by the spring of 1923, he had to leave Austro-Daimler.

It was less than six months before Hitler's Beer Hall coup when Porsche took his new engineering job at Daimler-Benz. The company was in Stuttgart, Germany, a prominent old town in the southern part of the country. His new job had no relation to the one he was leaving behind in Austria. Though the names were similar, the German Daimler was a whole new company, and that meant a whole new executive board, and a whole new philosophy about small cars, or so Porsche hoped. And so, as the buds were swelling and bursting into green, Porsche and his family eased along the curving and chaotic roads of the German countryside, spring weather streaming through their cars, preparing to start over once more.

Porsche had not left the Austrian company on good terms. His feuds with the executives and the board became extremely uncomfortable for all involved. Some at the Austrian company found Porsche too hard to work with: He wanted too much, and he was too impatient, they said. He might be a genius, but he made impossible demands. First there was the idea of a small car. Second, Porsche was adamant that the company should have a strong representation in racing, a strong marquee. By modern terms, race-car driving had now become a popular sport. Entire towns often turned out to watch or to welcome home their returning drivers. Spreading a car company's name through winning such races was not a bad marketing idea. But Austro-Daimler was not quick to see Porsche's point. Porsche wanted time and money to build an increasing number of racing cars, and when it came to such things, it was either his way or no way at all. Porsche was stubborn: When he wanted something, it was very hard for him to let any circumstance stop him from getting it. Arguments heated the air for months before exploding during a board meeting, which ended when Ferdinand rose in anger and left. The company no longer wanted him. Lawyers would be called in to settle the rest.

Relocating to Stuttgart so that Ferdinand could take his new job was not easy for the Porsche family. Austria and Germany were very different worlds at that time. In Germany, the Porsches were considered foreigners. They had a strange accent and unusual ways. Upon signing his name, and including the initials of the bestowed Austrian professorship, Ferdinand Porsche was told the new initials attached to his name would have to be taken off: The degree from Vienna was not legitimate in Germany.

Things were no smoother for the rest of the family. Ferry found he didn't fit in with his classmates so well, and they ridiculed him. Louise was set on art school back in Vienna. Aloisia and Ferdinand thus put great efforts into building the family a special home, the "Porsche villa" they would call it, though it

Ferdinand Porsche carrying his young
son, Ferry, on his shoulders.

was more like a modest country home. Porsche designed part of it himself, and the house felt good to them all. It would become the center of their lives, a place of comfort and warmth.

Porsche too had a bit of a rocky start at work. The men at the Stuttgart factory (which Porsche insisted on calling a "workshop") were not used to the boss being so hands-on. Paul Daimler, the man who had been their boss before Porsche, was a behind-the-scenes manager and had rarely shown his face on the floor. But Porsche was almost always in their midst. Stuttgart was a place where distance was a part of the work environment and certain lines were just not crossed. Porsche crossed them. The engineers in their clean white coats were offended when the plump little "professor" climbed under their test cars and growled at them for not having figured out things he could see quite clearly. They had to get their hands dirty, he said, and stop all this standing around.

Porsche was used to eliciting a strong response. He had no time to waste, however, and those who didn't see his point were simply left behind. Some found him self-absorbed and rude, and whispered about his lack of education and his rough, country ways. Others, however, thought he was an inventive sage of some sort and respected him immensely, men who would follow Porsche anywhere. One such man was Karl Rabe.

In 1913, the twenty-year-old Rabe had been working at Austro-Daimler when he impressed Porsche by coming up with a solution to a design problem that had had everyone in the design office stymied for months, a problem having to do with how to provide adequate "claws" on the sides of military vehicles to help get them out of mud. The gentle, bespectacled Rabe came up with a beautifully simple design, and Porsche soon made him one of his right-hand men. But it was just this kind of behavior that made it easy for some to find fault with Porsche. He did not follow protocol. When Rabe was only twenty-four years old, for instance, Porsche promoted him to departmental chief of design, a position many older and more experienced men in the office felt belonged to them. But Porsche liked Rabe, and he trusted him. When Porsche left Austro-Daimler, Rabe had to stay in Austria for the time being, but the two would surely meet again.

Arriving in Stuttgart in the first half of the 1920s, Porsche soon realized that it was not a good time to be doing business in Germany. Inflation was making life difficult, to say the least. It took so much money for his son Ferry to pay his streetcar fare to school that the boy could not even carry it all alone! To pay the men at the Daimler-Benz factory, the bills had to be brought over from the bank on a gigantic lorry. The entire world was on the brink of the Depression, but there was a brief moment of calm before the storm. Not long after Porsche arrived in Germany, some began to talk of recovery and hope. The introduction of a new currency in 1924, the reichsmark, created a new stability and the stirrings of an optimistic spirit. A man named Gustav Stresemann was leading Germany on a new course, finding ways to juggle the difficult demands still in place from the Treaty of Versailles. In 1926, he was awarded the Nobel Peace Prize for his efforts. Germany was welcomed into the League of Nations, a sign that Europe was ready to accept it again.

But as usual, depending on which class and political group you were part of, there were at least two realities. There was Hitler's party (and others) who were blaming the Weimar Republic for all the harsh conditions imposed after the First World War, and there were those who believed in what the new government was trying to do and saw real and visible strides there. On top of all this, there was the experimentation and creativity of Weimar Berlin. In Berlin, culture and art were flourishing in ways they never had in Germany, as some of the world's most inspiring and controversial people were gathering in a frenzy of music, writing, and art. This was a time when it was hard to walk ten steps down Berlin's main tree-lined street (the Kurfürstendamm) and not see some important writer or artist sitting in one of the myriad cafés. Playwright Bertolt Brecht was easy to spot, for example, and people were often on the lookout for the artist George Grosz.

• • •

The city of Stuttgart was much more traditional and conservative compared to Berlin, and it took Ferdinand almost a year to win its respect. He did get their attention, though, by designing a race car that blew the competition away. In fact, there are few times on record when the town of Stuttgart came together to welcome home a hero that can outshine the day in 1924 when race-car driver Christian Werner returned as victor of the Targa Florio with the Mercedes that had been designed by Porsche. The main town square was filled with people smiling and cheering. The mayor even gave a speech. Porsche was asked to sign his name in the great golden book of the town (a bit like being offered the "key to the city" in the United States), and he was also awarded an honorary German doctorate from the technical college. The award was dedicated to Porsche "in recognition of his outstanding merit in the field of motor car construction and particularly as designer of the winning car in the Targa Florio 1924." Stuttgart was offering Porsche a home.

It was a shining moment for both Stuttgart and Porsche, but as the years passed, even as Porsche designed some of the world's best racing and luxury cars, the same old problems began cropping up: The German Daimler was no more interested in giving Porsche funds for trying a People's Car than the Austrian company had been. It was only after years of negotiations that Porsche managed to proceed with several designs he had for a smaller car, and was able to produce thirty test samples. But he was not happy with his work. He had tried to make a scaled-down version of a typical luxury car; but to build a Volkswagen, he would have to throw out these old blueprints and start from scratch.

Porsche was impatient, and once again, some executives at the company were frustrated with him, exhausted by his tirelessness, his constant demands for more money to build new kinds of cars. After Daimler decided to merge with Benz in

1926, Porsche found himself in yet another fix. Take a vacation, his bosses said, go to America for a while, have a look at the industry there, and when you come back, perhaps we can find another place for you, something other than head engineer. Never a man to compromise, Porsche knew he had to find another job. The work he eventually found was for Steyr, a company in Austria, which meant the family would have to move countries once again. The family was able to keep their house in Stuttgart, however. Germany was not through with them yet.

Austria received Porsche back into their fold as though he were a hero coming back from war. But the Depression was close at hand now, and Porsche would be affected by it quickly. At the Paris Exhibition of 1929, thirty years after he'd shown his first car there, he exhibited his new Steyr models to a warm reception. He went back to his hotel room that night feeling confident, but as soon as he saw the evening paper, that feeling vanished: A main bank in Austria was closing its doors. Unfortunately, the bank that was failing was Steyr's bank, and the bank that was surviving—there were only two at the time—was the bank of Austro-Daimler, the very company Porsche had left with such angry words years before. Porsche knew what this meant: Steyr would soon be bought out by Austro-Daimler. And there was no way Porsche could work for Austro-Daimler again. It seemed there was no company where he truly belonged.

It was not an easy time. Here was a man who had designed some of the best luxury and racing cars in the world, and yet he didn't own even one of those cars or designs: They all belonged to the companies for which he worked when he made them. None of the cars he'd designed for production carried his own name. He was almost fifty-five years old and weary from trying to work for others. It seemed the only option left to him was the option of striking out on his own.

$$11$$

During the 1920s, another young man was coming of age in Berlin: slender, blond, blue-eyed, with one of those oddly attractive gaps between his two front teeth, Heinrich Nordhoff was finishing his technical studies and looking for work. He'd set his hopes on finding a job in the United States. It was an unusual decision for a young man in those days, but by going to America, Heinrich felt he'd learn the most about modern methods of automobile production and design. Like Porsche and Hitler, he too was an admirer of Henry Ford. But unlike them, Heinrich was equally energized by the ideas of the market economy and its role in industrialization. He was taken by Henry Ford's ideas of service. Ford had motorized a population, but he had also been the first to pay his factory workers a high enough wage so that they too could participate in the marketplace and aspire to buying cars and owning homes of their own. Hitler would make use of this in terms of propaganda; Nordhoff was interested in the literal possibilities of innovation and growth.

Heinrich came into the world on January 6, 1899, born just one year before the Paris Exhibition where Ferdinand Porsche received accolades for his electric automobile. He was the second son of a banker in a small German town called Hildesheim. Heinrich was eleven when his father's company failed and the family, suddenly penniless, moved to Berlin to start a new life. It was a difficult time for the young boy, made even harder when, shortly after they'd settled in Berlin, his mother fell ill and never recovered. Her untimely death left the three boys and their sister to be cared for by their father alone.

Throughout those years of his boyhood and adolescence, Heinrich watched as his father gave every ounce of energy to his work and his family, rising from bankruptcy to become the director of an insurance firm. His commitment left a deep impression on Heinrich, as did his father's earnest Catholic faith.

*Heinrich Nordhoff, a complicated mix of
sensitivity and distance.*

Heinrich developed a religious sense of order and reverence, parts of him that only deepened with the loss of his mother and his encounter with the First World War, a war that he would experience firsthand. Just before his sixteenth birthday, Heinrich stopped his studies and became a private in the army, where he was sent into battle and wounded in both knees. Unable to walk, he was sent home to recover, which he later did in full.

As much as Heinrich respected his father, he'd decided early on that he did not want to follow in his footsteps and become a banker or an insurance man. Heinrich wanted to study mechanical engineering instead. After the war, he enrolled in a technical high school and upon graduating, moved on to the Technical University in Berlin. By then, the 1920s were roaring and Berlin was a city of such culture and experimentation that any artistically inclined young man could not help but be affected by the outpouring of emotion and expression. Heinrich was still living with his father, but the family had moved into an apartment that was in the heart of Berlin's "Museum Island." The streets he walked each day were streets packed with galleries, theaters, and museums. Heinrich had a sketch pad that he carried with him, often drawing what he saw and taking notes on his surroundings.

There was one young artist in particular that made a deep and lasting impression on him. It was just after his mother had gotten ill. He'd wandered into a nearby museum and soon found himself standing in front of a painting called *Tower of the Blue Horses* by Franz Marc, a near-cubist rendering of a family of blue horses stacked one behind the other in a landscape of yellow and red. In Marc's painting, the horses look stern, tender, and vulnerable all at once; their faces are basking in the light on the page, but they also appear nearly blinded by it. The painting radiates power, a natural animalistic power, sweet and disarming all at once. In the years before and during the war, museums throughout Germany had to protect Marc's blue horses and other paintings from people who wanted to destroy them, enraged by the feelings they conjured.

Heinrich stared at the painting of the blue horses for a long time that day. And he went back to look at it again and again. Something changed for him with that painting. He started reading the writings and letters of Franz Marc, writings about the power of the natural and animal world and about mankind's need for a renewal of feeling. Reserved and quiet with most, Heinrich only wrote about these things in long letters to a childhood playmate of his named Charlotte. She was his best friend, a girl he had met and become close to shortly after moving to Berlin. In his letters, he wondered if perhaps it was only in nature that beauty could be truly perceived in its full and honest form: "not halfway, not dishonest, not unfinished" is what he said.

Franz Marc fought in the same war that Heinrich fought in, but Marc died on the battlefield in 1916. In one of Marc's letters home dated June 21, 1915, the artist writes: "No one should pride himself on the belief that he is closer to 'essence' than others are. I prefer to have faith in others rather than in myself . . . The time of this world war is not more evil than any time of profoundest peace; within the loveliest peace, there is always a latent war; but the individual can free himself and can help others to do the same."

Heinrich, in the midst of reading Marc's work and thinking of him during this time, was inexplicably saddened by the news of the artist's death. What had been an emotional, adolescent attraction for Marc's work became something mature and rich for Heinrich now. Later, in his twenties, he would continue to think of Marc as he studied engineering, finding that the intrinsic power and design of natural forms also applied to technical and engineering ideas. Streamlining, for instance, was a process that looked to animals and insects for the principles of movement and speed, and these were then applied toward designing the shape and curves of the motor car.

Streamlining was a hot subject in industrial circles at the Technical University in Berlin, and debate about the upcoming "machine age" was another. Heinrich had one exceptional teacher toward whom he gravitated regarding these topics. His name was Georg Schlesinger, and he was a Jewish professor and designer acutely interested in how factories and machines could be integrated into the human side of labor and work. Schlesinger wondered at how an excitement for mass production could be understood and appreciated without the loss of man's soul: he feared that mass forms of communication and transportation were moving so quickly that if one did not stop to consider their sociological implications, the results could be economically disadvantageous and take a dangerous toll on the human spirit. Factories were not new, after all, and neither was industry: what was new was the relationship between men and the way they thought about their work. The new problems were psychological ones. As Schlesinger saw it, they stemmed from the effect of industry on a human's sense of worth: if people were beginning to be thought of as "the mass," where did that leave the individual? It was in such discussions with Schlesinger that Heinrich began to ponder the harder questions intrinsic to his various interests and beliefs. He began to think seriously about the intersections between machines, technology, ethics, and his Catholic faith.

Schlesinger had studied the type of assembly line that had been invented and introduced in the United States by Henry Ford; he was aware of the immense benefit and profit the moving assembly line was bringing to America (it would increase efficiency 25 percent, and between 1920 and 1929 the number of cars bought and sold in the United States would increase by 2.6 million), but he was equally aware of the problems the United States now had when it came to labor issues and discrimination. In Detroit, even with changes like Ford's five-dollar day, workers often found themselves stuck in monotonous jobs with no rights or voice in regard to the conditions of the factory or the amount of heavy labor they were expected to do. Workers' unions were struggling to form, and it was a battleground at times, with people getting beaten or even shot. Strikes became commonplace as workers tried to find and assert their own human rights in a machine age but were denied legal unionization. And business owners struggled to balance the new demands of the industrial world, one that (seemingly) required that more be produced for less.

It was one of the immediate problems that Fordism created. With the moving assembly line (started in 1913), Ford could produce many more cars at much cheaper prices, and the demand for cheaper cars was certainly there, but this required huge amounts of human energy. With the surge of customers, Ford needed more workers, but because the conditions of the factories were designed to maximize production, the conditions were unregulated and thus quickly became deplorable. Workers could not bear it for long; thus, in response, Ford had decided to double the average factory salary at that time, announcing that workers would now get a proper wage that in turn allowed Ford to run three shifts at the plant and workers flocked to get the high pay. Still, it wouldn't take long for them to demand better working conditions as well. In raising wages, Ford had only addressed one side of the problem. Nevertheless, it was the beginning of the modern American middle class—now workers could buy the inexpensive cars they were producing, and own their own homes. But it was also the beginning of a new consciousness about what workers were entitled to, and what work meant. And many of those workers were immigrants from Europe: In fact, in the early 1900s, the most common ethnic background to be found at Ford was German, and English came after that. It was this influx of foreign workers that allowed such rapid industrialization to take place. And it was also yet another factor adding to America's new sense of unrest.

Between 1877 and 1920, the United States was in the midst of its industrial revolution, shifting from a mainly agricultural-based economy to an economy that was mainly industrial. This new industrial market meant more jobs, more desired services, and eventually, more potential fear. During these years, the population of the country more than doubled, going from 36 million in 1870 to over 80 million by 1900. By 1910, over one million Jewish immigrants were living in New York City, most of them having fled persecution in their Eastern European homes. Bill Bernbach's mother and father came over in this wave, starting their family in the first ten years of the new century with their youngest, Bill, born on August 13, 1911. Likewise, Bill's future Catholic in-laws, the Carbones, came over with the more than 3.6 million Italians who became part of the American population between 1880 and 1920.

When Eastern European workers in the United States organized a massive strike against the steel industry in 1919, unrest vibrated through the country, causing riots in twenty-five American cities. This was all part of what became known as the Red Scare: Americans feared Communists were taking over the country, and many responded with violence. A bomb exploded at the house of Attorney General Palmer in Washington, D.C., on June 3, 1919 in protest, and was followed by seven more bombs in different cities across the country.

For everyone involved, so much change was both thrilling and frightening, causing women like Bill's mother to hold ever tighter to their religion, and causing many in America to pull closer together and protect themselves within familiar groups. It was a time of radical change: People could feel time speeding up, and distance shrinking. New colors and shades of everything were suddenly apparent: new faces, new landscapes, new kinds of work, new ideas.

In both America and in Europe, some people looked at what they saw as different from them, and talked of "being infected" by it. In both America and Europe, encountering so much change and difference continued to spur concerns about eugenics and diversity. And now that books and information could travel more easily, these theories were easily spread. In 1916, for example, a man named Madison Grant wrote a book called *The Passing of the Great Race,* about how America's diversity was going to eventually be its weakness. As it turned out, the opposite was true; America's diversity would be its strength, but at the time, many found it a valid argument. Hitler himself read the book in its German translation, and even wrote to the author to thank him for writing it, calling it his "bible," and keeping it in his library till the end of his life.

This whirlwind of change was not only attributable to an increase in travel and immigration, it was also a matter of the mixing and meeting of new ideas and new ways of life. This was especially true in the United States, as internally, the country began to move around and explore itself (thanks in large part to the cars of men like Ford). The more Model T's were sold, the more roads were built, and the more people migrated and mingled. In fact, by 1920, after the expenditure of education, road construction was the country's biggest public project and expense. As the country became more motorized, people explored new areas, they encountered more choices, and this affected their lifestyles. As the American John Keats wrote in *The Insolent Chariots,* "The automobile changed our dress, manners, social customs, vacation habits, the shape of our cities, consumer purchasing patterns, common tastes, and positions in intercourse." All that change was just beginning to roar in the 1920s, and with it came resistance and fear. It was exactly this kind of fear, for example, that made Bill Bernbach's Jewish family disown him for marrying an Italian girl.

When American cars first started coming over to Europe in the mid-1920s, it caused a similar shock. It was as if space aliens had arrived on four wheels. In the past decade, the United States had advanced at rapid speed, but to see firsthand the proof of how far advanced the "people over the pond" were was astonishing and unnerving. Companies in Europe reacted immediately, trying to readjust their own automotive plans, but they were still far behind, especially Germany. In 1928, there was already one car for every 5 Americans. In England, there was a car for every 38; in France, Germany's great rival across the Rhine, there was a car for every 43 people. And in Germany, the country that had once been the leader in technology and perhaps also the most powerful nation in the world, there was one car for every 134 citizens, a statistic that left them almost a decade in the past. By the time Hitler came to power in 1933, there would be only 489,270 automobiles registered in Germany, which meant about one percent of the population owned a car.

There were both economic and social reasons for this. The First World War had debilitated industry, which meant it had also stymied the way modern machines were viewed. Many in Germany still rejected mass forms of production such as assembly lines because they were antithetical to the idea of German Quality Work, of artisanship that came with seeing one's technical skills as something necessarily tied to one's own inner life, rather than just something to pay the bills. Assembly lines and machines did not appeal to the German way of life, and yet in-

dustry and progress certainly did, and the two things were looking more and more inseparable. Voices could be heard on all
ends of the spectrum: some felt Germany needed to embrace
these new ideas and develop itself along these lines or else fear
falling even further behind. Others felt no economic gain was
worth reducing jobs to one repetitive mechanical gesture; humans were not cogs on a wheel.

Through the twenties, the Weimar Republic debated and debated these things. Plans were drawn for a great highway system
that would connect Germany and pave the way, literally, for a
new way of thinking about the motor car. But none of those
ideas or plans got anywhere close to being unanimously favored
in the government, or in the public at large. German states kept
taxes high on oil and gasoline, advocating the intricate railway
network that had developed instead. Train fares were kept affordable, and many argued that it made little sense to invest in
motorizing Germany when the railway was so efficient. At the
same time, however, big German cities were selling out of the
books about industrial American pioneers such as Henry Ford,
and universities were beginning to teach new American models
of business. This push and pull of fascination with progress and
industry, and desire to remain true to past ideals, left the country at a standstill. The Germans wanted to go where the Americans had gone, but they did not want to take the same route.

At university in the midst of all of this, Nordhoff could see
that the future of German automobiles would be tied to the innovations already in use in America. He didn't see how it could
go any other way, but following the example of Henry Ford did
not mean having to make the same decisions, or even the same
kinds of cars. There were other American models coming to the
forefront now too, new cars being tested and sold in a competitive market no longer dominated by the Model T. For those who
could read English, as Heinrich did well (later, he would sub-
scribe to the *New Yorker* and diligently read every page), it was
possible to seek out these new methods and study them. He also
wanted to study them firsthand, which is why he applied for a

job at the Nash Motors Company in Detroit. It was a company that had been created by a former General Motors man, with a *give the customer more than he's paid for* philosophy that Nord-hoff found very appealing. Things looked good for Heinrich at first: The Nash Motors Company was interested in him and offered him a job. But by the time they'd started serious negotiations, it was 1929, and the United States was on the cusp of something Heinrich hadn't bargained for: the stock market crash. After Black Friday, Nash wrote to Heinrich to tell him they were sorry but things had changed. Suddenly there were not even enough jobs for Americans; Heinrich would have to find something else.

Luckily, there was another option for getting experience with the American production model. One big piece of news in Germany in the late 1920s was the interest that General Motors was showing for a car company in Germany called Adam Opel. GM was emerging as the largest automobile manufacturer in America at the time: In 1928, GM represented 40 percent of the American market with profits of over a quarter of a billion dollars. Alfred P. Sloan, charming but tough, with thick facial features and the rugged build of a Marlboro Man, toured the Adam Opel company, looking to expand into the European market.

By the end of the 1920s, Fordism had been widely accepted for well over a decade, and now another business model was also coming into play, the GM model. Alfred P. Sloan believed that GM was initiating a new era in automobiles, and he described the change as a historical progression of sorts: Luxury cars had come first—Sloan called this "the class market"—then there had come Ford's "mass market," where the population had become motorized, and now, ushered in by GM and Sloan, there was "the mass-class market," a time characterized primarily by choice, a time where money was no longer the problem but rather large amounts of consumers got to decide what they most desired from among an array of elegant options.

People were also learning how to feel richer with less. General Motors invented installment buying, for example, allowing the population to enjoy a product while earning the money to pay for it. By the mid-1920s, one out of every three cars that General Motors sold was financed through an internal loan with the General Motors Acceptance Corporation. American car companies were also becoming more aware of the international market and the possibilities of what we today refer to as globalization. Because of innovations in communications and transportation, the foreign market was being seen as a viable, untapped consumer base, full of millions of people who would one day buy cars.

The Ford Company had opened plants on its own in Germany, England, and France, selling cars under its own brand. But GM thought the best business move was to invest in the future of Europe from the inside, to be there when the inevitable auto industry boom did finally occur. GM was not interested in building a People's Car or in motorizing the German population as Ford had done in America with the Model T. What they wanted to do was "acquire companies in individual countries and build upon their existing reputations." Opel was the perfect company for that: not only did it have a solid, indestructibly German reputation, it was also the only company in Germany already equipped with an American-style factory. With over three million square feet of factory space, Opel was churning out nearly half of all German automobiles produced. Sloan was impressed with what he saw there. And with Germany's recent entry into the League of Nations, it looked like a good time to invest. Thus, in 1929, General Motors of America bought 80 percent of the shares of Opel stock and Germany's biggest family-owned company became a daughter of an automotive company from the United States. Thus, when working for Nash fell through, Heinrich Nordhoff naturally applied to Opel. New management was coming in to work with the German management already there, and Nordhoff soon found himself speaking English with an American man. On the day of the interview, he discovered his future boss suffering from a hangover and lying down on the couch in his office. They talked anyway, and Hein-rich got the job. A German man accustomed to slow and me-thodical processes, Heinrich said he'd be happy to start in two months. His new American boss smiled: It would be better if Heinrich could start *next week.*

At the Weintraub advertising agency in New York City, Bill Bern-bach was like a kid in a candy store. He had a steady job again. His days had structure. And there was so much to learn. Aside from the one ad he'd written at Schenley, Bill had yet to prove himself a capable copywriter: A powerful man had decided to take a chance on him, choosing him over two big-agency men who had applied for the same copywriting job. Bill was hired without a portfolio of any kind; hired because of a letter he'd written, and because of the warm recommendation from his for-mer boss at Schenley. It might seem like he was at a disadvan-tage, starting in such a way, but the novelty of it all gave him a fresh take and a powerful desire to prove himself. It provided all that energy humming in him a place to flow.

In those years, the advertising agencies lining Madison Ave-nue structured themselves as service industries with isolated departments and well-defined parts: there were those who pur-sued the customers and made the deals (the accounts depart-ment), those who negotiated for top ad space in magazines (the sales department), those who wrote the ads (the copywriting department), and those who created the look and added the im-ages (the art department). At Weintraub, Bill's concern would be the written message of the ad. As any new employee, Bill was expected to learn the previously established structure and fit in to the machine. But one of his first encounters in the advertising business would alert Bill to a rather radical notion he'd already sensed in his readings of men like Einstein—the established way of doing things was not always the better route.

Part of who we become often has a great deal to do with the people who inspire us, and at Weintraub, Bill met a man who inspired him immensely: Paul Rand. Only twenty-seven, Rand's manner was forward and jarring, but he had dimples and wore glasses as thick as the bottoms of Coke bottles, and the combination of it all somehow created a very real charm. By the time Bill met him, Rand was already a striking presence in the fledgling avant-garde media environment of New York, taking his cue from those in Europe who were using visual art within the commercial world. Rand was art directing for edgy magazines like *Esquire* and *Apparel Arts,* designing experimental covers for *Direction* magazine, and creating ads for Weintraub that were more like art posters than commercial pieces. It was unusual work in a time before "graphic design" had become its own vocation, a time when the covers of magazines or the images used to sell a product were considered commercial, a service rather than something to be noticed unto themselves: The image was usually the literal representation of what was being sold, more a sign than a statement, and meant to be more obligatory and information giving than creative or capable of standing on its own.

Paul Rand chose another direction though: He made covers and ads that were the point of the entire piece, rarely showing the item that was to be sold. Words were often superfluous, or were present as implications within the visual work. He was one of the first in America to use ideas of art coming out of Russia (Constructivist) and Germany (the Bauhaus) in the 1920s and '30s. Rand made the interaction between lines and circles and space into its own visual world, a place very different from the usual ad of the time. Ads in those days might cover the page with a giant car and write: *Spectacularly powered! Attractively priced!* In contrast, Rand's ads were delicate and often handdrawn, simple, using basic geometric figures and images to create a cohesive, gentle, powerful abstract whole; composition was a wakeful kind of work for him. He was not a commercial artist; he was something else: The ad business didn't quite have a name for·him yet.

Rand was aware of artistic developments in Europe at a time when few others in America cared. Heinrich Nordhoff had been moved by the work of Franz Marc, and though Marc had been killed in the war, some of the artists who had been his friends, men like Wassily Kandinsky and Paul Klee, had gone on to become part of another movement in Germany in the 1920s, the Bauhaus. The Bauhaus philosophy was a holistic one, and its visual characteristics were simple, colorful, and about as far away from "commercial" as one could get: their very simplicity exuded something more spiritual than physical, more ethereal than abstract. In that sense, looking at Rand's work was more like standing in front of a work by Kandinsky or Klee than it was like reading an ad. Bill was lucky to have made his acquaintance, and even luckier that meeting Rand was one of his first true experiences in both advertising and art. Because of this particular baptism into the world of ad agencies, Bill's notions of what made a great ad would remain less tied to commercial ideas and more to the ideas and inspirations associated with wakeful artistic work, images that offered not only information but communion as well.

Rand was also happy to meet Bill, and not only because of the fresh way the upstart saw the world, or because he liked hearing Bernbach's raspy voice, but also because the two shared another common interest: the world of books. Rand was as avid a reader as Bill, and the two were not afraid to talk of the work they were doing together at Weintraub in a larger context, one that touched on everything from philosophy to the latest novel to the newly translated work of the psychoanalyst Sigmund Freud. Rand and Bernbach went for long lunches, walking the bustling streets of Manhattan together, sitting at the deli on 45th Street, talking and brainstorming about all kinds of new possibilities for the combination of image and word. It was a time of education for Bill, and the interaction thrilled him. Back in the confines of the agency, he could be seen sparkling with excitement, practically running the halls as he told his colleagues that he'd just made *the greatest ad in the world!* It was an energy and an innocence that was too authentic to be made fun of: Bill was inspired.

Bernbach and Rand were in the midst of a new world. Advertising agencies had taken off after the First World War, thanks in large part to the new availability of products like aspirin and automobiles and thanks also to the new emphasis on mass appeal that the war had fostered. As Adam Hochschild writes in *To End All Wars*: "Just as warfare on an industrial scale required the mass production of new weapons like poison gas, so this new kind of conflict required the mass production of public support." And the social, political, and commercial systems that produced that support carried on after the war. As corporations grew wealthy, they spent more and more money on ads. The rise of national magazines also had a lot to do with it. A survey done in 1950 would find that 62.5 million people in the United States read at least one issue of *Life* magazine every three months. That was more than half the population. To reach all these potential consumers, big companies now sought out specialized firms rather than trying to create the ads in-house. Ad agencies auditioned for the giants of the consumer world, trying to prove they were the best place for the accounts of companies like Procter & Gamble, Marlboro, and GM.

It was a serious endeavor. America was becoming a consumer society. New forms of communication—national magazines, radios, films, and eventually television as well—were taking individual consumer tastes and interests and broadcasting them on a national scale, and the number of consumers was growing as a result. It was all tied to the rise of mass production and its role in that same free market economy described in the 1939 World's Fair lightbulb ads, one that by the 1950s would be in full swing.

Mass production and mass attraction went together: The more technological progression, the more people and places there were to reach. Companies wanted people to hear their messages, and as the audience size grew, so too did the prestige of the advertising agencies who created those messages. Advertising was becoming a medium of communication between companies and customers, the mirror that reflected and created tastes. In 1926, President Calvin Coolidge told these burgeoning agencies that they were playing a part in the "redemption of mankind," that they were tools of national education, and that industry was directly linked to the magazine advertisements and billboards then becoming so prominent in the average citizen's life. Coolidge told the advertisers that a great power had been entrusted to their keeping "with the high responsibility of inspiring and ennobling the commercial world."

In both politics and business, understanding why someone chose to buy a product or to vote in a certain way had become a crucial concern. The pivotal factor was the attempt to understand the psychological motivations behind choice. New forms of psychology were thus developing in natural parallel to the new forms of communication: to reach people, one needed to understand what motivated them. The First World War had made a dramatic point in this sense: The war was a testament to what masses of people could do (both creatively and destructively) when mobilized. But the war had also shown how much violence and unnecessary death can arise when people act irrationally. More and more, people became concerned with how to control their irrational, emotional side. In the years after the war, many Americans began to study and read about psychology, especially the work of Sigmund Freud, the Viennese man who had just given birth to psychoanalysis. Sigmund Freud's main philosophy was that irrational desires and impulses guide people's choices and that most of those impulses were subconscious.

The mass, and the idea of the mass, was also a focus of psychological study at the time. Crowd mentality caused people to act and react differently than they would when alone, and crowds could spur individuals toward dramatic, even violent, behavior.

"There is no one self always at work," the esteemed political writer Walter Lippmann observed soon after the war, suggesting humans are each a variety of "selves" depending on surrounding environments. Men like Lippmann (sincerely) suggested that the masses were a "bewildered herd" that needed direction and strong leadership.

Nations were composed of masses. Immigrants were masses. But consumers were masses too. The success of political slogans such as "making the world safe for democracy" in the First World War made it obvious that these various masses could be swayed by carefully sculpted messages, and not only in the political sphere, but in the economic sphere as well. The success of the wartime media campaigns had meant "high excitement in the booming field of peace-time propaganda" once the war had come to an end.

One man behind those pro-democracy slogans during the war was an American named Edward Bernays. The Wilson administration had employed Bernays to promote American war aims in the national and international press. He was the son of Viennese immigrants, and he also happened to be the nephew of Freud. He read his uncle's books and papers and applied them to his own war work. He saw propaganda as a rational, honest, beneficial enterprise. The point of propaganda, as Bernays understood it, was to marshal the irrationality of the masses toward positive ends.

"When I came back from the war," Bernays would later say, "I decided that if you could use propaganda for war, you could certainly use it for peace." In that spirit, Bernays set up the first public relations firm in the 1920s, a way of expanding the ideas behind propaganda to the commercial world as well as the political one. Bernays continued advising the government (President Calvin Coolidge got an image makeover thanks to his idea to invite celebrities to the White House), but he turned to businesses as well: How could companies best give the masses what they desired? And how could companies create an attractive image?

When cigarette companies in the 1920s wanted to open the market up to women, for example, Bernays advised that a group of young debutantes stage an event for the press where they pulled cigarettes out from under their skirts and called them "torches of freedom," and then boldly lit up. It worked. Before the war, a woman who smoked was an outcast. After the war, smoking became a sign of female emancipation. These kinds of campaigns—that appealed to competitive instincts and sexual desires—became the primary drive behind ads, especially ads trying to sell cars out of Detroit. These ads tried to speak to people's desire for a more exciting or fulfilling life; each product implicitly promised to fill a void: Women moaned when sitting in their new car for the first time, or gazed dreamily at the camera, big-eyed behind the wheel.

Though such tactics may sound malicious in retrospect, that wasn't the intent. At the time, spending money was equated with doing right by the country, and there was a rather unconscious no-holds-barred approach to consumerism. It was the first time that large groups of people were able to buy things for sheer pleasure rather than for functional reasons alone, and there was a sense of fun and freedom to it all. For a time, it seemed the market economy had only one direction it could go: up.

Thus the stock market crash of 1929 came like a slap, knocking everyone into an unrecognizable new world. Money value simply fell, disappeared overnight. The Great Depression set in, and with it, a sobering shock. After all those years of speeding up and garnering ever-increasing potential, 1930 left many people feeling as if they'd just crashed into an invisible wall. Advertising came under heavy attack for the first time, as people felt they had been tricked, manipulated by propaganda and by the idea of capitalism that had been sold to them. The manic rush of opening banks and the stock market to the public sphere, only to have it all come crashing down on them, produced a feeling of distrust in Big Business. People felt lost. Things weren't supposed to be like this. There had been a lot of "dreaming big" (a good thing) but unfortunately alongside those big dreams, people had forgotten that it was also equally essential that they think small. And those small details that had been pushed to the side in the desire for bigness would come back to haunt the market in a very dramatic way.

In the 1930s, very suddenly the country entered an uncomfortable adolescent stage where skepticism seemed the only answer to hard questions. At the same time, people still desperately wanted and needed to believe that something in the world was meaningful and worth working for. A balance had to be found. People did not want to be hoodwinked, but they did want to feel connected and inspired. People did not want to be disappointed, yet they did want to have hope. In that sense, advertising was transforming into a tightrope between power and desire, truth and deceit. Advertising was, after all, the medium between corporations and the people, and there was a great deal of responsibility in that. How could there be fantasy without exploitation? How could one feel connected without feeling subverted into a mass and taken advantage of?

The Depression pervaded all areas of an individual's life, and that was reflected in the larger life of the country and, to some extent, of the world. Politics, mass communication, transportation, the market economy: These were inherently connected now, and like one wheel turning the next, all these things in one Western country inevitably had their effect on those same things in other Western countries. During and after the First World War, through media, transportation, and the market, the Western hemisphere of the world had become more economically and socially interlinked; 1930 brought that realization into sharp relief.

Germany had many short-term loans from the United States, and when the Depression set in, all those loans were withdrawn. Germany defaulted on its bonds. The country no longer had credit anywhere; it was internationally bankrupt. Within the country, any signs of progress that had begun to emerge were quickly washed away, and the unemployment rate jumped to one-third of the workforce. Now the democratic Weimar Republic was held responsible not only for the First World War and its grueling aftermath in the 1920s but also for the economic tragedy beginning a whole new decade. For Hitler's Nazi Party, this was very good news. The world was beginning to look a lot more like the one Hitler had painted, and he was back on the streets and in the halls with his electrifying and manipulative speech. The stock market crash was a failure of democracy, he said, and democracy was linked to capitalism, so it must be a failure of capitalism too. It was exactly what so many were worried over. And for the moment, the evidence seemed to be on Hitler's side.

There could not have been a better moment (in his eyes) for a man like him to rise: Hitler had become skilled at noticing and then speaking to people's fears, and this was a time of immense fear. By stirring up hatred, he could use that energy for his own gain. Hitler was well aware of Edward Bernays and the propaganda campaigns of the First World War, and he knew that the irrational desires of the masses could be manipulated through image and speech. Thus, when the market crashed, Joseph Goebbels, the head of propaganda for the Nazi Party, went into overdrive. The goal was for Nazi events to get into the papers: It didn't matter if the press was good or bad, he realized, just so long as people were learning the party's name. In 1930, there were over 34,000 separate Nazi events. Most of these were beer hall speeches where people were whipped up into a feeling of communion with one another, united in their hatred and complaint, feeling part of a movement, a group: It gave them the illusion of control. In Berlin, Hitler began to draw crowds of up to 16,000 when he gave a speech.

In 1930 Hitler's party was able to garner 18.3 percent of the popular vote (6.5 million Germans voted for them), a political landslide that now made it the second largest party in the Reichstag. That was eight times as many votes than in 1928 when they had not even reached 3 percent of the popular vote. In 1932, the year Hitler was finally naturalized as a German citizen, the Nazi's got 37.4 percent of the popular vote. In his Berlin newspaper called *Angriff,* Goebbels wrote: "We are going into the Reichstag . . . like the wolf into the sheepflock." The Nazis were now the largest party in Germany and occupied 230 seats there. The Weimar Republic was fading out. One year later, Hitler would be appointed chancellor of Germany, arriving back to his apartment at the Kaiserhof Hotel in Berlin with tears in his eyes. He no longer felt "at odds with himself"; he had been accepted, voted in. And while he didn't have the amount of power he wanted quite yet, he was irrevocably in the door. But now that he was in, he was in until the end. He had no intention of ever relinquishing any of the power he had gained.

Martin Scorsese once did a documentary on Bob Dylan called *No Direction Home.* In the documentary, Dylan is being interviewed by Scorsese. He's talking about his early years in the 1950s when he first hitchhiked a ride to New York City and started singing in the bars and cafés of the West Village. There were so many others doing the same thing at that time, and Scorsese wonders what it was about Dylan that made a difference, that propelled him forward: Why was it Bob Dylan and not someone else who changed the world? Dylan shrugs it off as will and luck. He says: "I just snuck in the back door when they weren't looking, and then they couldn't get rid of me." Dylan came into America's consciousness through the back door, but soon his words reflected and helped to rearrange the entire house.

It's unusual to connect Dylan and Hitler, and this is not a comparison, it's a contrast. It's also a question: Both have captivated the world—why? These two names are so well known; each having become something distinct from the man himself, the symbol of an extreme or exceptional time—but the imprint they have left on the world, what they did once they were "in the door," could not be more distinct. Dylan created something, gave it to the people, and then let them use it as they wished: His songs became the people's songs. One is free to agree or disagree with the lyrics. The music moves you, or it doesn't. The very medium itself is one that invites unlimited points of view. In contrast, Hitler promised to give many things to the people, but those gifts came with conditions: The gift was no longer a gift but a manipulation based on his idea that he knew what was best. He used violence and brutality to try to make "his view" the only view. And he failed. Humans are capable of great creation and great destruction. The power of life runs through us all, and the only real measure of how much power we have felt is what we give. In that sense, perhaps it's wrong to think of *people* as powerful. Causing violence and brutality does not mean you are powerful. But neither does praise or fame.

Heinrich Nordhoff was a gentleman, but his veneer of polished manners sometimes made him very difficult to read. Brought up in Prussian schools and the Catholic Church, by the time Nordhoff was in his late twenties, he had an austerity and severity—a physical and mental neatness and height—that garnered respect but also forced people to keep their distance. There was a gentleness to him as well, but it was a side he kept in careful check, much like the slight lisp that occasionally teased the listener's ears when he spoke. His love of art and music and literature only deepened as he got older, but it was mainly his technical mind that others saw in those early years as he made his way up the ladder in Germany's elite automotive world.

Heinrich's first job at Opel was writing service manuals. The job was not his top choice, but he made the most of it, digging into the idea of service and learning as much as he could. The job gave him a steady income and thus he was able to ask his childhood friend Charlotte to marry him: would she come with him to Rüsselsheim? Could they start a family there? She said yes right away, having always imagined they would go through life together.

Distinguishing himself early on, Heinrich was promoted to manager of Opel's customer service branch within a year. Nordhoff was determined and ambitious, often working seven days a week and using his vacation days to observe other parts of the factory and learn as much as he could of the American-style machines there. Seeing his interest, the Opel executives sent him on study tours to the United States where he soaked up the American plants in Detroit and met with the American men at GM. Perhaps Charlotte had a difficult time with his constant working, or perhaps she had expected it from him and understood. Certainly, they were both happy that he had a good job at the time. Many of their friends were struggling in the darkness of the Depression. In Germany, Opel was the exception to the rule. It was an exciting time to be there; a feeling of expansion and discovery gave Opel employees the sense that whatever automotive future Germany might have, they would be playing a part. Incomes at Opel had risen in the twenties, and the American takeover in 1929 gave them an extra boost, allowing a level of stability few other companies in Germany could know in those years.

His time at Opel would set patterns that would follow Heinrich for the rest of his life. One early policy that would become ingrained in his way of thinking was Opel's decision to establish an extensive network of service shops and dealerships. Opel was owned by General Motors, but the management there nevertheless still took many of its cues from the early work of Henry Ford, planning ahead for a time when cars would be more ubiquitous, and Ford had always made it clear that a primary factor in the people's decision to buy a car was the knowledge that it could be taken care of if something went wrong. In that same sense, many at Opel knew the future would be in a

People's Car, but even the best minds there were unsure of what kind of car it would be, or when.

Opel was among the first to test the waters and experiment in making a small mass-produced vehicle. As early as 1924, Opel manufactured a two-seat, four-cylinder, compact vehicle called the Opel 4 PS. This vehicle came to be known as the "Tree Frog" because it was small and only came in green. It could not be taken on a highway because it would have fallen apart. It was shaky, cheaply made, meant for short distances and low speeds, more like a go-cart. It was a big step in Germany at the time because it sold well, a sign that the common man did indeed want greater mobility, but the Tree Frog was not a People's Car. The realization of a Volkswagen or Volksauto was still the great puzzle of the German automotive world.

Too much innovation had happened in the past ten years for Ford's Model T, the first People's Car in the world, to serve as anything more than a metaphorical example. At the same time, making a small version of one of the more advanced cars like Hitler's beloved Mercedes was an idea that proved both economically and technically flawed: The type of engine, the design, the materials, and especially the expense, simply did not allow for a car that was "the same, but smaller"; it was like trying to put a square peg in a round hole. The other proposed option—a three-wheeled vehicle based on the motorcycle, an idea pioneered by Karl Benz—now seemed just as inappropriate as a miniaturized luxury car. As one automotive writer named L. Betz stated in 1931 in *Das Volksauto*: "The one will be too heavy and too expensive to produce, the other ill suited in traffic and unusable for this purpose." What was needed was "no hopping tree frog, but a car designed for the street, offering a maximum of comfort but a minimum of luxury."

Ferdinand Porsche had realized this too, and at the age of fifty-five and out of a job once again, he found himself having to make some drastic decisions. Instead of seeking the job as head engineer from another of the elite automotive companies (an option that was hardly an option anymore, it must be said), he decided to do something many would have considered impossible: He would rally a team of the best German-speaking engineers and designers he knew and start not a car company or a factory—he didn't have the funds for that—but rather a consulting and design firm, one of the first of its kind. If he had his own company, he'd be in a better position to do things on his own terms. It was a risk. But Porsche was still considered a genius in the automotive world, and while there were many who did not want to work with him in their companies, Porsche was smart enough to realize that those same executives would still be glad to use him as a consultant on projects instead. They loved his innovations and designs; they just didn't like the effort it took to try to direct him.

Porsche was still living in Austria, but even so, the question of where to found his company and of where to live was easy for him and his family: They still had their beloved villa in Stuttgart, a city that was fast becoming one of the centers of the burgeoning German automotive world. It was also where companies like Bosch and Hirth, essential for supplying automotive materials and parts, were located. And the high concentration of auto firms in Germany would mean more clients for the firm than if they were Austria-based.

Deciding to open his own business and start over at age fifty-five was one thing, but even more remarkable was the fact that Porsche was able to convince twelve of the most talented designers and engineers in Europe to come with him to Stuttgart and work without a contract and with hardly any pay. The men Porsche collected were men who could have worked just about anyplace they'd liked, and nearly all of them would eventually be known throughout the world in their own right.

As Porsche opened his first office on Kronenstrasse in the heart of Stuttgart, the room must have practically crackled with energy and ideas. At the head of Porsche's team was the same young man Porsche had once so controversially promoted in his offices at Austro-Daimler, the kind, clear-eyed Karl Rabe. Rabe would become the secret weapon of any Porsche success, a man who truly made Porsche's future accomplishments possible by serving as a rational and intelligent anchor to the more obsessive and impulsive Porsche.

Porsche's son, Ferry, wanted to work on his father's team too. He was a young man now, and though he was the opposite of his father in many ways—introverted and shy—his own talents for design and engineering were undeniable. But Porsche was tough on Ferry and rarely complimented him or his skill. He was also adamant that Ferry not take the same route of his father and skip the all-important degrees that came with years of school. Porsche demanded that Ferry finish his education, and wanted that to be the priority before he came on board for full-time work. Porsche knew all too well how difficult it could be not to have the proper degrees, if not in terms of knowledge then in terms of the way he was perceived.

In the meantime, Porsche's daughter, Louise, had gone off to school as well, choosing to study art in Vienna. While there, she'd also fallen in love with a young lawyer whom Porsche had hired back in Austria to help him settle some disputes with Daimler when he'd had to leave the company. The hearty man's name was Anton Piëch, and not only would he become Porsche's son-in-law, he would also be a business partner in the new consultancy and a trusted friend. For Porsche, work was inseparable from his private, family life.

Porsche and his colleagues moved back to Germany to prepare their new business in December of 1930, just at the time that Hitler's party was starting its fated comeback and rise. On April 25, 1931, the first company to ever carry the Porsche name was entered into the official registry of Stuttgart as the *Dr. Ing. h. c. F. Porsche Gesellschaft mit beschränkter Haftung, Konstruktionen und Beratungen für Motoren und Fahrzeugbau,* or, the Dr. Professor Porsche Company for the Assembly, Consultation, and Design of Automobiles and Engines. Louise and her husband, Anton Piëch, invested 15 percent of the funds necessary to open the business. Porsche himself contributed 70 percent of the capital, and the remaining 15 percent was invested by a Jewish man named Adolf Rosenberger, a man who—due to the rise of Hitler—would soon have to escape the country.

Porsche wasted no time in getting to work on a Volkswagen. In that first year, he worked on a small car design for a man named Fritz Neumeyer. Neumeyer was the head of Zuendapp, a successful motorcycle company, and he was known to talk about his ideas for what he called a *Volksauto*. He and Porsche met as motorcycle sales began to slump in 1931 and Neumeyer felt ready to try out ideas for a Volkswagen instead. The Porsche guys called this Zuendapp commission Project 12. It would be

*Ferdinand's daughter, Louise, with her husband,
Anton Piëch, and her cousin, Ghislaine Kaes (left).
Anton would later become the head of the
Volkswagen factory, while Ghislaine served as
Porsche's valued secretary and personal assistant
for most of Porsche's life.*

Porsche's first attempt at building not a small luxury wagon or a small racing car but rather a whole new kind of vehicle, one that could compete on all levels with the more luxurious cars of the time but that would be affordable for the common man. Porsche and his team already had a kind of ideal image of the car in mind, and sketches soon littered the shop as they tried to make their own ideas materialize, each of them brainstorming and experimenting with all aspects of the car. As it began to come together, Project 12 looked strikingly different from the long, right-angle civilian automobiles that Porsche had designed in the past. This one had a strange shape to its back, and a body draped over rear wheels like half-closed eyelids. The exaggerated curve of the car's body dropped into plump fenders, the effect being one of an unusual simplicity and line. Their final sketch was for a streamlined two-door body, its engine in the rear, and a spare tire up front.

Looking at the drawings and sketches from this time, one can't help but see that the Beetle's personality (so to speak) is already there, but has not yet fully emerged. There is a familiar face in it, blurry, but coming into focus. Here is an iconic image

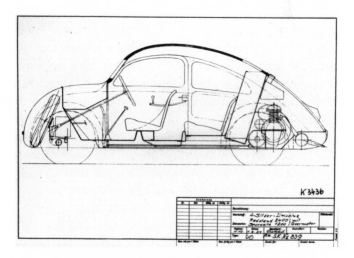

The future Beetle is slowly taking shape (sketch from 1933).

in its rawest form, a little chick that has just been born but not yet grown; clumsy, wobbling, but sure to make its mark. It's just a car, of course, and there were plenty of ideas going around for streamlining at the time that were similar to it—but none of those sketches became "The Love Bug," so it's hard not to see it as a kind of "family resemblance," as if one is looking at photos of the ancestors of a good friend. In fact, following that same idea, it really does feel as though every Beetle ever made has actually been only *one* car, the same car living a million different lives in a million different shades. But back in 1931, the car didn't yet exist in that form. Its characteristics were still developing; nothing was set. And there were plenty of problems.

While many good ideas emerged in all the early brainstorming, the guys in the Porsche workshop had trouble getting those ideas to gel as a unit, to hold together in real life. Porsche and his team found that if they perfected one part of the car, another would then slip beyond their control. As they experimented with suspension systems, the engines and torsion bars would sputter and leak hot oil, gears would snap, slivers of steel would shatter like ice. Cars would run too hard, or just stop dead in their tracks.

But as frustrating as the process was at times, in the long run, such experimentation had its rewards. In the process of creating this car, the Porsche workshop invented a workable torsion bar, for example, and the patent they received for this helped bring in funds and customers. In addition, there were sketches for a flat three- or four-cylinder engine that would not need water to be cooled, but early attempts at this engine proved frustrating and flawed. Cooling an engine by air was a rather new idea at the time (a Czech company named Tatra had been the first to try it), but Porsche could not get away with every idea he had, and Neumeyer insisted on a water-cooled five-cylinder radial engine instead. The gearbox would go in front of the axle, and the car would run about 25 hp from 1,000 cc. Amid the workshop clutter, there were also sketches on how to perfect the weight-bearing springs of the suspension system between each set of wheels and for a windshield glass that would sit straight up rather than having any slant or curve.

Though the shop had other projects in the works as well, Porsche was obsessed with getting the small car exactly right. He consumed any automotive writing he could find on new ideas of streamlining and weight, trying to rearrange all available theories into something new. By 1932, the Project 12 prototypes were ready to test and were sent all over the roads and through all sorts of trials, their inventors tweaking and adjusting them constantly, still trying to find just the right balance. All this testing took more funds than Neumeyer had allocated, but Porsche put his own money into the project, unable to stop. Adolf Rosenberger, the firm's investor and accountant, was often at his wit's end with the professor, trying to get him to stay within the monetary bounds. At one point, Porsche even went so far as to borrow on his own life insurance in order to pay the salaries of his men. Sometimes those salaries came a few days late, and sometimes they felt a great deal of stress over this, but none of them quit: they were caught up in the energy now too, and they were doing what they loved.

But when Neumeyer saw the prototypes, he wasn't sure what to make of Porsche's car. Something felt off. It didn't help matters that motorcycle sales had also picked up again, and like so many others in Germany, Neumeyer was thinking maybe it was better to stick with what he knew already worked; it would have been very difficult for him to produce a small car and still make a profit. In the end, Porsche and his engineers were fully paid but the project was canceled; they would not get to see their car produced. Porsche was frustrated but rolled right through that frustration: He already had another project lined up. This one was for a company called NSU. The story was the same: NSU was a motorcycle company flirting with venturing into the business of automobiles, wondering if a mass-produced car for everyman might be the way to break in. In the workshop, the

The prototype of the NSU car designed by Porsche's firm but never produced. It already has that familiar aerodynamic rounded hood.

Porsche engineers called the NSU car Project 32, because it was 1932 by then, and they slid all the designs and ideas from Project 12 into this new prototype.

They initially had more experimental freedom with this car than the Zuendapp job had allowed and the result was that the car got even odder-looking, the edges further curved, the front even softer. With Project 32 they were also able to try out their designs for an air-cooled engine, one that could be mounted in the back of the car rather than up front. Three prototypes were built and tested and the workshop bustled, but word came that this project would be canceled too. The pattern felt relentless. NSU got cold feet, and they claimed they'd forgotten about a former contract that kept them from building small cars. Just like so many before, NSU decided to stay in the motorcycle business where it was safe: At the time, Germany had the biggest motorcycle market in the world. All this hesitation was agonizing for Porsche's team, but the intense trial and error would not go to waste. Porsche and his men were innovating and tweaking with every seeming failure they experienced, and the overall design was getting better and better as a result. Porsche had been in business for only a year and a half, and he'd already gotten closer to building his Volkswagen than he had in the past decade of working for other firms.

A politician's first moves in office are watched carefully, thus it was telling that in his initial days as chancellor, Hitler showed up at the Berlin Auto Show to give a speech. It was also no accident that the theme of this show was *The Will to Motorization.* Before Hitler, no German chancellor had ever attended any such automotive event. But on February 11, 1933, less than two weeks after coming to office, Hitler stood before Germany's top automotive men and promised that the motor car would be one of his party's primary concerns. "The motor vehicle," he said, "has become, next to the airplane, one of humanity's most ingenious means of transportation . . . The German nation can be proud in knowing that it has played a major part in the design and development of this great instrument. . . ." And yet, Hitler went on to say, Germany has fallen behind in the automotive market and it was time to take steps to rectify that. There would be no more debate and hesitation, Hitler promised, and he would underline these comments at the following Auto Show of 1934. Starting immediately, he wanted Germany to embark on two major projects: The first was road construction, and the second was a car that could be owned and driven by the common man.

His first automotive speeches shocked the German automotive world. Not only did Hitler promise tax relief for all auto companies, he also promised more money for racing cars, more resources allocated for motoring events, and less interference from state government when it came to owning and building cars. Hitler was going to take such concerns out of the hands of the state governments and put them into the hands of the national government instead. In his eyes, it was the previous Weimar (which in his mind meant Jewish, Communist, Capitalist, and Democratic) government that was to blame for Germany having fallen so far behind other countries when it came to the automobile. With his appointment as chancellor, that would change. No country could be strong if it was weak in transportation, he said. Roads, a new automobile, tax relief, subsidies, and incentives for race cars—it was a lot for a politician's first full year in office, and the executives gathered at the Auto Shows didn't know what to believe and what to dismiss: was this just politics, or was he serious? It was hard to tell.

Included among those elite German automotive men who were following Hitler's first automotive speech that cold winter day in 1933 was Heinrich Nordhoff, now a primary player on Opel's automotive board. Hitler could be a captivating speaker, even Nordhoff would admit to that, but all the frenzy the new chancellor whipped up around him made it hard to see what was really there. On the one hand, Heinrich liked what Hitler was saying about automobiles, but he did not like or trust the rise of the National Socialists, or the frenzied feeling that was spreading through so many German streets and even affecting some of his peers. Heinrich hadn't joined the Nazi Party, and he didn't plan to now. For one thing, the party's ideas threatened Nordhoff's Catholic faith, something he held very dear. Hitler saw the power of the Church as a danger (priests were expected to obey Nazi dictates without question, including placing swastikas inside their churches).

But for Nordhoff and his colleagues at Opel, there was another side to consider as well. Even before Hitler had been elected to office, a conflicted relationship between the GM-owned company and the Nazis had emerged. With Sloan's company owning 80 percent of their shares, Opel was technically in the hands of the Americans, and Hitler found that deeply offensive. He saw it as a surrender: In his eyes, one of the crown jewels of German industry had been conquered by another land. Likewise, in the early years, there were many at Opel who did not like Hitler and were not afraid to say as much: In 1932, for instance, Opel executives refused to allow Hitler to use the Opel auto racing track for a campaign rally. It was something Hitler would not forget.

Later that same year, Hitler's henchman, Hermann Goering— a man who also loved industry and automobiles—unabashedly told an American embassy official in Berlin that it would eventually become impossible for Opel to remain under American control: As soon as Hitler's party came to power, Goering said, the National Socialists would take it back from GM. German companies had to be German-owned. It was a point Hitler had made early on: Even before coming to power, he had forced the members of the Nazi Automobile Club to sign an agreement promising they would not buy any foreign cars. He wanted German citizens to feel guilty if they participated in the global market: Instead, he felt Germany's borders should be open to exporting, but largely closed when it came to what they took in. Hitler wanted an autarky, an expanded German landmass that would eat up more and more area and thus acquire more and more industry. The German economy, he insisted, must provide everything for itself.

The feeling of hysteria that Nordhoff and many others felt descending on Germany was even more apparent a few weeks after Hitler's first appearance at the Berlin Auto Show. On February 27, 1933, a terrorist attack sent fear soaring through Germany. The Reichstag, the main governmental building comparable to the Pentagon or the Capitol in the United States, was set on fire by a young man who had once been affiliated with the Communist Party. It would become a pivotal moment for the Nazis. After the fire, a sense of order and control was in demand, and Hitler parlayed that desire into a chance to give himself and his party much more control. In order to deal swiftly with those who were threatening Germany, the country must have a stronger executive, a führer, he said, and in the panic of it all, he was able to blame the Communists and push new legislation through; legislation that would in effect take power away from other branches of the German government and more fully localize it in him. It was such a perfect situation for the Nazis that many would later wonder if they'd started the fire themselves.

In the following months, as the Führer Principle (Hitler's belief that the will of the people could be expressed only through the will of their leader) rapidly moved toward becoming the law of the land, Hitler was careful to follow through on his campaign promises with incredible speed, keeping the trust of the people on his side. This was especially true when it came to transportation. In the summer of 1933, the Reich Automobile Law was passed, absolving German states of any responsibility in matters concerning the automobile. Now the construction of streets, the ability to tax auto companies, and all other such automotive decisions would be conducted at the national level. And having such control at the national level—and thus, in Hitler's hands—did indeed produce speed: Three months after this law went into effect, and using plans that had been drawn up in the 1920s but gone unimplemented, widespread construction of the first modern German highways began. And Hitler was sure to be there for the groundbreaking. On September 23, 1933, the new chancellor earnestly shoveled out the first plot of earth of the coming autobahns. He was wearing his knee-high black boots, and he continually reached up to sweep his hair out of his eyes as he worked. He looked sincere: As the German magazine *Die Strasse* wrote at the time: "No symbolic groundbreaking, this was real work in the dirt."

In speeches that followed, Hitler tied the idea of national progress directly to the progress made in transportation: "Just as horse-drawn vehicles once had to create paths and the railroad had to build rail lines, so must motorized transportation be granted the streets it needs," he said: "If in earlier times one attempted to measure people's relative standard of living according to kilometers of railway track, in the future one will have to plot the kilometers of streets suited to motor traffic. . . ." The more roads that were built, the more the country would prosper. But prosperity was not Hitler's primary concern. There was another side to it too: The more roads the country had, the easier it would be to engage in war maneuvers, the smoother it would be acquire more *Lebensraum,* living space. It wasn't as sly as it looked: For Hitler, motorization, war, and renewing Germany were interlinked, and he did not pretend otherwise. In the words of German automotive writer Wolfgang Sachs: "The erasure of stubborn differences was supposed to be effected by 'eliminating opposition' and the highways were the spatial expression of this venture."

Today, perhaps it is hard to understand what a bold move the autobahn project was, but the scale of the street construction project Hitler initiated was unprecedented. Again, like so many defining characteristics of the Nazi government, the *idea* of the autobahn was one Hitler co-opted from other sources (most notably from his hero Benito Mussolini). Still, when it came to the actual creation of a network of such highways, nothing had been done like it in any other country in the world. The plan called for 6,500 kilometers of road, about 4,039 miles. And in fact 3,500 kilometers (2,175 miles) of road would be built over the next seven years. It was a huge public works project, and it was described in grandiose terms: The Nazis spoke of these new roads as "monuments" and presented them as natural accentuations of the landscape. This view melded the Nazi Party's philosophy of a return to nature with its philosophy of industrial progress in one fell swoop. One of their announcements called *Not Roads, but Works of Art* reads: "Nothing is to cramp or delay you in your swing from one horizon to the other, . . ." then adds that with highways the German landscape "will sparkle like a stone in an artfully wrought ring."

Road building was undeniably an important project to the power the Nazis wanted to acquire. Not only was it a way to give unemployed Germans a sense of work and purpose again, thus inspiring political loyalty to the man who had provided that work, but the new network of roads also gave the country a sense of literal unity, connecting areas of Germany that had never been physically connected before, bringing Germans from opposite parts of the country together to work on a common project, and providing a kind of metaphorical image for the population, to give them the sense of being one. The spirit it created was a hopeful one. And while the workers themselves would in truth have no direct control over what was to come from their government, for the moment, they would be made to feel as if they did. Working on Nazi programs such as this, the people could think of themselves as part of a grand project, doing what was best for Germany, acting not for individual gain, but for the greater cause.

Perhaps the strongest immediate benefit of the new road construction project was that it provided jobs for citizens in dire need of work. As many as a million new jobs came from motorization policies like this, and alongside the parallel project of rearmament, it helped the Third Reich bring the country out of its economic misery very fast. Before Hitler became chancellor, more than a third of Germans were unemployed. By 1938, the country would be working at full employment again. Automobile production tripled in Hitler's very first year: Private car production would rise 74 percent between 1934 and 1939, and truck production would increase by 263 percent. These were extraordinary numbers, and at the time, much of the world thought Hitler was doing something right. As early as 1935, the British magazine *Motor* wrote: "German car makers have made great progress during the past few years and have shown marked initiative in design. The encouragement which they receive from the German government, both directly and in respect of the national road-building program, is in sharp contrast with the anti-motoring policy of most British politicians."

People liked the idea of mobility, and Hitler was certainly taking advantage of the element of fantasy within it, but one had to ask: Who was expected to travel on all those new roads? If one had looked long and hard, it might have become obvious that the first likely advantage of such roads would be a military one. With less than one percent of the country motorized in those early years, the roads being built were nearly always completely empty and only the rich were buying more cars. In that sense, the project to build a People's Car was necessary in order to get the common people to believe in the idea of mobility Hitler wanted to present. One in which the focus was not on "war" but rather on "Lebensraum" and a higher quality of life. The fact that this mobility would *require* war was, at least in Hitler's mind, beyond question. But that did not diminish the importance of the automobile, or the goal of *Volksmotorisierung*.

Still, at first, most car companies dismissed Hitler's call for a Volkswagen as political rhetoric meant to get "the little man's" vote. But after Hitler followed through on tax relief, new automobile laws, and street construction, the big auto companies began to realize that he might be serious about the Volkswagen too. Of all Hitler's automotive moves, this one would be the most controversial. The other actions he'd taken were of clear benefit to the elite auto industry, but building a Volkswagen was an idea that they feared. Auto companies liked the thought of building a cheap car for the masses, something along the lines of a three-wheeled motorcycle perhaps, but they did not like the idea of building a car that was just as good as an expensive model, but could be sold at half the price. Not only were they feeling sure that such a thing was technologically impossible, they were also worried about having the government so involved in stipulating what kind of car should or should not be sold. In terms of the long-term health of the market, dictation of that sort was a threat.

But Hitler knew all along that he was leading the country into war, and all the momentum of reviving industry through road construction and rearmament was to be channeled into exactly that. Without war, all the money the Nazis were spending on such projects would have eventually resulted in a crash much like the one in 1929, and some economists of the time already knew it. In some sense, the Nazis knew it too: To avoid a looming economic crisis in 1936, they instated something called "The Four Year Plan." It was a plan to be fully prepared for war within four years, essentially creating a wartime economy in the midst of peace. This plan put nearly all of the country's industry into the hands of the NSDAP, making Goering, in effect, every German company's boss. Normal Germans considered The Four Year Plan a defensive measure, thinking the idea was not to go to war but rather to move into a position equal to the other countries in Europe that were already sufficiently armed. But Hitler's wartime economy would eventually require a literal battle or it would collapse.

With plans like the road construction project and rearmament, Hitler was rallying the country in one direction, and the nation's businesses were being trained to work in unison toward a common goal. Because Germany had been disarmed and much of its industry dramatically scaled down by the Treaty of Versailles, by (openly but illegally) restarting armament, Hitler was able to have a wartime economy for years before he had to actually have a war. All that energy and industrial activity was a way of catching up to other countries, making up for the time Germany had lost after the First World War. Soon, the internal lack of competition and the growing centralization would have proven detrimental—even Nazi economists tried at times to warn Hitler of such—but because of the strange situation Germany was in, he was able to keep the economic subservient to the political even while companies were still legally "private" ones.

The Volkswagen, however, was not merely a political ploy. Certainly Hitler knew the propagandist power in the idea, but he was also serious about providing Germans with cars: He could see no Germania that was not a motorized one. In fact, he and his Daimler dealer friend Jakob Werlin had been meeting and discussing the idea of a Volkswagen for years. Werlin often told the story of driving along with Hitler one day in the rain and seeing a man on a motorbike drenched and struggling along the road. In this story, Hitler invites the young man into his own elegant car for a ride (who knows what they did with the man's motorcycle!) while turning to Werlin and saying that one day he intends to give every such man a proper car. The story is most likely pure propaganda, or exaggerated at the very least. But Hitler went to great lengths to try to inspire enthusiasm for the project. He even targeted the young: Under his rule, toy stores abounded with tiny car figurines, including a black limousine modeled after the one that carried Hitler around Berlin, a toy complete with little working headlamps and an action figure of the führer sitting alongside the driver.

Automobiles were a passion for Hitler, and it was a passion he wanted others to share in, but he was a snob when it came to taking automotive advice. He considered himself an automotive expert, and he believed he knew how a People's Car would have to be designed. According to another oft-repeated story, upon discussing the Volkswagen, Hitler reportedly told Werlin: "It should look like a beetle. You only have to observe nature to learn how best to achieve streamlining." In truth, Hitler probably did make a similar remark at some point, but it is likely that he was merely repeating, and co-opting, ideas he'd read about in elite automotive magazines of the time. Hitler was not shy about taking popular ideas and claiming them as his own, and that was true when it came to all his passions, especially art, architecture, and the automobile. He had not had much formal education, and he tried to make up for that by reading, or skimming, as many books as he could get, and quoting from them extensively (and without attribution to the person being quoted). He also took measures to try to silence and extinguish the very sources from which he was likely getting those same views, especially if those were Jewish voices.

Heinrich Nordhoff's influential professor at the Technical University in Berlin, Georg Schlesinger, was accused of being "a spy for the enemy," for instance, and had to leave the country and teach in exile. And the popular Jewish automotive writer

and early Volkswagen advocate, Josef Ganz, a man who designed cars that had the look of a beetle, and who it is hard to
imagine Hitler had not read, was banished as well. On that note,
it is necessary to point out that when designing a car for the
people, Hitler believed it was his own authority that could determine *who* those people were. All Jews in Germany, for instance, were forced to give up their driver's licenses and were
banned from driving cars. Hitler's Volkswagen project did not
escape the ugliness of his racist thoughts. Nor would the country that had elected him.

As the leaves were turning colors on the trees outside the Porsche
home in Stuttgart and autumn pushed 1933 into its final months,
Ferdinand was in his office sweating over designs for a new race
car he was building. He was so caught up in the work that he'd
lost track of time and missed lunch. When Karl Rabe, often referred to as Porsche's gentler "second self," came in to tell him
there was a visitor, perhaps Porsche was just about to reach into
his pocket for last night's dinner roll: He had a habit of stashing
them there in the mornings before he left and eating them
throughout the day, and I imagine Aloisia had long ago gotten
used to dumping the crumbs from the pockets of his well-worn
pants and coats.

Porsche was never happy to be interrupted in the midst of
work, and it was no different when Jakob Werlin stopped by for
a chat that day. Porsche and Werlin had known each other for
quite a while, having both worked together for a time at Daimler, and thus Porsche's first thought upon seeing Werlin was that
he had come to spy, sent over from Daimler-Benz to get a look at
his designs for the new race car. That might have been true to

*Karl Rabe, often referred to as Porsche's "gentler,
second self." Rabe was Porsche's best friend. He even
kept a photograph of Porsche on his desk.*

some extent, though if Jakob Werlin were spying, it was probably not for Daimler, but rather for Hitler himself.

At the 1933 Berlin Auto Show, Hitler had promised to fund
new efforts in racing and to make Germany into a strong force in
the international racing world. He wanted a strong German marquee and he announced that the state would sponsor motor racing with a 500,000-RM annual stipend. The money was to be
awarded to one of Germany's foremost car companies and to be
used to build a top-of-the-line racing car. Everyone expected the
money to be given to Daimler-Benz toward building a Mercedes,
as the Mercedes was Hitler's favorite car. But a company called
Auto Union—a new firm that had formed when four small car
companies merged to survive the Depression—wanted a shot at

building such a car too, and they wanted to do it with a design by Ferdinand Porsche.

Just about anyone you'd asked at the time would have said Auto Union's chances of getting any of the Nazi race-car funds were close to zero: Auto Union was a new company and did not have the history or the prestige attached to it that Hitler sought. Ferdinand Porsche, however, was a name that did have that history and prestige, and it was a name Adolf Hitler knew well. He'd kept track of Porsche's cars and designs, and he'd read about him in the papers in Vienna all those years before. During a race of one of Porsche's cars in the early 1920s, long before Hitler had any real power, the two men had been introduced at Hitler's behest. Porsche never remembered that introduction, but Hitler did. It may have even been one reason Auto Union was able to get a meeting with the German chancellor: Porsche, alongside a famous race-car driver named Hans Stuck, agreed to go with the Auto Union executives on May 10, 1933, to try to convince Hitler to allocate them some of the new race-car funds.

Upon receiving the group, however, none of Hitler's admiration for Porsche was apparent. Hitler was distant at first, even going so far as to call the men rude for attempting to ask for money, shocked that such a "no-name" company would dare to ask for Nazi funds. But once Porsche began to speak, the vibe of the room changed. As Porsche poured out a monologue that lasted for more than half an hour, talking exclusively about his design for a new race car, brimming with the energy he always felt when talking about new automotive ideas, Hitler was rapt. The chancellor's secretaries would later say that it was the first time they'd ever seen Hitler listen to a man for so long without interrupting him. Porsche's passion for his cars filled the room, and by the end of the meeting, the impossible occurred: Hitler took a third of the money away from his beloved Daimler-Benz and promised it to Porsche to build an Auto Union racing car.

It was about a year later when Werlin unexpectedly dropped by to visit Porsche at his workshop, and it was that very Auto Union design that Porsche and his team were working on. Before they got the race-car commission, his guys at Porsche had been living hand to mouth. Being awarded the government funds was a big relief, but Porsche was less excited about the money and more excited about getting to build the race car. Werlin's visit, however, was for another reason entirely: He'd heard about Porsche's attempts at building a People's Car. Thus, in Porsche's office that day, sometime in late Autumn of 1933, it was the Volkswagen project that he and Werlin discussed. Hitler was interested in seeing a car produced for the people, Werlin said. Eager to discuss this, Porsche told Werlin about the designs for a small car he'd created on the projects with Zuendapp and NSU, and showed him some of the notes and figures he'd been compiling toward the construction of a whole new kind of car.

Werlin must have gone back to Berlin and told Hitler about Porsche's ideas because a few weeks later, Porsche received a call from Werlin asking him to leave Stuttgart as soon as possible and come to Berlin. They had some important things to discuss, he said, but it wasn't safe to talk about it over the phone; could Porsche come to the Kaiserhof Hotel the next day? Porsche was not one to arbitrarily change his schedule, but this time he obliged. He would leave for Berlin the very next day. He knew very well what this meeting could mean.

At the grand Kaiserhof Hotel in Berlin, Porsche met Werlin in the lobby and the two of them were shown into a lush room upstairs where they continued their talk about the People's Car. Moments later, the door opened and Hitler walked in. In their first meeting about the racing car, Porsche had held the floor, but now it was Hitler's turn to talk. Porsche listened as Hitler discussed his desire for a four-wheel-drive, 30-bhp car, one with a three-cylinder, air-cooled diesel engine, all ideas Porsche himself had already been working on with the NSU car and that he had shared with Werlin when they met. The car should also be able to hold two adults and three children, Hitler said. Porsche could probably tell that Hitler was regurgitating his own ideas, but he was nevertheless impressed by the depth of Hitler's knowledge of cars and his ability to converse about them.

On the surface, sitting there together near the large windows that looked out toward the Brandenburg Gate, Porsche and Hitler must have looked like opposites: Hitler in his perfectly tailored Nazi suit, not a stitch out of place, Porsche wearing his oversized work coat, his pants a bit too short, the edges of his shirt a touch frayed. But on some level, the two men probably recognized each other as well, both having been born in the Austrian countryside, both having come to their positions in untraditional ways, both passionate to the point of obsession. In time, the ease of the relationship between Hitler and Porsche, and their inability to discuss anything aside from automobiles when they were together, would annoy Nazi officials in Hitler's cabinet: Albert Speer, for instance, would avoid being in the same room with the two of them, finding their conversation frivolous in the face of daily politics and, eventually, of war.

But at the time, Porsche had no idea he would soon become so entwined in Hitler's government. Standing in the grand hallway of the Kaiserhof after that first official meeting with Hitler, marble arches and ornament stretching high above his balding head, scribbling ideas into his notebook, Porsche, as usual, was focused only on the immediate. Which is not to say he wasn't skeptical: How many times had he gotten his hopes up about this car, only to be let down at the last moment? Hitler seemed serious, but maybe it was just a lot of political hot air. And what about that price! Just moments ago, Hitler had said very clearly that the Volkswagen he envisioned should not exceed the cost of 1,000 marks. The average German at the time was not capable of saving more than 1000 marks, Hitler said, and so the price must be under that line. The car Porsche had in mind, however, would surely cost at least double that price. Once he was back at the shop, he told all this to Karl Rabe, and Rabe was as surprised by it as Porsche was. It is easy to imagine the two friends laughing about this price or simply shaking their heads in amused disbelief.

Nevertheless, in the following days, Porsche prepared a detailed plan incorporating all he and Hitler had discussed. It would later be known as "the Exposé" and would contain the most precise rendering of Porsche's thoughts about the car to date. He'd already written pages and pages on the car, but he specified and scaled those down in the Exposé, working on it for hours with his team. Werlin wanted it as soon as possible, but Porsche carried a final draft around in his chest pocket for days, pulling it out to make slight revisions, reading it again and again. In one section of the proposal, Porsche wrote: "In my opinion, a people's car does not have to be a small car with its dimensions, power output, weight and etc. being reduced in the misdirected manner adopted for previous efforts in this area . . . For me, a people's car must be a full-scale, practical model that can stand comparison with any other car intended for day-to-day use. [To create] a people's car, I believe that a fundamentally new approach has to be adopted."

In sending this document to Werlin at the Transport Ministry, Porsche knew he was submitting an application of sorts, and he knew what it would mean to have that application accepted. He tried desperately to get the price down to under 1000 marks, but he finally had to leave the price at about 500 marks higher than he'd been asked, and even that felt like a stretch. Porsche told Karl Rabe that he'd given Hitler the best price he could without compromising the solidity of his design; it was all he could do for now. He sent two copies of the plan off to the government offices in Berlin—one for Werlin and one for Hitler. It was received on January 17th, 1934. Then there was nothing to do but wait.

Hummingbird **was** the code name for the purge. Now, it's often referred to as the Night of the Long Knives. The Reichstag fire had helped precipitate Germany's change into a one-party state and had given Hitler more power, but there was still a great deal of resistance and threat to that power, most of it found in the chaos of the NSDAP itself. In 1934, a part of Hitler's own party had gotten out of hand, and its leader, the restless Ernst Roehm—one of the earliest members of the Nazi Party—had become a threat. In the early years, the NSDAP had been an assimilation of many anti-Weimar forces: the SA had emerged from the Freikorps, a nationalistic organization that carried machine guns and targeted Communists in particular with their wrath. The Nazis had used this army to their own benefit—the hundreds of street battles and deaths that the SA caused in 1932 had contributed greatly to the sentiment that had ushered Hitler into power—but now its volatile leader had become too much for him, and the two men were at odds about what role the SA should play.

Roehm's storm troopers had minds of their own, getting drunk and attacking citizens, and making it obvious that Hitler did not have complete control. Rather than the SA, Hitler had named the SS to be his personal military. But Roehm was still ready for a German revolution, and his SA was full of men with guns who were ready for it too. There were many calling for Hitler to rein in the SA, so it was not hard for him to bend the story and events of that night into what today is still sometimes referred to as the Roehm Coup: In short, it was made to seem that Roehm and his SA were planning to take over the government. And for such behavior, the only answer was death. The Roehm putsch, combined with the Reichstag fire and another manufactured event called the Blomberg-Fritsche affair, gave Hitler full control of both the police and the army, and thus complete dictatorial control. It was also a chance for the Nazis to do away not only with members of the SA, but also with any Communists, Social Democrats, or others Hitler wanted out of the way. Many prominent Germans were executed. In this final move, what Goebbels called a "chess match for power," Hitler broke loose of all restraints. And he got away with it. The nation helped him make it look like a legitimate legal move.

The Night of the Long Knives started on June 30, 1934, and ended two days later. On July 3, the German cabinet issued an official statement saying that the killings had been necessary matters of the state. Hindenburg, Germany's well-respected war hero, even wrote a letter expressing his gratitude to Hitler for getting rid of such treacherous influences. The brutality and lies and secrecy, the focus on traitors and punishment, set a tone for the country and for Hitler's reign, as did the fact that all this was done under a rational guise, another "emergency situation" that required "emergency measures." With usual ideas of morality now being stretched and warped, it was hard to know where one might safely stand: The truly "safe" bet was to do as Hitler wished. His governing maxim was "Whatever is best for the Reich." The catch was: He was the only person who could decide what was best.

Things were no different when it came to matters concerning the automobile. And Ferdinand Porsche would have been naïve to think he was the only man Hitler was turning to for plans of a People's Car. Numerous other German auto companies were also being courted. Back at Opel, for instance, managers had reconsidered their initial dismissal of Hitler's Volkswagen plan and were discussing ideas with his advisors. The Nazis did not like the fact that Opel was owned by an American company, but Opel had the factory, the infrastructure, and the workforce to build such a car (and of course, the Nazis felt sure that Opel would not remain American-owned). Porsche was a designer. His shop was not made for building or producing cars. Hitler was well aware of this, and he sent his advisors out to explore the issue from every angle. Hitler also went so far as to meet with the head of General Motors' overseas operations, the American James Mooney, about a possible deal. Mooney immediately went back to the United States with the thought that the German Volkswagen would surely be produced and designed by GM. In the company's monthly publication, Mooney wrote a piece gushing over Hitler and talking excitedly about the possibilities of partnership. It was in the midst of all of this that Ferdinand Porsche, his son, Ferry, and the rest of their team finished the Exposé and sent it in. Hitler was flirting with everyone.

On March 3, at the Berlin Auto Show of 1934, two months after Porsche sent in his plans, and just a few months before the Night of the Long Knives, Hitler spoke to all the gathered auto men once again. This time he talked about the Volkswagen, being very clear about the importance he attached to it. Porsche was at the Auto Show that day, and he recognized his own words in Hitler's speech: Hitler was speaking of things the two of them had discussed at the Kaiserhof and using ideas and specifications that Porsche had written about in his Exposé. It seemed like a good sign.

Opel thought they saw good signs too. At that same Auto Show, Hitler made a point of stopping by Opel's rented stage and paying particular attention to their "Opel-Volkswagen." Word had gotten out about Porsche's Exposé by then, but one of Hitler's advisors had also "leaked" information that Hitler was unimpressed with Porsche's design, which put the engine in the rear. If the members of Germany's Automobile Association, known in Germany as the RDA, had made bets in the summer of 1934 about who would be working with Hitler on his car, they'd surely have put their money on General Motors and Opel, not Porsche. And they would have been very wrong.

Behind the scenes, there was a very different story brewing. In actuality, Hitler had been deeply offended and annoyed by the article that Mooney, the American representative for GM, had written; it infuriated him that Mooney talked with such arrogance, as if the whole account had already gone to GM. At the Auto Show, Hitler had also been deeply disturbed to see Opel calling their car the German "Volkswagen": Hitler now felt that the word "Volkswagen," "People's Car," or any such variation of the term, was a word that belonged to him. By the spring of 1934, Opel and GM had in truth moved even further away from getting the project, though they imagined things were just the opposite. In typical Hitler fashion, he allowed people to believe one thing in order to give himself more time to act in exactly the opposite way.

Finally, eight weeks after Porsche had sent the Exposé to Berlin, Jakob Werlin called the Porsche firm. Karl Rabe took the call because Porsche was away in another city testing one of their cars. Werlin explained that he would be coming to Stuttgart the very next day: Could Porsche see him? Rabe, knowing how much the project meant to Porsche, answered *Yes, of course.* As soon as he hung up the phone with Werlin, Rabe began trying to reach Porsche, who was hundreds of miles away and difficult to track down. Once Porsche got the news, he left for Stuttgart, breathlessly arriving just hours before Werlin appeared.

It had been worth the rush: Werlin told Porsche that he had been chosen to design the German Volkswagen—the Porsche firm would get the job. There was just one small catch: Hitler was still unhappy about Porsche's price and he'd come to the conclusion that the best way to get it down to where he wanted it was to get the German Automobile Association involved. The RDA could provide materials and tools, Hitler thought, and this would reduce the overall cost. In having to work with the RDA, Ferdinand would be working with representatives from all the main car companies in Germany, some of whom were old enemies of his. Werlin and Hitler kept this decision as cloaked as possible, while Hitler continued his dance with the other auto companies, but by the following Berlin Auto Show, word was out. In February of 1935, Hitler gave his third Auto Show speech, announcing that a "designer genius" had been chosen to create the German Volkswagen and that the RDA was expected to work with this genius to produce the German People's Car. Even before Hitler spoke his name, everyone, including Nordhoff and the other Opel executives, knew exactly what that meant: The contract would go to Porsche.

There was no time to waste. Hitler wanted Porsche and the members of the RDA to have a prototype ready for production within the year. By 1938, Hitler wanted one million cars produced. This, of course, sounded insane. Nevertheless, the members of the RDA were ordered to assist Porsche in every way possible, and to keep tabs and reports of his progress that were to be sent regularly to the government offices in Berlin. All the major car companies had members in the RDA, but only Opel tried to rebel against Hitler's order, still feeling sure enough about their position and power in the country to be able to do such a thing. They were so close to having a small car ready for production themselves that they did not want to give it up. Opel executives tried to win the other members of the RDA to their side. Heinrich Nordhoff, being Opel's primary representative in the RDA, argued for his company, reiterating how impractical Hitler's ideas were. Nordhoff did not think that the government had the engineering and technical skills to be able to decide what kind of car should get built, and upon looking at Porsche's engine designs later, he said it was "built for an airplane, not a car." To him, the entire project seemed a waste of resources, and while the idea of a People's Car was not a bad one, this was simply no way to go about building such an automobile. But Hitler's word was now the word of the land. On August 19, 1934, a German plebiscite, a direct government vote, had vested sole executive power in Adolf Hitler. He was officially the führer now.

Ferdinand Porsche had a British-born nephew named Ghislaine. Young Ghislaine was thin and fine, chiseled and prim. He'd moved from London to Stuttgart to work for his favorite uncle, acting as Porsche's personal secretary. On December 17, 1934, as his uncle and the other men were in the garage working on the first prototypes of the coming People's Car, Ghislaine opened a letter from the Nazi authorities that was addressed to his uncle

Ferdinand and marked urgent. The letter strongly suggested that Ferdinand Porsche immediately apply to become a German citizen. It must have given Ghislaine's young heart a shock to read such words, for he too carried a foreign passport. In fact, most of the men in Porsche's shop were not German citizens, nearly all of them having come from Austria or Czechoslovakia to work for Porsche.

In the months since Hitler had given the People's Car project to Porsche, he and the other Nazis had been tirelessly praising Porsche as the "great German engineer," but in reality, Porsche was not even German; in the new nations that had developed with the fall of the Austro-Hungarian Empire, he was now considered Czech. Since his early years, Hitler had always claimed to hate the Czechs, seeing them as one of the main menaces in the empire of his youth. And now his great engineer held the passport of a Czech, and in fact, many of the ideas that went into the People's Car had come from Czech companies like Tatra and from Czech members of Porsche's team. This little fact about Porsche's Czech citizenship had been discovered by a jealous member of the RDA and brought to Hitler's attention. Perhaps the informer hoped to get in the führer's good graces with the revelation, or perhaps he imagined such news would change Hitler's mind about Porsche. It didn't work out that way, though. Hitler knew all too well how difficult it was to get German citizenship; he'd tried for nearly ten years to do so himself, having succeeded only a year before he was elected chancellor.

When Ghislaine told his uncle about the letter, Porsche looked it over and hesitated only a moment: "Well, I suppose there's nothing we can do about it. Go ahead and proceed," he said. A few months later, Ferdinand Porsche was a German citizen. Problem solved. It was yet another sign that when it came to race and citizenship, there was no solid Nazi policy aside from the dictates of their own imaginations and moods. The Nazis persecuted the Jews, but "Jew" was never completely definable by Nazi terms: Some Nazis reportedly had Jewish relatives; others had Jewish friends. In the co-opted words of

Goering, "Who is a Jew? That is a question I alone decide." Even so, one devastating thing would soon become clear: Those whom the Nazis did consider Jewish were people they did not feel deserved to live.

Sometimes Ferdinand's son, Ferry, would try to talk to his father about Hitler and the direction Germany was heading, but Porsche only wanted to talk about two things: family and cars. If he said anything about the political situation, it was only to tell his son that there was no way Herr Hitler—Porsche was perhaps the only man in Germany not to call Hitler "Führer" but rather "Herr Hitler" and get away with it—was planning to lead the country into war; how would they possibly produce a People's Car in the midst of a war? And wasn't Hitler serious about this People's Car? To Ferdinand, whose life revolved around automobiles, this seemed a foolproof argument, an obvious point.

Remarkably, many people in both Europe and America felt the same in the early thirties: They saw signs of progress in Germany, of increased work and a new stability. The country seemed to be emerging from the misery of the twenties, and business was picking up. Porsche's firm was no different: They'd gotten two large new contracts for the things Porsche cared about most—the race car and the Volkswagen. For the first time, Porsche had the freedom and the money to do exactly what he had always wanted to do. Almost. In truth, he had *the promise* of freedom and money, but in reality, he and his team were still barely getting by, beholden to the impossible time schedules and conflicting demands now being imposed on them by the German automotive men who comprised the RDA. Porsche was once again working for all the men he'd once been unable to work for, and it would be no easier this time around.

A bank account called "Volkswagen" had been opened for Porsche; 200,000 RM was to be allocated for the building of the car, and small deposits of that amount were given as the RDA saw fit. In an attempt to keep the project in private hands, they had met with Hitler and decided the German auto companies should pay for the car, thus Porsche's funds were monitored and given by them, not by the government. In the contract signed between Porsche and the RDA on June 22, 1934, Porsche was given ten months to produce his first car with 25,000 RM. Everyone knew it was an impossibly small fund, an impossible deadline, and that it would basically be a miracle if Porsche's team managed to achieve a working design for a whole new car under such conditions. Especially without a factory: None of the car companies offered to help or to lend factories or facilities. Because they had no other choice, Porsche and his team decided to use Ferdinand's own garage to build the first cars, and they quickly installed a milling machine, power drills, and two lathes in the tiny space.

The price of the car remained a problem as well. The contract with the RDA had stipulated that Porsche's car should cost 990 marks. Not only was this practically impossible from an engineering point of view, it was also unlikely that even if Porsche could make a car to sell at such a low price, there would be anyone to buy it. At 990 marks, one People's Car would still equal about 800 working hours for the normal citizen. If one compares those numbers to the Model T, the German citizen would be giving three times the amount of his or her wage to get a People's Car than the average American had given to pay for theirs. The impossibility of it all didn't seem to matter, though; Porsche's obsession pushed like a steam engine through anything that got in its way.

Even after the RDA signed their contract with Porsche, Heinrich Nordhoff and the others at Opel persisted in making their own small car, increasingly distancing themselves from the other auto companies that made up the RDA. They would eventually create a model called the P4, which could run at 200 RM and be sold at the price of 1,450 RM. That meant the price was 50 RM less than the one Porsche originally proposed in his Exposé, and Opel had the facilities for it to be mass produced. This Opel car was still a scaled-down version of a luxury car, but it was the most impressive effort toward a Volkswagen that anyone had come up with yet. Hitler did not appreciate Opel's attempt. Bringing his fist down hard against the table in front of him at another Berlin Auto Show, Hitler would tell them: "Gentleman! There can be only one Volkswagen, not ten!" And that meant *his* Volkswagen, the one being designed by Porsche. Opel would have to give up its idea of the small car. The P4 would never be produced.

Meanwhile, more than a dozen men worked together in Porsche's small garage, laboring day after day on the first three Volkswagen cars. They changed the engine type numerous times, going from a two-cylinder, two-cycle, water-cooled engine to an air-cooled, four-cycle, two-cylinder engine. The first did poorly when tested over long distances; the latter didn't have adequate power in the lower ranges. They tried all sorts of bodies: The three early cars were made of different materials— one wood, one a thin metal, and finally one that was all steel. Eighteen months after signing the contract with the RDA, Porsche had a drivable handmade prototype ready to show, and Porsche and his team took the car to Munich to let Hitler have a look. Hitler was deeply impressed and told Porsche that it was an amazing piece of work. The RDA men were furious that they were neither informed nor invited when Porsche showed Hitler the cars.

A full year of tests now commenced. Porsche and his engineers drove the V3 all over Germany, day and night, in inclement weather and in sun. (A little explanation about the term "V3": "V" stands for *Versuch,* which means something like *test model* in this context. There had been *one* car that was the V1 model and *one* car that was the V2 model, but because the V3 model showed the most promise, *three* V3 models were eventually tested, the third, fourth, and fifth prototypes ever made.)

The cars were always kept outside in the cold air rather than in garages so their start-up could be tested in all kinds of humidity and cold. (Most Germans did not have garages, so Hitler wanted the cars to be able to start in even the coldest of weather.) A member of the RDA often rode in the cars during these tests,

An early VW prototype coming out of the gate of
Porsche's home. In the background is the garage
where the first Beetle was made, and connected to it is
the beloved "Porsche villa," the family's home.

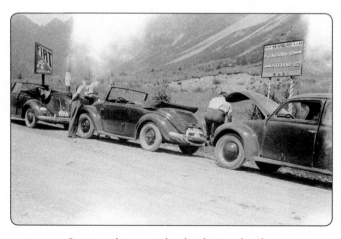

Prototypes being tested to their limits in the Alps.

taking careful notes. Sometimes the drivers did as much as 500 miles a day. Headlights went out, gearshifts and crankshafts cracked and broke, front wheels wobbled too much, shock absorbers dissolved, the brakes kept giving out. There were crashes with motorcycles and deer; there were times when they could hardly get the cars back home. People worked overnight to repair them just so they could be subjected to ever more testing the next day. The V3 covered over 30,000 miles and kept on going until December 23, 1936, the team trying to get the kinks out before the RDA issued its official report. Exhausted, Porsche and his team rested and relaxed with their families over Christmas into the new year of 1937 and the RDA compiled its report. Porsche wasn't too worried about the report by that time though. He knew the RDA was losing control. Once again, there was much more going on behind the scenes than most people realized.

In 1936, Hitler had sent his "designer genius" off on his first trip to the United States. Porsche had long wanted to go on such a trip, curious to see the factories and machines of America for himself. Ferdinand could not speak English, and he did not want to be alone for the trip, so he took his nephew Ghislaine with him as translator and secretary. The two men took a boat from Cherbourg and arrived in New York City on October 8, just as the autumn light was hitting the buildings, contrasts of dark and light allowing every angle to stand out against the sky. Porsche bubbled over with observations, bombarding Ghislaine with thoughts to record. His notebooks of those first days are awed sketches of the buildings as they frame the long straight roads, compliments about how nice and patient American drivers are, notes about Radio City Music Hall and the cleanliness and regality of the Hotel Commodore where Porsche and Ghislaine shared a room, and observations about the Roosevelt Raceway out on Long Island. (Porsche had Ghislaine take notes on the cars and the track, and Porsche himself sent a car to win the entire race the next year.)

From New York, Porsche and his nephew took a train to the crown jewel of America's automotive world, Detroit. Every moment was scheduled to the hilt with tours of the automotive plants, but it was the tour of the Ford plant that mattered most to Porsche. Work on Ford's River Rouge plant had begun just before 1917 and was completed in 1928. By the time Porsche was to visit, the place had become famous around the world. An issue of *Vanity Fair* from February 1938 gives a good idea of how it was perceived, calling River Rouge "the most significant public monument in America, throwing its shadows across the land probably more widely and more intimately than the United States Senate, the Metropolitan Museum of Art, [or] the Statue of Liberty. . . . In a landscape where size, quantity, and speed are the cardinal virtues, it is natural that the largest factory turning out the most cars in the least time should come to have the quality of America's Mecca toward which the pious journey for prayer."

Porsche and his team were now making that "religious" journey, and Porsche prepared a list of questions for Ghislaine to ask: How much money did the workers make? What kind of hours did they work? How much vacation time did they get?

Porsche sailing into New York City, gazing at the Statue of Liberty.

*Ghislaine, Porsche's loyal nephew, while traveling
with his uncle in the States.*

How did the people there buy their homes? What was this new
idea of credit, or installment plans, that they'd been hearing
about? From where did they get their materials and supplies?
Did they all have automobiles? What kinds of appliances were
popular in their homes? According to Ghislaine's notes, they
were both amazed at how prosperous everyone seemed, and
also at how clean they kept the workplaces.

They wanted an American car to take back with them on the
ship. At Ford, they tried to buy a car, but the model Porsche re-
quested wasn't ready and he ended up paying one thousand
dollars for a Packard instead. The car was a six-cylinder and he
and Ghislaine drove back to New York City in it, stopping in
Chicago en route. In his photo album from this trip, which is
now in the Porsche archives in Stuttgart, there is one photo
Ghislaine snapped of a sign in Chicago that reads: "Some of
life's keenest satisfaction comes from doing things we thought
we could not do."

Their last stop before New York was to take a moment to
stand and gaze at Niagara Falls. Porsche felt energized there,
standing and looking out at the water, feeling the tickle of mist.
It had been a long trip, but he still wasn't tired. In fact, he was

already pestering Ghislaine to find a way to get him on the *Queen Mary* that was soon to sail out of New York City. At the time, the *Queen Mary* was all the rage; the most modern ship of its time, and Porsche refused to take the ship they'd originally been booked on, once he'd heard the *Queen Mary* set sail that same day. On board, Porsche excitedly toured the ship's engine room, but the rest of the journey proved more difficult for him. There was a violent storm, and one regal passenger actually jumped to his death. Porsche was distressed by the suicide, and once they reached Britain, he was less enthusiastic about their plans to visit the factories there; after a morose tour through the Austin factory, Ghislaine packed Porsche away on the next train home.

But there was little time to rest. As soon as Porsche was back, Hitler wanted to hear from him. There was something important they needed to discuss. Hitler had recently met with the other auto executives of the RDA and asked them what price they would charge to mass-produce Porsche's Volkswagen design at one of their own plants. The RDA had come back saying there would be a 200-mark subsidy for each car built. The more Hitler

A photo from Ghislaine's photo album: "Some of life's keenest satisfaction comes from doing things we thought we could not do."

thought about it, the more he realized that if the government was going to pay an extra 200 marks for every car produced, it might make just as much sense to use that money and build the car in its own plant instead. Hitler asked Porsche if he thought it might be possible to build a factory based on the American model: Now that he'd seen the machines and moving assembly lines in America, did he think he might be able to organize such a thing himself? Ferdinand Porsche showed no hesitation in saying yes. But when Hitler suggested they call the new factory "the Porsche plant," Porsche declined. The factory was for the car, not for him; he insisted it should be known as "the Volkswagen factory" instead.

Jesse Owens was a black man from America, and he was riding the public subway in Berlin. Had he been in the Southern United States in 1936, the Olympic track star would not have been allowed to ride with white passengers—public facilities such as buses and trains were legally segregated according to race—but in Berlin, he mingled with white faces and was met with expressions of awe and appreciation, not disgust. Berlin was a bleeding sore of another sort of racism, of course, but for the Berlin Olympics, all of that had been tucked neatly out of sight. The decision to hold the 1936 Olympics in Berlin had been made in 1931, before Hitler had come to power. By 1935 Hitler was an admired man, sometimes spoken of as "Germany's savior." Hysterical women waited for him outside his mountain retreat, treating him like a pop star, taking away the stones on which he tread. After all those years of practice, his voice and manners had become as sharp as the blade of a knife. But the precipice was nearing.

Alongside Hitler's rise to full control, everything in Germany had become a mass event. It was a mood that Joachim Fest would later describe as "a psychological balance between fear and the fairground." It was the peak of the Nazi powers of propaganda, and it was the moment where propaganda was becoming an ugly word. Hitler and his party had realized that the best way to start a war was to convince everyone that they had no plans of starting one; to whip everyone into a state of wartime effort and emergency, but to talk to them only of peace. In fact, Hitler was busy signing peace treaties all over the Western world. "We will not lie and we will not cheat," he said. He talked to the British about Germany's navy, promising them he had no desire to challenge the British. He told Poland he did not want to take its land. To Austria, he said "Germany needs and desires peace" and "neither intends nor wishes to interfere in the internal affairs of Austria, to annex Austria, or to conclude an Anschluss." To the British, he reiterated: "We respect the national rights also of other peoples" and we "wish from the innermost heart to live with them in peace and friendship." Even as he said all of these things, however, plans were under way toward doing exactly the opposite.

In retrospect, it is odd to imagine the international world coming to Berlin to celebrate the Olympic Games. For Germany at the time, though, having the games held in Berlin felt like a crowning award to the success and growth Hitler's government had brought. Which isn't to say there weren't already doubts and rumors spreading; there were. So much so that an American delegation was sent to Germany to find out if there was any Jewish persecution there. Unfortunately, the delegation came back saying all was clear.

In truth, by the mid-1930s, it was getting harder to avoid issues of discrimination and race no matter where one lived. In the United States, for instance, race relations were experiencing a dramatic turn. President Roosevelt's New Deal, and especially the work program known as the WPA, had given many African Americans relief from the Depression. This, alongside Roosevelt's anti-lynching stance, his appointments of black men and women to councils like the National Youth Administration, and his wife Eleanor's open support of civil rights—had turned 75 percent of black voters away from Abraham Lincoln's Republican Party and toward voting Democrat instead. Still, President Roosevelt had also bowed to discrimination. In order to pass much of his New Deal programs, he'd compromised for the sake of votes, agreeing to separate and lower pay scales for blacks, and he'd bowed out of the lynching issue when things got too hot. The country, especially the southern part of the country, had been boiling over race issues for the past hundred years, and in 1936, mobs were still known to form and hunt down black men and lynch them for presumed crimes.

These lynchings were violent, ugly affairs of torture and disgrace, and senators in Congress were trying desperately to pass an anti-lynching bill to make such acts a federal crime. Congress fought dramatically and intensely and the event garnered a lot of press. Still, after a long filibuster by southern senators, the bill was eventually blocked. It was a bleak picture, one hard to swallow from the perspective of today, but even then awareness of the ugliness and despicability in such things was beginning to grow, largely due to new forms of mass communication. People were seeing themselves and their actions reflected in a wider and deeper way—shown to them in newspapers, magazines, spoken out through radio waves. Thus, even though the anti-lynching bill did not pass, it had an effect on the public consciousness, and the number of lynchings fell by two-thirds the following year. The angry mass found it was no longer an anonymous one. Being reflected in the media made the ugliness of such crimes more visible. And people did not want their faces spread across the newspapers as culprits of such horrifying crimes.

In the Porsche garage, no one was keeping up with Olympic scores. Ferry and Rabe spent most of 1936 relentlessly testing Volkswagen prototypes until they were ready for a full report by the RDA that was officially submitted at the beginning of 1937.

Looking at the photos from this time, there's no question about it: The Beetle has arrived. Oddly enough though, it looks older and more weathered in those years than it would fifty years down the road, as if it were born an old man and would grow younger as time passed on. And if a car could feel, in those days, it probably would have said it felt exhausted: The wear and tear the model experienced in those months was unprecedented for any other automobile of its time. And yet Porsche and his team were still finding all kinds of problems and kinks that needed to be worked out before the car could run well. The RDA demanded that the car needed more time and more tests. Hitler was not pleased, feeling it was them, not Porsche, who were responsible for the delay. At the Berlin Auto Show of 1937, Hitler's consecutive fifth, he scolded the RDA for their behavior. His voice was so loud that those in the first rows visibly straightened their backs a bit. With his left fist clenched, his stubbed mustache pumping along with his upper lip, and his eyes flaring, Hitler shouted: "Let there be no doubt: Private companies are either capable of solving this problem or they are not capable of continuing at all!" The little car had become personal for him. It was his *lieblingskind,* or favorite child, as Jakob Werlin now called it. He scolded them that day, but in truth, Hitler must have known that he was already finished with the RDA; they'd played their part. Nevertheless, the scolding did its job. Daimler-Benz scrambled to build thirty Volkswagen prototypes to be sent out for thousands of miles of further tests, and Heinrich Himmler sent 60 of his SS men to serve as test drivers for the cars. Now even those who tested the car had to be directly connected to the Nazi machine.

Heinrich Nordhoff, now the technical representative for Opel's sales line, gave a talk at that same Auto Show where he reiterated Opel's deep concern with quality products, saying it was the unregulated market that had allowed for the constant improvement of their cars. But his words sounded like an obituary for the free market. With the implementation of The Four Year Plan and with all of Germany's industry now effectively under the Nazi leadership of Goering, rational concerns for the future of German industry seemed to fall on deaf ears. The centralization of the auto industry was in full swing, and the members of the RDA must have known they were losing control, even as Hitler professed to be on their side.

Thus it was no surprise when shortly after scolding them at the Auto Show, Hitler took the RDA off the Volkswagen project altogether. On May 28, 1937, the Company for the Preparation of the German Volkswagen, Ltd. was formed to step in as the head of the project. Less than a year later, the name would be shortened to simply Volkswagen. Ferdinand Porsche and Jakob Werlin were at the new company's head. Rather than being funded by the private automobile companies that comprised the RDA, the money and structure would now come from the Nazi government's German Labor Front.

The German Labor Front was a financial empire headed by the importunate Robert Ley, and his organization was the most corrupt in all of Germany. Upon its creation in 1933, Ley had confiscated all labor union assets and liquidated all union funds. He'd also imposed monthly fees on German workers and made membership mandatory. It was supposed to work like a giant union—replacing the traditional workers' councils that had risen up as elected worker bodies within businesses—but instead of representing the workers it became the opposite: an oppressive and monopolizing threat. Because all workers had no choice but to join, Ley's Labor Front boasted the largest membership of any Nazi organization and generated copious amounts of cash, often raking in as much as $200 million a year. All that money was basically free money for the Nazis to use as they wished: Ley's accounting was private and did not have to be reported to anyone. Ten percent of those funds would now be set aside for the People's Car. The German Labor Front would be its official sponsor and owner, which meant the Volkswagen had truly become an enterprise of the Nazi government, and Ferdinand Porsche an official employee. The next step was to build their own factory, and the research for this project intensified.

Backed by Nazi funds, in the summer of 1937, Porsche, Ghislaine, Werlin, Ferry, and Porsche's son-in-law, Anton, all got to go on another extended learning trip to the United States. Now that they were building a factory of their own, they wanted another look at American plants, and they also used this time to recruit American workers to come back to Germany and work for them. Ferry liked America. He told his dad it was a wonderful feeling to be in a country where a man could act and work "without having to be supervised all the time." He even contemplated moving there, but as he'd later write, "the success of the Volkswagen at that stage, after all the work we had put into it, meant a great deal to us." He wanted to see the car finally come to life.

One thing Ferry and his dad were especially looking forward to was an appointment they had set up with Henry Ford. He was still their hero, and on this trip they got the chance to meet with him personally. It was just before lunch when Werlin and the

Ferry Porsche on a ship to the United States in 1937.

male members of the Porsche family, all of them in suits, filed into Ford's office, some sitting, others standing nervously; Porsche (with Ghislaine trying to keep up and translate) excitedly began to tell Ford all about the plans for a People's Car. He went on and on about its design and the tests it had been through and the hopes he had for it: Perhaps Ford might even like to work with him somehow? Ford came right out and said that no car designed by European standards would ever take hold in the United States; Porsche's People's Car was of no use to him. But Porsche didn't seem to be listening. Instead, he invited Ford to come over and see the car and the factory once it was built. Porsche would personally show him around. Ford declined: A visit to Germany simply would not be possible, he said, because Europe was heading into war. *War?* Porsche stared at Ford with a kind of frustrated disbelief: *Why did everyone think there was going to be a war?* (Among many Germans, this seemed to be a common reaction, and an honest one. Closed from the world to a large extent, they were shocked at how different their own country looked from afar. Even as late as May of 1939, for example, an elite German banker visiting the City of London was reportedly mystified at the preparations being made there for war.)

But it was probably not only the conflicting views and the souring of relations between Germany and the United States that made the visit with the legendary automotive man a rather cold one: Ford might also have been a bit distant with Porsche because at the very moment of their visit, he was in the midst of one of the hardest battles of his life, and his relations with Germany were tangled up in it. A newspaper Ford owned had published some terribly misinformed pieces about Jews, pieces with titles like "Does a Definite Jewish World Program Exist?" and "Will Jewish Zionism Bring Armageddon?" These articles were stupid and dangerous, to be sure, but one must realize that such stupidity did not mean Henry Ford wanted to exterminate Jews, as Hitler eventually would. Even so, it had been these articles, eventually published as a book called *The International*

Jew, that had become one of Hitler's favorite books, one he passed out to people on his staff. In 1926, Ford had issued a public apology about his campaign against the Jewish people, but not everyone believed he was sincere.

Thus, Ford was getting lumped together with Hitler, and many felt that he wasn't doing enough to change that view. In fact, Ford sometimes seemed to have turned into a different man altogether. Whereas he had once been considered an international hero and the most popular man in America, he was now the recipient of a lot of animosity, and it had made him bitter.

A lot of that bitterness came from his problems with his workers. Workers had once been Ford's main focus and his most loyal fans. But things had changed, and conditions in the plants had not evolved; indeed, they had worsened. Ford was not the only automaker in the States experiencing such problems. The whole country was experiencing a wave of uprisings. Workers had started forming groups and asserting their rights in ways corporations and the government could no longer avoid. By the end of the 1930s, those problems that Nordhoff's old professor, Georg Schlesinger, had noticed back in the 1920s had now become political problems that threatened chaos and violence in Detroit.

The national economy of the United States was changing and with it, so were expectations for a better quality of life: Industry, especially automotive industry, was an essential part of that. President Roosevelt understood this, and in an attempt to alleviate the tension, he established the Automobile Labor Board. This board conducted hearings that scrutinized the production centers and factories of automotive companies all across the country, exposing subhuman working conditions, hours, and pay. Until this point, workers had no legal representation, as unions were not sanctioned. Their treatment within the factories had gone unheeded and had thus deteriorated. Roosevelt's administration worked to pass controversial laws that would protect workers: The National Industrial Recovery Act and the Wagner Act gave American workers the right to organize legally.

The Congress of Industrial Organizations was formed, and from this, the United Automobile Workers Union, known as the UAW, gathered workers from all the major automotive companies together in 1935 in an open campaign demanding adequate working conditions and pay from the corporations that employed them. In 1936, the UAW took on the nation's largest corporation—GM. A forty-four-day sit-down strike against General Motors began in Flint, Michigan, and swept across the nation to other General Motors plants. The strikes turned violent. The public opinion of General Motors began to suffer—which meant business began to suffer—so the company acceded to the workers' demands and met with the UAW to officially work out a deal. It was the first time an automotive workers union had been recognized by a major company as having a direct say in their conditions, of where and for how much they worked. Many business owners felt Roosevelt had given the workers too much power, and at their expense. The proper balance between the workers and their bosses was still being sought.

Henry Ford resisted the United Automobile Workers Union for as long as he could, but in the spring of 1937, that resistance erupted into violence, sparking an event now known as the Battle of the Overpass, a day when members of the Auto Worker Union clashed with Ford's security force. Men and women from the unions were beaten and thrown down steps. Much of it was recorded in photographs. One man's back was broken. Ford was soon charged and ordered into court. The company claimed that the entire thing—even the back breaking—had been staged by the union, but Ford signed an agreement with the UAW nevertheless.

Porsche and the others visiting the United States on that 1937 learning trip were oblivious to this rioting and violence that had occurred just months before their arrival at Ford. Their eyes were trained on different things; they wanted a River Rouge of their own—the factory, and its machines and technology, was the filter for what they experienced there. Their notes are unemotional and precise. In one of the voluminous notebooks of thoughts and ideas from this time, Ghislaine wrote:

> There are 75,000 Ford workers employed at the River Rouge plant, and 140,000 in the United States . . . Ford is the only large company in the USA that hires Negroes and Whites without distinction in its plants. The Negroes are primarily assigned to physically hard tasks, such as in the forge and the foundry.

The new Volkswagen factory would use Ford's River Rouge plant as its structural and technological model, but it was taking its cues from American plants in more ways than one, and it would take them to even uglier extremes. Whatever lessons Ford was learning were lessons Germany would have to learn for itself, and even more violently. In a more extreme echo of Ghislaine's notes, the technical director and general manager of the Volkswagenwerk in 1941, Otto Dyckhoff, would deliver a lecture entitled "Automation in Production, with Special Reference to the Volkswagen Plant":

> Automated operations require a workforce composition differing from that used in normal operations . . . The actual machine operators . . . can be unskilled workers or trained on the job, since German skilled workers will regard mere insertion and removal of production pieces as beneath them. . . . In the not-too-distant future, we anticipate using more primitive people from the East and the South to operate the automatic machines, while making better use of our more highly qualified workers to set up machines and as toolmakers.

As had been the case during America's industrialization, great amounts of workers would be needed and would be thought of as a "mass" rather than as individuals: It was easier to avoid the inhuman connotations of this thought process if the mass was from a faraway place or of a different race. The assembly-line production employed at the factory and this mind-set would, for a while, go hand in hand. Ultimately, however, it would prove an impossible way to proceed economically, socially, and psychologically—just as Ford and America had learned, so too would Europe have to learn that to be profitable in the long-term, inhumane conditions could not endure. Ignoring basic human rights might produce more in the short-term, but it always inevitably proves to be an unsustainable, unprofitable path.

Upon returning from this second trip to the United States, in much the same way he had been made a German citizen, Porsche was made an official member of the NSDAP. And while he never officially signed his Nazi card—though he was prompted and urged numerous times to do so—there is no denying that he had made a Faustian bargain. Having the chance to build his own car in its own factory was the undisclosed dream of Porsche's life; it was also the beginning of the end for him.

19

Hitler sounds nearly schizophrenic at the 1939 Berlin Auto Show as he makes a sincere plea to German drivers to be more careful on the streets. It is extremely distressing, he says, that the death toll from traffic accidents has risen so sharply during his rule. The number of Germans killed by cars has reached the same number of deaths that occurred in the Franco-Prussian War. This cannot be tolerated, he tells the audience: Anyone who causes a traffic accident is "an unscrupulous criminal who sheds the precious blood of the nation." In the next five years, millions of Germans would die in Hitler's war, but he was lecturing them about traffic accidents.

There were no angry words at the 1939 Auto Show for the other companies of the RDA, though. All of that was in the past. The Volkswagen was on its way to production now. The factory was planned and rising, and once completed, the towering brick façade would be unlike anything that had ever been built in Germany. Modeled on the American style that had been pioneered by Henry Ford's chosen architect, Albert Kahn, the huge rooms were built to be spacious and bright. The Volkswagen factory, like Ford's factory at River Rouge, was a stark contrast to the dark, tight factory spaces that had come before: This new style of factory had a "sense of spaciousness almost unmarred by interior columns." They were, and still are, majestic pieces of architecture that catch and hold the eye.

A promotional flier for the 1939 Berlin Auto Show, with an illustration of the Strength through Joy Car.

In the shadow of this looming factory, an entirely new town would eventually rise: The Town of the Strength through Joy Car. Designs for it were already being made, having been delegated by Hitler's favorite architect, Albert Speer, to a young architect named Peter Koeller. Under Nazi patronage, thirty-year-old Koeller was told to design a "workers' city" to accommodate 90,000 inhabitants, one that would accentuate the factory and its automobile. In his designs, Koeller looked at the empty farmland and tried to predict what functional traffic patterns might emerge there once a motorized population arrived. With Nazi social-utopian ideas in mind, Koeller wanted to meld a "return to nature"—an idea popular at the time that prescribed living close to the earth and growing one's own fruits and vegetables as the native tribes once did—with the industrialization of city life and autobahns. He resolved this seeming contradiction by creating a town that had forested housing communities and estates dotting its circumference, all of which linked back through looping roads to the industrial heart. The diameter of this circle would be cut by the town's main street, a line stretching from the factory up to a little hill known as the Klieversberg that formed the other visual boundary of the town. This long straight pathway would be the heart of the city, eventually replete with bakeries, grocery stores, small businesses, and clothing shops.

Koeller aimed this main road at the car factory on purpose in order to connect the factory "visually with the center of town . . . and establish it in the consciousness of each citizen." For that reason, even today, all subsequent developers have "considered this axis more or less sacrosanct." This particular area had been chosen for the new town because it was close to the train line and close to the water—two things that would help when it came to transporting supplies and parts. The town was also located centrally in Germany, which would give everyone fairly easy access to come and pick up their new cars.

It was an extraordinary project, and an expensive one, which is precisely why Hitler had chosen the German Labor Front to fund it, headed by the hard-drinking Ley. In fact, it was from the

German Labor Front that the town and the car got their names: Since motorizing the population was inherently tied to ideas of labor and recreation, Hitler felt he'd found the perfect match in the division of the Labor Front known as Strength through Joy. This particular division of Ley's organization dealt with holidays and free-time activities. Strength through Joy offered an array of carefully chosen cultural activities and opportunities to travel, always accenting the idea of the *Volksgemeinschaft,* the people's community: The trips were supposed to unite people through participation. By calling the new car the "Strength through Joy Car," and the town "The Town of the Strength through Joy Car," Hitler and Ley attached the Volkswagen to the usual Strength through Joy mottos such as "Service not Self," and made it feel like a community project.

From the very beginning, Robert Ley loved the idea of the Volkswagen, calling it "the greatest social work of all time," and Hitler's "great pet." To Hitler's immense delight, Ley threw himself into the work of promoting the car, using the Labor Front

Ferdinand Porsche (left front), Robert Ley (center front), leader of the Nazi German Labor Front, and the city's young architect Peter Koeller (right front) walking through The Town of the Strength through Joy Car, 1938.

and Strength through Joy as a public relations company for it, and launching an unprecedented ad campaign with posters, speeches, and toys. As part of this great propaganda push, another thirty prototypes of Hitler's "pet" were built for exhibition purposes and sent through Germany—sometimes with Ferry Porsche at the wheel—on special motor tours that paraded through town and village streets. Exhibitions were held so people could see the cars up close: Wagnerian sets and sunbursts gave these exhibitions the feeling of a fairy tale. Leaflets given out at the shows called it *The Strength through Joy Car, as willed by the Führer.*

The fantasy was exciting, as fantasies often are. In reality, no cars were anywhere near the point of being produced. But there were grand plans. The first massive hall of the factory would be ready by the end of 1939, and two further equally large halls were supposed to be added in the following three years. Just the first section alone was designed to be larger than any other car factory of the time. According to the plan, a hundred thousand vehicles were to be produced before the end of 1940, and then two hundred thousand more in 1941. This would need a workforce of more than seventeen thousand men each working two shifts. By the final phase, thirty thousand workers would be making close to one million Volkswagens each year. As there were nowhere near enough customers in Germany to sustain such a plan, Hitler expected to export more than half of those cars (which, in large part, meant he expected to sell them in the countries he was preparing to conquer).

All that was an elaborate dream, however. The reality of 1939 was that The Town of the Strength through Joy Car was still a pasture with one giant brick building rising out of it and none of the necessary manpower to run such a plant. For that reason, training camps for German workers were set up in the nearby town of Brunswick instead, and recruitment began. As it was hard to find German workers to come and build the town— Germany had full employment now—Italy's leader Mussolini sent three thousand Italians over to join the German workers and help build the factory; they were housed in makeshift wooden barracks. Overseen by Ley's Nazi forces, they swarmed toward the canal each morning and back again each night. The popular German magazine *Der Spiegel* reported that "Chianti bottle and dagger ruled" alongside the "crocodile whip in the wooden watchtower of the SS." There was also talk of all the babies of "Mussolini's unemployed" that soon began to appear in women's arms along nearby German streets.

Needless to say, the Volkswagen project had turned into an extravagant enterprise. The scale of the project would have been impossible for any other car company in Europe, but even for the German government it was not an easy task. By the end of 1939, the plant had already cost 215 million RM, and only eighty percent of the first section was complete. For that reason, Robert Ley came up with another way of getting immediate funds—the Strength through Joy Car Savings Book Plan. Perhaps drawing on ideas from the United States first initiated by General Motors and their installment plans, the Volkswagen Savings Book Plan was a noncancelable and nontransferable contract with the German government. It was created, Ley said, to help Germans save their money for the purchase of a car: The people would pay about $2 a week (5 RM). For every such payment, they were given a stamp to place in their booklet. Once that booklet was full of stamps, the customers could come to the factory and receive their car.

The idea was drenched in expectation: There was so much propaganda leading up to its introduction that on the day the stamp books were officially available, long lines snaked around the post offices where the books could be purchased. In practice, however, trying to keep up with the stamps would eventually prove too difficult for most people: the fee of two dollars a week was still beyond their budgets and had to be lowered to two dollars *a month*. That meant a subscriber could expect to have his or her car in about sixteen years! Nonetheless, 253,000 German citizens subscribed to the program before the war broke out. And another 83,000 Germans would sign up even after the war had begun, pushing a total of 267 million RM into the Nazis' Strength through Joy Car account.

Once the factory was up and the machines ordered from America were flowing in to fill the rooms, Porsche wanted to be as close as possible while things were gearing up for the production of his car. He found a clearing he liked on the Klieversberg, the hill that is the city's highest point, and had a lonely little cabin built for himself there, fir trees and wilderness all around. From the back door of this cabin, he could step out and look over the space that would eventually be the town and watch the factory rising in the distance just over the canal. Porsche planted yellow tulips in the cleared area around his house. On their off days, some of the guys liked to hunt in the forests behind Porsche's hut. Ferdinand often went on those expeditions, but according to a later story told by Ferry, "nothing would induce him to pull the trigger." He'd shot a roebuck once, and that had been the end of it.

By 1939, all the things Porsche had wished for seemed to be coming true. More than $12 million had been spent on testing and perfecting his Volkswagen design, and in the midst of all this, a rounded little car had appeared. It looked plump, to be sure, but in reality there was hardly an extraneous inch of metal or steel to be found on it. The car had been tested and tweaked more than any other single car model in history to that point, and it was now as simple and precise as a Mies van der Rohe chair, its headlights a little larger than most, perhaps, giving it a perpetual look of youth. A majestic factory was being built for it, as was an entire city. For Porsche and his car, things looked good. Few on his team expected that the darkest times were drawing near.

Heinrich Nordhoff, however, was much less excited about the way things were going in his country, and even less enthusiastic by Ferdinand Porsche's fat little car. He'd set foot in one of them only one time—a friend of his from the RDA had once picked him up from the train station in the little car—but he had not been impressed. The whole idea of the car and its factory and town seemed ridiculous to him. In fact, there were a lot of things in Germany that were beginning to feel ridiculous to him. And he wasn't the only one thinking in such a way. In 1939, not long after the redbrick factory in Wolfsburg had begun to rise, Nordhoff took what would be his last visit to the United States for Opel, though he would never have suspected such a thing at the time. Still, he did feel trouble was coming. Walking through the General Motors plant in Detroit, another colleague would later remember how Heinrich took a long and pensive look at the humming machines and lines of metal and steel, and then wondered aloud if all those machines might soon be working against Germany in a war.

By that time, Nordhoff was the father of two little girls, Barbara and Elisabeth, and perhaps he was also thinking of them as he looked at the machines and considered the possibility of war. After all, he'd been standing in just that same town when he'd received the call telling him that his second daughter, Barbara, had been born. Even for Nordhoff, it was hard to believe that only twenty years after the First World War—a war he'd fought in as a boy—the world was already gearing up for a second one. Few in Germany thought it was coming, and even fewer thought

Porsche, Ley, and Hitler all admire the model of the
Strength through Joy Car (the KdF Wagen).

it would last long if it did arrive. Certainly, it wouldn't be nearly as bad as the last. But Nordhoff could feel the darkness closing in. When he boarded the ship back to his country, there were only a few dozen passengers on the entire ship. No one wanted to go to Germany; it was about to become the enemy again.

Part Two

o o

The Darkest Hours Come Just Before Dawn

It is weakness rather than wickedness which renders men unfit to be trusted with unlimited power.

—John Adams

It was a celebration of the first incandescent lightbulb. It was also a tribute to the life of America's father of electric light, eighty-two-year-old Thomas Edison. All the big men of business were there: philanthropist and Standard Oil heir John D. Rockefeller Jr.; one of the brothers who had experienced the first successful flight, Orville Wright; the first leader to explicitly champion capitalism as an essential part of democracy, President Hoover; banker, industrialist, and current treasury secretary Andrew Mellon; and the man who had changed the economic and geographic face of America by building the world's first People's Car, Henry Ford. The event was held in Ford's hometown—the Edison Institute was being opened there under Ford's watch—and a very big deal was made about the meeting of these two men, the work of whom had changed the nation in rapid and extraordinary ways. Reporters of the most prominent newspapers in the country were also invited, as were a slew of photographers. The main man behind the event was Edward Bernays, the nephew of Sigmund Freud and the personality who had made public relations into a new field. In 1929, Bernays was hired by Westinghouse and General Electric to coordinate a nationwide event to mark the lightbulb's fiftieth anniversary. Bernays called it *Light's Golden Jubilee.*

During the 1920s, electric light had experienced a rise similar to the automotive boom in customers and profits, and while state regulation had played a part in that success, *Light's Golden Jubilee* was sculpted as a tribute to the innovation of the individual and the private sector. Stories about Thomas Edison were sent out to the managing editors of newspapers in cities all over the country. Reading about the upcoming national event, citizens began planning local light celebrations in their own towns. A commemorative stamp was issued. On the day newly elected President Hoover dedicated the Edison Institute in Dearborn, Michigan, there was a "moment of silence" as utility companies all shut off their power at the same time in Edison's honor. The event set a new bar for public relations, showing that mass communication could be joined with the interests of big business and used to unite the country in a feeling of celebration, joy, and respect. It was a crowning moment for the power of the free market and for all the important businessmen gathered there, but in the midst of the celebration, news began trickling in from Wall Street that something was wrong. *Light's Golden Jubilee* ended on October 21, 1929. Just a little over a week later, on October 29, the stock market crashed. Men like Ford and Edison had created a new industrial wave in the United States and the social and economic wake from it would be rough.

The big dreams and big contributions to the American economy that were represented by men like Edison and Ford had improved the American quality of life. At the same time, however, that same wave had led to certain excesses and unhealthy actions, and those would become obvious in the 1930s. These excesses, and the country's failure to dream big *and* simultaneously remain awake and aware of the consequences of their actions (to think small), would devastate the country from the inside out—both economically and environmentally. It would take everyone in America—from the Edisons and the Fords to the farmers and the young men working for the Civilian Conservation Corps—to get the country back to a state of health. And those deep changes would not come without a great amount of frustrating debate.

Economics in America had always been a balance between government intervention and the laissez-faire practice of leaving private enterprise alone. The debate over this balance extended as far back as the country's foundation, to arguments represented by Alexander Hamilton and Thomas Jefferson. There were groups lobbying for more government aid on one side, and groups wanting less government intervention on the other. Over the years, the friction between regulation and deregulation had produced the lasting (though always controversial) mainstays of America: the modern banking system, "natural monopolies" in transportation (providing necessities like train tracks and roads, public works and utility services), and a boom in private enterprise that had made businesses like General Electric, General Motors, and Ford into national stars. The prosperity of the twenties in the United States made it clear that the government needed private corporations. The 1930s would make it clear that the private corporations needed the government as well. It was a relationship of "can't live with them, can't live without them" in every sense.

Laissez-faire has always been the underlying philosophy of the American market. (At least in theory, most everyone agrees there should be no permanent centralization or control). And yet, neither the citizen-staffed government nor the citizen-staffed corporations have ever been able to truly leave things alone. The paradox, as many began to discover (or rediscover) in the thirties and forties, is that leaving something alone often requires regulation: Over the years, it's come to light that a lot of discipline is necessary for the market to "naturally flow." Consumption in economic concerns is related to private consumption: It can feel so good to indulge, but too much indulgence can make a system sick, just as too much indulgence in food or drink can make a body sick. In the early 1930s, America was sick, and the symptoms were environmental and economic.

Still, corporations and bankers and the free market had indeed brought a lot of good things to America. And for that reason, government had stepped back, so much so that when the market crashed, President Hoover refused to have the government directly intervene in the domestic market, trusting that it would correct itself. And while Hoover was actually a believer in the beneficent hand (he believed that by being on the side of

big business, the government could help the American economy, and thus the American people themselves), those American people (the consumers) soon began to mistrust big business,
understandably confused about where big business ended and
Wall Street began. This new consumer mood, and the desperate
situation of the Depression, meant that Herbert Hoover did not
win a second term. Instead, Franklin Roosevelt came to office, a
man who was not afraid to let the government directly intervene
in the country's economics: He set up the New Deal. With its
philosophy of relief, recovery, and reform, millions of dollars
were poured into government projects such as the Tennessee
Valley Authority (TVA) and the Civilian Conservation Corps
(CCC), to stimulate the economy, making men like Wendell
Wilkie, the president of Commonwealth and Southern, furious
about the government's interference (one of the primary goals of
the TVA was to provide poor, rural areas of the country with
electricity).

But Roosevelt was aware that it was not only money that
would help; it was a change in mood. "After all," he said in his
fireside chat of March 12, 1933, "there is an element in the read-
justment of our financial system more important than currency,
more important than gold, and that is the confidence of the people. Confidence and courage are the essentials of success in carrying out our plan. You people must have faith; you must not be
stampeded by rumors or guesses. Let us unite in banishing fear.
We have provided the machinery to restore our financial system; it is up to you to support and make it work. It is your problem no less than it is mine. Together we cannot fail." The real
problem was one of thought and meaning, of how to connect
one's work and pay back to something inspiring again. The jolt
of the Depression came from many changes, but perhaps the
most significant was that the powering of the United States was
no longer agricultural but rather industrially-based. And the
country's overall mind-set—reflected in everything from factory
conditional to farms to the rules of Wall Street—now had to
evolve to adjust to that change.

Roosevelt's election and the New Deal signaled a political re-alignment away from the corporations and toward their employ-ees: Workers' rights and civil rights would now become the object of focus in the papers and the press. The United Auto Workers Union would be formed. Because the New Deal was a giant project with its hands everywhere in the market, many cor-porations resisted Roosevelt's administration, and that included men like Wendell Wilkie, Alfred P. Sloan and Henry Ford. Throughout the 1930s, American government and American cor-porations began a domestic battle to "win" American citizens; public relations and advertising would be the battleground. The people, Congress, big business, and the administration of the president—all would make mistakes, but those mistakes would not go unnoticed: A healthy rivalry (healthy only because it ex-isted within a system of checks and balances) would ensure that a delicate balance was maintained.

The struggle between big business and government was a paradoxical fight in some ways—even Edward Bernays would say that "Politics was the first big business in America"—but it would prove to be an important one, essential to America's health in the long-term. In Hitler's Germany, for example, there would be no such debate allowed, and Germany would feel the consequences of having a government with total control. Still, in those dramatic years of the 1930s, this long zoom view was by no means obvious. To some, it seemed the American model was too messy, too volatile, and might indeed collapse. Democ-racy and capitalism did not look strong. In fact, in the limited view of that decade, there was the sense that Germany's model was the one gaining speed and power.

After all, in the 1930s, such centralization of both the econ-omy and the power of the government worked in Germany. Re-armament gave the country a giant economic and psychological boost, as did the road construction project. But even more im-portant, there had been a dearth of motivation, and now people were motivated again. And yet the foundations for all that growth were corrupt and unsustainable: while on the surface it looked like industry was flourishing, underneath it all, the German economy was broken and in dire need of a war. By 1939, economists knew that the growth was a mere façade: the director of the Reichsbank, for example, sent Hitler a note demanding restraint in finances and predicting an imminent and dangerous inflation. Hitler sacked the Reichsbank man and called his words "mutiny," but he must have known they were true. The country's demands for raw materials and food, alongside its need for even more workers, meant it had to conquer new areas in order to get its hands on both. Austria, Czechoslovakia, and Poland would be the first areas that would feel Germany's push.

The truth always comes out eventually, and by the end of the 1930s, it was rearing its head. German people began to feel the weight of both price controls and rationing. But the inertia that had been garnered made it difficult to change economic paths or build a resistance. Hitler's reign had started with the vote, but by 1939, the NSDAP had accumulated six years of authoritarian power. It was no longer necessary for them to hide their intentions. Domestically and internationally, the German government became openly totalitarian. People were brought into the NSDAP without such niceties as asking for their consent. It was in 1939, for instance, that all forms of police and protection became part of Heinrich Himmler's SS: Whereas state and local police forces had been allowed to remain separate, in 1939, they all became part of Hitler's machine. The picture Germany had painted for the international community was crumbling as well. Hitler's peace speeches proved a ruse as he took Austria and invaded Czechoslovakia. Next came Poland, leaving France and Britain no choice but to respond in defense. In the autumn of 1939, just as Ferdinand Porsche was setting up his little hut in The Town of the Strength through Joy Car and preparing to finally build the automobile he'd spent more than twenty years of his life discovering and inventing, Europe entered an open and official state of war. Once again, Porsche and his little car had met a seemingly insurmountable wall.

(21)

Heinrich Nordhoff was walking the same Berlin streets he'd once explored as a child, taking his daughters to the same museums he'd visited all those years before. As a young man, Berlin had offered the culture, music, and art that Nordhoff needed in his life, things he soaked in hungrily every chance he got. And his desire for such things had only grown. He was always reading and learning and looking for the connections between disparate things. Perhaps for this reason, his young daughters thought their father knew everything. Sometimes they would try to find the hardest questions they could—even searching their schoolbooks for subjects about which they could quiz him—but their father always seemed to know the answer to whatever question they posed. Still, there were some things he could not explain at the time, had he been asked. He didn't know how to explain what was happening in his country or how to judge his own complicity in it, and he didn't understand why they were going to war, though he and his family were soon to be deeply affected by it.

Just as Hitler was beginning to invade Czechoslovakia, Opel had transferred Heinrich to their executive offices in Berlin. But it was no longer the town of his youth. The mood he found there was very different from the one he'd known in the 1920s. Long gone were the artists and writers and musicians who had once packed Berlin's streets. Now the capital had been rearranged to fit a Nazi fantasy—bloodred flags with swastikas hung from windows, parades of Nazi officials marched down the streets, and Germans of the "wrong race" were fleeing, hiding, or being rooted out and killed. Much of the modern art that Heinrich had so loved as a teenager was gone—masterpieces labeled as "degenerate" by the Nazi Party, including Nordhoff's favorite painting from his youth, the *Tower of Blue Horses* by Franz Marc. Schlesinger, Nordhoff's favorite professor, had been forced out by then, too, and many of the city's brightest minds had fled long ago. Anxiety hung thick in the air, unspoken but ever present. But Heinrich was given a nice executive job in Berlin, and the surrounding unrest was not enough to make him pack up his family and move. He stayed.

In retrospect, one can't help but wonder how Germans who were not part of the Nazi Party were able to stay during this time, but in those days, things were not so clear, which is why even those most in danger often refused to leave. After the Reichstag fire in 1934 and the Night of the Long Knives, Jewish people were warned and encouraged to emigrate, but many refused. Even at the end of 1938, when the *Kristallnacht* occurred, many Jewish families continued to stay. But of course leaving was a much harder task by then, impossible for some. In his autobiography, Marcel Reich-Ranicki, a prominent literary critic in Germany and a Jewish man who survived the Holocaust, talks of these days in Berlin. He was among those who had stayed, and would ultimately be sent to a concentration camp. He writes that two conflicting attitudes emerged among his Jewish family and friends in the mid-1930s:

> One stated: After what has happened there is no longer any place for us in this country; we should not indulge in any illusions but emigrate as soon as possible. The other held: Let us not lose our heads, but rather let us wait and see; nothing is eaten as hot as it is cooked.

He goes on to say that many Jews felt the hatred of the Nazi regime was directed toward Jewish immigrants rather than those who were native-born. And what about the Jewish men who had served Germany in the First World War? Ranicki says that these people felt invincible: After what they had sacrificed, how could Germany not treat them well? Jewish and German friends tried to mutually assure one another:

> . . . surely an inhuman regime such as the Nazis was unthinkable in Germany in the long run. After two, or at most three,

years the party would be overthrown. So it made no sense to dispose of one's possessions and abandon one's home.

But if the Jewish people knew how other Jews were being treated, how could they bear to stay? To ask that question in hindsight is to have no right to ask it at all. Home is a word so close to the heart that it can transcend reason. Sometimes propelling yourself into a frightening and foreign landscape—especially when there is no clear place to go—and leaving all you've ever known, looks worse than suffering the possibilities of what might come by staying. One cannot underestimate the connection humanity feels between individual identity and a particular geographical place. As Ranicki continues:

> From today's perspective, it is astonishing, to say the least, that the number of Jews leaving Germany did not increase despite their systematic persecution . . . What kept the overwhelming majority of Jews from emigrating for so long is easily explained—it was their faith in Germany.

This is something that perhaps many of us can understand. Even if one disagrees with the politics and practices of one's country, one still has faith in the overall place, and one can't help but believe that things will take a turn for the better, somehow.

By all accounts, when war broke out, Ferdinand Porsche was in a state of shock. He had not believed the war would come, even though, in the Volkswagen town and factory, there had been numerous red flags. The elite housing of the Steimker Berg—the first area finished, and the one where the Nazi officials were to live—came equipped with reinforced basements in case of air raids, and bunkers had been added for the same reason. In addition, the Volkswagen factory's floors and walls had been specifically reinforced with heavy concrete at a great deal of extra time and cost in order that they would be able to withstand bombing.

Even so, at the VW factory, Ferdinand was certainly not the only man stunned when the Second World War began. The factory itself had no specific war plan, and none of the major players in the town had ever discussed what they would do in the case of a war: Their only concern was with building People's Cars. All the design, all the construction, all the plans for housing, all the relocations, all the hiring, all the money that had gone into the factory—all of this stalled now as Nazi officers tried to figure out what to do with the place. For the first year or so of the war, up until 1940, it was more or less idle—everyone approached each day with the sense that the war would end soon and the hope that any day now they'd start making cars. Then, the German armaments department began to pressure the factory into doing small tasks for the military, simple things like fixing old vehicles or producing needed parts. But as the war continued, that pressure grew greater. Soon the factory was on the verge of being an armaments plant.

Porsche was furious about this upheaval, and was not afraid to make that fact known. He refused to cooperate when he was told that the factory's assembly lines needed to be rearranged to better aid the production of armaments. When a Nazi general came to visit him to talk about these new plans, suggesting that perhaps Porsche could dismantle the lines meant to make People's Car parts and hide them in the woods nearby—Ferdinand exploded. He often threw his hat on the ground and stomped on it when he was mad, but this time he was too angry even for that. He simply refused to deal with the man, demanding to speak to no one but Hitler himself. Eventually he took one of his cars out to Hitler's Obersalzberg retreat in the Alps.

Until that moment, Hitler and Porsche had not discussed the war, though it wouldn't be long before the two of them would be meeting to talk about military vehicles and tanks. Still, in 1940, Hitler continued to give Porsche the impression that the war would be a quick one and that it would not disrupt all the Volkswagen plans they had made together. Perhaps Hitler was simply trying to please Porsche, or perhaps he really believed that idea himself; perhaps he didn't expect the war would hinder Volkswagen production or stop them from following through on their plans. In any case, on the day Porsche visited him in the mountain retreat at Obersalzberg, Porsche reportedly asked: *What am I supposed to be building? A car for peace or a car for war?*

I believe we've only ever discussed the Volkswagen together, Hitler said.

Porsche: *So I can assume that this plant is being built only for the Volkswagen?*

I gave you the assignment for the Volkswagen! Hitler reiterated. *Everything else follows from that!*

The exact words of their conversation are unknown, of course, though the above is reportedly what Porsche related upon his return. In any case, Porsche was satisfied after his impromptu meeting with Hitler. He zoomed back to the factory and told all the Nazi generals there to go and see Hitler in Obersalzberg themselves if they had a problem: They were only to build Volkswagens in this town.

In the nineteenth century, when German-speaking tribes, kingdoms, and states united as an empire under one flag, Prussian war generals interpreted their new imperial colors—three long bars of red, black, and white—using the saying *"Durch Nacht und Blut zur Licht,"* "Through night and blood to light." Night was falling in Europe. And too much blood would be spilled before it grew light again.

With Hitler's invasion of Poland on September 1, 1939, and the subsequent Allied declaration of war, President Roosevelt immediately called a meeting with his cabinet and the country's top military advisors to discuss the United States' position. On September 3, his voice streamed through the air: "Until four-thirty this morning," he said, "I had hoped against hope that some miracle would prevent a devastating war in Europe and bring an end to the invasion of Poland by Germany." That miracle hadn't come. So what was America to do? The horrors of the First World War had not been forgotten, and Congress had recently passed the Neutrality Act saying war would never again happen unless it was to defend a threat to America's own soil. The act had been signed into law in 1936, and renewed and strengthened in subsequent years. Now, in 1939, Roosevelt and many in Washington's conservative Congress were determined to stick to that pact and not get involved.

According to a military poll taken at the time, 94 percent of Americans were against entering the Second World War. This time no slogans of "making the world safe for democracy" were going to work, and yet it was exactly the idea of democracy that was under threat. As much as any Western nation might have wanted to be neutral, separating itself from Europe was no longer a true political or economic choice. Markets and nations were intertwined, and what hurt Europe eventually hurt America. And if Europe fell into the hands of a dictator, the consequences felt in America would indeed be vast. This was not as easy to see in 1939, however, and Roosevelt and his advisors hoped that by staying out of the war they would benefit from the needs and increased demands of Europe's wartime economy without having to get directly involved or risking American lives.

The United States was in the midst of its own fierce inner conflicts at the time after all, and those conflicts were largely taking place through the medium of mass communication. Likewise, the new balance of power in Europe was in large part due to innovations in mass communication. Hitler made that clear. As Marshall McLuhan wrote in *The Mechanical Bride*: "That Hitler came into political existence at all is directly owing to radio and public-address systems . . ." Hitler's power was his voice and the image he presented, and radio and print made it possible for Germans to hear that voice, to experience collective images and rallying cries. The blurring between real news and "news as entertainment," and between public relations and persuasion and manipulation, made it a confusing time to form a true opinion. In the States, this blurred communication battle was one between the government and private enterprise, not a new battle but a battle that had new tools. The Depression had weakened people's belief in capitalism and the products being sold, and because programs like the New Deal had put the economy into government hands, those businesses now found themselves trying to "win back" the public at large.

Corporations wanted to restore consumer confidence in buying and selling again, which was something the government was also trying to do, but neither side understood that they were on the same team. Corporations made commercials warning of the perils of Big Government; members of the government warned of the perils of Big Business (sometimes also called Big Money and caricatured by men like Huey Long as "corrupt oil giants and millionaires"). It wasn't as simple as the Democrats (represented by Roosevelt) being against oil executives and rich capitalists and the Republicans (or industrialists like Hearst, Rockefeller, and Mellon) being on the other side of the coin. In fact, it was all mixed up, and people were constantly switching sides. Underneath all the various criticisms of both corporations and government, however, all the groups professed a desire to see the same end, prosperity in America, and each of them blamed the other for putting the country in danger or damaging that prosperity. The media became the arena in which all these battles raged. And at the center of it was Edward Bernays. His clout had risen throughout the twenties, and with the crash of the thirties, he found himself working with American businesses to try to revive customer trust.

It was in this spirit that in 1939 Bernays became an advisor for General Motors, helping to dream up the Futurama ride and the transportation zone at the New York World's Fair. His work with GM was geared in part toward reidentifying democracy with capitalism in a positive way. The Fair's popular GM transportation zone presented a vision of the future that linked progress to industry and the free market. But Roosevelt was also interested in using public relations to find better ways of connecting with the voters and their needs, though he was not a fan of the Bernays style of PR. In contrast, Roosevelt and his administration identified with a man named George Gallup.

During the 1930s, Gallup (and others) had started a new branch of public relations, one that he thought spoke more to the rational side of the human psyche. Rather than trying to figure out irrational desires and then covertly speak to them, one could simply ask the people what they needed and wanted and they would get a straight answer. Of course Bernays considered his style of public relations rational too, but his style was based on using rationality to speak to the irrational or unconscious desires of the masses. Gallup wanted to speak rationally to those masses, and he devised new methods of doing so. It was the beginning of surveys and polls. In these lists of questions, men such as Gallup were careful to try not to manipulate desires; the emphasis was on avoiding emotion rather than trying to stimulate it. It was more like science, they said; it relied on research and data.

Public relations was easily mixed up with advertising and with news: Men like Bernays, for instance, used advertising and newspapers as part of their public relations campaigns. And the surveys and research done by men like Gallup were used to make advertising campaigns or to create material for political campaigns. All this created a very blurry battleground for the public's loyalty and attention. Depending on what station one tuned in to and what publications one read, the American government was either saving the country or it was leading the country toward becoming an authoritarian state; big business was either manipulating you and stealing your money or it was bringing all kinds of beneficial products and opportunities into your life. It was difficult to know what sources of information could be trusted. As Roosevelt said in another radio address, "You, the people of this country, are receiving news through your radios and your newspapers at every hour of the day. You are, I believe, the most enlightened and the best informed people in all the world at this moment . . . At the same time . . . it is of the highest importance that the press and the radio use the utmost caution to discriminate between actual verified fact on the one hand, and mere rumor on the other . . . Do not believe of necessity everything you hear or read. Check up on it."

The world had to be wary of its sources of information. But the world had to be wary of government as well. In Nazi Germany, Joseph Goebbels could be heard openly praising Edward Bernays and his use of propaganda, but he could also be heard praising Roosevelt's unprecedented government intervention through programs like the New Deal. In America, however, the government's overall intentions were not the same as those of the NSDAP, nor were the corporations' use of public relations and propaganda. In the States, while each individual group had its own agenda, the overall direction was one that championed checks and balances; thus while people were certainly greedy and power-hungry at times, there was a greater chance that those inclinations would be caught and culled before they could grow too large. But in Germany under the Nazi Party, there was no questioning of the government, and the government was now in charge of the businesses as well. There were no checks and balances. Still, it was the *intentions* rather than the methods that differed when it came to German and American use of the media. Hitler and Goebbels believed that the people were blind creatures who had to be manipulated into doing what was best for them, but to a certain extent, so did American men like Walter Lippmann and Edward Bernays. Roosevelt supported yet another view, namely that the people can think clearly and participate rationally in government by telling their leaders what they need and want. Hitler and Bernays thought new forms of mass communication spoke to the irrational side of humans.

Gallup thought it could speak to the rational side. Both were right.

Meanwhile, Hitler's armies were sweeping through Europe as France and Britain tried to fend them off. The German tanks known as Panzers swarmed like ants. London was hammered with bombs. One by one, countries began to fall to the Nazi army. Yugoslavia surrendered. Greece surrendered. Norway surrendered. And once Mussolini joined his troops with Hitler's, France was forced to surrender to Germany too. Now Britain found itself the last European bastion for democracy. In retrospect, it looks unavoidable that the United States would enter: How could they let a totalitarian regime conquer all of Europe? But even with the defeat of France, Americans still hoped they would not have to become entangled in a world war again. In 1939, Roosevelt had assured the country that the United States would remain neutral, but he'd also said "Even a neutral [person] cannot be asked to close his mind or his conscience." Now it was a year later and Europe was weighing much heavier on the mind of his administration, and he asked the people to help, not by sending their sons to fight, but by sending money and supplies instead: "Tonight over the once peaceful roads of Belgium and France millions are . . . running from their homes to escape bombs and shells and fire," Roosevelt told the country in the spring of 1940; "They stumble on, knowing not where the end of the road will be . . . each one of you that is listening to me tonight has a way of helping them. The American Red Cross, that represents each of us, is rushing food and clothing and medical supplies to these destitute civilian millions. Please, I beg you, please give according to your means . . . give as generously as you can. I ask this in the name of our common humanity."

Now the whole world was debating the importance of democracy and the new threat posed by Hitler. One of Bill Bernbach's favorite writers was the British philosopher Bertrand Russell, a prominent intellectual in both the United States and Britain at the time. Russell had been an outspoken pacifist during the First World War. For his views, Russell had been thrown in jail and fired from his job, but he stood strong by his beliefs. Now, twenty years later, Russell was not afraid to change his mind, knowing that what was right yesterday might not always be right today. As the Second World War hit, he urged the United States to intervene, saying that Adolf Hitler had shifted the balance. Sometimes war was the lesser of two evils, he said; if Hitler were allowed to conquer Europe, it would forever damage democracy everywhere. But it wasn't a matter of rage; it was a matter of action. "It is a waste of time to be angry with a man who behaves badly, just as it is a waste of time to be angry at a car that won't go," Russell wrote. It was necessary that words mean something, he said; strong action must back them up.

That strong action did eventually arrive, but not as anyone had expected. It was December 7, 1941. The Weintraub advertising offices where Bill Bernbach would soon work were as sober as any other office in New York City on that cold Monday when people returned to work with the knowledge that Pearl Harbor had been attacked by the Japanese. Suddenly the United States had been jolted out of its isolationism. They had not gone to the war, but the war had come to their doorstep. "We are now in this war," Roosevelt told the country that Monday, "We are all in it—all the way."

Sometimes public opinion really does change in a day. All the squabbles and competition and mistrust between corporations and government, between workers and corporations, between citizens and state now had to be overcome for the good of the country: The foundation they all shared had been attacked. To win the war, it would take private business, government intervention, union support, and the lives of millions of citizens. "Private industry will continue to be the source of most of this [war] material . . . Private industry will have the responsibility of providing the best . . . most efficient mass production. . . ." Roosevelt said. What days before had seemed like giant problems, now no longer looked so monumental. People were ready to do whatever it might take for freedom, as the threat to democracy and their country became immediate and real. Taxes were raised. Price and wage controls were introduced, and nearly every sector of production turned toward aiding the troops. Civilian car production came to a halt and the great factories in Detroit were retooled for war. (Even Sloan and Ford reluctantly joined in and agreed to produce equipment for the war.) Unions made a no-strike deal with the government. Immigrants flooded in, welcomed as some of the country's best assets, many of them working as scientists and engineers for the United States military, others helping to fill factory jobs as men went off to fight. Women stepped out of their homes to assume new roles, providing a large push in the nation's factory and business force. And young men joined (and were conscripted) into the U.S. army in droves. Everyone's work mattered again.

Bill Bernbach was one of those men drafted shortly after Pearl Harbor was attacked. But aside from a little taste of training camp, he wouldn't directly experience army life. He was deemed too weak for military purposes. Due to an astonishingly high pulse during his examination at boot camp, he was sent to the sick bay for a few days so that "whatever drug he must have taken could wear off." But Bill hadn't taken any drugs. Days later when he was released from his confinement, his heartbeat was still the same, a ridiculous 148 beats per minute. Bill was dismissed and sent back home. The world had another path in store for him.

Albert Speer's very first position in the Nazi Party was as head of his local chapter of the National Socialist Motor Corps, a paramilitary drivers' organization—part AAA roadside service, part sports club—that Hitler formed in 1931 as part of his platform toward election. Many of Hitler's closest acquaintances and

some of the earlier Nazi Party members were a part of this organization, a crew that would later be known as Hitler's *"chauffer-
ska."* The point of the National Socialist Motor Club was to train
people to drive well and to engender attachment to the automobile. It also assisted people when their cars broke down. At the
time of its formation, Albert Speer was only in his twenties, still
with baby fat and the soft features of a boy. He was also the only
person in his area of Berlin (known as Wannsee) who owned a
car. Speer was hesitant about the Nazi Party at first, but he was
impressed the first time he saw Hitler speak and eventually
grew so enamored with the party that he joined. In later years,
Speer would be considered one of Hitler's closest associates,
someone Hitler believed had an artistic soul close to his own. At
the Nuremberg Trials, Speer would testify: "I belonged to a circle which consisted of other artists and his personal staff. If Hitler had had any friends at all, I certainly would have been one
of his close friends."

In part because they both shared unique relationships with
Hitler, Ferdinand Porsche and Albert Speer did not get along.
Despite their common interest in the motor car, the two men ag-
gravated each other to no end. After the unexpected death of
Fritz Todt, a friend of Porsche's and an engineer he had respected greatly, Speer took over Todt's job as minister of armaments and war production with a fervor to put some order into
a Nazi war machine he felt was chaotic and out of hand. And
that meant, in his opinion, reining in men like Porsche.

The facts around Todt's death were blurry and Porsche might
have suspected Speer was complicit in it somehow; in any case,
he didn't like the young man and they had very different ideas
about what was important during the war. Speer was concerned
with efficiency. Porsche was not. And their very different energies seemed to collide any time they were in the same room.
Speer was especially annoyed at the way Porsche and Hitler
dreamed up crazy transportation ideas together and pored over
ideas for the German tanks that Porsche was commissioned to
design, one of which was a supertank called the Maus that

proved almost too fat to move. According to Ferry, it was Speer who took Porsche to see his first group of concentration camp prisoners, men who were laboring at breaking stones in a quarry. Speer then turned to Porsche and warned him that if he wasn't careful, that's where he'd end up. But Porsche was no better with Speer, always hesitating and delaying orders he did not like, doing what he wanted to do rather than what he was told. And it certainly must have annoyed Speer that Porsche seemed to have somehow escaped Hitler's control. Porsche was one of the only men in Germany at the time who seemed safe from Nazi punishment. As historians Hans Mommsen and Manfred Grieger would later write:

> With the success of a sleepwalker Porsche succeeded to a great extent in staying aloof from the chronic power struggles between the satraps of National Socialism, and, admittedly backed by the unarguable respect he enjoyed from Adolf Hitler, he was able to maintain a largely independent stance. His unorthodox manner, his relaxed and never subservient way of dealing with the Party notables, his international renown as a motor car designer, and his spectacular success in racing car construction, gave him an exceptional position within the regime, which in some respects allowed him to break ranks from time to time.

As always, Porsche seemed to be operating in a different universe, concerned only with his own very specific plans. Speer found Porsche's ideas of war juvenile and hated having to witness conversations such as the one where Porsche told Hitler that he should put an end to the war because the country was short on fuel, as if it were as simple as that. There was also the time when Porsche told Hitler, very seriously, that it would be better if only small men were put into the tanks, because then he could make the tanks smaller. Hitler apparently found this comment rather charming and went out of his way not to embarrass Porsche, saying "I think you have a very good idea there,

Professor . . ." and explaining to others in the room that it was a known fact that short people tended to be very courageous, and citing Napoleon as an example. It's no stretch to imagine that Speer would rather have left the room than listen to such talk. And there was also the fact that Speer was still a young man, and thus thought that Porsche, who was now approaching his late sixties, was far too old to have official power. Speer believed that no man over the age of fifty should be in a position of management, and he tried very hard to implement this rule. Speer eventually became so annoyed with Porsche and his age and inefficiency that he "promoted" him to "Reich Armaments Councilor," to get Porsche out of his direct vicinity, never mind that Porsche was now the head of an organization that did not really exist!

In 1942, Porsche was sixty-seven years old, and it had become clear that the war would not be ending anytime soon and that his beloved car factory would not be producing any Strength through Joy Cars as had been promised and planned. Instead, the plant would be rearranged to produce vehicles and armaments for war. It was a chaotic mix of projects: fuel tanks, airplane wing repairs, mines, bazookas, and (perhaps more notably) 20,000 V1 flying bombs. Porsche was also commissioned to turn his designs for a People's Car into wartime vehicles of various sorts, some of which were tough-guy Beetles with big wheels and raised frames, others that were more like jeeps and known as Kübelwagens or Bucket Seat Cars. The lines for Porsche's original cars were finally taken down and a second assembly line was set up for Kübelwagen production. This vehicle had an engine of 25 hp and a body that was redesigned to provide more ground area while remaining lightweight. It looked more like a jeep than a Bug, a pumped-up version with bigger wheels and a tougher spine. These gutsy little pug-nosed vehicles had the same air-cooled engine design and chassis as the People's Car and they were a hit among both the Allied and Axis armies by the end of the war. The Volkswagen factory would eventually produce more than 66,000 of them. In addition to the Bucket Seat Cars, Porsche also revamped the VW design and made an amphibious vehicle that could either move through the water like a boat or drive over dry land. These strange creations were called Schwimmwagens and they were completely waterproof, with retractable propellers. In 1943, production of the military versions of Porsche's design accounted for 41.5 percent of factory sales, pulling in a total of 93 million RM out of the 225 million RM the factory made that year.

Having worked on wartime projects for Austria in the First World War, it was not an unfamiliar mode for Porsche. But this time he had many more responsibilities and was constantly traveling between his company in Stuttgart, the factory in Wolfsburg, and numerous other factories and cities that required his presence during the war. His offices and workshop in Stuttgart grew considerably, employing hundreds as they tried to keep up with airplane, tank, and automotive design demands. Because Ferdinand was kept so busy with his wartime designs, it was his son-in-law, Anton Piëch, who, in 1941, took over as head of the Volkswagen plant in The Town of the Strength through Joy Car, moving with Louise to the little Porsche hut on the Klieversberg hill, so Porsche himself was around less and less as the factory retooled itself for war.

As the war progressed, Heinrich Nordhoff was removed from his executive position in Berlin and made the director of Opel's nearby Brandenburg truck plant. Brandenburg, less than an hour from Berlin, was a town of castles with an old Prussian heart, and the Opel truck factory there had come into existence under Nazi patronage and in large part through Nazi behest. Because it was connected to the United States, Opel's main factory was not trusted enough to be given any of the main tasks, such as building tanks, airplanes, or weapons for the war. But it was a primary source of wartime trucks. Now Heinrich had to deal with as many Nazi elites as Porsche did, including Hitler's old automotive friend Jakob Werlin. In addition to his job as an official director of the factory in The Town of the Strength through Joy Car, Werlin had also become a member of the SS and carried the title of *Generalinspektor des Führer fuer das Kraftfahrwesen*—he was Hitler's automotive inspector, more or less, and that meant factory heads like Nordhoff had to please him when he came around to inspect the plant. Werlin made his rounds to all the car companies, ensuring all things were "working toward the Führer." Nordhoff also found himself having to work with Goering, often referred to as the second most powerful man in the Nazi Party, because (thanks to the Four Year Plan) Goering was the official manager and administrator of every industrial company in Germany. And Opel's truck factory had a special place in the eyes of Goering since it had been built under his watch.

Even before coming to office, the Nazis had planned to put Opel back into German hands, and as the war progressed, it looked as if they had succeeded. General Motors declared Opel a tax loss and for a time the factory was indeed completely under Nazi control. At the plant, Nordhoff was given the new title and rank of *Wehrwirtschaftsfüher,* or War Economy Leader, a standard title for someone in his position but a term that would later prove very difficult to explain. Nordhoff still refused to join the Nazi Party, but even so, he was working directly for the Nazi machine. Since Brandenburg was less than an hour from Berlin, at first Charlotte and the girls stayed where they were while Nordhoff commuted back and forth. But as his hours grew longer and ever more tedious, he was eventually forced to take an apartment in Brandenburg and see much less of Charlotte and his girls.

Nordhoff was now immersed in the midst of an ugly world. In 1943, in a letter to Charlotte, he celebrated their wedding anniversary from afar with melancholic thoughts: "The future looks dark," he wrote. "I long for a time when we are free to live in our own way, when a better life will begin for all of us and we can raise our girls to be happy and competent citizens in this world." People working with him would later say that Nordhoff experienced an "inner emigration" during these years. He was as diligent as ever about his work, but there was a part of him that seemed to have simply gone away.

During Nordhoff's first year at the Brandenburg factory, the war seemed to be going well for Germany, but by 1943 it would all turn around and Hitler's winning streak would disappear. Soon, conditions all over Germany would begin to deteriorate, even more quickly than they had improved when Hitler had come to power. And Hitler's health would experience a steep decline; he would grow less and less social, no longer wanting to see or speak to the German people, claiming he was waiting until the tide turned again so he could give them better news.

He did seem to believe the tide would eventually turn. And neither he nor Porsche had yet given up on the idea of their People's Car. Even when Hitler was holed up in his mountain retreat (the Berghof near Berchtesgaden), isolated from the destruction he was causing in the world, the Strength through Joy Car was still part of his daily life. Hitler didn't drink, but he liked to have nightly tea sessions—tedious and uncomfortable hours for the others who were present, but seemingly enjoyable for him. At one such late-night session in 1942, Hitler sketched the People's Car for everyone present and spoke once more about "the great designer" Ferdinand Porsche. "He is a real genius," Hitler said, "even though he seems so modest and self-effacing." According to a secretary of Hitler's who was nearly always nearby, Hitler drove around the country near the Berghof in a Volkswagen. It was a "specially made cabriolet with black paint and leather upholstery. Apart from the Führer and his chauffeur, only his valet and Blondi ever traveled in it." Blondi was Hitler's dog; she was always by his side, even in the bunker. And the special Volkswagen had been a birthday gift from Ferdinand Porsche.

It's hard to say why the old designer had such an effect on

Hitler, but he was always sure to take care of Porsche. Once, when Porsche had to go to the front lines to see how the Panzers were performing in action, Hitler insisted that he use the Führer's official pilot and aircraft. "Let the generals fly in the regular planes," Hitler said, "I have many generals but only one Porsche." Porsche was also the only person in authority who did not have to wear a uniform at the time—by 1942 everyone

Factory workers and staff living together in the cramped barracks in The Town of the Strength through Joy Car.

was wearing a uniform—and he was the only man who did not address Hitler as "the Führer." Ferry would later say that he sometimes felt as if Hitler considered himself Porsche's son as well. In Ferry's own words, "at most a half-dozen men in all of Germany dared to speak their minds openly before Hitler, and my father was one of them . . . The situation, in fact, was in some respects as though my father were also Hitler's father." But such a comparison can only go so far. After all, out of a desire to get back to making his car, Porsche suggested numerous times that Hitler should end the war, and it's extremely doubtful Hitler ever gave that idea even the slightest bit of thought.

By 1943, The Town of the Strength through Joy Car had all

but been abandoned by those who had founded it. None of the men who had started the town were able to give it much attention or care now. In fact, it was hard to say that a town even existed at all: Construction had been abandoned when the war started, and much of the area was still a giant building site. Trees had been cleared, but nothing had been erected to fill the space. Materials and supplies were left abandoned in piles. Roads ended abruptly into the grass, leading nowhere. Aside from a medieval castle tucked into a nearby grove of trees, the only structural presence in the area was that of the towering brick factory, rising out of the emptiness and mess. The workers lived together in overcrowded dorms around it, and clusters of their makeshift barracks dotted the surrounding landscape. Only the sweet and fully finished area of the Steimker Berg, with its white thatch-style houses and idyllic tree-lined estates, gave the sense of something civilized, but those homes were occupied mainly by Nazi and SS men. Whatever experiment had been attempted with the project of The Town of the Strength through Joy Car, it was beginning to look like it had horribly failed.

The use of forced labor spread quickly throughout Germany as Nazi forces captured ever more foreign towns and brought people back from them to work in their German plants; this was a common practice during the Second World War, not only for Germany but also for the Allied countries. Nationalities were scrambled and mixed in factories all over the Continent during that time, though in Germany and the Soviet Union, the conditions were especially brutal. After 1942, nearly all German plants, including those owned by General Motors and Ford, relied heavily on forced labor for work. None of the factories would have been able to produce the wartime weapons and transportation that were needed had they not. After all, Germany had already been at full employment in 1938, and for wartime, the country needed millions of additional workers.

The Volkswagen factory was no different: In fact, the Volkswagen factory, having never had a full staff to begin with, was even more in need of foreign help than most. Likewise, because the town and the factory were a direct project of the Nazi Party, the factory experienced an even greater extent of Nazi presence and control. The Gestapo had its own office there. Everyone in charge was part of the Nazi Party. And there was an additional policing force called the Werkschutz that patrolled the plant and the housing compounds and barracks, keeping a close eye on the workers—especially the foreign ones—and operating as an instrument of punishment and surveillance, ensuring no one could escape. Beatings and brutality were commonplace, and for any workers who dared to rebel, including the Germans, there were "reeducation camps" where, according to the reports of the workers, torture was the norm.

The average amount of staff in German companies during the war that were forced laborers was 30 percent. Because of its unusually high lack of labor from the beginning, at the VW factory during the height of the war, *80* percent of the staff was forced. Indeed, foreign prisoners of war were, to a large degree, the factory's first real employees. The town that Hitler had hoped to be a model industrial city for Germany was in reality perhaps one of the most mixed and international areas in the country, but violently and involuntarily so.

Slave labor is not a horror the Germans invented—the world knew it long before the Nazis, and today there are still millions of forced laborers in the world. But forced labor in Germany was brutally tied to the tragic ideas of race and class that Hitler and his party had been trying to prove. Hitler's *Mein Kampf* was often read over loudspeakers, and Nazi officers imposed public humiliations on Eastern laborers who were deemed a lower "breed." For example, in June of 1940, 300 young Polish women were among the first forced laborers brought to the plant, many of them having been randomly plucked from their homes with no time to say goodbye or pack. Some did not even have shoes when they arrived. To make it clear to all the other workers that the women were from Poland—a country that was seen as full of *volkspolitische Gefahren* (contaminating influences)—the women were immediately given patches of the letter "P" to sew onto all their dresses.

There were many Soviet prisoners of war brought to work at the factory too. They had "SU" patches sewn to their clothes, and of all the prisoners, they were treated the worst. Many Soviet prisoners of war never made it to work at the factory but died from malnutrition, outbreaks of typhus, and other diseases, not to mention the mass shootings that sometimes took place in camps outside the factory grounds.

For other nationalities, classification was more fluid: The Italians who were also working at the plant, for example, were treated well so long as Italy was fighting on Germany's side; but once they united with the Allies, they were treated as traitors. One Italian prisoner at the Volkswagen factory, Cesare Pilesi, would later tell of the day he burned his foot on purpose by holding it to the red-hot wall of a stove. He was very sick, and burning himself was the only way he could think to get taken off the relentless winter construction work.

Even from its earliest days, this factory had been a mix of nationality. Before the outbreak of war, more than a thousand French boys had been coerced into coming to the plant to work. Young Dutch boys came too. And when the war began, many of those French and Dutch boys found themselves stuck. They had "higher racial status" than those from the east and thus received better treatment and compensation when it came to housing, wages, and food. But they were by no means free. When the Dutch boys tried to have a musical evening with the French, for instance, the SS came with guns strapped to their backs and took people away to the reeducation camps. Letters were also monitored. One Dutch boy named Marinus Kop was sentenced to death and shot by the Nazis on the grounds that his letters home "betrayed" the Nazi Party in some inexplicable way.

Concentration camp prisoners were used at the Volkswagen factory too. As early as 1941, Heinrich Himmler suggested using Jewish forced labor to finish building the still-incomplete town, but Hitler did not want Jewish people in the town, so the idea was put on hold. Eventually Robert Ley established a Jewish camp that was to be a light metals foundry toward the creation of Strength through Joy Cars. But as it became clear that no Strength through Joy Cars were going to get made, the camp quickly closed and the prisoners were sent elsewhere. By 1944, however, it looked as though Germany was losing the war, and as nearly every German man and boy was being sent to fight, the push for workers for the factories became even more desperate, and Albert Speer, who had become head of the Nazi Armaments Division, gave official authorization for the use of concentration camp inmates in producing vehicles at German automotive plants. Thus in 1944, skilled Hungarian Jewish metalworkers were plucked out of Auschwitz to come to The Town of the Strength through Joy Car and build V1 bombs. These prisoners had access to the shower facilities that were inside the factory, and they each had their own bed, which was, some wrote in their letters, an unheard of joy after having been at Auschwitz. After they'd worked on the V1, however, most of these men were sent to concentration camp Dora and many of them died just months before the end of the war. Hungarian Jewish women were brought to the factory from Auschwitz too, as were Jewish women from Bergen-Belsen. The women later testified that this time felt like an escape from the usual "*Vernichtung durch Arbeit*" or "death through labor" that was common in the other camps during these last, and worst, years of the war.

It is amazing that the times were so grim in Germany that escaping *Vernichtung durch Arbeit* was considered a lucky break. Perhaps one of the most astonishing things, however, is how strong these people were in the face of so much darkness and suffering, and the ways they found to stay connected to creativity and a sense of life. In fact, there was a whole underground world of close relationships forming between prisoners as they got to know each other. In letters and stories from this time, it becomes clear they had formed strong bonds with one another. In their camps at night, they told stories, recited plays, sang songs. Some of them prayed together. They met late at night to discuss their former lives. They drew and painted and wrote letters to one another as they were shifted from camp to camp, devising all kinds of ways to deliver them. They used old clothes to make new dresses and little items, like purses, to give each other as gifts. In one story, a man tells of smuggling in a radio and of all the prisoners crowding around it to hear the news. Another laborer remembers seeing that a Frenchman from another camp had written graffiti on the side of a train: *Le jour de gloire va arriver* . . . The day of victory is coming. Dire as their conditions were, many still dared to dream, and many still had hope.

Throughout 1944 and 1945, the focus at the factory was less about production and more about trying to save the machines and equipment there. As the bombings of the German countryside increased, steps were taken to move many operations to more areas off-site. As the grounds around the factory had been cleared in order to build the city, the massive building was completely out in the open and an easy target for bombs. As early as 1943, when it was still believed the Germans might be able to win, workers in The Town of the Strength through Joy Car began moving equipment to remote areas in nearby forests and caves. In one large-scale project, the equipment was relocated to an iron mine and reassembled so the workers could continue producing war armaments under cover. The mine was converted into an underground factory within six months. At other sites, as they moved equipment, the laborers were forced to live in tents until they'd built their own housing by hand. Inside the factory itself, bales of straw and giant sandbags were piled up around all the best machines to try to reduce the effects of the bombs when they hit. Air-raid shelters were separated according to nationality, and prisoners often woke two or three times a night and hustled to the bunkers for safety. As the days and months passed and the bombing grew more frequent, the air became more electric, and minds more preoccupied with wondering "what might come." Some laborers took comfort in the old saying that it always gets worse right before the end.

When Ferry was a little boy, Porsche would usually arrive home from a long day of work just as Aloisia was putting their son to bed, and he would always plead with her to allow Ferry to stay up just a few minutes longer. But as Ferry grew, and as he developed his own taste for cars, the father and son found they had a great deal of time together. Ferry had followed in his father's footsteps, and his father's obsession for automobiles was now also his. It wasn't an easy relationship, as relationships between fathers and sons rarely are, but it was certainly a crucial one in both their lives, and it would forever remain inseparable from their work. Ferry, who was much softer and more emotional than Porsche, and who thought of himself as "a mother's boy," nevertheless wanted his father's approval and struggled to make his mark in a world where his father was the "designer genius" whose name and reputation would follow Ferry like a shadow for the rest of his life. As Porsche's only son, Ferry was both privileged and at a disadvantage: His father was harder on him than on anyone (and that was saying a lot), but he was also very concerned about Ferry and focused on him in a way he did not focus on any of the other men in his life. The closeness between the two men was especially apparent, even if Ferry's position was not always an enviable one.

Ferry's cousin, Ghislaine, however, who was Porsche's personal secretary for much of his life, would probably have done just about anything to be able to switch places with Ferry and be Porsche's son. Whereas Ferry came into the world with a clear and solid idea of a very particular world—the automotive one—Ghislaine's life was less certain. He often occupied a

*Ferry as a child in the car his father made for him. His cousin
Ghislaine is trying to get into the car with him. There seemed to
always be a part of Ghislaine that wished he was Porsche's son.*

rather gray place in the daily Porsche automotive world—
important to his uncle on one level, and yet never having access
in full. Ghislaine also inhabited a gray middle ground when it
came to his nationality: Having been born in Britain, he carried
a British passport even during his time in Germany. In the years
after Hitler came to power, surely he felt he was in a precarious
position.

Ferdinand and his nephew did not discuss Ghislaine's British citizenship. When Ghislaine listened to the BBC (an illegal
thing to do by Nazi rules), Porsche saw no problem with it and
at times even asked him to translate what he'd heard. But once
war began, and the tide began to turn against Germany, Ghislaine's connection to "the enemy" could not go overlooked. Despite Porsche's high standing with Hitler, once the Nazi military
became starved for soldiers, Ghislaine was targeted and deported to a German punishment battalion on the eastern front
where he was forced to fight. In one gruesome battle against the
Soviets, he was wounded and eventually sent to a Nazi wartime
medical facility in Copenhagen. Denmark was still under German control, but it was 1944 and it was clear to most that Ger-

many had already lost. When Ghislaine saw a British flag flying over the city, he rushed to the British embassy to ask them for help. They didn't believe that he was a British citizen, however, and he was handed over to local resistance fighters who threatened to kill him, shoving the end of a pistol into the back of his neck. His execution was thwarted at the last moment by a Dutch officer who had another look at Ghislaine's British passport and thought it best if they sent him to jail instead. He would eventually convince the Allies of his British birth, though he was made to stand trial in a British court for treason because he had fought for the Germans. The exact details of this time in his life are rather hard to trace now. Certainly, his loyalties must have been conflicted ones, and it was probably difficult for him to explain his actions or intentions in those years, even to himself.

In fact, things were becoming difficult for all the Porsches in 1944. Germany was being bombed heavily, and Albert Speer ordered Porsche to leave the country and to move his offices to a safe place. In the autumn of that year, Porsche began relocating his entire workshop to Gmünd, a place near his summer home at Zell am See in Austria. The place they chose was a former woodworking factory. According to Ferry, Speer had first ordered them to Czechoslovakia but they'd found this place instead and had been given permission to go. Gmünd was a village in Carinthia, nestled between the mountains of the southern province of Austria. Karl Rabe and the other Porsche engineers and workers left Stuttgart, along with the rest of the Porsche family, including Ferry's wife and sons. But Ferry and his father stayed back at the Stuttgart villa a bit longer, finding it difficult to say goodbye.

As they were preparing to close down their beloved home and leave, bomb sirens rang out over Stuttgart, and Ferry and Porsche had to stay in the city bomb shelter until it was safe to come out. Afterward, they walked up the hill to their home, not saying a word, both silently fearing it had been destroyed. When they arrived, they found that the garage where the first VWs had been built was still standing, untouched. And though the house had shattered windows, and part of the roof was missing, it was still there. Neither Porsche nor his son went inside; instead they leaned together against the front wall and tried to take it all in. Ferry would later say that his father's face was frozen in a state of "anguish and disbelief and bewilderment," a man "finally overwhelmed by the futility and madness of the Wagnerian roller coaster the country had been on."

Ferry knew it was the wrong time to bring it up, but being his father's son he couldn't help but remind Porsche of earlier times when he'd tried to talk to him about Hitler and the war. Porsche hated to be contradicted, especially by his son. In the past, if Ferry ever dared to question his father in public, he would cruelly shut him down, even if (or especially if) what he was saying was correct. But in this case, Porsche nodded and withdrew; it was perhaps the first time he had ever conceded to his son. Ferry had been correct back in 1939, Porsche said, and he now admitted that there was no way anything good could come of this.

A tired Ferdinand Porsche sitting in his Volkswagen at the Wörthersee in 1940; war has broken out, and it looks like the little car will not get produced after all.

In the following months, Porsche seemed to grow visibly smaller and weaker, and by the end of the year there were some days when he did not get out of bed once they'd returned to the farm at Zell am See. Since none of his family was still in Wolfsburg, no one knew what was happening at the VW factory, but the outlook was not good. Even if by some chance the factory managed to escape being bombed or destroyed, it was very unlikely that Porsche would ever get a chance to build his car there after the war: The entire place, after all, had been a project of the very man who had caused this war, and there was no reason to think the Allies would allow any remnant of his rule to persist. In fact, the Porsches themselves must have realized they were complicit with the Nazi Party to some degree, and with the fall of Germany, it was unclear what would become of them. They were safe and they were together for now, and reading Ferry's account of those days, it seems they tried to make the best of it. Their farm was overflowing with all the friends and workers who had come with them from Stuttgart, twenty-five people staying over and working and living off the Porsche farm. They baked their own bread and smoked their own meat, waiting for the war to end and wondering what was going to happen to them.

No one is really sure exactly how many people died in the war, but there are estimates of up to 60 million, with 40 million civilian deaths. That means one-third of the victims were soldiers and two-thirds were people who had nothing directly to do with the war, a shocking number the likes of which had never been seen before (or after). This extreme amount of civilian casualties came in part because of the use of airplanes and air bombings. Before the Second World War, no one had made cities the indiscriminate targets of strategic bombing to such an extent. With Hitler's first blitz campaigns, the Allies watched in horror as innocent civilians were killed, so shocked by Hitler's actions that they believed they would never be able to retaliate in kind. But it was a slippery slope. By the end of the war, the Allies would have bombed Germany to such an extent that some cities were more than 80 percent destroyed. The decimation caused by the war was so extensive as to seem almost unbelievable and in many ways it still is: It's very difficult to imagine so many cities, streets, and homes reduced to rubble and ash. But they were. And it had all started with the desires and ideas of one man. It was a situation that had seemed impossible, until it was real.

In retrospect, there are many signs that things had gotten out of control very early on in Germany and that its leaders were living in an unsustainable world of personal myth. It's probably safe to say, for instance, that when a political party passes a law to make their current active leader's birthday into a national holiday, that's a sure sign that something has gone wrong. Hitler's birthday was a Nazi national holiday, and stamps were often issued to commemorate the event. It was a matter of perpetuating the mythic feeling of immortality that Hitler cultivated around himself: By doing things that were usually only done for someone after their death, such events made him seem larger than life. But the image of Hitler as savior and hero was not something he'd created on his own. People had been looking for a hero and he'd stepped into that role, believing it himself so sincerely that others around him got caught up in that belief as it took on a life of its own. Goebbels above everyone seemed ready to talk of Hitler with religious fervor. Every year on Hitler's birthday, Goebbels gave speeches praising him, usually just before the Philharmonie played a tribute concert in Berlin.

However, in 1943, on Hitler's fifty-fourth birthday, the mood of the country was hardly celebratory. Hitler avoided the masses. He'd become too worried about his safety and too embarrassed by German losses to be seen much in public anymore. Instead, he celebrated with his "*chauffeurska*" on a lonely section of the autobahn. German roads were still white elephants, empty because most people in the country still did not have cars. Standing together there on the distant slice of concrete surrounded by a rolling and empty landscape, it was difficult even for Hitler's entourage to rally their spirits. Hitler himself had lost that determined and confident gleam he'd once had. He was not the same man who had shoveled dirt nine years ago to commemorate the first autobahn.

That same year, even Goebbels began Hitler's birthday speech in Berlin with the words: "The German people celebrate the Führer's birthday this year in a particularly somber manner." As Hitler and his crew stood on the empty autobahn, Goebbels continued on to say: "Confidence is the best moral weapon of war . . . When it begins to fail, the beginning of the end has arrived. No matter where we look, we see no cause for such concern. It exists only in the propaganda dreams of our enemy. The more hopes they put in the moral weakness of the German people, the greater will be their disappointment." Now that the war was going wrong for Germany, Goebbels said it was not Germany but "the wicked forces" of the Allies that had wanted and waged this war, a statement impossible to prove in any way. While the Allies were confronting reality, Hitler was avoiding it. The German people wrote him letters daily asking him to come out and see the destruction of their towns, but he ignored them. Not once did he reach out to comfort any of the citizens or the families of those who had been killed. Goebbels lamented this turn more than anyone, and as propaganda minister, was constantly trying to get Hitler to talk to the masses, knowing that his ability to speak had been his only real strength. But Hitler could not talk because he no longer had the confidence or the energy to present "a strong will": He waited on a miracle instead, hoping against the very clear (to others, at least) odds that things would turn in Germany's favor again. He would only talk to the people, Hitler said, once that miracle had occurred.

25

In 1945, the atmosphere of The Town of the Strength through Joy Car suddenly changed. It could be felt in the camps. The SS was on edge. The guards were jittery. For the foreign laborers, 1944 had been a year of bombing and constant sirens, of being herded into bomb shelters in the middle of the night, of less food than usual, of days of picking through debris, and of that hysterical middle ground between the fear of death and the dream of being rescued. Over half the factory had been damaged to some extent, but wartime production crawled on. No one was getting much sleep. Everyone scanned the skies for planes.

Just before 9:00 on the morning of April 10, the factory sirens blasted once more, this time with a Panzer alert meaning enemy tanks were near. The Allies had come. German workers were ordered to go to their houses. Prisoners were sent to their camps. People whispered that the Americans were coming. Or was it the Soviets? Good news spread, but an equal number of horror stories were told. Tensions were high. Everything was overcrowded. The trains carrying concentration camp prisoners and foreign laborers—the town had become a crossroads of sorts—stalled and backed up. The telephone services had been disconnected days before; there was no way of getting outside news. Communication and transportation were breaking down, and Nazi authority was breaking down too.

Twelve hours after the first alert, at 9:00 p.m., another shrill alarm broke through town. German workers barricaded themselves indoors. Some Nazi officials began to destroy documents, trying to erase their existence and their names. Nazi uniforms were burned; official photos of Hitler were quickly hidden or annihilated; SS leaders fled. Those still loyal to the Nazi government talked of destroying the factory, of burning it to the ground. All the highest officials knew about the NSDAP's policy of "scorched earth": If the Third Reich was to go down, all was to be set afire. At one point, Hitler told Albert Speer: "If the war is lost, the nation will also perish. This fate is inevitable. There's no reason to take into consideration what the people will need to continue a most primitive existence. On the contrary, it will be better to destroy these things ourselves because the nation will have proven itself to be the weaker one. . . ." As Speer later recalled, the list of things that were to be destroyed included "all industrial plants, all important electrical facilities, water works and gas works; all stocks of food and clothing, all bridges, all railways and communications installations, all waterways, all shipping, inland as well as oceanic, all freight cars and all locomotives."

At the close of the war, the Germans began carrying out such plans not only in their own country—which was already to a great degree destroyed—but in the countries they occupied. As they retreated, they burned or destroyed as much as they could along the way. In cities of great culture such as Florence, bridges and sacred works of art were burned or blown up. In Russia, the original scores of Tchaikovsky were thrown out into the yard, and Leo Tolstoy's house was wrecked. The mood was one of total war, and the climax of destruction had begun. There was no reason to think it would be any different for The Town of the Strength through Joy Car.

But those who had been given orders were hesitant to follow through. Two such officers went to the mayor of the town and told him they'd been instructed to blow up the factory's power station, the Kraftwerk, and the canal bridges connecting the factory to the rest of town. The mayor pleaded with them to reconsider their orders: The factory's generators were the lifeblood of electricity and services for the entire town. And the Nazi Party hardly had the power to punish the two officers for disobeying now, the mayor pointed out. Many were already on the run.

Outside the camps and around the factory, the group of SS guards continued to thin. Men left their posts and slipped off into the night. A feeling of freedom blew through the barracks and camps, but few had any clear direction of where to actually go once they were free. After these past five years, what was home, and how could they travel when the infrastructure of their countries was being destroyed? Stories circulated among the Russian prisoners that it wasn't safe to cross into the Soviet-occupied areas of Germany: So much time among the enemy meant they were likely to be seen as "contaminated" and thus would be locked away or killed. The next day, a few last battles raged on. Soon, word came that the nearby village of Fallersleben had been taken by American troops. But no one showed up in the Volkswagen town: They didn't know it was there. The city was too young to have made it onto any of the American army's official land maps. (The factory had only made it onto aerial maps by then.)

The chaos increased around the factory; more Nazi officials and SS troopers escaped into the night. As morning broke on April 11, the camps of the forced laborers could no longer be guarded and the prisoners—some starving, aggressive, seething with pent-up rage—broke free and moved like gangs through the town in search of retribution, attention, food. Other prisoners stayed huddled in the camps and met among themselves, sending search parties through the factory for vittles; the more clearheaded realized that to flee would be even more dangerous than staying: The only thing to do was wait.

Still, those prisoners intent on revenge were of a large enough number to send a new wave of fear through the still-unoccupied town. German families boarded up their windows and went up to the attics to hide, watching from the highest windows as groups of prisoners celebrated and shouted on the streets. The grocery stores were looted, a local butcher was shot, there was sporadic violence and a few hand grenades were thrown. Some discovered stores of alcohol and their drunkenness added a further layer of release. Some drank industrial alcohol and methanol in the pharmacy and died from it. Another group of laborers broke into a pharmacy storage closet and found a large bag of rice. Starving, they cooked it into a pudding, unaware that the rice was laced with poison and had been used to kill rats.

The rioting continued the entire day, escalating to a near frenzy in some places before the initial euphoria began to wear off and things quieted down. Remarkably, in all the looting and destruction, no one destroyed the factory's machinery, and the power station remained unharmed.

The Americans were so close, but unless someone told them that the town needed help, it was doubtful they would seek out the factory themselves. A French Franciscan friar who had been a laborer in the camp—the SS men had been particularly cruel to him because of his religious ties—spoke a bit of English and offered to help; a German priest who had helped the French friar as much as he could over the past years came to him, and together, the two decided to take a Red Cross jeep over to the nearby village to talk to the Americans. A German-born American citizen, an autoworker who had moved to Wolfsburg from Detroit in 1937, volunteered to go with the priests and help too.

The first American they found was a red-haired army soldier who was kind but cautious, not sure what to make of a German factory worker who spoke English with an American accent. That same man also claimed there were American children—sons and daughters of those who had been recruited by Volkswagen before the onset of war—living in Wolfsburg who needed help. The priests nodded in confirmation. Eventually the Americans loaded up their jeeps and gear and moved into The Town of the Strength through Joy Car.

U.S. troops first entered the Volkswagen city late in the afternoon on April 12. American officers and tanks patrolled the streets and broke up what rowdy groups were left, arresting Nazi soldiers and collecting weapons. The noise decreased; the town grew quieter. Germans began to take the boards off their windows and came out to watch the American tanks. Soon, various officials and other citizens of the city created a small local patrol to help keep order and to try to decide what else could be done to assist.

Three days after entering the town, American officers set up a U.S. Army post at the factory and another one by the old Cas-

A heavily damaged area of the factory. One Volkswagen can be seen parked in the wreckage.

tle Wolfsburg, which had existed since the Middle Ages. For the next weeks, the army tried to find food and supplies for the town. The factory was in good enough shape for the Americans to set up a repair shop for their own vehicles. Urging from the factory staff also led the Americans to consider restarting production of vehicles, a very significant decision at the time and one that may have saved the plant. Compared to the rest of Germany, the Volkswagen factory survived the war surprisingly unscathed. A study done by the United States Strategic Bombing Survey Team shows that there were large gaping holes throughout the buildings, but that overall, the main infrastructure was still strong. More than 2,000 bombs had been dropped in the area, but only 263 had actually hit the factory. Legend has it that during the inspection, a dud bomb was found sitting snug between the two main turbines of the power plant. It would have been the end of the factory and town's power and electricity source had it gone off.

In the official report, the team concluded that half of the factory was damaged to some extent—missing roofs, busted windows, gaping holes—but that only about 20 percent had been completely destroyed. Much of the machinery—expensive new technologies brought over from the United States—had been protected by the heavily reinforced walls of the factory and by steps taken from workers to pack sandbags and bales of hay around them. The press shop, which is the part of the plant where the metals are shaped, was miraculously still operable, meaning production could be started again, though at a limp.

The U.S. officers appointed a plant manager from the remaining German staff and the factory was ordered to continue building the jeeplike vehicles for Allied troops. At the end of April 1945 production started up again, and in the next two months the Volkswagen factory pieced together 133 Bucket Seat Cars for the U.S. forces stationed there, many of the same German and foreign workers working together as they had before the war. The Americans also took another crucial step in ensuring the future of the plant: They had a map made, compiling the knowledge of the workers and the German staff that remained, showing where many of the parts and machines that had been taken away could be found.

As the town tried to take stock, one of the first orders of business by the community was to change the city's name. No one wanted it to be called The Town of the Strength through Joy Car anymore. On the 25th of May, the city decided to name itself after the castle that had been there long before the Nazis, and would remain long after they had left. The town would be called Wolfsburg from that day forward.

Around the same time that the Volkswagen town was being occupied by American troops, Erich Kempka, Hitler's private driver and friend, got a phone call from the führer's bunker. It was the 30th of April and the call was an urgent order for 200 liters of petrol. Kempka could not believe the request. Berlin was in the midst of being taken by the Russians and the need for such a large amount of gasoline made little sense. The only stores of gasoline were in a bunker near Berlin's central Zoolo-gischer Garten train station, a place being heavily fired upon and bombed. It was impossible to send men there in the middle of the day under such heavy fire, but his commander refused to listen. *Do whatever it takes, just get the gasoline and come to the Führer immediately.*

The years had not been good for Hitler. He looked like an old man, and the rapid aging and deterioration that the last two years had caused were striking to those who saw him. Long be-fore the war's end, he'd developed a condition like Parkinson's, trembling constantly. In the last year, there were some days he did not get out of bed. He was totally reliant on his doctor for medications. Methamphetamines were now being given out to the German military, and it is speculated that Hitler was ingest-ing those as well. At the time Kempka was called for the gaso-line, it was just days after Hitler's fifty-sixth birthday: There had been no speeches from Goebbels, and little celebration. The en-tire country was being overrun by the Allies; it was just a matter of time before the Russians would make their way to the bunker too.

In the heat of battle, Kempka refused to send his men to the Zoologischer Garten. Instead, he had them spread out and find parked or damaged vehicles and siphon gasoline from those. Collecting as much petrol from the cars as he could, Kempka rushed to the bunker, still fuming over being made to take such a risk. When he arrived, however, all that anger dissolved. The Führer was dead, he was told. The petrol he'd just gathered would be used to burn the body before the Russians arrived.

Hitler's Thousand-Year Reich had lasted twelve years. And the Volkswagen factory he'd promised would build millions of passenger cars had produced 66,285 military vehicles for the war. By the time Wolfsburg was taken by the Americans, it was clear that Germany's once all-power and all-knowing head, the man many had believed was ordained by Providence to save Germany, had been deeply wrong. The power of his propaganda

had crumbled, shown itself an empty shell, with nothing of lasting substance behind it, nothing true.

What was known as the *Stunde Null,* the Zero Hour, fell over
the country soon after Hitler's death and the army's surrender, a
kind of motionless hour where the whole world seemed either
to end or restart, or both. In the calm of the postwar air, visions
of the rubble and debris weighed heavily. Nearly three tons of
bombs had been dropped on Germany and almost three-fourths
of that amount had come within the last year. After such destruction and noise, the silence was almost impossible to endure. Some German families locked themselves in rooms and
committed suicide together. Others began trying to remove the
wreckage and start again, even though it felt like an impossible
feat. And the truth about the numerous concentration camps,
where so many innocent lives had been taken through the most
horrific means, could no longer be hidden or denied.

As production resumed at the factory he had helped to design
and build, Ferdinand Porsche was in Austria, unable to get any
news about what was happening there. Over the past year and a
half, communication with the factory had become more and
more difficult, until it finally had simply ceased. His large staff
of laborers, and his twelve original men (with Karl Rabe at the
head) were now in Gmünd, in the new workshop they'd set up,
where they were busy building things for the local farmers like
wheelbarrows, tractors, and carts.

In the early spring of 1945, in the heat of the war's slow end,
an Allied CIOS (Combined Intelligence Objectives Sub-
Committee) technical commission sought Ferdinand Porsche
out and questioned him about his wartime work, taking him
back to Zell am See and placing armed guards in front of his
house for a few weeks. Two and a half months later, just before
Porsche's seventieth birthday, he was summoned by the Americans to Frankfurt for a trial. He was allowed to drive there him-

self, but he was aging now—the kind of aging that did not necessarily have to do with years. Not sure he could make the drive alone, he took his long-standing family chauffeur (and friend) with him. Soon, the men arrived in the American Zone for Porsche's trial, joining Albert Speer and a host of others who'd been singled out as prominent members of the Third Reich.

The trials were called "Operation Dustbin," and the men were kept in a large castle and questioned one by one. The process took nearly three months. From all the reports, Porsche seemed to exude a kind of simple innocence while he was there. He was quieter than usual. He seemed lost. Some commented that it felt strange to see him there. Even Albert Speer was upset by Porsche's presence, feeling it was wrong that he'd been called to trial. Speer told the Americans that it was pointless to continue interrogating Porsche over political matters; the engineer had never been privy to such things, nor would he be able to discuss them. The Americans eventually released Porsche uncharged and allowed him to go directly to his home at Zell am See.

Porsche did not seem to understand what a close call he'd just had: Many of the prominent Nazis he'd just been with would eventually be sent to Nuremberg and get the death penalty for what they'd done. Porsche was free, but was given explicit instructions to leave the country at once. Yet, he couldn't help going by Stuttgart, wanting to know if his old home and workshop were still intact. He was happy to see that they were both still there, and he hoped the Americans occupying it would let him come inside for a quick look. But the generals in charge of the estate refused to come out and talk to him, and he was reprimanded and warned to return to Austria at once. Porsche did as he was told this time. Ferry and Louise and the rest of the family were happy to have him back at Zell am See. But their joy was short-lived. Porsche was home now, but the Allies would come for him again soon.

People who were there often comment on how bright the sun was the summer when Germany fell. The color footage of Berlin at the time does indeed paint a striking picture: The intense blue sky seems a profane backdrop for the piles of rubble, skeletons of buildings, and lines of people—mostly women—emerging from the wreckage and venturing into the open air. People formed chains, passing bricks or pails of rubble to one another, starting what seemed an impossible task. An aerial view of Berlin is even more striking: Every building is a shell, streets are unrecognizable, it doesn't look as if anything could still be alive down there at all. And for those who were still alive, what was next?

There were many differing policy ideas about what measures would be best once the war ended, but the one overwhelmingly supported by Roosevelt in 1944 and 1945 was the Morgenthau Plan. This plan would destroy Germany's capacity of waging war by turning the country into an agricultural nation, eliminating all its heavy industry and ensuring much of its machinery was dismantled and destroyed. This meant that the automotive industries (alongside others) were to be crippled. Germany's economic and industrial heart—the Ruhr area, a powerhouse of coal and steel—was to be taken over by the Allies, and much of the mining was to be shut down. In the heat of battle, with so much unnecessary loss, these measures seemed to Roosevelt, and many others, as the only way to ensure that Germany was no longer a threat. Hitler had used industry to rearm and revive his country, and that dependency was now the glowing red target that many wanted destroyed.

Not all the Allied countries were so gung ho about the Morgenthau Plan. Being so close (geographically) to Germany and thus more economically invested, and having seen what happened with the punitive measures taken after the First World War, many in Europe sensed that turning the country into a pastoral land would do more damage than good. Winston Churchill, the prime minister of the United Kingdom, was especially hard to convince. He was shocked upon hearing Roosevelt's call for "unconditional surrender" and he did not agree with the Morgenthau Plan: "England would be chained to a dead body," he said.

One thing the Second World War had proved, however, was that the United States was in a new position of power in the world. After the First World War, the United States had wobbled; this time, it would not. As Harry Truman, then a senator gaining his reputation with the Truman Committee's investigation into wartime business concerns, said: "History has bestowed on us a solemn responsibility. . . . We failed before to give a genuine peace—we dare not fail this time . . . We must not repeat the blunders of the past." And the blunders were not only ideological ones, they were also economic. By the end of the First World War, the Weimar government paid about $7 billion in reparations, but not a dime of it went to the United States. Instead, according to Edwin Hartrich, an American historian and journalist who was working in Germany during this time, "the German government floated one big bond issue after another in the U.S., to which the Americans subscribed approximately $7 billion of their own wealth," exactly the amount the Germans were paying to the other Allies, as it turned out. Needless to say, when the Depression hit, the Germans defaulted on all those bonds, in essence going bankrupt, unable to get any more monetary help from the United States, but also inadvertently causing Germany's $7 billion of reparation bills to be paid by American investors. Having learned that lesson the hard way, no one in the American government wanted to end up footing the entire bill for the Second World War as well.

Roosevelt and his staff got Churchill to at least nod in agreement to their terms, and the Morgenthau Plan, though never officially implemented, had the strongest influence on the occupying armies' stance toward Germany as the war came to an end. While there was bitter arguing among those in charge about how best to deal with Germany, the Joint Chiefs of Staff (JCS) Policy 1067 was passed, directing occupying forces to "take no steps looking toward the economic rehabilitation of Germany." It called for Germany's "excessive concentrations of economic power" to be broken apart. In this plan, automotive plants were referred to as "surplus," meaning they could be destroyed because they did not provide a basic need. Automotive production in Germany was to be scaled back so that it would be operating at just 10 percent of what it had been before the start of the war. At least, that was the American idea of the plan.

Germany surrendered unconditionally on May 7, 1945, and the Allies came together at the Potsdam Conference to determine the terms. In the end, it was decided that Germany would be divided equally among the Soviets, French, American, and British troops for an indefinite occupation. The United States took control of the southeast fourth of Germany and the British were given the northwest. The Soviets got the northeast, and the French the southwest. East Prussia, Pomerania, and Silesia were taken from Germany and broken up, to be annexed by Poland and the Soviet Union. This move would send refugees flooding into Germany, many moving through Wolfsburg on their way. Lower Saxony, the area that contains the city of Wolfsburg, became part of the British Zone. Under Control Council Act Number 52, in June of 1945 the Volkswagen factory came under official British control.

While the Americans had a very big economic voice and a very big stick, they did not have control of the areas of Germany with the highest concentration of industry and industrial supplies (the Ruhrgebiet was with the British, the Saar with the French, and the Silesian industrial basin had been given to the Soviets for occupation). All this made for a very interesting Allied tug-of-war; but one item all of the zones agreed on was the need to uncover any technological secrets Germany was housing, because they knew that all the money Hitler and the Nazi Party had put into industrial innovation had produced some strong results. In that spirit, the Allies harvested copious amounts of technology from German factories, offices, and think tanks, rooting it out from underground hiding places and questioning the country's scientific elite. As a result, the formulas and plans for innovations in electric condensers, jet propulsion, guided missiles, milk storage, and the production of colored dye (just to name a few) were sent back to all the Allied countries.

Together, the United States and Britain set up a special committee, the CIOS, to deal with this technological harvesting. Its specific aim was to find and use any information of an industrial or scientific nature to help the Allies win the ongoing war with Japan. CIOS was eventually split into two divisions: The British side took the name BIOS while the Americans continued using CIOS. Even after all fighting ceased, these organizations would continue collecting information that could advance civil industry. The technological secrets were written up as reports and sent to universities, research centers, libraries, and journals. Sometimes, the actual technical objects that were found were collected and displayed on traveling shows throughout Allied countries. Through its Office of Technical Services, the United States made all German technological secrets available in the public domain. According to a *Harper's Magazine* article from 1946, "a certain American aircraft company" used one such secret to save "at least a hundred thousand dollars." And another businessman at the OTS offices claimed that the information he found there was worth at least a half a million dollars in business for him.

In the American sector, it had been just this group, the CIOS, that had first sought out and questioned Ferdinand Porsche. Then, Porsche's recently orphaned Volkswagen project had been entrusted to British soldiers for foster care, and once it was in the British sector, one of the missions of BIOS was to evaluate its technology and create a report. The first British reports were positive; they thought the original car design showed promise, and they were also fairly impressed with the modern machinery in the factory. They even said that the VW might offer "with a few modifications, a possible solution of the cheap utility vehicle which would be acceptable to [Britain] and in overseas markets." When the British had a Volkswagen sent to Britain for tests by the Reparations Assessment Team, the people there did not agree with BIOS's first reports. The officials in Britain said the car was "uncomfortable," "noisy," and "backward," claiming British designers had nothing to learn from Germany when it came to automobiles. It sounds bad, but those negative reports might actually have helped the VW survive: Because of them, few believed the Volkswagen posed a threat to their own country's automotive business, and no one was in a rush to carry away its machines or harvest its secrets and close it down. Even so, the VW plant existed in a perpetual state of *perhaps,* a gray area where no one knew how long it would last. But the plant had an advantage as well: the British.

Had it fallen into any other Allied zone, it's hard to say the VW would have had the same support, though it's true the American soldiers did seem to see a bright future for the car, even in those very early days. The Soviets, had they gotten the plant, would probably have done what they did to the other industry in their area: take it all down and ship the parts to Russia to be reassembled, leaving a trail of machines and mess along the roads between. And though the French were certainly interested in the Volkswagen, they did not want it to continue as a German-based company.

But the plant was with the British, and they were less keen on turning Germany into a pastoral, deindustrialized country, and more concerned with figuring out a way for the Volkswagen to play a role in helping to revitalize Germany. Without the British, it is doubtful the world would have ever known the Bug.

(27)

Just weeks into his presidency, following the shock of Franklin D. Roosevelt's death from a cerebral hemorrhage, Harry Truman was confronted with the decision of whether or not to proceed with the Manhattan Project, dropping a new kind of weapon into worldwide consciousness; one of the most important and devastating single decisions in history. FDR, who had not lived long enought to see the Germans surrender (missing it by only a matter of weeks) had overseen the secret creation of the nuclear weapon. But it was President Truman who would have to decide whether or not to use that bomb. With George Marshall and the other Joint Chiefs of Staff, Truman weighed the matter heavily; ultimately, they chose to proceed, dropping atomic bombs on Hiroshima and Nagasaki, leading to Japan's surrender on August 5, 1945.

It was in this same violent and historic week that British REME (Royal Electric and Mechanical Engineers) soldier Ivan Hirst came to the former Town of the Strength through Joy Car. He came alone, though he was newly married. He was twenty-nine years old and he was tall; too tall, he'd often thought. He wore glasses: black perfect-circle frames. His wife had to stay in Britain because living conditions in the town were not adequate, so Hirst came prepared to give all his attention to the factory for now.

The day Hirst first laid eyes on the Volkswagen factory was warm and sunny. He would later say that Wolfsburg did indeed look like an abandoned construction site. There were 25,000 people living there, and many of them were displaced persons (often known as DP's, and including former forced laborers) or refugees. The streets were overgrown with weeds. Most of the German men were missing. Because there was little material for clothes, the girls wore red skirts that had been made from old Nazi flags. The giant brick factory seemed out of place in that

British officer Ivan Hirst, the first man to champion the Beetle and help bring it to life after the war.

landscape so full of holes but nevertheless a clear survivor of the war, almost majestic compared to the shacks and camps that made up the majority of the town. No matter though, Hirst was optimistic; surely this place could be set right again.

Ivan Hirst's optimism was characteristic of the British soldiers who came to occupy the plant. A high emphasis was placed on finding ways to cooperate with the foreign staff, and with dividing labor and decentralizing authority, though this would prove a difficult task. While the British were much less idealistic about democratization, they did feel it was their job to provide a new template, a new example and a new start for the German workers. In his first days at the factory, Hirst made a point of meeting and talking with the workers at the Volkswagen plant face-to-face, a practice he would continue throughout his time there, hoping to give the workers a sense of independence and a chance to make decisions for themselves. This was a hard balance to achieve, however, because some of the Germans and members of the strange, transitory town still felt a desire to be extreme and right-wing, sometimes "smearing the walls with swastikas and National Socialist slogans," a trend that would continue throughout the British rule, more than two years after the end of the war. In finding a balance between democratization and occupation—two things that are in many ways inherently at odds—the British often found themselves struggling. When the workers came to Hirst and wanted to start a workers' council, for example, he supported this initiative, but nevertheless kept them under strict watch, being sure he approved all of their agendas, and giving them only the opportunity to deal with internal social relations, not with any big decisions about the plant itself. In essence, the workers were allowed to form their own council, but the council was not allowed to influence any real decisions. This is what the British thought of as a policy of "constructive pragmatism"; they had one eye on democracy for Germany, but as occupiers, they readied themselves for the long haul.

Ivan Hirst was only one of many who had a hand in the day-to-day operations in Wolfsburg. At the head of the factory, there was a kindly walruslike colonel named Charles Radclyffe: In January 1946, he had become the head of the Mechanical Engineering Branch of the Industry Division in the headquarters of the British Zone, which made him the main authority in matters regarding the Volkswagen plant. Ivan Hirst was just below Radclyffe in the hierarchy, with the official title of senior residence officer, but he was the man who had the most direct contact with the factory itself.

Walking through Wolfsburg his first day, Hirst heard languages from all over Europe, a Babellian brew of Russian, French, Polish, Danish, Serbo-Croatian, South African, Mexican, Iranian, Cuban, Turkish, Australian, Swedish, Mexican, Hungarian, and English. There were also the numerous German dialects—so different that sometimes even Germans claimed to find other Germans impossible to understand. Everyone seemed shell-shocked, Hirst thought, as he handed out cigarettes to the workers; they appeared unable to do anything unless directly told. But Hirst, as he himself would later say, knew he'd need the help of just about every person there in order to set the plant right.

According to Hirst, some parts of the factory looked as though they'd not seen a human in years, and the worst thing about the place was the smell. All the plumbing and drainage systems had been damaged in the bombing and were in desperate need of repair. It was a mess, and there was little time to clean it up because the VW factory already had quotas to fill. Thanks to British labor officials like Leslie Barber (the British Labour representative responsible for the financial and proprietary matters of the Volkswagen plant for a time), the factory had been told to build 20,000 Volkswagens for the British military and basic German transportation needs. The cars produced at the time were still the jeeplike military model, because that was what the lines were set to make. But Hirst didn't like the idea of producing a military car in a time of peace. The British occupation was to be a civilian administration, he thought, not a further act of war. Hirst had discovered an old original VW on the factory premises, and he felt that it was the car that should be produced, Porsche's original design. Hirst liked it so much that he had one of these early models fixed up and painted green, and he sent it over to the British headquarters to see what they thought. The military government liked the car too; they told Hirst if that was what he wanted to build, he had their blessing.

But in practice, it was not so simple. Every decision about the car was entangled in hesitation and debate, with pressures coming not only from the British, but from the other Allies as well. Labor officials made it clear to Hirst that the car was only temporary; under no conditions was it to be mass-produced. On the other hand, some army representatives and British officials were making the argument that the VW case was special: If they took out this factory, they'd be taking out an entire town. The factory should be allowed to rebuild itself, they argued, and that would mean allowing it to sell and export cars. But British authorities in London reacted strongly, reiterating that the VW factory was being retained only in order to serve the basic needs of the city and to furnish what the occupying powers needed while they were there. Exports were out of the question.

Just simply getting permission to build the original People's Car was a victory, though. It meant all the wartime assembly lines would be taken down and the jigs and machines and tools would now be set up according to their original plans. Things remained ambiguous, however, as the Level of Industry Plan in March 1946 stipulated only 20,000 cars and 21,000 trucks for the total zone were to be produced. Many felt these vehicles should be produced not by VW but by the Ford plant in Cologne. VW's factory was listed as "surplus." And once again, it looked like the factory would not survive. For his part, however, Hirst decided to more or less ignore all this bureaucratic back-and-forth and just get busy making cars.

Sensing his dedication, the workers tried to do their best for him. The town itself was in terrible shape, though: Old labor camps were being used as housing, some of which were little more than breezy wooden shacks, with between two and four beds in each room. The old lodgings of the SS were also being used. And most of those still a part of VW management had homes in the only fully finished neighborhood in Wolfsburg, the Steimker Berg. For the majority of workers, accommodations felt temporary and inadequate. Many families had to separate in order to be housed. The idea in many workers' minds was not how to make a life there, but how to move on.

It didn't help that the factory work was grueling and that food was extremely scarce. In the spring of 1946, workers were on an allowance of 1,014 calories a day, less than half of what doctors determined an adequate provision for heavy laborers. Much of the workforce had to attend to things like rubble removal, filling craters that bombs had made, and restoring tooling and factory halls. In addition, there was no catalog or inventory of tools, so it was easy for things to be lost, taken, or simply overlooked.

Because of the lack of housing and food, workforce was in constant turnover. The town served as a kind of crossroads. Workers rarely gave notice before leaving: They would be there one day and the next day they'd disappear. By the end of 1946, more than half the employees who had been on register at the beginning of the year were gone.

In the midst of all this chaos, it was difficult to train workers or to be sure people with the right skills were performing the right jobs. The Works Council and the German executives and British officers at the plant did their best to sort out the multitude of problems that presented themselves, but it was rarely quick or neat. The British soldiers—while waiting for official policies between the Allies to be solved in terms of the factory—decided to allow the workers to produce 4,000 cars per month (for the military), but that number began to look comical with time. It was all the workers could do, in fact, to produce just over 1,000 of them in March 1946, one full year after Germany's surrender. Still, they were doing better than most companies in Germany. Being a publicly owned British undertaking, a *Regiebetrieb,* was an advantage for the factory: In a country experiencing a dearth of supplies, the VW factory's status as an Allied undertaking gave it first dibs in acquiring resources.

The British staff there also made some crucial decisions about VW service and sales, changes that would profoundly affect the following years. One of the first orders of business, for example, was to initiate a service department staffed with experts to train the other workers. The British also worked on setting up an organization of dealerships and distributors for the car—something the Nazis had wanted to avoid in their policy to "cut out the middleman." An old colleague, friend, and sometimes rival of Porsche's named Karl Feuereissen was at the VW factory during this time too, and he worked with the British to develop a philosophy for the company that would later evolve into "the Volkswagen way." Feuereissen's central tenet was that service must always come before sales. In other words, the entire factory must be geared toward the customer, not toward what would produce the most money in the short-term. Their goal was that any dealership that sold a Volkswagen should be equipped to service it too, or at least be in proximity to a station that could. A service school was set up to train the staff. Classes were taught in both English and German, and bilingual service bulletins were published as well. In these classes, workers discussed possible problems with the car and brainstormed ways to fix them. In such chaotic and unstable conditions, it's amazing that Feuereissen and the British were able to focus on the bigger picture in such a direct way.

Reading back over the notes and bulletins from these meetings, one finds the issues discussed were of a wide variety; there are pages on the development of "silent engine techniques" and those discussing "anti-boom compound" that could take away the original Volkswagen's classic air-cooled engine noise (it didn't work). Paint problems were also a big concern: There was no good place to store the cars after they were painted, and thick layers of dust that still swarmed through the plant would settle on the cars as they dried. To deal with such problems, an inspection department was initiated and put into full force. In 1947, more than 200 vehicles were singled out as "inadequate for the customer" and had to be resprayed.

Ivan Hirst was a real stickler about these types of concerns. He could often be found driving cars off the assembly line in order to check them as thoroughly as possible. Under Hirst's watch, the car's Solex carburetors were modified in such a way that a faultless idling and transition to acceleration was achieved. A host of other changes took place: A "noise monitoring apparatus" was set up to give readouts on the volume of noise emitted when the car shifted gears or accelerated. Deflectors and new felt-element air filters helped the engine not to overheat. A change in the amount of alloy used on the cylinders gave them longer life. The crankshaft production line was modified for greater efficiency. The loosening of the camshaft wheel was eliminated by improved riveting. Frequently occurring running noises from the crown wheel and bevel gear disappeared thanks to a new device that allowed more exact adjustment. The dimensional precision and surface quality of the gears, running parts, and bearings were improved so that the rattling of the front axle disappeared and the jar of the steering lessened considerably. When they'd first restarted making the car, its doors often wouldn't close properly, and the front hood would not stay shut. By 1947, the car design was much more durable thanks in large part to Hirst and his constant rallying cries for improvement. The workers called him "Major" and liked seeing him around. On his birthday—March 1, 1946—they gave him a birthday card that read: "For our energetic British officer Major Hirst, the rebuilder of the Volkswagen factory."

The other British officials there were also doing a lot for Wolfsburg as a city, not just the car and the factory. They set up a makeshift cinema inside the factory and showed whatever films they could find, sometimes as many as two a week. At Christmas, they threw a party for the workers and their children, and all the kids got tiny aluminum Beetles as gifts. Everyone was provided with an evening meal: mashed potatoes and goulash, with jelly for dessert. It was exceptionally generous at the time, as the scarcity of food was foremost on everyone's mind.

But relations were not always smooth between the British and the German staff. Denazification was a big concern for the Allies, and for many Germans as well, and not one Hirst wanted to deal with for very long: He felt he needed every man he could get at the time, so he didn't ask them about their pasts. Those senior to him, including many Germans, found his don't-ask policy too lax and took the matter into their own hands. In June 1946, authorities notified 179 people of their dismissal, including the main factory director, the technical manager, a divisional manager, and four department heads. A second wave of denazification later sent the total up to 226 dismissed workers.

Many of the main staff Hirst had been working with were gone in an instant. These stringent measures created a strong feeling of unrest around the plant; some claimed the "real

Nazis" had been allowed to stay, while those who were innocent had been forced out. It was a touchy subject, to be sure, and
the tension was felt on a daily basis. Sometimes when machines
broke down, for example, it was due not to technical difficulties
but to workers venting their frustration about certain decisions
that had been made.

The Nazi issue was a potent one in the city at large as well.
Because shelter, food, and clothing were in such short supply,
the desire for a portion of these resources played a part in people's attitudes. Campaigns were waged to remove former NSDAP
members from their homes, and from the town. Similar campaigns were waged against Displaced Persons and refugees, a
drastic push to clear the town so that there would be more
space. At the same time, the factory was still in desperate need
of every worker it could get. The more people they sent away,
the fewer people they had to work at the plant. But the more
people who came to work, the harder it was to feed them or
provide housing. Every day felt like an emergency situation,
and nearly every problem felt like an impossible one.

Even so, by the end of 1946, Hirst and the VW staff had managed to pull together a total of 10,000 People's Cars. It was only
a fraction of what had been originally planned, but it was a large
accomplishment for Wolfsburg, and a truly extraordinary feat
for the time. Two of the surviving photos from that day attest to
this contradictory situation. One photo shows the tall, regal,
smiling Ivan Hirst, flanked by the workers and their 10,000th
car. The second photo, one taken by workers without the eyes of
management, shows that same car; but beside it there is a handwritten sign, a "list of wants," including a hot meal, a beer, and
an existence of less unbearable stress. Another handwritten sign
on the car says "Ten thousand cars, and an empty stomach. How
can we endure?"

Such desperation might be hard for us to imagine now, but at
the time hunger was literally a matter of life and death in many
parts of Europe. Allied-enforced price controls, a continuation
from wartime, had made nourishment so hard to find that often

people did not come to work simply because they had to go out and forage for food. In *Mainsprings of the German Revival,* Henry Wallich, an economist at Yale University, writes that "hungry people traveled sometimes hundreds of miles at a snail's pace to where they hoped to find something to eat. They took their wares—personal effects, old clothes, sticks of furniture, whatever bombed-out remnants they had—and came back with grain or potatoes for a week or two." At the time, this was the natural condition for the majority of the population.

The black market often seemed the only market. In such an environment, cigarettes glowed like hundred-dollar bills. As Hermann Abs, chairman of the German Reconstruction Bank in 1947, said: "There was one genuine currency . . . American cigarettes. Even wage was expressed in cigarettes because that was something of value." By some estimates, half of all business going on in the U.S. and British zones in 1946 and 1947 was done through this kind of barter. With their signs in the photograph, the VW workers were asking the crucial question of the time: What good was industry if those laboring could not be properly fed? Still, the Volkswagen cars proved beneficial. Money itself was practically worthless, but one People's Car could be bartered for 150 tons of cement or 200,000 bricks. Lightbulbs, steel, shoes, clothing, food—all of these at one time or another were paid for in Volkswagens.

From all this, one thing became very clear: The German economy was broken and its industrial aims had hit a wall. The factory system—the mass amount of people needed, the assembly lines, the large consumer base—was not possible unless basic social and economic conditions were met first. Supplies were there—there was plenty of coal and steel in Germany, to be sure—but those supplies were kept under lock and key, and there was tremendous dissonance about how to move and manage them, or who should be allowed access to them at all. Just securing basic necessities took a lot of time and work. Every month, for example, Ivan Hirst had to take "iron tickets" and travel to headquarters to get the coal needed to run the factory and town. Wolfsburg had the advantage of having its own power station—the factory—but coal was necessary for it to run, and when the coal was held back, or the transportation of the coal broke down, things could get very grim very fast. For many who experienced it, for example, the winter of 1946–1947 would stand out forever as the harshest of their lives. This was one moment when the factory could not get adequate supplies. Europe was literally frozen; in some of the factory halls the temperature got as low as minus 7° Celsius (about 19° Fahrenheit). It wasn't possible to expect anyone to work. Machines broke down from the cold. Because the shipments of coal had not arrived, there was no heat. People cut down trees and made constant fires to stay warm.

In 1947, industry in Germany was a third of the size that it had been before the country went to war, and that number was descending. Food production was at 51 percent of what it had been in 1938, making malnutrition worse than it had ever been during the war. At the factory, it was not unusual to see men faint or curl up on the floor in exhaustion. One cold evening, Hirst heard an argument outside his door. A man was trying to steal another man's potatoes. The first man killed the second with his garden tools. The situation was so bad that stealing one vegetable could get you murdered. Living in such conditions, it's no wonder there was little enthusiasm for building cars. For the majority of Germans, buying a car was the last thing on their minds.

28

Heinrich Nordhoff had a front row seat for the last year of the war. The Opel truck factory he managed had suffered heavy bombings. Berlin, the city where Heinrich and Charlotte were raising their family, was no longer a safe place to live. In 1944, Charlotte and the girls left and found shelter at a friend's house in the Harz Mountains. Heinrich was alone in Brandenburg, working many more hours than he slept. As the bombs worsened, he rarely left the factory grounds, spending his nights in the damp air-raid shelters beneath the plant, nights that were long, full of unexpressed questions and concern for his colleagues, his family, and the future of his country. The lack of sleep and the intensity of stress weighed heavily on him, and eventually Nordhoff fell ill with pneumonia. In 1945, when it got to the point where he could barely stand up anymore, he was ordered to go to the mountains so he could be nursed back to health by Charlotte. As spring brought a whisper of warmth to the cool mountain air, Heinrich, Charlotte, and their two girls lived together in a single room, surrounded by the rolling hills and fir trees of the Harz. The area was still quiet, but there was no telling how much longer that would remain true. The Allied forces were on the move.

Even in the mountains, Heinrich had trouble sleeping. He felt guilty for leaving his colleagues. He had been in charge of hundreds of men, and now he was alone with his girls, removed from the noise and relatively safe. The moment he was almost fully recovered from his sickness, he told Charlotte that he wanted to go back to work. Charlotte thought the risk too great; the bombs were everywhere now, and much of Germany was already occupied by the various Allied troops. Falling into the hands of the Soviets meant sure death, if one judged by the stories being heard, and the Soviets could be in Berlin. She pleaded with him to stay. He said he'd sleep on it one more night, but he felt he had a responsibility to his men he couldn't avoid, even though he of course also felt a responsibility to his wife and his girls.

The next day was clear and crisp, and Charlotte and Heinrich decided to go for a walk along the ridge of the mountain and talk. As they left the house, Nordhoff grabbed a pair of bird-watching binoculars and hung them around his neck. Once they were out in the trees, they were startled by the sound of gunfire. They found their way to a place where they had a view into the valley, and Heinrich took out the binoculars to gaze below before passing them to Charlotte so she could look. American troops had arrived, and German soldiers were putting up a futile fight. Heinrich and Charlotte watched the battle in silence, conflicted emotions pounding away in their chests.

Some hours later, American jeeps pulled up to the little house where they were staying. Because of all his studies and trips to the States, Heinrich spoke very good English, and the soldiers found that a relief. The troops eventually moved into the house and set up a post in its living room area, and Heinrich and his family found themselves living alongside American soldiers for a time. One of Nordhoff's daughters had fallen ill by then—perhaps with the same pneumonia her father had recently recovered from—and an American soldier, who also happened to be the army doctor, took care of her, often sitting with her by her bed and telling her stories to raise her spirits and teaching her English too. Heinrich tried to stay out of the way, but the Americans liked him and invited him to come and sit with them and talk. They had a large map spread out on the table and they showed him what areas had been taken by the Allies. The Soviets were entering Berlin, he was told, and that meant nearby Brandenburg and the Opel factory were probably in their control. The question was settled: Nordhoff couldn't go back. In fact, as he'd later discover, he had left the plant only days before the Soviets arrived there. They had confiscated its machinery and started disassembling the plant. Nearly all of his coworkers were arrested and deported to Russia, most of them never to be seen again. Heinrich had barely escaped the same fate.

In the Harz Mountains, however, Heinrich still didn't know these details and he was concerned for his colleagues. He decided to travel to the main Opel plant, the one a good 200 miles outside of Berlin, in Rüsselsheim, an American-occupied area. He found a truck that could run on charcoal. He took his youngest daughter with him, while the eldest stayed back with Charlotte; Heinrich managed to return for them in a few weeks, and once they were in Rüsselsheim he was able to rent a hotel room where they could all live.

For months after the end of the war, Nordhoff would put on his suit, comb his hair down, and go to the main Opel offices. But he felt out of place. There was no real position for him there, and a lack of work left him depressed. It seemed people were only humoring him, letting him hang around because they knew his own job was gone. His future looked more uncertain every day. According to the American policies of the time, his former position as head of the truck factory meant he'd collaborated with the Nazi government, and under their rules of denazification, it looked as if Nordhoff would not be allowed to work in any position of management again. In the autumn of 1945, Nordhoff's employment eligibility at Opel was suspended indefinitely: The Americans needed time to deliberate his case. Nordhoff saw such measures as understandable, as necessary, and yet he held out hope: He'd never joined the NSDAP, all those who knew him knew he'd never liked or supported the Nazi Party. He imagined the Americans would eventually see this and allow him to continue his work with GM. It was an idealistic thought perhaps, but it kept him going.

After 1942, once General Motors had lost control of the Opel plant and declared it a tax loss, Alfred P. Sloan found (for the moment) he had no further desire to try to build an American presence in Germany; thus, once the war came to an end, he and the others at GM were very slow in resuming operations there. It was not until more than three years after the war, in November 1948, that GM made the decision to resume official control. In the interim, the Opel plant was in a strange state of flux, officially in the hands of the American military government, still unclaimed by its owners. Many former employees hoped that once GM took control, the job situation would be sorted out. But until then, their fate was in the hands of the American occupying government. Time passed at a grueling pace, and Nordhoff soon found himself in desperate need of work. And work did come, just not in the way he'd hoped. In the winter of 1946, an unexpected message arrived from Hamburg, a port city about three hours northwest of Berlin. An old friend of his, Herr Praesent, had died, and the message asked if Heinrich could come to Hamburg; the man's wife, Lisa, who was also a friend, needed someone to manage Dello & Co., the small Opel garage that her husband had left. Nordhoff took the job, packing a few bags, and moving to Hamburg.

Heinrich and his family had lost their home and possessions in the bombings of Berlin, and Berlin itself was little more than a pile of rubble now, but still, the city of Hamburg had suffered even more damage than any other city Nordhoff had seen yet. The Allies had considered Hamburg a "war center" of Nazi Germany and thus its industries and ports had been bombed extensively. The time Nordhoff spent there would be a straining time for his marriage, as Charlotte and the girls stayed in Rüsselsheim in the company of family and friends. And it would be straining on his confidence as well: By taking a garage management position, Heinrich found himself at the bottom of a ladder he'd spent most of his adult life trying to climb. It didn't look like he would ever be in charge of an automotive factory again, at least not in the American sector as he wished. Many of his friends and colleagues wrote to the Americans and testified on Nordhoff's behalf, but month after month passed and still Nordhoff did not receive any definitive word on his former job.

Heinrich's situation was only too common at the time. No one knew what kind of rules, or what kind of government, would eventually rise in Germany. Opinions and plans changed by the hour, as the complication of so many occupying forces in one area began to take its toll. For decades, the very countries now joined together in occupation of Germany had been arguing about what kinds of policies were best when it came to international trade, and now they found themselves packed together in one place, in a situation that required an even more intimate kind of exchange. The biggest problem they faced had existed long before the First World War: In an increasingly connected world, how could different countries put their products into an unrestricted international market, and buy products from foreign countries, without weakening themselves or feeling threatened? If America bought coal from England, did that mean the United States was the weaker country? If Russia traded with France, did that mean they were bowing to the capitalist principles they were so against?

Germany now became a heated microcosm of this question and conflict. In the agreements set out at the Potsdam Conference, the various zones were supposed to exchange Germany's resources among themselves. Each zone contained its own precious raw materials. Exchange was necessary to keep everyone supplied. It soon became clear, however, that the Soviets were not going to comply. They didn't keep their word or send the supplies as stipulated, and in retaliation, other zones stopped sending their supplies to the Soviets. And that was only the most flagrant of the disagreements; this kind of behavior meant Germany was desperate for just about every resource and raw material it had. It was part of the reason why the winter of 1946 and 1947 was so unforgettably painful and cold: The veins of the country were no longer operating; nothing could flow.

On May 26, 1946, the military governor General Clay sent a memo to the Pentagon trying to explain the German situation. The Allies, especially the French and the Russians, were not cooperating with American ideas, he wrote. Neither Russia nor France wanted to see a united Germany again, and this view directly opposed that of America and Britain. There was also a degree of desperation and a lack of resources in France and Britain that the Americans did not always understand, and this exacerbated the lack of cooperation. These disagreements, as Clay claims in his report, meant that communication had shut down among the four zones to the point that there was "almost no free exchange of commodities, persons and ideas." In Clay's view, the only hope for the situation was if there was some way for all the countries to unite their zones economically. Knowing that France and Russia would probably reject the idea, Clay went on to suggest that at the very least, Britain and the United States should join forces. Having *one* united zone would be better than having none.

The authorities in Washington were listening, and by the following July, at the Foreign Ministers Conference in Paris, Clay was able to convince Secretary of State Byrnes, as well as two important members of the Senate Foreign Relations Committee, Tom Connally and Arthur Vandenberg, that the British and the American zones must be fused: Economically, the more agricultural areas that were in American control would be joined with the industrial Ruhr areas of the British Zone. Alongside this change, there would be a change in America's position on Germany: They would begin trying to help rebuild German industry, rather than trying to control it and take it apart. Together, they agreed that Byrnes would make a public statement about this on his visit to Stuttgart a few months later. Byrnes would eventually title his speech the "Restatement of Policy on Germany."

This change in America's posture toward Germany happened just in the nick of time. Conditions in much of Europe were deplorable. Germany was bad, but people in both France and Britain were struggling to find food and shelter too, and all this was happening while Britain and France were meant to be using their own resources to maintain their occupied zones in Germany. As Secretary Clark Clifford, who was counsel to President Truman in 1947, later said: "Here was a situation that was not ever going to get better by itself. There was no way for the Western countries to pull themselves up by their bootstraps. There weren't any boots, there weren't any straps." Or, in the words of Ambassador Hervé Alphand, who was the French foreign minister at the time, "We needed everything. We needed raw materials. We needed food. We needed machinery. And we needed credits and foreign currency to pay for it."

Truman realized that in considering what was to be done for Europe, it was imperative that he listen to the advice of men who had seen the destruction firsthand: He was especially interested in talking with General George Marshall and General Lucius Clay, and both generals felt that it made little sense to keep German factories and workers from producing the items that the entire continent was desperate to get. In addition, by keeping Germany's factories from working, they were keeping Germany from making money, meaning it would only become more dependent on the Allies. If Germany would be able to pay the Allies back all this money spent in the occupation, they needed their industry. On top of all this, there was the new threat rising from the Soviets, which was beginning to look a lot like the threat that had just been faced with Hitler. Winston Churchill, in his letters to President Truman, had already started to speak of the "iron curtain."

In other words, as 1946 eased into 1947, Germany began to look less like the enemy and a lot more like a possible ally in a new war—the Cold War, as it was already being called. Having Germans think of Americans as "dictators of democracy" (a term Hartrich heard being used at the time) did not bode well for such a war, nor did it make sense to continue with a policy of turning Germany into a "farming state." Other influential Americans were coming to this conclusion too. When former U.S. president Herbert Hoover toured Germany in 1947 at the behest of Truman, he was horrified by what he saw: thousands of homeless children, millions of refugees, and a quickly deteriorating condition of life. There was no way to convert Germany to an agricultural state, Hoover said, "unless we exterminate or move twenty-five million people out of it."

The event announcing America's policy change toward Germany took place in Stuttgart on September 6, 1946, and it was one that would have made PR man Edward Bernays proud. It was held just miles away from where Porsche had once worked, and all of Stuttgart was swarming with press from the Allied countries. Members of the United States Senate were there, as was General Clay. In many places, the event would make the cover of the papers. In his speech, Secretary of State Byrnes said that America was dedicated to staying in Germany for as long as it might take to help them recover. But he also said that it was time for the German people to begin to experience their own sense of freedom again, and to find ways of creating their own systems of government and industry. Byrnes stated that by merging the British and the American zones—making their industrial, political, and economic policies into one—the Allies were taking one step further toward unifying Germany itself. In the end, Byrnes said: "The American people want to help the German people win their way back to an honorable place among the free and peace-loving nations of the world." His speech was translated live and broadcast across German radio. It became known as the *Rede der Hoffourg* (speech of Hope) because it was the first time the German public was given the chance to believe they would indeed be allowed to control their own destinies again.

Morally and emotionally, it was a stirring speech for many. But as usual, it was only one side of the coin. There were also those in Germany who said that if they were to be occupied, the occupation ought to be complete: In other words, it wasn't a matter of Germans becoming more responsible and developing their own self-government, but rather it was a matter of the Allies handling the full burden of getting Germany back on its feet again.

Nevertheless, this new attitude toward Germany addressed the dissonance that many Germans felt between the American philosophy of democracy—one that promoted freedom in politics and economics—and the actual policy decisions that had been made thus far (guided by the Morgenthau Plan). Hartrich writes that America's democratic ideology initially "did not coincide with what the German encountered in his daily existence under Allied military-government rule. He enjoyed no basic civil rights. His residence could be searched without a warrant. He could be arrested and held indefinitely without habeas corpus or a chance to confer with a lawyer. . . . Phones were tapped; mail was opened and subjected to arbitrary censorship. . . . There was an abstract, out-of-this-world quality about the democracy that the Americans pushed . . ." Nevertheless, it should be noted that after the horrors the Nazis had inflicted upon the world, it was equally understandable that the Americans were cautious and that it took time for their policies to shift toward giving control back to Germany.

The American policy changes were important for another reason as well; by 1947, Germany was becoming a stage for the battle between democracy and communism. And, in the reality of the postwar world, separating politics from economics was no longer possible, if it had ever been. Thus the battle was also one of *communism versus capitalism.* General Clay often said that "democracy will only be acceptable to the Germans when their economic and political affairs are in good order," arguing that "job security and decent living, buttressed by a stable economy must come first." And crucial to whatever new economic system would rise in Germany was the question of international exchange: What did Germany have to sell in the marketplace, and how open would it be to trade?

Even before the war's end, there had been plans like those heard in 1944 at Bretton Woods, which sought to open up industry through international trade. In 1944, the idea of more international monetary cooperation—of less international tariffs and more trade—felt fresh. At that time, high tariffs (adding a tax to the price of an imported good in order that it cannot be acquired more cheaply from a different country) had been long debated. With the increase of mass production, the world felt like it was getting smaller. High tariffs and fears over international trade were getting in the way of a healthy, open market. In fact, some believed that such restrictions played a large part in

British soldiers standing proudly beside their Volkswagens with the bomb-damaged Volkswagen factory behind them. Ivan Hirst stands second from the front.

starting both the First and the Second World Wars. Men like Cordell Hull, who had been Roosevelt's secretary of state during Bretton Woods, were confident that by *not* allowing free trade to occur naturally, countries were setting themselves up to fight. Trading with one another with less restriction, Hull reasoned, not only increased one country's desire for other countries to be free and democratic, it also provided a natural kind of competition that exhausted certain violent instincts. At Bretton Woods in 1944, the Allies thus agreed that after this war, they would further open up international trade and decrease tariffs. They also vowed to extend free trade to the Axis powers. In the heat of the Morgenthau Plan, some of those ideas and energies seemed to have dissipated or gotten lost, but by 1947, they were coming back again.

Germany was slowly beginning to look like proof of those Bretton Woods theories: When one European country suffered economically, the others suffered too. Getting Germany back on solid economic feet was necessary to everyone's recovery now. They needed Germany to contribute to the pool of money and resources again. Even those strident voices pushing for punish-

ment and extreme denazification shared the same overall intention as those who understood the deeper nuance of how difficult
it would be to punish Germans excessively without also punish-
ing themselves.

At the Volkswagen factory, these issues were paramount too:
the British were engaging in "constructive pragmatism," a policy that was passed down to them from the occupying British
military government itself. The British had studied the German
situation in depth, publishing a long article about it in their official military journal, the *British Zone Review*. That article
spoke of how the Germans would have to go through a long process of reeducation and that it would not come from an outside
force trying to impose their idea of democracy on them, especially at a time when the people had to work every hour of the
day just to find enough food to eat. If the Americans went too far
in their optimism about democratic ideology, then it could be
said that the British went too far in their pessimism, speaking of
how they expected a resistance movement to form in response
to the intense denazification, and writing in the *British Zone
Review* that:

> *Napoleon sought to impose democracy on Germany and the
> German people; but instead merely intensified their national-
> ism. In the days of the Weimar Republic democracy came
> again, after a lost war, as an imposed blessing, and was re-
> jected. Today, for the third time, the victor nations bring the
> opportunity of democracy to the German people, but synchro-
> nized with its arrival come hunger and distress.*

But then again, maybe it was not that the British went too far
in their pessimism or that the Americans went too far in their
idealistic quest to cleanse the country of Nazism. Perhaps these
two views were exactly right, but right only because they were
existing together in one space, and so had to butt up against
each another and fight it out. In some strange way, certainly not
obvious to anyone at the time, the Allies (and that even includes

the Soviets up until around 1947 or so) were engaged in a very democratic push and pull about democracy as they tried to find the best way to step ahead.

By the time American troops started returning from the Second World War, Bill Bernbach had become the father of two little boys, John Lincoln and Paul. He had also left Weintraub and become the chief copywriter of another ad agency called Grey. Perhaps it was something about fatherhood, or perhaps it was the war, the bombs, the rapid change of the past few years, or even the fact that Bill was in his late thirties now—but whatever the reason, Bill had found a new confidence and clarity. He was less of a follower and more of a leader now, and he wasn't afraid to speak his mind.

The war had been a wake-up call in more ways than one. Before it, anti-Semitism, racism, and discrimination toward women all had been accepted behavior in many parts of the United States; few had felt compelled to take a public stand against such inequality or bias. Hitler made people aware of the existence of such attitudes in their own backyards, and finally many were beginning to voice their concerns about them. But at the same time, many people—especially the older generation— felt that this kind of questioning, and the uncertainty it brought, was the last thing the country needed. They were exhausted from the Depression and the war. They didn't want to turn inward and ruminate, but they did want to feel peaceful: They wanted to feel free, but also safe. They wanted order, but also release. How were all these things supposed to fit together now? The country was richer than it had ever been, and it was also being forced to reevaluate its ideals. It was not easy to see how to deal with so much change.

What was obvious was that the war had damaged the psyche of the American people, especially those who had witnessed it firsthand. The effect was so profound that President Truman passed the National Mental Health Act, clearly recognizing that the country was experiencing a particularly high level of mental strain and psychological disorder. It was a consequence of increased self-awareness, and it was occurring not only on an individual level, but also on a national one. It was a search for balance. People were trying to understand their emotions, and yet remain reasonable, civilized, under control. Hitler's legacy was one of hysteria, of the masses getting carried away; thus falling prey to too much emotion was equated with a dangerous lack of self-control. In truth, however, the emotion Americans were feeling was more potent than ever, as would be evident in the paradoxical explosion of buying and selling that would soon commence: one that professed to bring satisfaction but could never quite deliver, one that praised reason but appealed to emotion instead.

Economically, Germany struggled after the war, but the United States experienced a lift. There seemed to be a lot more money to spend, but that came with a new kind of stress. If the 1920s had been a time of decadence and letting go, the 1950s would be a time of consuming excessively while pretending to be calm and in control. The country's media would reflect these developments as they occurred. By the late 1940s, public relations had become a full-fledged field, and its boundaries blurred with those of the advertising world. Experts were everywhere, people judging and measuring the public's wants and needs, trying to determine what would sell and how to sell it. What had started with Bernays and Gallup was now a thriving industry with branches in all directions. And one overwhelming conclusion at the time was that what people wanted was *more*. The 1950s would be one long push toward bigger. Big cars and big houses were considered visible markers of progress and success.

Working at Grey Advertising at the end of the 1940s, Bill's own world was getting bigger as he rose through the ranks, pitching and winning important accounts, channeling his restlessness into moving up the ladder, eventually becoming the vice president of the copy department. But Bill sensed that the spirit he'd once shared with Paul Rand was getting lost in all the constant desire for more, to look the same as everyone else, to fit in. Trying to impress, Bill thought, could too easily leave one feeling vacuous. It wasn't that big cars and houses were wrong, but did people really think these possessions were all they needed, the answer to their ills?

For the next few weeks, as he took the train back and forth from his home in Brooklyn to his office on 42nd Street, Bill wondered about the role of advertising in the world. He tried to put those feelings into words, and on May 15, 1947, he sent a memo to everyone in his office at Grey. He chose his statements carefully, and what he said was direct and from his heart. "Our agency is getting big," he wrote. "That's something to be happy about. But it's something to worry about, too . . ." There was danger in embracing "big" blindly, he said: "I'm worried that we're going to fall into the trap of bigness, that we're going to worship techniques instead of substance; that we're going to follow history instead of making it . . . There are a lot of great technicians in advertising . . . They know all the rules . . . They can give you fact after fact after fact. They are the scientists of advertising. But there's one little rub. Advertising is fundamentally about persuasion and persuasion happens to be not a science, but an art."

For 1947, these were radical words: Bill was trying to connect people to a sense of risk again, and he was trying to wake them from the very consumer slumber that seemed to be protecting them from their pain. In his short memo, Bill used the word "creative" three times. He spoke of "art" three times as well. "I don't want academicians. I don't want scientists," he wrote. "I don't want people who do the right things. I want people who do inspiring things. . . ." In other words, dreaming big was one thing, but actually being creative and inspiring—achieving big things—would also require a lot of hard work, focus, and mindfulness: It would require thinking small, and thinking strange.

Today such a note would be sent via email. In 1947, each copy was typed and hand-delivered. Imagining Bill that day, I can't help but think of those painful opening moments in the film *Jerry Maguire* where Tom Cruise's character Jerry is so inspired by his new ideas for bringing honesty and personal relationship into the sports agency where he works that he stays up all night to type and print his mission statement (titled *The Things We Think and Do Not Say*). He arrives early the next day and puts a copy in each person's mailbox, confident that he has had an epiphany, and that, upon reading his words, his colleagues will have the same feeling. Instead, Jerry finds it to be one of the most embarrassing moments of his life: No one seems to have a clue what he is talking about. Bill, like Jerry, discovered that thinking strange is rarely easy. The very reason it is "strange" is because, for a while (sometimes a very long while) there are few others who "get" what you're talking about or who are willing to jump in and do the hard work with you. Bill's memo would garner a similar reaction to Jerry's mission statement at first. But just as that moment in the film is actually the beginning of Jerry's rise, so too was Bill's memo, in many ways, the beginning of his.

Ferdinand Porsche was being courted by the French. Not long after he'd returned from his American trial in 1946, a French official named Lecomte, a man who was working on behalf of the French politician Marcel Paul, knocked on Porsche's door and invited him to come to an elegant spa town called

Baden-Baden, a place with hot springs in the western foothills of the Black Forest that had been popular since the time of the Holy Roman Empire. The French authorities wanted to talk to Porsche about his People's Car, Lecomte told him.

At first, Porsche was skeptical and politely declined. Lecomte was persistent, however, and knocked on his door again a few weeks later, this time with a trusted German engineer in tow. While Ferry continued to doubt, Porsche couldn't help but feel excited; maybe the invitation is legitimate, Ferdinand told his son. His son-in-law Anton agreed: If the German engineer—a man Porsche had worked with in Stuttgart—believed the offer was legitimate, then maybe it was.

At that time, Porsche had no way of knowing what was happening at the VW plant he had worked so hard to build. He was not allowed to return to Germany, let alone the factory in Wolfsburg. The rumor was that the VW plant was being used as a proxy for British vehicles, but that it would soon be dismantled and closed. That meant, after all these years, Porsche would not see the production of his little car. Thus, it's understandable that he would want the French proposal to be a real one. And in some ways, it was. But Ferry wanted to be cautious; he decided he would go to Baden-Baden first and meet with the French. Once he was sure it was legitimate, his father could join him.

Ferry's initial trip was a good one, and he returned to his father in Zell am See in good spirits. It seemed to him that the French were sincere, and he felt confident enough about it to ensure his father the coast was clear. What Ferry couldn't have known, however, was that not everyone in France was necessarily on the same side in those chaotic, postwar days. Ferry met with one group, but there was a whole world of political maneuvering and jealousy raging between French carmakers, not to mention between politicians trying to gain a foothold after the war. The Porsches were stepping into the middle of a very ugly fight.

In high spirits, Ferry, Ferdinand, and Anton Piëch all piled into one of Porsche's cars and made their way to the beautiful spa town near the border of France. Wined and dined by the French, the men had a good time together and let themselves relax a bit. After Porsche talked with the French commission, and then privately with Ferry and Anton, he decided he would do as the French asked. Once again, he would embark on a project to build a Volkswagen. The next morning, details were sorted out over a breakfast of French pastries and champagne. It would take two days for communication to get to Paris and return. Relax and enjoy the spa for the weekend, the French officials told Porsche. Word will arrive soon.

To everyone's surprise, there was a knock at the door within days. Ferdinand opened it excitedly, only to find a group of French policemen standing outside. Without any word of explanation they arrested Porsche along with Ferry and Anton. Soon, they found themselves locked in a dreary cell that had been used by the Nazi SS up until the end of the war. Lecomte hadn't expected such a turn of events either. He kept repeating that there must be some mistake, and promised that he would alert the rest of Porsche's family. In a state of panic, Lecomte drove back to Austria to talk to Aloisia and Louise. He assured them that everything was fine and that this would all clear up very soon.

In some ways, however, things would never be clarified. Even today, it's hard to say exactly what happened in those convoluted months after the war. In France, it had become clear that the next step in automotive business was to motorize the masses and a mad rush began to get there first. Porsche's idea of a whole new type of automobile, one that was not just a miniaturized version of the elite old cars, but rather an original rhythmic whole, had gone from impossible to inevitable. Having worked on such a design and tested it endlessly for so many years, Porsche was clearly the man who had the technological answers that so many now desired. But that same expertise was also seen by some as a threat.

The French automotive world was chaotic. Having been occupied by Germany during the war, some of France's automotive men had cooperated with the Nazis, and some had not. Now that the Nazis were gone, it was a scramble to try to piece together stories and reputations. Just before Porsche's arrest, the French carmaker Louis Renault had also been arrested (by the French) for war crimes. According to one account, it was Renault who had supplied the Allies and it was Peugeot who had supplied the Nazis. According to another version, it was just the opposite. In any case, the already ailing Renault was taken from his villa and placed in a jail cell where he died (or was murdered, depending on which story you hear) within a month. Now Ferdinand Porsche was in a similar position: The French wanted his plans for the Volkswagen, or they wanted the threat of competition he posed to be contained.

Trying to distance himself from the Nazis, automotive executive Jean Peugeot had charged Ferdinand Porsche with war crimes. Upon his arrest, Ferdinand was accused of violating the 1907 Hague Convention that dealt with the treatment of prisoners of war. It was claimed that Porsche had abused the men at Peugeot's automotive plant after it had been seized by the Nazis and placed under Porsche's command. Porsche did have frequent contact with men at the Peugeot plant, including Jean Peugeot himself. Ferry would later claim that Peugeot willingly helped the Nazis and made a lot of money working for the Germans during the war. But Peugeot also visited The Town of the Strength through Joy Car once, at which time the Gestapo tried to arrest him, so it's not clear that Peugeot and the Nazis were on the best of terms. And yet, the reason Peugeot was *not* arrested was because Porsche intervened on his behalf and helped him get safely back to Paris! And it had been Porsche who had convinced German officials not to remove workers from the Peugeot plant in France and force them to work in Germany: *It's better if they can stay near their homes and families,* Porsche argued; *A man is more productive when he is near his home and his wife.*

The question of Porsche's participation with the forced labor is a difficult one, much like it was for Nordhoff at Opel and for Volkswagen as a company once it emerged from the war. It must be said that the Porsche family certainly knew that forced labor was being used at the Volkswagen plant, and Porsche's own Stuttgart workshop was likely employing forced laborers and prisoners of war as well, considering that in 1933, Porsche had employed 23 men, but by the middle of the war in 1943, he was responsible for a staff of 600. By all reports, the workers were modestly paid and well fed: Porsche felt they did their best work that way, and it was their work he was interested in. According to one account, when he happened to be at the Volkswagen factory as a large group of emaciated Russians arrived, he flew into a rage upon seeing their condition, took pictures of them, and went to the Wolf's Lair to show the photos to Hitler. *How can men do any work if they have to live like this?* Perhaps it was a clever way for Porsche to get the men some help, or perhaps he was simply focused on producing as much as he could: Either way Hitler acquiesced, and for a time Volkswagen laborers were fed by the factory's own farms, and, according to Ferry Porsche, food became decent enough for the Nazi officials to complain that workers were being "pampered," which was of course a terrible warping of the truth, but perhaps comparatively accurate.

In any case, Porsche *had* been complicit in the use of forced labor, to the extent that *every* executive of any factory in Germany had been complicit during the war. The amount of punishment this kind of complicity deserved is exactly the issue that the Allies were confronting as they occupied Germany and tried to proceed with denazification. To some extent, everyone in Germany, merely by being a part of that nation, was guilty. To an even greater extent, everyone who had worked in an industry during the war had worked for the Nazi Party, whether they had joined that party or not, because all such companies had been taken over by the government. It would have been nearly impossible to place all those people in jail; after all, wouldn't that include not only the executives, but each individual worker as well? And trying to pursue such an inherently ambiguous project, as the British were adamantly stating, could possibly lead to some further uprising, or to a very weak and incapacitated Europe at the least. It was a situation that was excruciating on both a psychological and an economic level. In any case, Porsche was held by the French on pretenses not of the condition of laborers in Germany, but of those in Nazi-occupied France, and he was being held without a trial. Once again, Porsche's dream of seeing his car produced seemed to have met its end.

Around this same time, Ghislaine, Porsche's British nephew, was put on trial in Britain for being a traitor, but was then acquitted and released. Upon making his way back to Germany, one of the first people he wanted to see was his uncle, but when Ghislaine arrived at the workshop in Gmünd, Karl Rabe had to tell him the unfortunate news. Upon hearing what had happened, Ghislaine rushed to Baden-Baden and found his uncle in jail, just as Rabe had said, so he stayed in the town and took to bringing Porsche home-cooked meals each day (a woman in town cooked them for him), having to bribe the guards to get into the jail with every visit, and then bribe them again to get back out. But some French authorities began pressuring Ghislaine too, threatening him and threatening his uncle's life. During one of his visits to the jail, Porsche told Ghislaine it was time to get another country involved: He should go to the British and tell them the whole story from beginning to end, and ask for their help.

Anton was still in the same jail as Porsche, but Ferry, as Porsche's son and heir, had been separated from them in hopes that the younger man would talk. Ferry was taken to a nearby spa in the Black Forest, where a different set of French officers tried to schmooze VW secrets from him. He was kept under constant surveillance, but because of his sweeter, softer ways, he was treated much better than his father. Even so, Ferry refused to give any information about the Volkswagen: "My thoughts are with my family," he reportedly said. "And a prisoner is not a colleague. There's no true collaboration when it involves a gun."

Back at the Porsche homestead, Rabe and Louise were running the workshop and trying to keep Aloisia healthy and calm. Louise was as tough as her father (maybe even tougher), with a piercing intellect and clarity that could be daunting to those she knew. Now, with both her father and her husband in jail, she held the home together, and she played a very big role assisting Rabe in the business affairs as well. Together, they were able to house, clothe, and feed hundreds of workers and keep the business profitable. In December 1946 there were 222 people working for Porsche in Gmünd. Only 53 of them were executives and engineers, which means many of them were likely former laborers who had come with them from Stuttgart and stayed.

On March 17, 1946, Ghislaine reappeared at the Porsche home in Zell am See, trailed closely by Lecomte, who had now grown desperate and no longer seemed to have the safety of Porsche foremost on his mind: He too wanted the plans to the Volkswagen. Late that night, Ghislaine, Louise, and Rabe sat together around the kitchen table and tried to come up with a plan. There was no way they were handing the VW plans over to the French, Rabe said. Louise agreed: Giving up the plans would do nothing to bring their family back home. They needed to try for the British again; after all, the Volkswagen factory was in their zone. They might see the plans for the car as their property. Ghislaine had already gone once to see the British officials, but nothing had come of it.

But now he left again, driving forty miles out of the Alps, Lecomte still in tow. And the British finally took interest in the situation, though it was not quite in the manner Ghislaine had hoped. While Lecomte was eventually banished from Germany, Ghislaine himself was also arrested and handed over to intelligence officers, where he was questioned constantly for nearly a week and then placed in an internment camp. Once again, the British wondered at his excellent English, and they were also suspicious about what was really taking place between Porsche and the French. Karl Rabe, Aloisia, and Louise waited back in Austria, still with no word or idea of what was happening. Now four Porsche men were in prison and under examination, and all of it was over the plans for one little car.

Meanwhile, back in the Grey Advertising offices in New York, there had been little response to the memo Bill had sent, his version of *The Things We Think and Do Not Say.* Bill was realizing that there were simply a lot of people in the advertising business who were not ready for his ideas, and there was a reason that people think things they are afraid to say: Taking such a risk can be potentially alienating. After the memo he sent about "blazing new trails," there was no outpouring of agreement, no collective sigh of relief; if he'd thought his memo was going to change anything at Grey, he was wrong. Nevertheless, there were a few who understood what he wrote. They came to him quietly over the next few months, and they came up with a plan. If they couldn't change things at Grey, they probably wouldn't have much luck anywhere else: It was doubtful any big agency would have given Bill's memo a serious look. The more they talked about it, the more they realized that if they really wanted to change things, they'd have to strike out on their own.

One of the first people to express solidarity with Bill was the calm and cool Phyllis Robinson. She'd originally been in the fashion promotion section, but Bill had noticed her creative work and brought her into copywriting with him. Robinson was talented, young, and confident; she didn't have to search for ideas, they just came. She'd graduated from Barnard College in 1942 and began her career writing plays and musicals around Broadway. She had poise, a no-nonsense but elegant approach, evident in the colorful silk scarves she would wear to complement a simple gray dress, evident in the way she listened neutrally but completely and then gave an honest opinion of what she'd heard. Advertising felt simple to her. She was just good at it. Becoming part of the senior management at DDB seemed a natural step: The fact that she was a woman didn't matter at all. It might have been unusual at the time, but it didn't feel unusual to the unique team that was slowly forming.

Robert Gage was a warm exceptionally talented young man who also strongly identified with what Bill had written, and he too had found great inspiration in the work of Paul Rand. If Rand had introduced Bill to the idea of collaboration and given him the desire to write copy in a way that could aspire to be artistic, then it was Gage, in his white shirts and simple ties, his hair neatly parted and combed but still unable to resist a curl, often taking pensive drags of a cigarette, that made Bill's ideas come to life. It's likely that Bill knew Gage would agree with the memo before he even sent it: His respect for Gage, and the interaction the two had at Grey, was one of the things that had given Bill his confidence in the first place.

Phyllis could write. Gage had the artistic instinct. Bill had the guiding inspiration and energy. But they needed partners, and preferably ones who could understand and generate capital. They needed someone with a strong mind for the practical side, someone who understood the business from an accounting point of view. And they needed someone experienced in dealing with clients, someone older, wiser; someone with contacts, someone who knew the field.

Ned Doyle had already realized Bill Bernbach had potential. While his first impression of Bill was of "a nice little guy, very creative, with gold-rimmed glasses, a little on the scared side," working with him at Grey and watching him rise through the ranks, Doyle couldn't deny Bill's unusual outlook and growing confidence. Like Bill, Doyle's path to advertising hadn't been clear-cut. He was the vice president of business accounts at Grey, but before that he'd been a captain in the Marine Corps and fought in the Pacific Rim during the Second World War. He'd played quarterback for his high school football team, and had gone to Fordham and studied law while juggling a job selling magazine space. He passed the bar in 1931, but stayed with selling magazine space because, oddly enough, he could make much more money there. Women were always attracted to Doyle, and he was attracted right back. The guys around the industry might say he was a player, a joker, but there was no one else they'd rather hear a story from, and when it came down to it, they always knew his word was word they could trust. Doyle seemed to know just about everybody in town, and nearly everyone was happy to take his call. He was good company, and genuine too. He didn't like flattery, and he didn't say things just to please. He knew he went overboard with the drinking and the flirting at times, and he'd admit as much.

Bill looked up to Doyle in those years. Doyle was heroic, large in both physical stature and self-assurance. At Grey, Bill would often drop in and sit with Doyle in his office, learning from Doyle but also sharing his own ideas, using Doyle as a sounding board. And as Doyle listened, he began to realize that this "nice little guy" wasn't so timid after all, that he could really identify with this man. So when Bill approached him about the new agency, Doyle was more than ready to go in as a partner. They now had Doyle and Bernbach for the masthead, but there would also be one more name.

Ned Doyle had once worked with Maxwell Dane at *Look* magazine. Dane was a bit of a bore in some people's eyes—George Lois would describe him as "the agency bean counter"—but his sober business sense and disciplined ideas about work and money would prove essential to any success the agency might have. Dane knew something about media and mass communication: he'd been the retail promotion manager at the *New York Evening Post* and he'd help to arrange the first "top of the hour" news bulletins during the war. Not too long before Bill sent his memo, Dane had opened up his own advertising agency, a small office in an attic room off Madison Avenue. But while Dane had the business sense, he didn't seem to have the creativity or the drive to make his agency a success. Doyle knew Dane was looking for some help, and he called him up and talked with him about Bill. Soon, Dane was ready to go in as a partner too. He even offered the use of his office space—so long as they didn't mind that it was a floor and a half up from the last elevator stop! Bill was lucky to have found Doyle and Dane, and he knew it. In a later interview, he would admit one of his biggest advantages was "having with me partners who did what I didn't do well," going on to say DDB would've been "a bankrupt agency" if he'd been running it himself. But the success was yet to come; in 1947 they were still looking for their first account, and Bill had an idea. Maybe, just maybe, he could get Ohrbach to go with them.

Bill hadn't seen his father in years. His brothers and sisters had tried to bring the two back together again, but his mother simply refused to acknowledge her youngest son, and his father—so independent in all other areas of his life—found it too hard to go against his wife's wishes when it came to this. It was no doubt a crushing situation for them all. As a child, Bill had loved his mother immensely. She'd filled the house with music and books, memories he still carried with him. He'd been an exceptional piano student when he was young—his mother

The founders of DDB: Maxwell Dane, Bill Bernbach,
and Ned Doyle.

had never ceased to brag about him—and though he rarely played the piano anymore, he was always quick to quote Beethoven or Thelonius Monk. True to their estrangement, though, Bill never uttered a word about his parents or his personal past. It was one subject that would draw only a blank and icy stare, even from his own sons.

Nathan Ohrbach probably reminded Bill a little bit of his father. Ohrbach was a first-generation American, a Jewish businessman whose presence filled a room both literally and figuratively. He was a self-made success story, the owner of a flourishing clothing store in New York that he'd opened in 1923 under his own name. He was used to getting what he wanted, and he'd learned how to play it hard and smart. But he was also, like so many in Bill's life, a man who was not afraid to take a well-thought-out chance. Especially on someone he liked.

Ohrbach was a client at Grey, and he'd already worked with Robert Gage and Bill. The Ohrbach's campaign had originally been in the hands of Bill and Paul Rand at Weintraub. Ohrbach liked the way Bill was ready and willing to listen and learn. But part of the reason he said he'd go with DDB was probably because he liked the idea of being their most important customer. For Bill, this was an essential account, the only way to pay the first month's rent, and Ohrbach knew it. So he went with them. As the years passed, Bill's relationship with him would come to mean as much as any other in his professional life. In fact, one piece of advice that sprang from Ohrbach's lips was to become the keystone to DDB's approach: At one meeting, as the men were discussing the "angle" from which to develop their next ad, Ohrbach quieted the room: *I've got a great gimmick,* he said. *Let's tell the truth.*

On paper, Bill knew starting his own advertising agency did not look like the best move, but he felt he had to trust his intuition. "Only true intuition, jumping from knowledge to an idea, is yours and yours alone," he'd later say. Bill had an idea, and he was ready to take responsibility for it. Come what may, he was ready to follow through. Perhaps he remembered something Rand had once told him, about there being no exception to the impulse of creation. Or maybe it was something he'd heard Einstein say about how the only real and valuable asset we have is our intuition. But then again, maybe Bill simply recalled that advice Grover Whalen had given him all those years ago when Bill and Evelyn had first fallen in love: *Follow your heart.* It hadn't been easy, but so far he had no regrets.

In 1947, the "democracy versus communism" question was beginning to burn. In a speech by Harry Truman, given around the same time Bill sent his memo out at Grey, the American president compared these two worldviews: "One way of life is based upon the will of the majority, and is distinguished by free institutions, representative government, free elections, guarantees of individual liberty, freedom of speech and religion, and freedom from political oppression. The second way of life is based upon the will of a minority forcibly imposed upon the majority. It relies upon terror and oppression, a controlled press and radio, fixed elections, and the suppression of personal freedoms." The debate raged around politics and economics, but both those things were inherently dependent on another aspect that went less noticed at the time: education. Not necessarily education in schools or universities—though that too—but rather education as *access to ideas* and *fostering the conditions whereby people can learn.* In practice, a very real difference in the Red Army–style Communism and the American-style democracy was the freedom of access to new information and new ideas, i.e., the freedom to be curious. Stalin's method of Communism wanted to squelch curiosity and ideas—seeing them as threats—while American-style democracy wanted to embrace them as assets. The American administration had the understanding that in the long run a country is only as strong as its ideas, and ideas only flourish with freedom. The administration might not always live up to that bar, but at least the bar had been set.

The automobile was very much tied to revolutions in thought. In fact, it had been a revolution in education that had allowed the first cars to be created: Karl Benz and Gottfried Daimler, the men who got the first patents for the modern automobile and who later created some of the world's first auto companies, were part of the "revolution of thought" in the mid-1800s. At that time, before there was a united Germany, people experienced a new way of approaching education and the first Open University was created. It was a school open to all classes and all people, not just the elite, and it was where Daimler got his technical education, the education that led him toward the innovations he brought to the motor car. Porsche also learned much from his small technical college, but even more from Ginzkey and from auto magazines, and from the bubbling environment of fin-de-siècle Vienna. Learning was the essential ingredient for innovation, and it required curiosity, the feeling that comes from being free to have questions and seek out answers. Learning could come from many places, but however it came, it always required access. And access—whether to books or radios, schools or debates—was something Stalin wanted to deny the majority of his people.

If learning requires being open to new perspectives, then perhaps being free is, at heart, a matter of learning how to think and learning to both question and respect what others have thought before you. Stalin did not want that kind of learning in his country. In his own oft-repeated words: "Education is a weapon whose effects depend on who holds it in his hands and at whom it is aimed." In another famous quote, he spoke of his people, saying: "We don't let them have guns. Why would we let them have ideas?" He knew very well that with learning comes questioning, and with questioning comes the threat that people will demand a change. Learning also meant people taking responsibility for their own lives, rather than letting their lives be dictated by an authority outside themselves. Access, openness, experimentation, reflective thought: These are the things that lead to sustained innovation, and it is perhaps why countries with healthy democracies flourish economically.

It was this access to learning—to curiosity and creativity—that the Americans were really offering the Germans when they changed their policy toward the country: They were asking Germans to come to the foreground and create a new society for themselves. It was a matter of national security now, President Truman said in July 1947, as the administration rescinded the punitive JCS 1067 and replaced it with JCS 1779. Under this new law, the United States took a nearly opposite approach to the one that had come before. For Europe to prosper, this policy created by Washington's Joint Chiefs stated it was necessary that a "stable and productive Germany" supplement the Continent's economy. Germany's industrial base would have to remain intact—oil, rubber, coal, steel—and these goods would have to flow freely again. Germans could once again create their own products, and they would be trusted to buy and sell those products in the free market.

Naturally, all of this had direct consequences on the Volkswagen plant. The factory was tied to the British pocketbook, thus when the British and American zones merged, the VW factory received a nice push. By the beginning of 1947, Ivan Hirst was able to assure workers that the factory would not be shut down. For years, those workers had lived with the constant anxiety that their jobs could end at any time, and naturally it affected their work. Now the Allies were telling the workers that it was time for them to become participants in their own country again. Slowly, the factory began to see itself through new eyes.

British officials who were representing the VW plant in London had continued pushing hard to get permission for exports during all these changes. Those requests had all been denied, but as the Soviet threat began to grow, the option was reconsidered. Now the VW factory looked like a potential way of bringing money in and easing the British expenses. In March 1947, the VW factory's quotas were raised: It would be allowed to produce more cars; it would be allowed to sell those cars to Germans; and it was decided that Wolfsburg would be allowed to export Volkswagens to the Netherlands, Belgium, and France. The first official export happened in August 1947 when a jolly man named Ben Pon took five Volkswagens home to the Netherlands. It was only five cars, and the whole process was a difficult one, but it was a monumental shift: Selling "Hitler's car" to countries Hitler had just tried to conquer seemed absurd, but it wasn't Hitler's car anymore. The tide was turning.

In May 1947, about a year and a half after the end of the war, the Bizone powers set up a quasi-German parliament and focused on putting recovery of the country, at least in their shared zone, back into German hands. At the end of 1946, in anticipation of the merger of their zones, they had set up the Joint Export-Import Agency as a means of trying to revive the flow of goods in and out of Germany. There were so many areas in such dire need of so many items that it became clear that getting those goods to the people, no matter what country they were from, should be the priority. This same organization was in charge of Volkswagen export and import, and thus with the new Bizone, the factory found itself with much more room for growth in both production and sales. In August 1947, an all-German administration was set up at Volkswagen to work with the new national German authorities. It was hoped that someday the Board of Control (still British and still in ultimate command at VW) would be turned over to Germans too. Figuring out who really had the most authority at the plant became a bit difficult; the British military government was still in control, but the German managers were supposed to have an independent influence, and this caused some tension.

One example of this tension was apparent in the relationship between Ivan Hirst and the man who was the acting German director of the plant, Hermann Münch. Hirst and Münch rarely saw eye to eye. Hirst was a technical man; Münch was not. In

Hirst's eyes, Münch was a good enough man, but he was a lawyer and someone who'd been chosen out of necessity, not skill.
He didn't know how to interact with the engineers, and he
didn't understand the industry. Münch was doing the best he
could, and in the records, one finds he was indeed a very important voice in those first two years after the war, but it was true
that he was not an engineer and that he did not have the industrial background needed to run a plant. Hirst was ready to
slowly hand over control, but he was not ready to leave the
plant in the hands of people he felt were unqualified. In truth,
few at the VW plant felt very confident that the current German
staff would be able to control things properly should the British
leave. Those suspicions seemed to have been confirmed around
the end of 1946 when Ivan Hirst had been briefly taken off the
VW project. Chaos quickly ensued and he was immediately
brought back again.

It was clear that if the still-shaky plant were to return to German hands, it would need someone at the helm who had experience running a large factory, who knew the ins and outs of
engineering, and who could deal gracefully with the large numbers of men and the problems that came with mass production.
As of yet, there was no defining rhythm to the work, no way to
mark the pace. The factory needed someone who could give the
men direction, confidence, a sense that it mattered if they
showed up each day—and that man needed to be German. Ivan
Hirst and Colonel Radclyffe began asking around the automotive circles: Did anyone know of such a man?

For the last time in his life, Heinrich Nordhoff prepared to move
to a new town. It was just after New Year's; 1947 had come to an
end. He'd spent an extended Christmas holiday with Charlotte

and their daughters—going to church, praying, celebrating, opening gifts—and now he was saying his goodbyes, not sure how long it would be until he saw them again. He left late Sunday, January 4, 1948. A friend drove him through the night so he'd arrive just in time to start his first day. Nordhoff had no furniture or luggage to speak of, just his clothes, a fold-up cot, and some books, all things that had been sent on ahead. The town he was arriving in was still incomplete: There was little available housing and no hotel. He would live in the Volkswagen factory for now. He'd set up his cot behind a cardboard wall.

When they arrived, the roads of Wolfsburg were so bad that his friend dropped him off across from the factory, on the opposing side of the canal. Heinrich walked the passenger bridge alone, stopping halfway across to have a long look. The factory looked about the same as it had at the end of the war. Only the most necessary repairs had been made. On his walk, Nordhoff also noticed that many of the signs around the factory were in English only; very few of the original German signs were left.

A road ends abruptly in Wolfsburg, late 1940s, around the time of Nardhoff's arrival.

Stepping inside the factory for the first time, tripping through the dust and debris, surely he must have seen those famous wide-eyed headlights watching him and wondered how in the world his life had come to this. If a car could have feelings, perhaps the VW would have felt a bit the same, looking at Nordhoff: The car had been through so much, and here was yet another man coming into the picture. What was next? Nordhoff's attitude toward the car could have been only one of business-like tolerance at first, but it wouldn't be long before that would change.

Over the holidays Nordhoff had thought about calling a meeting with all the workers once he'd arrived. Getting himself rather worked up about the Nazis, he prepared a speech that denounced all they'd done and talked about the importance of finding a new course. When he arrived at the factory, however, he began speaking with a man named Frank Novotny. Novotny had set up the first VW press office, and he told Heinrich that as much as everyone might agree with him, using such a tone might not set a good opening mood. The denazification process at the plant over the last two years had not been easy, and wounds were still raw. There were also refugees and foreign workers there, and they had their own painful reactions each time the word "Nazi" was uttered. Novotny's advice struck a chord with Heinrich, and he spent some nights sleeping alone in the factory, rethinking his words. He'd wanted to condemn their past, but perhaps the best way to move forward was to create a present moment that offered a new direction. How could he give the workers a new sense of communion? How could he motivate them, rouse them enough to move toward a common goal?

When he finally did give that speech, he simply talked from his heart. His tone was precise, studied and calm, but his words were a kind that had never been offered from a German manager to a warehouse full of laborers before. He called the men his "fellow workers" (Meine Arbeitskameraden) and told them the future of the factory depended on them as much as it did on him: We are all in this equally here, he said, and we have the chance to create something that could have a positive effect on our country and the greater Western world, but it's going to take not only our hands but also our hearts and our minds. The workers looked at each other nervously and wondered if maybe this man was a little confused. Did he absolutely know where he was?

And did he? Certainly Heinrich never expected to find himself sleeping in the Volkswagen plant. It had all happened in the blink of an eye. Just months ago, he'd been working in Hamburg, managing the garage, with no signs of change coming anytime soon. There'd been no news about his old job at Opel, but month after month he'd continued to hope for the best, exchanging multiple letters with former colleagues, men trying to persuade the Americans on his behalf. But nearly two years had passed since the war's end, and by then, many of Nordhoff's old friends from Opel were working in the British sector, and their advocacy on his behalf was heard not by the Americans, but by Colonel Radclyffe and Ivan Hirst.

Needless to say, Nordhoff's experience with the VW had not been love at first sight. He'd had trouble with Hitler over the project; he'd been one of the RDA members criticizing both the car and Porsche's design, and the one time he'd ridden in one, he'd found it a bit like riding inside a noisy egg. So when that first call came from the Volkswagen factory, Heinrich had hesitated: Not only was he still hoping the Americans would change their minds and let him work at GM, he also wondered if trying to rehabilitate the Volkswagen factory was not something of a lost cause. Still, he did miss working with a large group of people and being in a position of authority where he could learn and be challenged, where he could make use of his experience and skills. But the Volkswagen? It didn't sit well with him. And how would he possibly explain it to Charlotte and the girls? Moving again! And this time to a town that barely even has a working traffic light!

Thus Nordhoff told Colonel Radclyffe and Major Hirst that he'd have to say no for now; he was still waiting to hear what the Americans would say about Opel. They told him to think it over, that they'd try their offer again someday soon. In the days that followed, Nordhoff did wonder if he'd done the right thing. Especially when he opened his mailbox to find a letter from the American military government reiterating that no person who had been an industry manager in the time of the Nazis would be allowed into a position of management in the American Sector again. It was a standard letter, but it felt like an omen. He wondered if he should go to Wolfsburg and have a look. Contemplating, he called up an old colleague and asked if he might come by and talk some things over with him. He needed some advice. That friend would later recall how serious Heinrich had been, and how uncertain he was about taking the VW job. He also remembered that Heinrich had gone through the trouble of finding and purchasing a bag of coffee for him, something quite hard to come by at the time. Listening to his own thoughts and ideas pouring out as he talked to his friend, and listening to the man's return advice, Heinrich made his way back home that night with his mind made up. He would go to Wolfsburg and see how it felt, and he would trust his intuition. But one thing was certain—if they offered him the job, it would have to be all or nothing for him. When Radclyffe finally called Heinrich a second time, Nordhoff accepted his invitation and began preparing to travel to the factory to meet Ivan Hirst.

One thing about Nordhoff, he was easy on the eye. Something about him was so elegant and friendly. And his English was excellent, Ivan Hirst would later recount. At dinner with Hirst and his wife, Nordhoff made a strong impression. Hirst found him a relief. Heinrich was clean and well-kept, Hirst's wife told Ivan later that night, and he seemed to bring a new air to all the mess. Hirst was as charmed by Nordhoff as his wife had been. Here was a man with a deep sense of technical knowledge, something Hirst had sorely missed in Münch. Hirst and Nordhoff spent two days together. The original idea was that Nordhoff might make a good technical director, but after their meetings and conversations, Hirst had something else in mind.

According to the story Ivan Hirst told later, in their final meeting before Nordhoff was scheduled to leave, Hirst kept his head down and put on a serious face. "I'm sorry," he told Nordhoff, "but I'm afraid I won't be able to recommend you for the technical director job after all." Heinrich slumped a moment, but recovered quickly, reaching down to pick up his briefcase. "Hold on a minute now," Hirst said. "What I was going to say is that I'm going to recommend that our general director retire and that you be given that job instead." Heinrich met his eye and smiled. "It's not totally my decision in the end, though," Hirst explained. "You'll have to go and meet with Colonel Radclyffe first, and the rest of the British board."

Within a month, Heinrich had been to the main offices in Minden and met with the jovial Colonel Radclyffe and the other members of the Board of Control. Nordhoff and Radclyffe already knew each other from their phone conversations, but in person they felt a genuine warmth for each other and they got along well. A full background check was done on Heinrich—they had to be sure he had never joined the Nazi Party—but once he was cleared, they offered him a contract to become general director of the VW plant starting January 5, 1948. Nordhoff said yes, but only after a serious talk with Colonel Radclyffe: If he were to be put in charge, he'd need full authority, he said. That meant the British would have to recede from the daily managerial tasks. Radclyffe agreed. But, unaware of Nordhoff's stipulation, Ivan Hirst was in for a shock.

When Nordhoff arrived for his first day on the grounds, a subtle but noticeable change spread through the factory. He was friendly with Hirst, respectful, but over the Christmas holiday Heinrich had thought long and hard about what kind of mood needed to be set at the place. Bowing down to Hirst would not work. If he was going to be successful with the workers, with this factory, he was going to have to distance himself from everything that had come before, he thought, and that included the old German management and the British officers. Nordhoff would later say it was the hardest thing he'd ever had to do, but that it was necessary. It was his decision to make, and he'd been clear from the beginning with Radclyffe about his plans. He could have been clearer with Hirst, however, and with men like Hermann Münch. But Nordhoff knew how to be quiet and how to be aloof. In Hirst's words, while Nordhoff was never cruel to him, he didn't feel any "warmth of contact" coming his way. His relations with Nordhoff were "close but cold." To Hirst, Nordhoff distanced himself from almost everyone even as he spent every waking moment at the factory. He worked incessantly, he slept in the plant, reading and thinking alone in the giant space each night, waking and giving each day his all, and yet, he also seemed inaccessible. He made the decisions; he didn't discuss them.

Hirst had not expected the change to be so swift, and he found himself wondering where his place was now: As much as he wanted what was best for the factory, and even though he'd known that someday he'd be expected to leave, there was also a part of him that imagined he'd find a permanent place in this world, somehow. But now, suddenly, a new man had arrived— a man he'd handpicked—and Hirst no longer felt needed. He had to search for things to do. Though he was officially supposed to be looking after Nordhoff and making sure he was up to the job—other German executives had tried before Nordhoff to work at the factory and had failed—it was obvious very quickly that in this case, the relationship had irrevocably flipped. From the very beginning, it was Hirst who reported to Nordhoff's office. Heinrich also had all the English signs taken down and replaced with German ones again. The British did not try to stop him, and no one dared to complain.

34

For Professor Porsche, 1947 had not been a good year. The French officials had eventually transferred both him and Anton out of Germany and into another jail in France. Keeping the men deep in France, it was reasoned, would give them more incentive to help design the cars. However, in the Black Forest, the other French officials had decided they'd had enough of the entire situation, and they released Ferry and let him return to Austria. Finally, Ferry was able to inquire about his father, and he soon discovered that both Porsche and Anton had been hidden away somewhere near Paris.

Carmaker Louis Renault's villa had been confiscated upon his arrest, and its attic had become the new prison for Anton and Porsche. They were kept there for nearly a year while Ferry, Karl Rabe, and Louise did all they could to try to get them released. Though they were treated well enough in Renault's attic, they had little privacy; French engineers and officials came and went as they pleased, asking for Porsche's automotive ideas and his advice. Nothing very tangible came from it all, however, largely because Porsche was such a different man when away from the only two things that mattered to him—his family and his workshop. When he did not have a medium and an outlet for his passion, it broke his enthusiasm and his spirit. He suggested a few basic changes to the Renault 4CV, but had no real hand in any part of its essential design. He needed to be creative on his own terms; it had always been that way for him.

Seeing how futile their efforts were, the French finally grew weary of Porsche. In the spring of 1947, he and Anton were moved once again, this time to a damp and unheated dungeon in Dijon where they did not even have beds. Porsche, a man who thrived on working and collaborating, a man who was used to hot soups and pockets full of bread, a man who felt a deep and visceral tie to his environment and to the land and shelter he called home and was used to being cared for and attended to by a large family and a loving wife, was no longer able to cope. He wrote to Ferry that he was lonely and cold. His sentences grew shorter. He no longer issued any commands. In confinement, he was chilled and sick most of the time. One of the only visitors allowed to see him was a Benedictine priest who lived nearby. Perhaps Porsche talked to him about things he would never again tell a soul. He certainly had a lot of time to think. He was over seventy years old now, and it didn't look as though he'd ever see his own home again, much less the actual production of his car.

The other men who had once worked with Porsche at the Volkswagen plant were also in jail now, or worse, dead. Robert Ley, the man who had headed the German Labor Front, and the Strength through Joy project, had been arrested along with other major Nazis and was to be tried at Nuremberg. From jail, he wrote to Henry Ford II asking for a job. He also desperately proposed a "conciliation court" between the Nazis and the surviving Jews, but before any of those requests were answered he committed suicide, using a towel to hang himself in his cell.

Around the time of his birthday, in May 1945, Hitler's old automotive consultant Jakob Werlin was arrested and put into an interment camp by U.S. soldiers. He was an SS Oberführer by then, party number 3208977. He was considered a principal offender and would remain in prison until November 1949. When he was released, he went back to work in the automotive industry, setting up a small Mercedes-Benz dealership that he called Jakob Werlin & Sons.

Joeseph Goebbels, Hitler's minister of propaganda during the Reich, committed suicide with his wife in the Hitler bunker. Their six children were given morphine to make them sleep, then tablets of cyanide were crushed in their mouths by Hitler's doctor. The entire family died in the same room.

Albert Speer was arrested and placed in jail until the Nuremberg Trials in Bavaria. There it was decided that he had contributed to the inhumane conditions of the concentration camps and forced laborers; he was found guilty of war crimes, but he did not receive the death sentence as most other top Nazi officials did at the time. Instead, he was given twenty years in prison. Speer was one of the few who accepted responsibility for his actions during the court's proceedings, saying: "Who else is to be held responsible for the course of events, if not the closest associates around the chief of state?"

For many, there was a sense of closure that came from seeing men held accountable for the viciousness of their crimes. There was also something healing in the ability to put a face to the men who had been so intimately responsible for the war. In fact, it might have been these trials that allowed for the shift of mood that came to Germany in 1947, along with more magnanimous economic efforts like the Marshall Plan. The apocalypse had lingered for so long. After such darkness, when the light finally does begin to trickle back in, one sees paths that had not even seemed possible before.

Part Three

o o

Ooh . . .
Growing Up

All our progress is an unfolding . . .
Trust the instinct to the end, though you can render no reason.

—Ralph Waldo Emerson

In the Tate Modern in London, a museum that sits on the south bank of the River Thames, it's possible to walk in for free, ride up the escalator, and see a Paul Klee painting called *Walpurgis-nacht*. This painting is a wash of swirling blues, adept but play-ful, and after looking at it for a moment, the dancing eyes of spirits materialize, tucked between its thick strokes. Klee's title, *Walpurgisnacht* (Walpurgis Night), refers to a kind of "Day of the Dead" or Halloween-like holiday celebrated by some people in Germany. But Walpurgis Night is not a time for costumes and candy; rather it's a night that celebrates the coming spring, a time for communing with nature, a time when spirits and fairies and witches might haunt the night. Observed mainly in the mountain towns of Germany now, people gather together to build bonfires and dance. It's a potent night in German litera-ture, playing a role in Goethe's *Faust* as well as in *The Magic Mountain* by Thomas Mann.

Walpurgis Night is also the night before the 1st of May (May Day). May 1 has a long history, having been previously cele-brated in Wilhelmine Germany as "International Workers' Day"; but the holiday took a bloody turn in 1929 as workers' parties clashed and over thirty people were killed. Capitalizing on the split in workers' parties at the time, the NSDAP used the distur-bance to gain more support. Once the Nazis came to power, May 1 was transformed into an official national holiday, and was re-named "Day of Work" by Adolf Hitler. The Nazis made it into a mass event. Today, it is still called "Day of Work" in Germany, but it's hard to say what the event is really about anymore. In

Berlin, for example, there are usually riots that start on Walpurgis Night; in my experience, they have a young, anarchist feel, charged with energy, but vague in intent. One thing is certainly clear, though: While work was, and is, important in all countries, Germany has had an especially long history of meditating about it *as an idea*. A big part of this is well articulated by the close tie between Walpurgis Night and May Day; together, the two holidays are a matter of both spirit and body, and the line where they meet. Walpurgis Night is ethereal and easily romanticized, but May Day speaks to an inner, stolid self-reliance, a belief in the individual's right and responsibility to contribute to his or her community. This contribution was an essential and uncompromising part of the German idea of labor, and every party that has come to power in the country has understood as much, especially the NSDAP. As it so happens, the evening of the day Adolf Hitler killed himself was the start of Walpurgis Night (April 30, 1945), and the following day was May 1, the Day of Work. And three years after his suicide, Hitler's legacy had come to weigh heavily on Germany and its industries.

Heinrich Nordhoff was experiencing this for himself at Volkswagen. He'd been on the job for five months, was still sleeping in the factory, and the problems were as numerous as ever. Wolfsburg and the plant were plagued by a lack of housing, a lack of raw materials, a lack of men, and a lack of motivation and unity. Because of all this lack, sometimes cars that were started could not even be finished; rubber door seals might suddenly be unavailable, or there would be a shortage of side panels to install. At one point the entire upholstery line had to shut down because there were no springs for the front seats. Some months, the turnover rate was more than 90 percent. The town, and the work, offered little incentive for people to stay.

In part, this was because inflation had made money practically worthless, but there was also an imbalance in what Karl Marx called a "metabolism with nature," the symbiosis between a person's productivity and his or her inner experience of labor and work between the manual and the spiritual, body and mind.

Nordhoff knew all about the problems that could arise when such a balance was off. He'd first studied the possibility of such complications in his days with Schlesinger, then had followed them from afar by paying close attention to the news about the labor and union fights at the leading factories in America (especially GM, as he was technically one of its employees). Now, he found himself face-to-face with them in his own factory. Nordhoff knew the VW factory workers were missing this: They had no real connection to the factory, the country, or the job.

The very words "labor" and "work" had accumulated all kinds of connotations over the years, having been explicitly associated with the revolution, with Communism, and most recently with socialism and the Nazi regime. Work was still deeply important to Germans, but the relationship of that work to authority was tenuous. As Ivan Hirst had found upon his arrival, many workers were so used to being told what to do that taking initiative on their own did not come easily, and yet, there was also a lack of respect for authority, a lack of trust. The real difficulty faced at Volkswagen and elsewhere in the country was no longer how to mass-produce or whether mass production was necessary—the past ten years had made those things obvious—but rather how to do it *in Germany again.* How could German workers take pride in their craft? Feel a sense of loyalty without hurting anyone or being hurt? Would Germany ever again be able to think of itself as a positive contributor to Europe and the Western world? Because of Hitler, Germany was no longer respected or trusted by much of the Western community, and the situation was still volatile. Totalitarianism had been defeated in the war, but it was not necessarily dead. As the right-wing graffiti at the Volkswagen factory showed, that extremist tendency was still there, and it could rise again. The trick was figuring out how to ease into healthy forms of leadership instead. Tied up in that was the fact that government and industry needed to develop a responsible relationship; not only would they have to coexist, they would have to help one another to grow.

Heinrich thought about such things, and worried over them. With prominent German publications like *Die Zeit* insinuating that the Volkswagen factory was still under Hitler's dark cloud, with umbrellas still being used throughout the plant to shield workers and staff when it rained, with cars being made mainly for the occupying forces, and with new bids and the threat of possible takeovers in the air at every step, the potential for following through on the original idea of the Volkswagen and motorizing the population looked grim. Germany was a poor country now. And for those who did have money, the Volkswagen either conjured uncomfortable images of Nazi times, or else was written off as a product of "the Allies' plant." The British had saved the Volkswagen factory. But saving the factory and getting it to run smoothly as a German company were very different things.

On top of these concerns, Nordhoff also found the factory itself strikingly inefficient. When he arrived, he calculated that it was taking the workers at least 300 hours to build just *one* car. This inefficiency was due to a great lack of communication, both between the men on the line, between different areas of the company, and also because there was no standardization of the actual assembly procedure, with the machines laid out chaotically on the factory floor. Nordhoff had seen enough of Detroit to know that proper arrangement was necessary for maximum efficiency. He reshuffled the lines and machines, slowly putting the puzzle together again, restoring and augmenting Porsche's original floor plan. The station for the final assembly of the car's body, for example, was shifted so that it was in the same area as the paint shop (which was the car's next stop), and both these stations were placed in Hall 3. The press shop, where the outer chassis of the car was made, was placed in the preceding hall, Hall 2. He also divided tasks and streamlined assembly so that each worker had a very clear outline of what he was supposed to do and how to quality-check that specific task.

There was no Technical Development Department before Nordhoff decided that a much greater emphasis needed to be placed on improving and developing the inner workings of the car. This was the kind of necessary initiative that Ivan Hirst had found lacking in Hermann Münch, the man who led the plant before Heinrich arrived. Nordhoff was also constantly on the lookout for new kinds of machinery and made steps toward bringing in new equipment as soon as possible, so that the teams working to improve and innovate the car had all they might need. The war had actually destroyed many old procedures and obsolescent equipment, thus moving production forward was not always a matter of rebuilding so much as it was of finding new, fresh methods. The situation *required* creativity, and Nordhoff noticed this early on and took advantage of it, giving workers the feeling that they were starting something new together, and being clear about his desire to rearrange the plant in a way that would raise the quality of the product while simultaneously reducing costs.

But that wasn't the only reshuffling that was done. Nordhoff also reconfigured the budget; 1949 was the first year the factory was given a firm fiscal plan based on selling 40,000 vehicles. Each individual department within the larger company was aware of this plan and of the part it must play. This kind of clarity had a very big effect on the change in efficiency at the plant. Expenditures were now accounted for, as was every piece of machinery and every tool within the plant. The attention to such details paid off considerably: Manufacturing costs of the Volkswagen car had been 3,312 DM at the start of 1949 and by the end of that same year they were 3,072 DM—more than 200 DM under budget, an amount that quickly added up. And that was for cars sold within the country. Exported cars also came in below their budgeted cost, the new fiscal plans resulting in a decrease of 138 DM per car. The budget was also set up so that a quarter of all profits went back into the factory to be used for updates and repairs. Looking all day at destroyed walls and crumbling roofs was not good for the psyche: To work as a whole, the optics needed to be whole too.

All these changes carried over to the management staff as

well. Heinrich wasted no time in reconfiguring the power structure and delegating new people to new tasks, a rather unpopular
move, but one he felt had to be done. In the postwar chaos, positions had been filled in a feverish dash. Now it was time to reevaluate. If things were going to work on a long-term basis,
Nordhoff thought, there needed to be a structure based on skill.
While he would always need the previous managers and the
Works Council more than he liked to admit, as the months
passed Nordhoff weaned himself from them as much as possible, putting aside the temptation (or some might say, the responsibility) of trying to please former executives and office staff.
According to historians Mommsen and Grieger, a kind of "industrial feudalism" ensued as Nordhoff created a management
that revolved around himself.

In this new structure, much of the decision-making power
was located with him, the general manager. Beneath him, much
like the organization of General Motors that had been developed
by Sloan, there were the heads of the departments such as production, personnel, and technical development. While such
structure is common today, it revolutionized the Volkswagen
factory and introduced a very modern and new kind of organization into German industry, one pioneered in the country by
Opel under GM. But at the time of all this new structure, the
factory was still an occupied organization, and though they now
stepped far into the background, the British board remained at
the helm: Heinrich was ultimately accountable to them.

Nordhoff was a complicated mix of Germany and America; he'd
learned a great deal from both countries. From Germany, there
came a desire for quality work and austere order, but so too
there came a belief in authority that was not always neutral.
From America, there came the innovative ideals of taking care
of the customer and the worker, of service and attention to the
conditions of labor within a plant—ideas that Heinrich often

implemented more sincerely than their American originators once had. Nordhoff believed, for example, that Henry Ford's initial practice of respecting the workers and giving them a good quality of life—allowing them the opportunity to be customers of the products of their own labor—had been the secret behind Ford's success. But he could also see how such practices fall apart, the workers themselves becoming power-hungry and losing track of their own best interests and goals. Ford had revolutionized working conditions in large part to solve the problem of attrition, of the large turnover rate. This decision had been praised as an act of good will—and it *was* an act of good will—but because it was also an act with an eye to maximize profits, it wasn't long before the profits became the sole focus and the workers again had to fight to keep and improve their rights.

Nordhoff didn't want unions and strikes and violence. To avoid them he'd have to try to give his workers what they wanted and needed before they even knew they wanted or needed it, and he'd have to do it with more awareness: Reciprocal altruism worked, as Ford's early years had proven, but it would last only if it truly took care of both sides (management and workers) proportionately. Thus, Nordhoff not only made radical moves in terms of payment and benefits for the workers, he also saw to more personal reformations, like ensuring that his workers' homes were equipped with real beds (up until May 1949, many individual workers slept on wood-shaving-filled sacks).

Nordhoff also noticed the conflicted feelings his men had about being occupied, and thus about the British staff, and he was able to capitalize on those feelings: He was "one of them," a statement that could generate great feelings of loyalty in those days. Nordhoff understood the need many had for an authoritative figure—much as Ivan Hirst himself had noticed when he arrived—and Heinrich was in a position to use that feeling to inspire a new sense of cohesion between the staff and the management of the plant; in essence, between the workers and himself. It was exactly what the factory needed: a figure of authority who believed in American-style business ideas but nevertheless was grounded in a German idea of work. An American could not have done it. But nor could a German who was still looking to the models of his country's past for solutions for the future.

Still, some asked: If Nordhoff became the figurehead of the plant, what would be *his* checks and balances? Some felt his policy of "workers first" was coupled with an authoritarianism that kept most decisions solely in his hands. But Nordhoff saw it more as "tough love," and he rather controversially made efforts to reduce the sway of the unions and Works Council, as he felt that he knew what the workers needed and could more quickly give them what they wanted. He was, in effect, centralizing management. In a later article written in praise of the plant, *The Times* of London would refer to Nordhoff's style as "cradle to grave paternalism."

It was hard to argue with Heinrich at the time because he was exceeding all expectations, proving magnanimous with the workers and earning their trust. A wages commission was set up, and with the important contribution of the Works Council, the factory saw a 50 percent increase for the lower wage groups by the end of Nordhoff's first eighteen months. Heinrich also set up a system that gave workers a 4 percent share in the company's yearly profit. In the early days, he installed a new kitchen and bartered cars with local farmers in order to get enough food for the VW workers to at least have one good meal a day. He also began regular "family-style" meetings in the colossal warehouse-like halls of the factory, where all the workers would put down their tools for a period and meet to hear Nordhoff speak. In these speeches, he used "we" instead of "I" and phrases that had been used by past Communist organizations in Germany—"work comrades" or "workmates" or "workers community"—seemed to take on another meaning in his leading of the postwar democratically inclined plant. He wanted to use words people knew, but redefine them: In doing so, he was redefining one's concept

Nordhoff (right) and a Volkswagen factory worker inspect one of the cars.

of work. "I am firmly convinced that there is no more natural an alliance," he told the men, "than that between a factory management and its employees." It would sound like propaganda, except for the fact that he actually meant what he said.

At one of the first of these meetings, he spoke to the same group of men who were building *one* car every 300 hours and said his goal for them was *one hundred cars* in *one hour.* One hundred cars in an hour! In another session, he talked of the factory's potential to prosper—an idea that felt fantastical at the time—and promised that Volkswagen could become one of the best car companies in Europe. Upon hearing this, the workers groaned. And yet, they also couldn't help but smile. They liked what he was saying, even if it did sound far-fetched. By setting such a high bar, Nordhoff brought a new energy into the plant. And after half a year on the job, there was a noticeable difference there, even Ivan Hirst had to admit as much. The factory had a full working German management and board; it looked and moved like an industry again. More men were coming to work regularly. And they were discussing Nordhoff on the lines. Nordhoff would often walk through the plant, not something German managers did at the time, and interact with the workers. He spoke in an even tone, never raising his voice, but his authority was clear, and his words and manner were unpretentious. Nordhoff knew, and openly said, that he would rise or fall with this factory, and with his men. And those words were true. Nordhoff had stepped into a very unusual moment in history, and he was meeting it with unusual means. No one was sure yet just what they were moving toward. The British were slowly relinquishing authority it seemed, but what would happen from there? After all of Hitler's motivating speeches, inspiring unity and pride through a paternal stance was a method that could not help but remind people of the very recent past. Many wondered if Nordhoff was seeing the situation clearly, or if he was overstepping his bounds. His intentions seemed honest, but were they? Only time would tell.

36

The doors of DDB officially opened on June 1, 1949. It was a hot summer day in New York City. The air in the stairwell was thick, but the mood was light. "Nothing will come between us," Bill Bernbach said to his new partners, "Not even punctuation." And he meant it *literally*: The name they'd chosen was a name without a comma or a dash—Doyle Dane Bernbach, just like that. It was the first time the masthead of an advertising agency had been written in such a way; a small difference perhaps, but one already hinting at changes to come. Seeing that name appear in the directory of advertising agencies, Madison Avenue had to stop for a moment and scratch its head. Who were these guys? No commas between their names? Was that a gross mistake, or had they done it on purpose?

"There was a spirit of high adventure," Phyllis Robinson said of those early days at the agency. When Bernbach, Doyle, Dane, Gage, and Robinson moved into their first office together at 350 Madison Avenue, an 1,800-square-foot space a flight above the building's last elevator stop, Bill had just turned thirty-eight years old. He was the youngest of the partners, but he was clearly the agency's creative head. The unusual young men and women that DDB would soon hire would be coming there because of him, lining up outside his office, wanting his opinion on their ideas and projects. When Bill got excited about an ad, the whole room would seem to glow from his enthusiasm. It made his small, loyal team work hard for him, stay late, come in early; they probably would have slept there if they'd had the chance. "We did it to see Bill's eyes light up," Robert Gage once said.

Bill was perhaps the only one who did not stay late at work—he always caught the train back to Brooklyn in time to have dinner with Evelyn and the boys—but he was totally and completely *present* every moment he was in the office. His door was always open. He would listen to any idea, take anyone's call. His eyes were everywhere. He was aware of every campaign DDB did. His presence set the temperature and mood of any room. Some people hid from him when they weren't ready to take what he would surely dish out: the truth.

In fact, telling the truth was just about the only rule at DDB, and that one rule was challenging enough to keep them all occupied, every moment of the day. The partners had agreed that they would start their agency with a clean slate. They'd do work that inspired them. When creating their accounts, they would still use research, but they would weigh that research with their own intuition, remaining aware that just because something had worked once didn't mean it was the only option, or even the best option, for a new situation that might have since emerged. In other words: Just because something was right yesterday, that doesn't necessarily make it right for today (but it could!). They weren't in it just to get rich, to schmooze and booze high-profile accounts—they'd done all that. They were looking for a deeper nourishment now, a way to creatively have an effect on the world. They were still a business—tuned in to their customers and accounts—but a business like none Madison Avenue had seen before. Even they did not know exactly where they were heading, only that it felt like they were heading in the right direction.

Whatever direction it was, it wasn't fancy. The office space was clean and neat, but little time was delegated to decorating (they would later use their ads to decorate their walls). When clients visited, Bill didn't want them to choose DDB because of the fancy art or pricey whiskey or quality leather couches, but rather because of the agency's approach. Decoration would only distract people from the thing that mattered: the work. Some clients might take such minimalism as an affront, but no matter, those weren't the kind of clients DDB wanted. DDB was going to be about the people, the relationships, *the ads*; perhaps an obvious, but nevertheless unique, idea. According to Bill, the client is not *always* right. In his eyes, it was important for his team at DDB to trust their own ideas and work, and he wanted the clients to give them room to do that. Bill knew that the clients would always have a big say—clearly they knew their products best—but he wanted the attitude of the clients they took on to be one of respect, not of power plays and veiled threats.

For that reason, every person creating an ad within the walls of DDB knew they could count on Bill to get behind them if what they were doing was honest and coming from the heart. If Bernbach thought their work was good, he'd back them, even if it meant losing a client, and he wasn't afraid of taking risks. Feeling that vibe from the boss reduced the debilitating fear of upsetting the client that so many on Madison Avenue must have suffered from at that time; Bill's trust opened up a space for real creativity, gave people the freedom to try and fail. It wasn't about cultivating giant egos—though giant egos would remain a peril of the trade—it was about finding a way *to connect*. In short, with DDB, Bernbach wanted to flip the focus. Instead of asking what the client or the customer wanted, DDB asked: What do we have to give? Ads were meant for an audience, and it was the audience that needed to be at the center of the ads, not the client. By focusing on the audience, Bill thought, his firm would inevitably do well by the client too: if those looking at the ads were taken care of, that could only bode well for the subject of that ad.

Bill would walk through Manhattan, or sit on the train, or watch people reading their magazines, and he soon realized that most of them were hardly even glancing at the ads surrounding them. In fact, they were often trying to avoid them, as if ads were an intrusion into their day, a giant sign of how polished and lovely their lives *should* be. In the heat of a stressful work-day, those ads always seemed too far from the reality—giant homes and smiling faces and beautiful ladies draped across the newest models of cars; such images created a status anxiety that only added to the frustration of everyday life. They also seemed to be using the same faces and colors, the same landscapes, the same words, as if there was a perfect, protected world; if people just kept spending, maybe they would get to that happy place too. The ads were meant to inspire, but they turned into a burden instead. People felt guilty for not being as happy as they were told they should be in such a modern and technologically advanced age. People jealously looked at their neighbors and colleagues and imagined they were the only ones who hadn't managed to reach that ideal happy place. But that place didn't exist, Bill knew; it had never existed, and it never would. With DDB, Bill wanted to make ads that would pleasantly surprise, something that would catch the eye, relate to the customer and remind them that they were alive. *Just look at all this opportu-*

nity, all these walls and billboards and train station walls, Bill thought. *And what are we doing with it? What are we really giving people here?* To him, it felt like a terrible waste.

Theirs was an easy enterprise to mock: too idealistic, too dreamy, too hard to bring to life. And for DDB, there would be days when they would wonder if their goals were naïve. After all, the system that had been in place in advertising agencies before them seemed to be pervasive for a reason: It worked. Why go against the norm? Because creativity required it: "Rules are what the artist breaks," Bernbach said. "The memorable never emerged from a formula." And breaking the rules at DDB meant being disciplined and confident enough to find something worth standing behind, even though it might be an angle or idea that had never been tried. It would be a lot of work, especially considering they had no precedent, but because Bill had thought it through so fully, the emotion and inspiration he felt weren't running away with him, and he was ready for whatever might come. Now that he had his own agency, he could change things from the ground up. To do new work, they'd have to create a whole new structure as well. They'd have to think strange.

At the time, the ad agency standard was to departmentalize work as much as possible. The accounts department acquired and decided on the companies and campaigns. On another floor, the copywriter received his or her account name and the "angle" that was to be used, an angle usually derived from research purchased from polling companies and focus groups. The copywriters would come up with the copy, then send it to another floor where the art department would give it images. This system was highly comparable to the automobile assembly line, and the process had been honed to the point where the guy putting the doors on, so to speak, wouldn't even talk to the guy designing those doors, or the person who had crafted them—it was all unnecessary. And it all worked well enough. But it wasn't good enough for Bill.

DDB wouldn't have any such floors. Bill wanted the agency to be a place that nurtured interaction, relationships like the one he and Rand had started and that he and Gage were cultivating. That meant doing away with certain departmental walls and allowing for more communication. Bill realized that juices flow when there is trial and error and messiness and moments of transcendence, things that come from two people interacting in a room, so he put the copywriter and the art director together as a team. It was a simple move, but until Bill, it had never been done before, and the very idea of it—common as it might seem to us now—was considered strange (at best). As Robert Gage described it: "Two people who respect each other sit in the same room for a length of time and arrive at a state of free association, where the mention of one idea will lead to another idea, and then to another." In this way, every ad was about "the combination of the visual and the words coming together and forming a third bigger thing." If the writer and the artist interacted, then the copy and the image of the ad would ultimately interact on the page, creating a stronger finished piece. They would use research. They would have their own offices and desks. Reason would certainly have its place, but they wouldn't keep churning out different sizes and shapes of that same happy-world ad that was so common. "Logic and overanalysis can immobilize and sterilize an idea," Bill said. "It's like love—the more you analyze it, the faster it disappears."

Thus, Bill developed a philosophy of sorts, a philosophy that resulted in a totally new structure, much like Nordhoff's presence was changing the Volkswagen factory during those same years. And if industry was a matter of technical innovation and efficiency, then media (at least as DDB saw it) was a matter of translating that innovation into a language that the everyday customer could understand. Bill's philosophies were ultimately shifting the very founding dynamics of advertising, just as Nordhoff was attempting to redefine what it meant to be a German business. If it worked, it would be revolutionary. *If.*

$$\left(\textbf{37}\right)$$

At the beginning of 1947, Porsche was still in a lonely Dijon cell, and so was his son-in-law, Anton. They were still being held without trial, without any clear charges, and the rest of the Porsche family was still trying in earnest to get them released. In the months since Ferdinand and Anton had been transferred into their solitary, cold, medieval cells, Ferry and Louise and Rabe had continued their convoluted negotiations with the French. In the spring of 1947, a deal was finally struck: The French authorities would let the two men go, but only if they were paid 500,000 francs for each man.

This felt like an impossible sum in 1947—such money simply could not be found in one lump sum, especially given the conversion rate. But it was the only option, and necessity tends to have its way. Amazingly, they managed to make the deal and scrape the funds together in July, thanks to the help they received from friends and colleagues living in France. A French Grand Prix driver named Raymond Sommer and a French automotive journalist named Charles Faroux helped to get messages to and from Ferdinand and his family. They also got food packages to Porsche and Anton and helped in the negotiations for their release. Once the French had agreed to let the men go on bail, other automotive men helped Ferry secure a large contract to make a car for Italian tycoon Piero Dusio. He commissioned Ferry and the Porsche team to design an all-wheel drive Formula One racing car, the Cisitalia 360 (and it turned out to be a very beautiful car indeed). The contract paid about $62,000 in today's terms, but at the time that was more than enough to cover the one million francs that constituted the bail. Even so, it was impossible for Ferry to get those funds transferred to France by himself, so the French Grand Prix driver Sommer served as the middleman and the Italians and French worked together to finally get the money delivered. It was less bail than ransom, really, as there had been no trial and Porsche and Anton had been held illegally the whole time. Even today, the details about this imprisonment are still murky, as the French files of those years have yet to be released. But such things didn't matter to the Porsche family: at that point, all they wanted was to get Ferdinand and Anton home again.

On August 1, 1947, well over two years after the end of the war, Porsche and Piëch were released. But Porsche emerged a broken man. All that exuberance and fierceness that had so characterized him before the war was lost, and it was clear that he would not resume his running of their company; those responsibilities would stay with Louise, Ferry, and Rabe, though for now Porsche would remain the company's figurehead. Now that they were all back together as one family, there were many things to be done. One such order of business was how to deal with the Volkswagen plant.

By early 1948, with Nordhoff managing the factory and with cars being produced and sold, it had become clear that a new agreement needed to be reached between Porsche and Volkswagen; it was his car they were selling after all, and it had come from the Porsche family firm. The old contracts that had been decided on between the Porsche family and the company in 1943 were completely outdated. Thanks to Louise, Ferry, and Rabe, the Porsche firm had done well in the years since the war. It now had over 300 employees, and many contracts abroad. Ferry had also been working on a new kind of car, and he needed to get things settled with Volkswagen before he could proceed in producing it. Upon being contacted by Ferry, Heinrich Nordhoff made immediate plans to go to Austria and speak with the Porsche family. They had to meet in Austria because Ferdinand Porsche was still not allowed to enter Germany. It would be 1949 before the Allies would allow him to return.

Ferry needed cash because the car he'd just designed was the remarkable Porsche 356, and he wanted to produce it, as the idea for the car had finally jelled in his mind while he was working on the Cisitalia project. The 356 Roadster (known as No. 1, and receiving its permit on June 8, 1948) had an aluminum body, was 35 hp, and could go about 85 mph. It was based on the Volkswagen platform, sharing its flat-four engine, gearbox, and suspension system, but the 356 was given a sportier shape and line. It was the first sports car in the way we think of sports cars today, not necessarily built only for the racetrack but for people to drive on the autobahns and streets. It was also the first car of what is today the very respected and elite Porsche brand. It was a landmark in Porsche history, and it is telling that the decision to proceed with production of the car came from Ferry, not from his father. Ferdinand Porsche had designed a car to be built in the factory in Wolfsburg under Nazi control. Now Ferry had taken that design, mixed it with other ideas his father had for making a race car, and turned it into one the Porsche company would produce on its own. When Ferry first showed the design and roadgoing chassis of the 356 to his father in February 1948, it's easy to imagine that he was nervous in the way only a son can be, a feeling mixed with excitement, but also frustration and fear.

Porsche looked at the car long and hard. The two men walked around it together quietly, both of their eyes alight. There wasn't a thing about it he would change, Ferdinand Porsche finally told his son: "If I'd created it myself, this is exactly how I would have wanted it." It's hard to imagine a greater compliment for a son, or one more fitting for that particular moment, a moment when the elder Porsche was clearly handing over the reins to his talented heir. In his father's absence, Ferry had shown that he could stand on his own.

Thus when Nordhoff, Ferry, and Ferdinand met at the edge of Austria near Berchtesgaden in the late summer of 1948 to discuss where things stood between Volkswagen and Porsche, it was Ferry (with the guiding help and advice of his sister, Louise) who was essentially in charge. And yet it was the pres-

Ferry with his sons and his "baby," the Porsche 356.

ence of the elder Porsche that set the mood of the meeting. Nordhoff, the man who had criticized Porsche's Volkswagen design many years ago, was now both humble and filled with words of praise. The little car was the center of both men's existence; Porsche had given it birth, the British had adopted it for a while, and now Nordhoff was steering it toward the new international commercial world that was beginning to emerge. It seemed the old was indeed giving way to the new, and while change is often subtle, this was a moment when the very near past and the present were in stark contrast, a break highlighted all the more by the fact that Nordhoff and the Porsches met near Berchtesgaden, a beautiful Alpine village where Adolf Hitler (just years before) had occupied his famed mountain home.

That meeting in the Alps was only a preliminary one, arranged more of out of respect for Porsche than of out of a sense of business. A few months later, Ferry would travel alone to Bad Reichenhall, a spa town in upper Bavaria, leaving his father at

*Ferdinand and Ferry look at sketches of the
Volkswagen Beetle in Stuttgart. By the time this picture
was taken (1950), the VW was almost entirely in
the hands of Nordhoff and was slowly beginning to
motorize the German population.*

home, and meet with Nordhoff and their respective lawyers to
sign the final plan. Ferry liked Nordhoff, and he would later
write in his autobiography that the meeting had been easy: The
two men immediately saw eye to eye. Indeed, Ferry and Heinrich were not strangers. They knew each other from the days of
the war, as they had both been part of the small and elite German automotive world. Both had seen the Nazi machine up
close, and both were keenly aware of the new conditions they
now found themselves in, and they wanted to make the best of
them.

In that sense, they both understood that the Volkswagen company and the Porsche company needed each other in order to be
strong, and they each respected what the other man was bring-

ing to the table. Together they decided that the Porsches would not build cars for any company that might be likely to come into competition with the Volkswagen, which was an essential point for Nordhoff. The Porsche patent for the Volkswagen—and the patents for its parts—could be used by the company in Wolfsburg free of charge. In turn, the Porsches would get royalties on every VW that Wolfsburg made and sold: In effect, VW would become Porsche's biggest client. The Porsche company, and any cars it made, were also entitled to use any of the Volkswagen service centers and chains. This would be a big incentive for the emerging Porsche firm in coming years as the Porsche 356, the car that Ferry created using his father's original Volkswagen design, was soon to be presented and sold. In an unshakable way, the original Volkswagen and the original Porsche would always be a bit like brother and sister, each eventually starting families of their own. (The 356 would soon lead to the Porsche 911, considered by many to be one of the most beautiful cars in the world, a car that, like the 356, was strongly modeled on Ferdinand Porsche's original VW design.) The sweet but sleek 356 was presented in its first auto show in Geneva in 1949. A new generation was emerging now, and in the tradition of innovation, the Porsches were again creating something the European world had never seen.

A year later, in 1950, Ferdinand Porsche and Ghislaine set off with Ferry's new model of the 356 for the Paris Auto Show. Porsche's family was worried about him taking such a long trip, but Ferdinand insisted that he be the one to go. For his part, Ghislaine was happy to have his uncle back, even if he now found himself having to care for the aging man in a whole new way. At that year's Paris Exhibition—the same one where Porsche and the American Max Hoffman would fortuitously meet, resulting in the Porsche sports car's United States debut—Ferdinand Porsche and Ghislaine showed Ferry's 356 with pride, though the decoration of the exhibit itself was sparse: just two cars and a banner overhead that read "1900 Porsche 1950."

As he and Ghislaine sat there together in the two folding chairs Ghislaine had brought along, perhaps Porsche recalled that day so long ago in 1900 when he'd been just starting out, a young man working for Jacob Lohner and showing his first car in this very same city, his future still uncertain but bright, his energy and ideas overflowing in all directions. Now he was an old man. The world had changed dramatically during his long life, and it was still changing. The rest of the twentieth century would see the realization of the ideas about mobility and speed that Ferdinand Porsche had been so determined to explore as a young man. The elder Porsche would not live to see the mass motorization of Europe in full, but the importance of his car, and his idea, had indeed proven itself: Porsche's intuition had been the right one. His passion for the automobile had started when he was a young man, in a time when very few people believed that the automobile would one day be the most ubiquitous and essential form of transportation. Porsche's passion for cars and movement had begun before the turn of the century, and now, as the 1950s were dawning, that passion was about to spread and reach millions.

The Porsche 356 at the 1950 Paris Auto Show.

Perhaps there was something comforting in seeing the automobile on the verge of taking off, especially after having watched its changes and evolutions, that process of growth that ran parallel to his own. Porsche was no longer as quick or as tough as he'd once been, but the importance of the automobile in his life had taken on a potent and tender tone. He had come to the end of his life, but in many ways the Porsche legacy was only just beginning: After all, only now was there a car being sold on the market bearing solely the Porsche name. He could not have known it at the time, but that name would soon grow into one of the most respected and admired automotive companies in the world: Today it's hard to find a person anywhere who has not heard of a Porsche. And it is even harder to find a person who has not heard of the Volkswagen Bug, a car that may not carry his name, but certainly carries his legacy.

Ferdinand Porsche in his Beetle.

$$\textbf{38}$$

Not all of Germany had supported Hitler hook, line, and sinker: Throughout the 1930s and 1940s, there were those who had indeed resisted and dared to speak out against him. And, perhaps surprisingly, one of the more vocal anti-Nazi groups was composed of a handful of Germany's key economists. A man named Walter Eucken, the son of a respected German philosopher and Nobel laureate, was the dean of the University of Freiburg during Hitler's reign. Eucken and most of his colleagues resisted the Nazis—some eventually having to flee because of it—and they came to be known as the "Freiburg School." Men like Franz Boehm, Erich Preiser, and Wilhelm Roepke were all part of this school, and they persisted, even in the midst of a Nazi regime and war, in designing what would eventually become the economic heart of West Germany. It was a system designed not on the teachings of any German thinker, but rather on those of the Scottish economist Adam Smith.

These German economists, all writing and publishing their papers as early as 1937, were aware of what Heinrich Nordhoff's professor Georg Schlesinger had been aware of—namely, that a change in labor division would change the economy. In their eyes, to accommodate such fluctuations, an economic system needed to be both responsible and flexible, ordered and yet not restrictive to the natural flow. Around the same time Hitler had been coming into his full power, the men in Freiburg were creating an economic system they called the *Soziale Marktwirtschaft,* or Social Market Economy. They wanted their "social market" to be a version of Smith's "free market"—things would be bought and sold internationally without tariffs and governmental control. However, they also realized that because humans are imperfect, part of the order meant a certain amount of government or societal action that could prevent unhealthy forms of monopoly and keep taxes fair and flexible as the market changed—

but the regulation *itself* would also have to be balanced and checked.

Needless to say, such ideas were in stark contrast to the Four Year Plan and economic policy of the Nazis, which encouraged excessive cartels and assumed command control. The Social Market Economy was more akin to economic developments that were happening in America around the same time, headed by men like Milton Friedman and the Chicago School. But still, it was not the same. It was a plan of economic liberalism, thus the emphasis was on freedom—but it was also an economy that was meant to be *observed,* contradicting the idea that economic freedom requires total deregulation.

One young German economist whose face would become synonymous with this new "capitalism with a conscience" theory was Ludwig Erhard. Erhard was a plump man with eyes spread far apart and an avuncular smile that could be mischievous and comforting all at once. He had been influenced by both the unregulated free market ideas of Adam Smith as well as by the more regulated ideas of J. M. Keynes. And while his economic stance was nuanced, his political one was not: he had *not* become a member of the Nazi Party, and his stance against them had been a public one. He had refused to join the Nazi Association of University Teachers, thus being denied a position at his university, and—so long as the Nazis were in power—kept from advancing in his field. Though he did find a long and lasting job at the Institute for Market Research in Nuremberg, his outspoken dislike of the Nazi Party meant he could not be offered a management position, even though his skills were above those he worked for. To get around these rules, he eventually began his own research company where he could consult with members of Eucken's group at the University of Freiburg. With their help, Erhard concluded that the Nazi system would fail, and even in the midst of the Second World War, he began preparing for a time when the Nazi government would be gone and Germany would need a new economic plan.

After the war, in large part because of his prominent anti-Nazi stance, the Allies trusted Erhard and made him a minister of finance in the southern U.S.-controlled area of Bavaria. This appointment would naturally propel him into a position of economic leadership in the new Germany. Once the Allied mood moved away from the Morgenthau Plan and toward a spirit of desired regeneration for Germany, men like Erhard were consulted as to how to strengthen the German economy; they stood out as possible leaders in the new *German-led* Germany that would inevitably have to emerge. There was also the simple fact that Erhard was one of the few economists who had a plan, who had been working on that plan for many years, and who had the zeal and confidence to promote and pursue that plan once the Third Reich crumbled. Thus in 1947, after America and Britain joined zones to create the Bizone, Erhard became their director of economic affairs.

Because his ideas still seemed so new and strange, at different times and in different ways, Erhard worried *everyone*—the Allies *and* his own countrymen were often at odds with him. But the young economist refused to conform, thus becoming a necessary part of Germany's recovery as he pushed and challenged both sides, something very few others could do at the time. Erhard, despite all that had happened in his country over the past ten years, had a great deal of faith in the German people. And from the very first day on the job, he was convinced that economic recovery would have to come from them: In his eyes, only by *freely and responsibly* buying and selling their own individual services and goods could they redeem both their confidence and their prosperity. Contradictorily perhaps, and a bit unconsciously, the American and British system that was in place was a system still fraught with Nazi economic policy. As occupiers, the British and the Americans had not wanted to disturb the country even more than it had already been disturbed, and thus they had left economic controls (controls originating with the Nazi plan for autarky and German self-sufficiency) as they were. Erhard wanted to demolish all those things, to break it all apart and start again. But laissez-faire didn't mean being passive so much as it meant actively getting out of the way: Regulation was needed in the sense that the old ingrained Nazi order had to be uprooted, and the market had to be freed. Erhard wanted government to guide but not direct.

Of all the changes that Erhard was bubbling to make, the most crucial parts of his plan were his belief in the need to eliminate price controls, and the need for a currency reform. In the postwar German economy, there was no longer any relation between objects and money; money had become meaningless and the objects were worth more: There was no medium for exchange. This was a condition that was easy to see, and while all agreed something had to be done, not everyone was sure that creating a new monetary unit was the best action to take. Erhard and his supporters wanted a whole new kind of money (deutschmarks) to be created to replace the now worthless reichsmark, but others felt it was essential to keep the reichsmark because healing the economy *was* a matter of healing the currency, of bringing it back to a state of health.

To many, including many Allied authorities, the details of Erhard's theory felt like "economic heresy," a recipe for total chaos. It was the same struggle that was happening at the VW plant: How much control was too much control? How little control was not enough? Some in Germany at the time, most notably the heads of the Social Democratic Party (SPD), argued that with Erhard's currency reform, all the "common people" would lose and big capitalist concerns would win. Erhard's detractors felt that the German economy was in a very precarious condition and that it needed to be taken care of and protected, that "it must grow in an incubator chamber" and not be required to carry too much weight. But after what he'd witnessed over the past decade of Nazi rule, Erhard was anything but naïve. He knew that any successful program would have to offer a delicate balance of order, freedom, and competition. Ideally, the economy that Erhard and the economists of the Freiburg School proposed would require companies and individuals to compete, but the very means of winning would require they also do right by their fellow men.

For a moment in the early months of 1948, all eyes focused on Prague's Czerin Palace when renowned Czech foreign minister Jan Masaryk was found dead in his pajamas in a courtyard just under his bathroom window. The scandal seemed to symbolize the growing problems of the Western world. Czechoslovakia had been free, but on February 28, 1948, it had been taken over by the Soviets. Masaryk's name was one on the Kremlin's list of men to be killed. Whether it was a Soviet plot or a suicide has never been resolved, but the event was evidence of the unrest that had once again mounted throughout the world. Stalin's coup d'état of Czechoslovakia demonstrated that he had no qualms about pursuing his own goals with defiance and aggression, in much the same way Hitler had. Democratic countries did not want an authoritarian antidemocratic regime spreading through Europe. Hitler was gone, but the danger he represented was still there. And, once again, Germany was the crux of the new battle: As London's *Economist* wrote at the time, ". . . the competition for the soul of Germany is now no longer avoidable—and it is the soul that must be won."

When the Soviets moved into Czechoslovakia, Britain, France, and the Benelux countries formed a defensive union. This was a dramatic move, for it brought France and Britain back into an alliance, and it marked a sizable shift in the French attitude toward Germany. France would join their zone with the American and British zones, effectively making it the Allies minus the Soviets. The French would also give up their plans of trying to separate and control the rich Ruhr area of Germany, and agree to help create the International Ruhr Authority to get the industrial veins of Germany fully flowing again.

In the Second World War, Russian soldiers had been a crucial reason for Allied victory. The Russian people suffered greatly—an estimated twenty-seven million of them died, more than any other nationality fighting at the time. The Allies were lucky to have the Soviets on their side in the war, but it was the Soviet people who had fought, not the Soviet government. And it was the Soviet government that the Allied governments were now beginning to see as a threat, one that became all the more daunting when combined with the condition that much of Europe was in at the time. It wasn't only Germany that was in need of help, after all. It was much of Europe. And for Europe to be strong, Germany needed to be able to function without relying on Allied support. The recognition of this need, alongside the rise in Soviet aggression, became the catalyst that changed the Allied attitude toward Germany, and toward the rest of Europe as well.

In the States, the attitude change was quite literal: General George Marshall replaced Byrnes as the secretary of state under Truman on June 5, 1947, and just five months later, gave a speech at Harvard that summed up this new way of seeing the world, introducing what would later be known as the Marshall Plan. "The truth of the matter," Marshall said that day in his speech, "is that Europe's requirements . . . are so much greater than her present ability to pay that she must have substantial additional help or face economic, social, and political deterioration of a very grave character." Marshall's plan called for a large amount of funds (what would eventually be just over $13 billion, something like $70 billion by today's terms) to be given to Europe. According to those who supported the plan, giving Europe money would be the best thing for the U.S. economy, because much of the money would be used to purchase goods from the United States and would ultimately be pumped back into the United States, erasing debts owed and strengthening the market as a whole.

It was a hard case to make to the American public and to

Congress though, especially in a time where the only ones who truly understood the desperation in Europe were those who had seen it firsthand. Many people felt it was time for Europe, and especially Germany, to take care of itself. But Marshall had thought of that too: One big part of his overall approach was that *before* American funds could be given, Europe needed to show that it was ready to deal with those funds; it needed to come up with a new structure and plan for itself. Only once that plan was made would America release the promised funds.

In Europe, Marshall's speech had a catalyzing effect. Word of it buzzed through the decimated countries—just the very possibility of getting help was enough to inspire a great deal of activity and work and they certainly had the clarity, intelligence, and integrity to create a competent plan. Sixteen countries arranged to meet in Paris and discuss how to set up a new European system as Marshall had suggested. The Organization for European Economic Cooperation, and later the European Steel and Coal Community—two organizations often seen as the first official steps toward what is today the European Union—were set up to find the best ways to allocate the funds and services of the Marshall Plan.

Though the Marshall Plan would be extended to the Axis powers as well, the Soviets did not stretch out their hands, but rather, created their own plan for the Eastern Bloc, the Molotov Plan (what eventually became COMECON). In this way, the Soviets formed their own economic enclave in Eastern Europe, creating market ties between the communist countries and organizing trade through the USSR. In truth, many Americans eventually got behind the Marshall Plan not because they were thrilled to send more money to Europe, but because they were worried about the Soviet threat. The Communist Soviet state had become the new enemy of the West.

As all this change was happening in the larger context of Germany, at the Volkswagen plant, Heinrich was still dealing with the possibility of the company being bought by an outside source. Henry Ford II was his biggest customer; a Volkswagen/Ford deal had come close to happening in 1947, but had fallen through because the British occupying force had been ensnared in difficult problems with the right-wing tendencies at the plant, and Ford had felt there was too much confusion about the best way to enforce denazification. But once Nordhoff began managing the plant, the negotiations with Ford began anew. At first, Nordhoff thought that joining forces with Ford might be a way to ensure the plant had a solid future. Joining with Ford would give the factory access to more capital and make it easier for them to repair and modernize the plant. Nordhoff also knew that merging with an American-owned company would loosen the restrictions that were then placed on foreign trade.

Ford was equally interested at the start, but that interest turned sour. In one of the legendary miscalculations in automotive management, the otherwise very astute Ford employee Ernie Breech—upon reviewing Volkswagen's proposal—offered his advice to Henry Ford II: "What we're being offered here," he said, "isn't worth a damn." But the real cause behind Ford's final decline of taking control of Volkswagen was likely the factory's proximity to the nearby Soviet line. The Ford company would later admit that they had serious reservations about controlling a plant that was just miles away from what was fast becoming the Soviet Bloc.

Nineteen forty-eight was a year when Germany's future felt very fragile. Since the war, the Volkswagen plant, and the country, had been hovering between options, teetering on the edge of "maybe this" and "maybe that." And it was in October 1948, just as Nordhoff was preparing a new home so that Charlotte and the girls could finally join him in Wolfsburg, that Ford backed out of any possible deals. For Nordhoff, it was a crucial moment of change: He realized that the factory would have to prove itself, on its own, as a German brand. And though it was possibly the biggest challenge anyone could have imagined for such a company at the time, he could suddenly see that it was exactly the path that had to be taken. Perhaps in the back of his mind he was also thinking of the health and future of his country: If a factory that had been a Nazi creation could transform itself into an instrument of the free market and its democratic ideas, then Germany would be able to do so as well. Volkswagen was to be a German company, come what may, and Nordhoff would proceed with that idea at the center of any future plans. This responsibility became clear to Nordhoff just as it was becoming clear on a larger political and economic scale to the Allies and the German authorities; a new way of thinking had arrived, and men like Erhard and Nordhoff began to realize that confidence in Germany was the next step, the only way to move forward now.

Behind the scenes in Germany, Ludwig Erhard was working furiously to push through a currency reform, and his actions did not stop there. At the same time, he was pushing for a price decontrol ordinance. In essence, and to simplify a very complex matter, this ordinance would wipe away all the old and lingering rules about how products were priced on the market, meaning that the most basic needs in any German's life—vegetables, eggs, milk, as well as the industrial supplies required to produce supplies, clothing, and large-ticket items such as cars— would no longer be regulated or rationed, as they had been for the past ten years. Control of that sort would be placed in the hands of the market again.

On the surface, this plan seemed highly illogical: The German people were experiencing a scarcity of vegetables and eggs and parts for cars, and so on, so deregulating the price of such things seemed absurd. It was an uphill battle to get his reforms

passed, but Erhard could not be deterred. His incessant lobbying coupled with his clear and deeply reasoned arguments
eventually provided him with the crucial support of General
Clay and other Allied officials. But everywhere he went, Erhard
had to explain himself. Hartrich tells of Erhard's confrontation
with a U.S. Army colonel named Oberst around that same time:

Colonel Oberst: *How dare you relax our rationing system,
when there is a widespread food shortage?*

Erhard: *But, Herr Oberst. I have not relaxed rationing; I have
abolished it! From now on, the only rationing ticket the people will need will be the deutschmark. And they will work
hard to get these deutschmarks, just wait and see.*

Erhard also cut high tax rates dramatically so that both the
workers and their employers would have more money to spend;
however, his tax reform did *not* include cutting taxes on high
incomes or tax cuts for those who were already rich. Those
would remain, helping to fund the rest. It's indeed easy to imagine how this combination of cutting taxes, abolishing price controls, and wiping away an old currency in one fell swoop looked
like a wild and dangerous move. And it's understandable that so
many were afraid it would result in a free-for-all fight for the
limited available resources. But, Erhard asked, what if those resources were not limited; what if they only *looked* limited? Perhaps, Erhard reasoned, there *was* an abundance of goods.
Perhaps goods had just been hoarded, congested, off-limits,
forced out of the natural flow. This sounded like wishful thinking, and maybe it was, but a dramatic move had to be made so
that the country could feel as though it had *assets* again.

Erhard's hope (and belief) was that the measures he was taking would provide a production push to German industry while
at the same time force German businesses to deal with competition from the rest of Europe (reducing tariffs, Erhard hoped,

would spur on the fighting spirit of capitalism) and yet allow German businesses to keep the prices of their goods low and affordable. Erhard knew that all of Europe was in need of the products that German industries could produce. Once German manufacturers got their factories running again, the market for their goods (both home and abroad) could be better and more profitable than anything they'd experienced before the war.

In making all these changes, Erhard was not really gambling on markets or systems; he was gambling on the Germans themselves. It boiled down to the question of whether or not, in all his study during the Nazi years, Erhard had indeed come to understand human behavior. With the implementation of his reforms, he was betting that "men were primarily motivated by their never-sleeping appetite for material gain, coupled with their deep-seated instinct for self-survival; in short, by their quest for security and protection against want and helplessness in a troubled and feckless world." And he was betting that people could do this without resorting to hurting one another. His notion of "capitalism with a conscience" was a belief in the ingenuity of German businessmen and German consumers, a belief that if given proper incentives, as well as large doses of responsibility and competition, the industry of his country would find its own way without having to be directed by a detailed top-down plan.

As word spread that a new currency was soon to become standard in Germany, the Volkswagen factory was bombarded with requests from customers to have their ration cards exchanged for vehicles before the currency changed. It was impossible for the factory to produce so many cars all at once—and because this was happening in many other industries in Germany at that time, it also became increasingly harder to get suppliers to provide enough materials to fulfill Volkswagen's *own* ration cards. Everyone was trying to trade in their cards before they became obsolete. But even such doubt and panic did not deter Erhard. He pushed his currency reform through and hoped for the best.

• • •

The days directly after Erhard implemented his reforms did not look auspicious for large German businesses, or for some small, industrial towns. There was now 90 percent less existing cash than there had been before the reform. Wolfsburg, for one, suffered almost immediately after Erhard's wild move. The change of currency hit the town and factory hard. All the town's land had been seized as former property of the German Labor Front, so all liquid and fixed assets were more or less null, which meant they had very little capital before the reform, and they had much less after it. Volkswagen was the town's biggest taxpayer and it too was having severe liquidity problems directly after the currency conversion. In fact, the town had to apply to the Allies for a bridging grant to get it through. To some, it was as if their bank accounts had been halved, even as their bills became twice as large.

Needless to say, Nordhoff's first few months after the currency exchange were extremely tough. In terms of exports, for instance, the external demand was there, but it became impossible to keep up with that demand because of exchange rates and because bilateral national trade agreements had not yet experienced the same loosening as the German economy had: The factory was doing well and had orders in other countries to fill, but with the currency exchange rate at the time, it was calculated that VW would *lose* about 1,596 DM for every exported car! Such a loss seemed to point to the immediate termination of such export agreements, but in a very brave (and unreasonable, or so many thought) move, Nordhoff remained true to Volkswagen's word; he decided to take the loss and hold his breath.

Nordhoff's newfound confidence in the plant had a lot to do with his shift in attitude toward the strange small car sitting at the center of it all. Nordhoff was beginning to appreciate what he had; indeed, he was captivated by the machine now. In a speech to his workers, he would later gush over his own baby blue Volkswagen Beetle, saying: "I have to tell you, it's really fantastic. It doesn't *go (lauft);* it *flies (fliegt)* . . ." Perhaps in the past, he might have thought of driving a Mercedes, he goes on to say, but such things no longer crossed his mind: "This car is so sweet and wonderful," he said: How could he ever drive anything else? Even the reserved, practical Nordhoff hinted that he thought of the car as being alive, calling it "an amazing automobile with a special personality." Nordhoff had clearly come a long way from his early days at Opel, when he'd criticized Porsche's design. In fact, he would later admit that his most important decision at Volkswagen was really a simple one: the decision to stick with the original design of Porsche.

If the most crucial moments in our lives are often a surprise, then realizing that he had fallen for the Volkswagen was Nordhoff's surprise crucial moment. And the little car had found a good caretaker as well. It was Porsche's brainchild, adopted and then abandoned by the Nazis, liberated by the Americans, given new life and nurtured by the British, especially by Ivan Hirst. Now it had finally landed in the careful hands of Heinrich.

For its time, the Volkswagen was a highly unique car. After all those years of constant testing, the car's combination of a swing axle, central-tube framing, torsion bars, and opposed air-cooled engine at the rear were indeed a fortuitous combination, as was its beetle-like, streamlined shape and (especially) its affordable price. After the war, it seemed to suddenly dawn on Europe that it was time to make and own just such a car— one that was inexpensive but still reliable and able to perform in the way a luxury car could. That meant the VW was actually ahead of its time. Nordhoff understood this, and came to think of the car as a gift. That was the main reason he stuck to his export agreements: The future looked exciting, and possibly rewarding, if only he was patient enough to wait it out.

(41)

July 1948 ushered a late San Francisco–style summer into Germany, and the warm air was like a balm. People opened their windows wide, letting the light flood in and the gentle breezes blow through. For the past seven years, shops and storefronts around Germany had gradually emptied to the point where even the most basic of objects, like toothbrushes and soap, were nowhere to be seen. But in the summer of 1948, with the currency reform and the end of price controls, suddenly all those basic objects—and many other objects besides—reappeared. One store after another began restocking shelves, brand-new goods displayed in their newly cleaned windows, opening their doors to welcome customers again. A sense of abundance spread quickly like dominoes falling across the land. Saucepans, papers, ink, coffee mugs, shoes, picture frames, silverware, jam, grains, brushes, furniture, clothing, books, medicine—all of these much-longed-for goods were suddenly available again. Life quickened. The change felt mystical. There was a kind of holiday mood across the country. Even the cows and chickens seemed to be happier: in the week after the currency reform, there was a jump in the supply of both butter and eggs!

In some areas of Germany, the change seemed to happen literally in one day. The new deutschmark, alongside a number of other reforms, went into effect on June 20, 1948. On June 21, many felt like they were living in a new world. One German American economist working for the American military government at the time claimed Erhard's move had "transformed the German scene from one day to the next . . . goods reappeared in the stores, money resumed its normal function, the black and grey markets reverted to a minor role. . . . The sprit of the country changed overnight. The grey, hungry and dead-looking figures wandering about the streets in their everlasting search for food came to life. . . ."

Still, it would be inaccurate to paint Germany as a country full of only smiling faces and shiny eyes that summer of 1948. The sudden change sparked a backlash of ill feeling in some areas, as people were shocked at the abundance that suddenly appeared. Clearly, many of the goods had existed before the currency reform, but people had been hiding or hoarding them, feigning a lack of stock or overcharging for what they did sell. Some even lashed out at the store owners or farmers who suddenly had an abundance of wares for sale. One woman in Frankfurt, for example, brought a fresh basket of eggs to the market only to have the crowd turn on her. "Where were those eggs last week?" they asked. The woman went home wearing her eggs on her clothes; the people pelted her with them.

The currency reform also drew a bright red line through Germany. The Soviet Zone responded to Erhard's changes by withdrawing from the Allied Control Authority. What to that point had been figurative was in a sense made official: There were now two Germanys. But the currency reform was not a reason for that division; it was simply one of many visual representations of it.

One thing certainly became clear in that summer of 1948 in West Germany: Erhard's bet on human behavior had proven right. When price controls and ration cards were taken out of the picture, the mentality of hoarding and fear all but vanished. Erhard's critics had been wrong: Removing controls did not make people more greedy and animal-like, but rather relaxed economic tension and allowed for an economic mutuality to begin. People *wanted* to buy and sell. It wasn't that conditions had changed overnight, but the way those conditions were *perceived* certainly had. Seeing things in shop windows and on shelves gave people a sense that everything was finally okay again, that there was no need to panic and hide what they had. The mentality had changed, and so the reality changed as well. The economy grew at an astonishing rate. It was referred to as the *Wirtschaftswunder,* the Economic Miracle. And Ludwig Erhard would go down in history as its father and guiding star.

It wasn't only the currency reform and new economics that were effecting change in Europe—it was also the new spirit that was arriving at just that same time, ushered in by programs like the Marshall Plan. While it's true that Germany would see only $1.4 billion of the tens of billions of dollars that would stream out of the United States and into Europe over the next four years (meaning that, even at its peak, Marshall Plan aid was less than 5 percent of Germany's national income), the money wasn't the important thing—it was what that money stood for, and it was why it was being given. It was the step of trust, the chance to start again, all things much harder to equate with numbers. Vernon Walters, the U.S. ambassador in the State Department in 1947, later said that the genius of the Marshall Plan "was to instill psychologically the idea that there would be a future, which also created a greater European economic and, eventually, political unity," going on to say that "the dramatic change in the last half of 1948 and the first half of 1949 in Europe was unbelievable. People had confidence. They began to build because they thought there would be a future and that future would be free."

The feeling of renewal eventually spread to Wolfsburg too. While the city didn't have shop windows to fill, it did have a factory, and alongside Nordhoff's new philosophies and plans, the currency reform and the ending of ration cards eventually turned in the Volkswagen's favor. Absenteeism plummeted at the plant. Before the reform, in May 1948, it had been estimated that each worker missed at least 9.5 hours of work every week: This was because many still had to go out and hunt for food or barter on the black market for their basic needs and supplies. In October 1948, the number of missed hours was down to 4.2 per week and would only descend more rapidly from there. In May 1948, VW made 1,135 cars. In June, that number was up to 1,520 cars. In July, 1,806. And by the end of the year, they were making over 2,300 cars per month. The increase in productivity was helped by the fact that the workers were eating better than they had in years. Food was no longer the focus of each day. In the records in 1947, one sees as much as 15 percent of the staff bringing in doctors' notes from sickness, many citing malnutrition. In December 1948, only 3 percent of the staff brought in such a note. People were growing healthier, and work was beginning to mean something to them again; indeed, some were even starting to feel a sense of pride and enjoyment about it.

The Marshall Plan did not provide aid for the Volkswagen plant directly. Nordhoff got by entirely on his own during the first hard months after the reform, sometimes asking his car dealers for loans in order to have something to pay his men. But as it took effect, the Marshall Plan helped VW inadvertently because it assisted the suppliers of the parts, which meant they got more quality parts, and they got them on time now. The plant also benefited greatly from the new attitude the Marshall Plan helped to instill: In Europe and America, it was becoming possible to think of Germany in a way other than "the enemy" again. But the biggest direct help for the Volkswagen factory came from Erhard's removal of price controls, because a lack of price controls eventually made trade with other countries much easier, indeed favorable. Between June and December of 1948, industrial production in Germany increased by 50 percent. But no other car company had the type of growth that the Volkswagen plant had. No other car company was in a position to make so many cars with a moving assembly line, nor did any other company have a People's Car.

By autumn of 1948, a rapid rise in car sales and car production at VW had solved early tax and liquidity problems. It was now possible to produce cars at a gain, and because Nordhoff had stuck to his export agreements even when the situation looked dire, there were plenty of potential customers, and it was now possible to produce cars for them. Among the reforms that occurred through Erhard's new "social market economy," there had also been a specific tax incentive, a remission of any profits earned on export sales. Volkswagen was the only car company in a position to export cars to any substantial extent. Just as Erhard's risk paid off, so had Nordhoff's. By October

1948, the loans that VW had taken in the summer to keep it afloat could be paid back in full.

It's not surprising that the export side of Volkswagen would eventually become so strong. From the very beginning, there were ways in which Volkswagen was a European company as much it was a German one: It originated from, and depended upon, many different people from many different places, and without each player, the company would not have succeeded.

Take Ben Pon, for example, the man responsible for helping to start exports in the first place by bringing the Volkswagen to the Netherlands, and a man who was also one of the People's Car's biggest and earliest fans; Pon was of great service to both the British and Nordhoff. In fact, it was Pon who first proposed to Nordhoff that he build a transport vehicle, an idea that Nordhoff followed through on, introducing the Volkswagen Type 2 (the Bulli), known in the States as the VW Bus, in November 1949.

Ben Pon had driven his first Volkswagen in 1938, before the factory had even been built. As a young man, he'd read about the German government's plans to build the car and the factory, and he and his father (a man who owned a car dealership in Holland) had journeyed all the way to The Town of the Strength through Joy Car to have a look. At the time, Wolfsburg was essentially an empty field surrounded by small villages, but Pon and his father did find Professor Porsche there. In fact, it was Ben who had given Porsche the vibrant yellow tulip bulbs that Porsche would later plant around his cabin on the hill. Pon met with Porsche and Nazi officials in Berlin months later, persistent in his desire to be involved with the car, and had eventually been promised that he'd have dealership access to the car for his Dutch franchise—he'd be allowed to sell the Volkswagen there. Then, according to Pon, Ferdinand Porsche—clad in "brocaded felt slippers"—took him for a ride in a Beetle on the empty Berlin autobahn.

Even during the war, the Volkswagen was still on Pon's mind. And once Germany had been defeated and the Volkswagen had come under the control of the British, he contacted them too with the same hopes of bringing the car to the Netherlands. (He even brought fish from Holland to give as a gift for the workers, knowing they were in need of food.) He and VW made plans at the Hannover Trade Show on August 8,1947, to begin export to the Netherlands. It was Pon's interest and the agreement that was reached between his dealership and the British that led to an export committee being set up at the factory, one that was aided and accentuated by Feuereissen's plan later known as "the Volkswagen way" of "service before sales."

Pon also played a role in the development and improvement of the car in those years, pointing out many defects and areas where the car could be improved that the British had not seen. On the first export models, the Volkswagen archives attribute to him having found "nonfunctioning blinkers, a defective hood lock, a handle for the heater that was not attached, sluggish gear shifting, dented hubcaps, a bumper that was poorly chrome-plated, a stain on the backrest, and handlebars that were impre-cisely installed"—all things that were immediately fixed by the Volkswagen factory workers.

Pon was the first major export dealer for VW, a side of the business that basically had started from scratch. These early ex-port contracts were a matter of individual cars. Ben Pon had five Volkswagens delivered to him at the beginning of October 1947 (there was supposed to be a sixth, but it didn't make it through inspection); those five little cars that were shipped to Pon made a sensation in the press. They were praised as "the rebirth of the German automobile export business." But really, little came from that first export, at least for a while. By the end of 1947, only 56 cars in total had been exported to the Netherlands and no new export agreements had been made. The British had hoped to make a profit on exports, but so far the only dollars trickling in were through sales to the Allies and the foreign press. Still, while on the surface the numbers and the profits were extremely small, the potential of the export possibilities had been released—it had become a tangible idea in German minds again. Thus, when Nordhoff arrived at the beginning of the following year, he was able to use his own experience, skills, and will to develop that side of the business.

Before the partnership between Pon and the British, it had seemed impossible that anyone would ever want to buy a German car again; the Nazi shadow was still too dark. But the gates had been opened, and Nordhoff kept them open through 1948, all the while improving the car to a level of quality that had also been thought impossible just a few years before.

As far as Heinrich was concerned, the problem was *not* one of demand—in Nordhoff's first months at VW, he received requests for Bugs from Switzerland, Denmark, Belgium, Sweden, and Norway—it was one of logistics. From the very beginning he had made it clear to the British that he wanted to have control of the plant when it came to the big decisions, and in his mind, exports fit the category of big decisions. A large part of the problem, Heinrich thought, was all the red tape he had to go through with the Bizone organizations before any agreements about exports could be finalized. Finally, he asked Colonel Radclyffe to back his request to make such decisions completely factory-based. "I would like to request with all possible urgency to be entitled to handle export business," Nordhoff told the British board once Radclyffe agreed. And he eventually got his way, thus paving the way for the jump in sales that was soon to follow.

By December 1949, there were 529 factory workers and 68 office workers in Wolfsburg. A Volkswagen now cost 5,300 DM. It could be had about one week after being ordered, and the Volkswagen factory was considered the leader in the field of sales and service in West Germany. By the end of 1949, Nordhoff was able to show that the VW plant was out of debt. In fact, Volkswagen was beginning to help boost the West German economy: It was now the leading German exporter of automobiles. Export figures rose to 7,128 vehicles in 1949, a huge increase from the fewer than two hundred total that had left the country in 1947. (Though, while VW was miles ahead of other German car companies—Opel exported a total of 12 cars that year—it was still far behind others in Europe. The British, for example, exported 180,000 cars in 1949.) Internal sales in West Germany were even more extraordinary: 37,500 Volkswagens were sold in 1949 and there were now 59 German VW wholesalers, 213 repair shops under contract with VW, and 164 subsidiaries. The German population was, finally, on its way to being motorized.

The Beetle was coming to life, like a black-and-white photo suddenly washed with color. It now had the eyes and hands of an entire factory caring for it. And the car did not have a single extraneous inch. The engineers at the Volkswagen plant found that even the tiniest change in the sheet metal would affect every other part of the car. As sales increased, Nordhoff began to focus more acutely on the details of the car. He wanted to keep improving the mechanics, but without changing the design itself: He wanted it done *organically,* he said, as though on a cellular level, step by step. Nordhoff assembled a specialized team to comb through every detail of the car, led by a man he'd known from his days at Opel whom he named as VW's chief engineer.

Between 1948 and 1954, every single part of the People's Car was inspected and improved. The old gearbox was forgone for one with synchromesh shifting, meaning manual clutching was no longer needed for the second, third, and fourth gears, and the wheel diameter was reduced from 16 to 15 inches, the rim width increasing from 3 inches to 4. Because Volkswagen was one of the first companies to weld its cars, all the welding work was still being done by hand when Nordhoff arrived (he called it "tinsmithing" and an "alchemist's kitichen"). It was a time-consuming, labor-intensive process and one that Nordhoff eventually decided to change, opening an automatic welding shop in

1953, thus nearly doubling the gross number of cars that could be made per person per day.

Nordhoff was especially displeased with the brakes on the car, the ones Hitler had refused to have upgraded because the better version was British-made. According to Nordhoff, the Volkswagen's brake power was only at about 10 percent of the power an Opel Olympia got at this time. He'd soon switched to Teves hydraulic brakes, so the Beetle could match the GM cars in braking action. According to the Volkswagen company archives, other "really burning issues" for Nordhoff in those days were the exhaust valves and the rear axle; the valves kept falling off, and the axle wasn't tight enough. There was also the problem of "the juddering clutch" and clutch discs that were of poor quality, alongside the fact that the front axle and the suspension system caused road-handling, steering, and balance concerns, and the bumper seemed a little crooked, a little off. The heater also didn't work well (and as all original Volkswagen Beetle owners of future days can attest, that was one area that never quite got fixed).

In the midst of all this improvement, the car was also fitted with better tires and would eventually lose the tiny pretzel window of the rear, getting a bigger, modern window instead, a change that increased rear visibility by almost 25 percent. The dashboard was redesigned to be easier on the eye: The speedometer was relocated to where the driver could actually see it without any strain, and the engine was enlarged from 1,131 to 1,192 cubic centimeters. Peak power went up from 26 to 36 hp. Larger valves, redesigned cylinder heads, and a higher compression ratio were all introduced as ways of improving the car's drivability. Fender-mounted lamps replaced the semaphore turn-signal arms. The fuel tank was reshaped in a way that gave the car more trunk space. The team also tried to give the car a new horn, one more elegant and "up to date," less "sweet." Complaints poured in, however: *Don't mess with the horn!* There were certain things about the car, Nordhoff was learning, that its drivers were very attached to and did not want changed.

And that was especially true when it came to the overall look: Porsche's original design was kept in place even as nearly every inch of the inner car was improved. It was a healing process that, at least metaphorically, mirrored the one that VW workers and the German population were undergoing: changing the inside rather than the outside.

It was also a microcosm of what was happening in West Germany. The Trizone Allies had put great time and effort into working with Germans like Erhard to designate and form new German states, and then to set up a committee toward the creation of a new constitution to unite those states. From August 10 until August 23, 1948, meetings were held at a convention on a Bavarian lake to discuss what would constitute this new "Basic Law." Other than the technical details concerning how the new German states would be governed under the new national government, the law dealt with social and psychological concerns: One of its main principles, for example, was the rejection of any belief in a "master race." On May 23, the Allies gave their official approval of the document and it came into effect as law. West Germany was no longer a "legal nonentity," but rather its own self-governed country again, the Federal Republic of Germany. In response to West Germany's actions, the Soviets came up with a constitution for East Germany, officially establishing the German Democratic Republic (GDR). The two Germanys had now been legally recognized.

Consequences from this shift of power between Germany and the Allies rained down on the still ambiguously owned VW plant. Volkswagen's strange history meant that it was not a private enterprise like most other automobile firms of the time. And with business picking up, everyone wanted a piece of the VW pie; the question was, who should get to own it, now that the Nazis were gone? The labor unions that had been dissolved, and whose money had been taken by the Nazis' German Labor Front, claimed it was their funds that had built the plant in part. The men and women who had signed up for Robert Ley's Volkswagen Savings Book Plan claimed they should get a part, since they'd paid for cars that had never been delivered (interestingly, all that money was found untouched in the Nazi VW bank account in Berlin—it really had been intended for the production of cars—but it was confiscated by the Soviets when they took over the capital). At the same time, the German state of Lower Saxony tried to claim the plant because it was physically in their region. And Erhard, now West Germany's minister of economic affairs, thought it would be best if the VW factory went to the federal government, to be doled out for privatization once it had matured. But the VW plant was technically in the hands of the British, so it was the British alone who would have to make the call. They wavered and wobbled, so earnest in trying to be fair that they ended up being completely unclear. In what Ian Turner called a "master of equivocation," the British said the plant was "under the terms of ordinance of Lower Saxony" but "on behalf of and under the Federal Government." So . . . who owned it exactly? The state government or the national one? In any case, the plant was officially given back to Germany on October 13, 1949.

This was a disturbing change for British men like Colonel Radclyffe and Ivan Hirst, who had devoted themselves to the factory for the past three years. They found it very difficult when they were told it was time for them to leave. Nordhoff wrote a warm letter to Colonel Radclyffe. In his letter, Nordhoff thanked Radclyffe for laying the foundation that saved the plant, and for the energy and spirit he had shared with Germany. He wrote the letter in English, and signed it "I am, dear Colonel, sincerely yours." The elder Radclyffe died just months after returning to England. It's been said that the change broke his heart.

On the other hand, Ivan Hirst was still very young, but he suddenly felt directionless. Those early years of urgency and perpetual emergency were giving way to a more peaceful, ordered time. Before Nordhoff came, before all the new laws and reforms, Hirst had felt like he was sailing in a violent storm. Suddenly, the waters were calm, and he was at a loss. The British assigned him a new position in Hamburg, assisting with the zone's transition from British to German hands. The factory workers wanted to make a special VW for Hirst, as both a thank-you and goodbye, but he would not allow it. So they gave him a handmade miniature Beetle instead, a little model he would keep with him for the rest of his life.

Oddly, Nordhoff was quite cool in his farewell to Hirst (and would grow all the cooler in the following years, as Hirst tried to stay in touch with the VW plant). He'd written to Radclyffe in English, but with Hirst, Nordhoff wrote in German and the tone of the letter was formal and austere. Perhaps the reason is obvious, if ugly: Hirst had been a threat to Nordhoff's power, a young and able man whom the workers liked. He'd been a constant presence at the plant over the past year, while Radclyffe, operating in the executive offices many miles away, had not. Perhaps it was evidence that no matter how neutral Nordhoff tried to be, and no matter how good he had been to the workers, he certainly was not above insecurity and jealousy. After all, it was to Ivan Hirst that the factory owed much of the success it was now experiencing. But it was probably exactly that which Nordhoff found so hard to accept.

"**In Manhattan** last week, newspapers ran double-truck ads with the word 'Go' in fifteen-inch-high type," *Time* magazine reported in September 1954, printing an entire story to commemorate the day Ohrbach's department store left its "at-the-heels quarters" on 14th Street and slid twenty blocks north to join the big fish uptown. *Go*—that was all the ad said, and yet everyone knew what it meant even before they took time to read the small print. DDB's language was a language New York City was starting to understand.

Ohrbach's was prospering, competing with Macy's head-to-head. Its growing popularity was, at least in part, thanks to the ads coming from DDB: Its campaign had the whole city thinking Ohrbach's was the best-kept secret in town. The day Ohrbach's opened its new store, it made half a million dollars in profits. That was the same amount of money DDB had brought in for its entire first year! But DDB was growing in both profits and popularity. Though they were not in the same league as agencies like J. Walter Thompson, which could bill $130 million in a year, DDB was holding steady at just under half that amount, but it was alive and on the move.

Nathan Ohrbach was still their primary customer. And they were doing well by him. DDB's elegant and intelligent ads made shoppers feel they could "bargain-buy" with their heads held high, seeing through the façade of shopping at an overpriced store. "I found out about Joan," one such ad read, going on to relate how the high society Joan had been spotted coming out of Ohrbach's: Oh! So *that's* how she affords to look so good! Today the idea of bargain shopping is pretty standard, but back then it was the first time such an idea had been raised. DDB catered perfectly to the 1950s obsession with shopping, all the while cutting through the usual lies and somehow getting to the heart of the matter. Everyone wants to look like they are wearing the best clothes, but it didn't matter how much the clothes actually cost. DDB was not only calling out the game of *keeping up with the Joneses,* it was also (rather than asking them to give up the game) giving shoppers a way to do so intelligently. The ads generated an immediate sense of community, making customers feel like they were simply getting some good advice from a benevolent friend.

That same style and element of communality would carry over to other ads at DDB. Take Levy's Jewish Rye, for example, an early client of theirs that would mature into one of their most celebrated accounts. The Levy ads took the fact that it was a Jewish product—something that could have seemed limiting in terms of the "focus group"—and spoke clearly and directly about just that "limitation," transforming it into the product's greatest strength. Getting on the subway, commuters looked up and saw Asian or Native American faces munching happily on Levy's, and underneath the pictures were the words "You don't have to be Jewish to love Levy's." It just made sense, but it was also witty and fun and unpretentious—all qualities that people could instantly relate to. "Say something meaningful—and say it in a fresh, provocative way." That was how a later VP of copywriting summarized DDB's overall approach, an approach that applied as much to the art as it did to the copy. It applied to the style and the copywriting, but it was also a new and risky way of thinking about the art. In the Levy's ad, for example, there is a great deal of white space, and only one image (the person munching the bread) is present to catch the reader's eye, and the overall effect is certainly one of humor, but not in a sneering or unintelligent way: The ad invites empathy, it doesn't "make fun." It's neither cruel nor sentimental; it's real.

Such ads stood out like sore thumbs in the 1950s, and they caught the attention of many young writers and art directors in New York. DDB started getting résumés by the hundreds, and it was Phyllis Robinson, hair cropped short, wearing trendy, thick black-rimmed glasses, who mainly took on the job of hiring them. She knew what kind of people Bill wanted. It wasn't a matter of big credentials or fancy degrees. Take Helmut Krone. Before he came to DDB, he wasn't exactly a rising star. In his own words, once Phyllis and Bill hired him, he more or less copied Robert Gage and his work until he could find a voice of his own. Helmut was never a very confident man, especially not in his early years. He took everything personally. He could be extremely hard on himself, and excessively scrupulous. As Gage would later say of Helmut; "He had the capacity for infinite pain." Nearly everything about him—from the language he used in daily conversation, to the style of the art he did—was geared toward precision, toward stripping things away, getting to the most essential. And rarely did he feel good about the result. At times it was as though he wanted to erase himself from the face of the earth.

Born in a German enclave of Manhattan called Yorkville in

the summer of 1925, as a boy, Helmut Krone was surrounded by a community of people reluctant to integrate. They spoke German. They talked of the Fatherland. And when Hitler came to power, many of them rejoiced. Helmut would later admit that his mother had been "very right wing," and somewhat "sympathetic with the Nazi Party." Helmut was sent to a Wagnerian camp in Long Island—Camp Siegfried—that was German-run and bore a close resemblance to the youth camps the Nazis were setting up for children in the Third Reich. Helmut would tell Julian Koenig that he'd been brought up as "a little Nazi," but that wasn't quite true. Helmut had always had a mind of his own. He distressed his mother, for instance, when he decided that Camp Siegfried simply was not for him; he had himself discharged and boarded the train back home on his own, just like that.

Amazingly enough, Helmut's parents were born in Germany very close to where Wolfsburg is today. They left Germany in the late twenties and his mother, Emilie, was pregnant at the time: Helmut was born just one month after they'd arrived on American shores. As Helmut grew, his parents told him many stories of Germany and their Lower Saxon village. But Helmut, as he would later say, always felt there was something about those stories that made the whole country seem unreal.

Helmut had a complex relationship with his mother. His classmates would remember how much he'd loved her, but she was not always easy on him. In fact, on more than one occasion, Helmut's mother told him he was worthless. Of course, in the very next sentence, she'd be telling him about all the great things she expected him to grow up and do. Around relatives and family friends, she would praise her son to the heavens— clearly smitten and proud—and yet Helmut always felt a heavy pressure or stress when he considered his mother's big dreams for him. In adult years, when talking about his childhood, Krone would often say "A German son is always wrong till he's proved himself to be right."

Helmut's father was the one who doted on the boy, at least when Helmut was a child. As he grew up, however, the two grew distant: Otto watched his son sitting inside on sunny days and drawing and he criticized him for being too solitary: *Why don't you go out and play with the other kids your age?* His father thought he needed to toughen his son up, make a man out of him. But when the Depression hit, Helmut's father found himself out of work and out of motivation, his health slowly deteriorated, and in 1939, just before the World's Fair in fact, Helmut's father died in his son's arms. Emilie had gone out to get pain medication for Otto when it happened. Helmut was the only one home with his father for those last moments of his life. Helmut was twelve, and suddenly he was the man of the house.

At school, acting on the advice of one of his teachers, Helmut began calling himself Bud; his own name felt far too German and sinister. As he matured into his teens, he styled himself a bit like a character from an Oscar Wilde play, wearing full suits to school, sometimes even accenting them with elegant leather gloves and a porkpie brimmed hat. All those days of drawing had also paid off and he was accepted into the elite High School for Industrial Art. His classmates there thought he was arrogant, but those closest to him realized it was only his deep and earnest struggle *to be clear* that made him appear as such. Even back then, he was always struggling to get to the meaning of things, frustrating himself with his inability to put things in the most crystal clear of terms. Arnold Burchess, one of "Bud's" teachers who saw this inner struggle, recommended that Bud have a look at the work of the artists who had comprised the Bauhaus school in Germany.

His teacher was right: Helmut was intoxicated by the art of Paul Klee and Wassily Kandinsky, and of the German Bauhaus as soon as he saw it, and that inspiration would lead him to study design and attend lectures at the "Design Laboratory" of Alexey Brodovitch's New School classes in Manhattan. But once there, Helmut could never quite seem to own the inspiration he felt. He spent time in the East Village, just wandering pensively. During World War II he was drafted into the navy and served time in the Pacific. Upon returning, he tried an ad job at

Sudler & Hennessey and eventually got fired. His work was good, but it was only when he made it to DDB that something extraordinary began to flower in him. Robert Gage and Bill Bernbach were men he felt comfortable with, men he looked up to and respected. Bill's openness freed him, Gage's seriousness and deep appreciation of the Bauhaus resonated with him. And there was of course that one essential link: Before being hired, in his interview with Phyllis Robinson, when Helmut was asked to name three people who'd had the most influence on his work, his answer was: "Paul Rand, Paul Rand, Paul Rand."

The first time Charlotte Nordhoff saw her new home in Wolfsburg, she burst into tears. She and the girls had been shuffled around so many times by then that she no longer expected their

The neighborhood of Steimker Berg in Wolfsburg, late 1940s or early 1950s. This is how it would have looked when Charlotte first arrived.

lives to proceed any differently. She hardly remembered what it was like to have a real home, and it's easy to understand why. When Heinrich finally felt ready to have his family join him, after nearly a year of separation, Charlotte did not go with high hopes. She'd not heard good things about Wolfsburg. She knew it was still little more than a factory surrounded by a rough construction site.

But in the midst of so much hastily built worker housing, the residential neighborhood known as the Steimker Berg presented quite a contrast. It had been Wolfsburg's first (and only) residential neighborhood completed by the Nazis, and only used by the party's elite, and then later by the British soldiers who occupied the town. Even today, the Steimker Berg is an idyllic neighborhood, by any country's terms: The houses are simple and elegant and they blend in naturally with the trees and the earth, giving one the feeling of being outside the city, but safe and protected. The houses are all off-white with green shutters and clay-shingled roofs. Some would say they look more like ideal country cottages, a place where people sit by the fire and read a good book, or take a walk and breathe in the fresh air, or work in the garden, surrounded by large, flourishing fir trees. The design of the neighborhood came from Hitler's nostalgia for Germania, from the Nazi *Blut und Boden* (Blood and Soil) ideology about the power of the past: The houses are *Heimatschutzstil* or "conserved heritage." Aesthetically, they are modeled on a feeling for the past, but from the very beginning, the interiors were designed to be very modern. Each house came equipped with the latest appliances and central heating, a very big deal at the time since most people were still using coal ovens for heat and cooking.

Riding in the car with her mother that day, Nordhoff's daughter later admitted that she'd thought: *Perhaps we will live in a house like this one day.* When the driver pulled into the driveway of one of the beautiful homes, no one in the car dared to move. It was only when Heinrich opened the front door, and Charlotte saw her husband, that they broke down.

The little cabin that Ferdinand Porsche had once built with such high hopes was just a few miles away from the new home where the Nordhoffs were restarting their lives. It sat alone in the midst of trees and a cleared field that offered a perfect view of the rest of Wolfsburg and of the Volkswagen factory. The cabin was closed in by a handmade wooden fence with a little gate. Resin-colored fir trees give the place a fairylike feel. By 1949, when Charlotte felt like her dreams were finally coming true, the dreams Porsche had once had of building his car for the people were being realized too, in that very same town, and Porsche himself could see it with his own eyes now—for the first time since the end of the war, he'd just been granted permission to enter Germany again.

Once the entire Porsche family was allowed to return to Germany in 1949, they moved their offices back to Stuttgart. Ferry would always remember the tears that came to his father's eyes the first time they drove down German streets and happened to see a Volkswagen pass by, the moment Porsche finally saw a People's Car being driven by *one of the people.* The elder Porsche even took to counting Volkswagens as he saw them "in the wild." One day Porsche told Ghislaine excitedly that out of the twenty cars he'd seen pass by that day, *eighteen* of them had been Volkswagens. (Ghislaine recorded that in his diary; nearly everything he wrote in his diary had something to do with his uncle Ferdinand.)

The car was obviously still extremely close to Porsche's heart. Thus, in the summer of 1950, he asked Ferry to drive him out to the Wolfsburg factory. It would be Ferdinand's first time returning there since the war had come to an end, and would be a very different city from the one Porsche had known. In an issue of *Autocar* from around that time, an article titled "Production Is Their Wealth" relates the following about Wolfsburg: ". . . some 9,000 Volkswagen employees live [there] with their families, making a total population of 25,000. Heating and light are supplied from the Volkswagen works, and their own bus service connects villages within a radius of 20 miles, providing transport for those employees who cannot be housed at present at the Volkswagenstadt . . . There is no one who can stop the German people from working hard; a people who have become fully aware . . . that production has become their wealth. The example of America is being followed by a European nation."

There were many reasons for the shift in the public's perception of the factory, but one part of it was certainly due to Heinrich Nordhoff's expert use of the media and the press. In 1948 when he'd arrived, the papers were still calling the VW plant "Hitler's pet" or "an Allied factory," but Nordhoff, with the expert help of his pressman Frank Novotny, courted those same reporters, sending out press releases and inviting them to meetings and events, opening up the factory for them to tour and inspect. Journalists liked Nordhoff. They often referred to him not as "Heinrich" but as "Heinz." He was friendly and articulate, always ready to answer their questions. And the Volkswagen was a sort of German Cinderella story that the papers were (eventually) happy to report on. A former Nazi town, saved by the British, redefining itself by using an American model, with Italian and German workers side by side on the assembly lines creating and exporting cars to all the European countries that had once been enemies—it was an inspirational tale for postwar Europe, for those who noticed. In 1950, the same year Ferdinand Porsche visited the factory again, the Volkswagen workers made their 100,000th car and many of Germany's top papers were there to cover the event. The photos taken as the car rolled off the line are a stark contrast to the ones taken during Hirst's days in 1946 when the 10,000th car had been produced. The photos of 1950 show healthier workers, men who look proud of their work and happy to be there.

Under Nordhoff and Novotny, Volkswagen made deliberate efforts to reach out to the German people as a consumer base, to try to cultivate a specific, warm feeling for the car. It wasn't really necessary for Volkswagen to advertise in Germany at the

time, as they were by far the leader in their market; by the end
of 1949, growing lists and orders constantly flooded in. One survey done in 1949 by the Bielefeld market research institute
(TNS Emnid) asked customers "Which personal vehicle being
built again today do you consider, independent of its size category, to be the best of its type?" The Volkswagen got 40 percent
of the votes, while Mercedes got about 24 percent and Opel
about 22 percent. Ford got close to 8 percent and BMW came in
last, with about 5 percent of the popular vote. For some reason,
people found it was easy to like the Volkswagen.

But Nordhoff and Novotny were thinking in terms of the future. It was a matter of providing customers with the feeling that
their cars were simple enough to be understood—because really,
they were—and thus the advertising was more of an informa-
tional service (indeed, this division of the factory was called
"Volkswagen Information Service"). The "ads" lent a feeling of
accessibility and warmth to the purchase of an automobile, and
this was important in a psychological sense: Because these were
the first cars working-class Germans (the burgeoning middle
class) were buying, the way they felt about the car and the company would forever impact how they thought of automobiles.
As the country moved forward, Nordhoff and Novotny understood that the car was writing its own postwar story. The men
who had championed this car had come to think of it in personal terms, and the advertising and promotion reflected that
same feeling.

One such effort, for example, was a series of films Nordhoff
commissioned. (Nordhoff was a bit of an amateur filmmaker
and films were a big interest of his.) One of the first was *Kleiner
Wagen, Grosse Liebe,* or *Little Car, Big Love,* which was screened
150 times in venues across Germany and was a big hit; as the
dealers would later attest, customers referenced that film when
they came in to buy their cars. To use the word "love" speaking
of the car, and to have that word accepted by the people, was
telling. "Love" is not a word that Germans use lightly.

It was easy to link Germany's Economic Miracle to the miracle occurring at the Volkswagen plant. The car factory provided a concrete example of the Social Market Economy and the new direction that West Germany had chosen. In an important sense, Germany's social and spiritual renewal in the 1950s is perhaps best understood through the country's relationship with the automobile. For the first time *ever,* everyday Germans were becoming motorized. The car was a symbol of ideas such as freedom and release as well as one of progress and stability; just as the car was reinventing itself, so too was Germany.

In that sense, when Ferdinand Porsche and Ferry entered Wolfsburg that day, it really was like entering a new world. Porsche was clearly shaken upon seeing the long brick factory again. It must have risen out of the Lower Saxon countryside like a ghost, bringing with it a strange mix of pain, guilt, and celebration. He told Ferry that it was strange how much easier it had been to build brand-new race cars than to build a People's Car. And yet, perhaps for that very reason—for all those memories of the years of testing it, of building it by hand in his garage with his close associates, of trying to get it mass-produced, of the dark regime that funded it, and of the dramatic way Porsche had lost control of the project and been placed in jail over it . . . it was the Volkswagen that held the most intimate threads of his past.

The elder Porsche hesitated for a moment when he and Ferry got out of the car. He didn't want to go directly into the factory, so they went up to Nordhoff's office instead. Porsche and Ferry were received reverently and warmly. Heinrich would later admit that this meeting with Porsche on the factory grounds in Wolfsburg had been unexpectedly difficult and moving for him. Nordhoff seemed to sense that it was the last time the two would meet. It was clear, he said, that Porsche was a man who was looking back over his life. It was as though Porsche had made this trip for closure, in order to say goodbye. He sat with Nordhoff for quite a while that day, but he declined the invitation to tour the factory halls, only peeping in for a moment to greet the

Ferdinand Porsche in the year after
he was released from prison.

workers as they built and worked on the car he had spent decades of his life trying to design. Before leaving, Porsche said something that Heinrich would recall for the rest of his life: "Only now do I have the feeling," he remarked, "that I have done something right."

It is fitting, in a way, that after all the movement in Ferdinand Porsche's seventy-five years, it was this trip to Wolfsburg that would be his last. Not long after returning, he had a stroke from which he never recovered. Porsche died on January 30, 1951. He was buried near his home at Zell am See.

In my research, one thing that has always struck me about Porsche is how, in nearly every picture of him, his face is quite serious and determined. It's rare to see him smiling. But in the few photos taken after his time in prison, he has a smile in nearly every one. There is a gentleness and warmth in his expression. Maybe it's just the grace of old age, or maybe Ferdi-

A picture taken less than a year before Porsche's death.

nand had suffered so much in jail and spent so many days alone that by the end of it, he'd found a new level of peace. In any case, Ferdinand Porsche would not be easily forgotten, nor would his little bug-shaped car.

45

When feisty young George Lois came on board at DDB in the 1950s, Helmut Krone was not thrilled. Here was a young man who was Helmut's opposite in nearly every way. George was a Greek boy who had grown up in the Bronx. He spoke loudly and forcefully; he was rowdy and extroverted, and supremely confident about his work. In the film *American Graffiti,* George would have been one of the tough guys in a white shirt, sleeves rolled up and a motorcycle between his scuffed leather boots. Helmut didn't like him. "What's wrong with that kid?" he asked.

George didn't like Helmut much either: "He's nasty to everybody," George would say, "except Bernbach. He kisses Bernbach's ass." George had a dirty mouth. He grew up in a rough neighborhood, a place "racist to the point of vulgarity," where on the night of a big boxing match, there'd be "500 radios screaming into the night." In those days, according to George, Irish guys in the Bronx didn't have much tolerance for tough-guy Greeks. He had his nose broken more than once, and everything about him said he was a fighter—his voice, his swagger, his un-inhibited use of the word f*ck—screamed troublemaker. And yet, he was also a Son of Pericles and a loyal son, happy to work long hours in his father's florist shop after school. George also had a love of art; even as a boy, he used to get up in the middle of the night to draw: "It was the only time I had to do it," he said. Those same nights, he pored over Paul Rand's work published for the first time in magazines like *Esquire, Direction,* and *Apparel Art*: "It was the first time I realized you could be part of that glamorous fast-moving media world but still be doing art."

His parents didn't quite get their son's obsession, but Mrs. Engle, one of his teachers at school, certainly did. It was her prodding that convinced him to apply to the prestigious High School of Music and Art in Manhattan. She even gave him the dime for the round-trip subway fare, sending him off to apply in 1945, just as the war was coming to an end. George took the school's entrance exam and passed.

In school, his art teachers were both frustrated and awed. Once, during an end-of-the-year exam, the students were given a white sheet of paper and told to make something "using a rect-angle as their form." George thought for a moment, then put his pencil down on the desk without drawing so much as a single mark. He just sat there quietly, an amused look in his eye, while the rest of the class scribbled furiously. Their teacher scowled at George, seeing the boy's calm as an attempt to provoke him. Just before the bell rang, as the teacher reached for George's empty sheet of white paper, George stopped him. Hold on a minute, he said; picking up his paper, he signed his name in the lower right corner, as though it were a work of art. And in many ways, it was. The paper was a simple white rectangle after all, about as Bauhaus or Constructivist and precise as one could get, and the teacher soon couldn't help but smile at what George had done.

"In that moment, I began to understand that everything you do has to be a surprise," George later said. "Everything I do should be seemingly outrageous, I thought. It should have that feeling of 'hey, you can't do that!' but in the next moment the realization of 'hey, that's really great.' " George was looking to give people something that would resonate, that would make them think.

Clearly George had a rollicking ride ahead of him, and a few years later, he broke the news to his dad: He wouldn't be working with him in the florist shop anymore; he was going to college. He'd been accepted into art school at the prestigious Pratt Institute. A little bit later, he had some shocking news to break to his mother too: He'd gotten married on the sly, and the girl wasn't Greek. His mom gave him a hug. Times change, she said. And indeed they did. Not too long after, George's artistic career was interrupted by the Korean War and he was sent overseas and wounded by a piece of flying shrapnel. He'd be fine though, recovering well enough to remain a major headache for the officers who had him under their command.

When he returned to the States, he had less patience than ever for the slow road. He had ideas, energy, and a surplus of ego to spend. He saw what was happening with Ohrbach's and Levy's, saw the other ads flowing out of DDB, and he knew that's where he wanted to be. He told his father that Bernbach was "the maestro" and that once he was ready, DDB would be the place for him. In the meantime, George flew around town at lightning speed, working with some of the biggest names in media: Herb Lubalin at Sudler & Hennessey, William Golden at CBS. He also managed to turn a few desks over in a rage when he didn't get his way. People loved George. His energy was undeniable. But he was a challenge, containing a plethora of ideas that could explode from him at any angle, any time; he shot ads out like darts.

Needless to say, the prickly and prim Helmut Krone simply didn't know what to make of such an aggressive young man. Helmut had come on board at DDB in 1954 when he was twenty-nine years old. Now he was nearly thirty-five and his apprenticeship to Robert Gage was ending. In campaigns such as Polaroid, as an art director, he was beginning to come into his own, and the younger George looked like competition. Lois walked DDB's halls like a bully ruling a high school, and he was indefatigable: By the time Helmut arrived at work in the morning, George would have already been there for hours, working furiously, ads covering his office floor. Helmut would take the long way around just to avoid George's door. George liked to work on six or seven ads at once; Helmut, according to George, "would do an account every two years." That was an exaggeration, but no one would have argued with George if he said Helmut worked slowly. Still, George wasn't just fast; he was manic. Copywriters complained to Bill. They found George and his ads a bit too vulgar, a bit too obvious. One such ad, for example, showed a giant ear with toothpicks, bent paper clips, and all kinds of other gruesome sharp objects sticking out of it: it was for a Q-tip product, of course. But Bill dismissed the complaints. He liked George. George was a curiosity, Bill thought, and that was a good thing.

On George's first day, when Bill came over to welcome the young man, he couldn't help but notice George's office had a shine uncharacteristic of the place. "They really fixed you up good," he said. George sheepishly told him that he'd actually snuck in over the weekend and repainted the room: "It was too dingy," he said. "Uh-huh," said Bill. "And look at that chair! Did Gage give you that chair?" "It's my chair," George said, "I brought it from home." The chair was a sleek Mies Brno, the product of a Bauhaus star.

George's arrival was a sign that a new generation was drifting into DDB—the agency was ten years old by now, successful enough to have moved out of its early cramped quarters and into a larger space just off Madison Avenue, on 42nd Street. And it was on the cutting edge of a still-unarticulated shift that was taking place, rearranging the face of the city itself. New styles of architecture were springing up, and not surprisingly, that was tied to the Bauhaus and Russian Constructivist mix that was also affecting magazines and art at the time. In 1958, the same year George started at DDB, one of the Bauhaus movement's leaders and stars, Ludwig Mies van der Rohe (the same man who'd designed George's office chair) was hired to design a new building for Seagram. The Seagram Building was like nothing the New York City skyline had ever displayed before: In Bauhaus terms, the functional utility of the building was also supposed to be its beauty. That meant all the building's structural elements were visible—everything was obvious and transparent, and there was no ornamentation. It looked so unfinished, people said, so raw. George loved it. Bill did too.

There was another powerful presence slinking in and out of the DDB offices around dusk at this time. Julian Koenig was tall, witty, and charming. Hired around the same time as George, the two young men fell into an instant friendship. George called Julian "the writer from Aqueduct," "the Columbia beatnik," the man in "horn-rims and rumpled suits." Julian was indeed an Ivy League combination of sharp and smooth; he wore narrow ties and oxford shirts with button-down collars. He was articulate, mischievous, but with a deliquescent voice.

Born in 1921, Julian grew up in an intellectual, sophisticated home, the kind Helmut Krone would later admit he'd always admired. Julian had been brought up in New York City and had

The Mad Men: Helmut Krone, George Lois, and Julian Koenig.

gone to grade school at P.S. 6. During his undergraduate years, he was considered one of the brightest and funniest in his class. He wrote for his college paper, and he dated beautiful blond women with names like Aquila. He loved baseball. And movies. And he loved the film persona Groucho Marx. He even looked a little bit like him, and maybe wrote in a style reminiscent of him too, gravitating toward the witty, the enlightened, the playful but suggestive phrase. Like Groucho, Julian seemed to always know just a bit more than he would ever let on, and yet, as many have attested over the years, he wasn't afraid to call his colleagues out if they said something imprecise. He was (usually) piercingly honest, but he wasn't sentimental. In fact, if he hadn't been so sophisticated and articulate, he might have come across as rude.

Julian's father was a judge in the Court of General Sessions and a well-respected man around town. For a while it looked as if Julian might follow in his father's footsteps. He attended law school at Columbia and did well there, until he realized that he didn't agree with his professors, or the rules. It all seemed so constrictive and false. At the time, Julian was reading authors like Hegel and Karl Marx, and their ideas didn't blend so well with the teachings of law school. He eventually dropped out and started hanging around art museums, trying his hand at writing radio scripts. He ended up writing advertising at an agency named Morton Freund for $20.50 a week, and soon started trying to unionize the place. That was how he first met Bill. It was back when Bill was still at Grey, head of the copywriting department and also the editor of an agency publication called *Grey Matter.* Julian's attempts to unionize the advertising business sparked quite a controversy in the pages of Grey's newsletter.

Unionizing was not so popular with company heads in 1947. For some, even traditional workers unions seemed "too collectivist" or too much of a threat, given the Red Scare. In such an environment, Julian soon found himself out of a job for voicing his ideas. But while Julian did indeed think of himself as a Marxist, it had nothing to do with the Soviet Union: He had no respect for Stalin and his politics. What he liked about Marx was best summed up in the statement, "From each according to his ability, to each according to his need." He thought that was a "splendid way to build a society," but the only problem was that "the instinct for power always corrupts." That's how the world ended up with men like Hitler and Stalin, he'd later say; they were the very antithesis of the Marxist ideas he liked.

After a few more attempts to make it in the advertising business, the dissatisfied Julian packed up and went for an extended trip to Europe to try to get a bit of perspective. He lived in France mostly, but he ventured into Germany as well. His new wife Aquila was with him. They'd gotten married in 1951, and a young photographer named Richard Avedon (a name not yet known at the time) had taken their wedding pictures. When Julian and Aquila finally made their way back to New York City, Julian resumed his career in advertising. He still wasn't satisfied, though. He was looking for something else, so he started working on "the book." The gambling book, that is.

In 1955, Julian had discovered horse racing. He'd been raised to think nobody could beat the horses, and that it was immoral to even try. The young Julian certainly had a rebellious streak in him, though, and when he came across the formula for a "secret system" in the pages of a magazine one day, he couldn't help but try. He went to the horse races with high hopes. In three days, he was bankrupt. But he'd been bitten by the gambling bug, and he couldn't stop. Sure he was on to something, he went to his boss at the advertising firm and said he'd like to take leave "to work on a book." Everyone had always expected Julian to become a writer, so he let that image hold. And, in the end, he hit it big. In 1957 alone, he made more money at the racetrack than he'd ever made in advertising. In the flush of the win, he quit his old job. He would work only because he wanted to work now, and there was only one place he really wanted to be: DDB.

Prior to his interview with Phyllis Robinson, Julian had sent his portfolio to DDB with a bit of hesitation: The only ad in it he liked was the one ad that every previous agency had refused to publish. When Bill had seen Julian's portfolio, he'd told Phyllis that he didn't like a single thing. *Except this.* Funny, Julian thought upon hearing this from Phyllis, but that's the only ad I like in there too. It was for root beer. The image was of a sweet kid sipping on a straw with the caption "Finest beer I ever had." In 1950s America, that was profane stuff. Bill didn't love the ad, but he liked it, and he thought he saw something in Julian. He might just have it. Might. It's worth a shot, Bill thought. And so Julian was hired.

He fit right in at DDB. "It's a disaster working with Julian," Helmut once said, perturbed by the fact that Julian did not sit at his desk all day; but in truth, Helmut liked Julian very much, and like Bill, he too thought he saw something in him. But unlike George, Julian wasn't seeking out the limelight, at least not overtly. He had a kind of internal humbleness, and it would manifest itself in his style of working: While Helmut pored over every ad to an almost comic degree, clearly wanting to impress, Julian worked on the fly, letting ideas roll out as they came and not worrying too much about them. Helmut just didn't understand this.

In a strange but fitting way, Julian became the intermediary and messenger between George and Helmut, helping to keep things peaceful between them. George and Helmut might not have gotten along, but they were curious about each other, and they respected each other's work. And all the sparring, all the insecurities, all the competition, all the doubt—created exactly the kind of atmosphere Bill had wanted, a high-energy, creative workplace. And a challenging one. Bill was honest, but that didn't mean he was easy. In fact, Julian found that getting his copy through at DDB was harder than it had been at any other place he'd ever worked! But there was a difference. The copy wasn't rejected. Instead, Bill kept making him work on it, and then work on it again. Julian remembers days of waking up at dawn and sitting in one of Manhattan's pocket parks before work, trying to get his copy exactly right before handing it to the fastidious Bill.

In an interview that Bernbach gave later, he said that some of the most talented people to have worked at DDB were the people that took a while to mature: They were chosen with care, he says, nurtured for what he and the others could see in them waiting to make its way out. "[It's such] a thrilling experience for me to see," Bill says, "one day—and it happens just like that, in one day . . . the person has it."

Photos of Wolfsburg from 1950 can be deceptive. Especially when placed beside photos of the city from 1955. There is one picture, for example, of the long, main road (now called Porsche Street)—the road that visually connects the high point of the city (and Porsche's old cabin) to the factory and castle. In 1950, this road is only half-paved, bare, and nearly deserted. There are a few figures, mostly women, in dark colors, standing in a circle by the end of the street. Near them, a little boy plays unwatched. A few houses are visible, under construction, spaced unevenly toward the horizon. There are some old barracks that resemble long thin barns. Seemingly out of place, there is one brick building, the most solid in the shot. In the caption, it says that this building is the *Buchhandlung Grosskopf* (Bookshop Grosskopf), a place Heinrich used to frequent with Charlotte.

Photos of Wolfsburg from 1955, however, look like advertisements of a shopping Utopia compared to that. All the buildings are uniform, built in fifties minimalist–style, but with a commercial feel. If it weren't for the line of (fully paved) road leading from Porsche's hill to the factory and castle, it would be hard to tell that it's the same city. But in the photos from 1955, there is not an inch of space on either side of Porsche Street; the road is lined with storefronts. People walk and shop, towing bags or pushing baby carriages. The place has the look of a movie set, almost as if it would blow over if a strong wind came

Porschestrasse, the main street in Wolfsburg, in 1950. If you look closely, you can see the Wolfsburg castle in the background.

along. All but the brick factory in the background, which looks solid and muscular, permanent. And in these later pictures, cars are everywhere. But not just any cars. Row after row of Beetles line the streets and fill the parking lots.

Looking at these pictures, and especially at those cars, they remind me of something I heard musician and punk rocker Patti Smith say about "relics." In a 2010 interview about her memoir, *Just Kids,* interviewer Michael Silverblatt asks Patti Smith about magic. In the memoir, Patti suggests that an object can be transformed when it is placed in a new context, and Silverblatt wants to explore that idea. "I think it's very Catholic," Patti Smith says. "I wasn't Catholic, but Robert [Mapplethorpe] was an altar boy . . . and I was always fascinated with Catholic imagery and saints . . . I think both of us had a very 'relic' sense of things, that once we infused an object with our own faith . . . it became almost like a holy relic, and you know, many relics are very humble but it's the reverence of the people, or its approximation to someone great, that makes it special."

In Germany in the 1950s, Porsche's Volkswagen was a car, a technological tool, a commonality—but it was also a symbol. In

Porschestrasse in 1955. The road is now bustling and full of life.

retrospect, after all the continents and peoples the car encountered, one can see how it transformed as it was placed into new contexts (from Nazi Germany to West Germany, then from West Germany to the rest of the world). It started out in the most racist nationalistic regime in Europe, and went on to become an epoch symbol in an "American-style" business and town where, according to a *New York Times* article from 1955, more than 80 percent of the population were refugees from the Soviet Union. "Nobody is from here," one Wolfsburg worker told the reporter.

Coming to life in Germany's *Stunde Null,* its Zero Hour, though difficult, was actually a benefit to Volkswagen in many ways. Coming out of the Zero Hour, there were no traditions to be followed, no clear path. So VW could take the best of General Motors and Ford and mix that with German work philosophies and German needs to create a product that was something entirely new, perfect for the emerging international market that was equally new. "That was a blessing for us," Nordhoff said in an interview he gave in 1953. "We solved our problems as we encountered them, in our own way, not by what the book told us, but usually by improvisation."

In a speech in 1952, Nordhoff could congratulate the workers for now being capable of building 1,200 cars per day. In that same year, 35 percent of Volkswagen's production was exports outside of Germany, mainly to Sweden, Holland, Belgium, and Switzerland. The Swiss registration figures for the year 1953 show that the Volkswagen accounted for 23 percent of all new bought and registered cars. A *New York Times* article from December 1952 reported that Volkswagen had produced a record 135,970 cars and that this was 28 percent above last year's number and still rising. Output was rising so fast, in fact, that by 1954, every other car on German roads was a Volkswagen, and there were 200,000 exported cars, with plans to export to Japan, Hong Kong, Burma, and Indonesia. Volkswagen was leading Europe in exports, and Nordhoff kept cutting prices to speed up those sales all the more, always a step ahead of competitors like Renault and Fiat. Wolfsburg might have been the oddest city in all of Germany, but it had found a formula that worked.

And much of West Germany was experiencing that same growth, the "Economic Miracle." One can find a million and one reasons for why prosperity suddenly washed over West Germany as quickly as it did. Some said it was the Social Market Economy, others credited the Marshall Plan. Some said it was denazification, others said it was the deep gratitude people had for having survived the NSDAP and the war. Some said it was the influence of the Allies, others said it was the threat of the Soviets. In Wolfsburg, it was a combination of all of those reasons, and the Volkswagen factory, a place that people could see from just about anywhere in the city, was a giant reminder to its citizens of every single one.

The acceleration of growth was so dramatic that by 1955, Wolfsburg was making its millionth People's Car. Around that time, the Allied High Commission that had been watching over Germany was dissolved and West Germany's Federal Republic was accepted into the North Atlantic Treaty Organization (NATO). At the NATO ceremony in Paris, fourteen foreign ministers gave speeches to welcome West Germany into the fold.

Workers coming over the footbridge that connected the VW factory to the town center, spanning the Mitteland Canal, 1954.

The French refused to play Germany's national anthem (understandably perhaps, as it was "Germany Over All"), but Norway's foreign minister Halward Lange, a Jewish man who had endured two years in a German concentration camp, called the day a "decisive moment in the history of our continent." Konrad Adenauer, the new chancellor of West Germany, said: "Today, everywhere in Germany, peace and freedom are felt to be the greatest treasures of all. . . ." Just a few months before that speech, Adenauer had been at the Volkswagen plant for a photo op: Heinrich Nordhoff drove him through the factory in a Bug.

In Wolfsburg, Nordhoff had come to be known as "the king," a term people still use when referring to him in Wolfsburg today. The first time the term was used was in a ten-page cover story for Germany's well-respected magazine *Der Spiegel,* with the title "In Heinrich Nordhoff's Kingdom": the kingdom was Wolfsburg, of course. And the comparison said a lot. Like Germany's new Social Market Economy, Nordhoff's methods were successful ones, but they were controversial for their ties to an authoritarian past, especially with a totalitarian present sitting just a few miles away over the East German line. Like the Social Market, the Volkswagen company was a partnership between government, business, and a centralized management, a confusing mix of paternalism, regulation, and an embrace of ideas typical of laissez-faire. Even the German press spoke of Wolfsburg as a "social-political enclave," and Nordhoff himself called his way of doing business "social capitalism."

Nordhoff, though far from perfect, gave the workers big salaries and benefits, policies that spread to become standard in new West German industries. It wasn't really all that different from what Ford had done in America back in 1914, except Nordhoff had the advantage of hindsight. According to that same article in *Der Spiegel,* his workers hadn't had a single day of strike. Somehow Nordhoff had made the factory feel like a home, a family, a place where the people were taken care of and well fed. It came with all the warmth and drama and discomfort that any family knows, but also with the loyalty. *The car is our castle,* people in Wolfsburg liked to say.

A big part of Nordhoff's "reign," and of this familial feeling that developed with respect to the factory and the town, had to do with the cultural support he gave. He commissioned churches to be built by the great Finnish architect Alvar Aalto, a multipurpose exhibition space called the Stadthalle to be used for music and entertainment, and the Cultural Center located in the middle of town, equipped with a public library, an outdoor terrace, and numerous rooms where painting, drawing, dance, and other cultural programs were set up for the young. And then there was the music. In 1951, in a rather wild but brilliant move, Nordhoff convinced the famous Prussian conductor Wilhelm Furtwängler to bring his Berlin Philharmonie to the Volkswagen factory. (Imagine the New York Philharmonic packing up their instruments and going to play inside a factory in Detroit!) The concert was actually held in one of the main factory halls, and it was for the Volkswagen employees only. Most of them came there directly from their shifts. Furtwängler himself had been quite skeptical at first about playing in a factory, but the response, and the attention he and the orchestra received, left him in awe. The musician Johnny Cash once said that the crowd at Folsom Prison was the best crowd he had ever played for. Not that the workers and the prisoners are in any way comparable, but perhaps the attention and gratitude they gave to the performers was similar, a crowd more focused and appreciative than a typical audience, one for which such shows were easily accessible, would have been. It must have felt rather mystical to hear that music filling the halls of the Volkswagen plant. The orchestra was deeply moved by the experience too; they came back every year for the next ten years.

Because of all the success, Wolfsburg was often referred to as a "gold rush town." Certainly Heinrich knew he had a lot to be grateful for, and yet he still wasn't satisfied. One very big piece of the puzzle was missing, and Nordhoff couldn't stop thinking about that one piece: the United States. For both economic and personal reasons, the United States was the place Nordhoff and the Volkswagen company needed most. But it was also the country that seemed to want the least to do with them.

The Volkswagen was undoubtedly a German car. And yet it was also an international car, and in a way, some of its ancestors

A parade of Bugs. Wolfsburg, 1953.

(and its diverse origins) were American. The United States had been the model for designing the car, the factory, and the town. And now Wolfsburg was living "the American dream"—it had gone from rags to riches, both literally and metaphorically. But the United States was still playing hard to get when it came to embracing and buying the car itself. In 1953, even though Wolfsburg was booming, Volkswagen sold only 2,100 cars in the States, and just getting that many sold had been an uphill battle. All the innovations Nordhoff still wanted to implement at the factory would require machines that were made in America. The best way to do that was with dollars, and the best way to get dollars was to sell cars to America, but that just wasn't happening.

It was a problem that Nordhoff had already been working on for many years. In fact, not long after he'd arrived on the job, he'd met the Bug-loving Ben Pon and, learning how much Pon had done for exports, he'd asked if Pon would try his luck selling the car to the United States. And so, on January 17, 1949, Pon and the little car had taken the long transatlantic journey, traveling together aboard the MS *Westerdam.*

But in America, Pon's luck simply hadn't held. Even though a friend of his had arranged a press conference upon their arrival, and although Pon had high hopes, he soon found that the spirit washing over the car in Germany had certainly not reached U.S. shores. People in America still thought of it as "Hitler's car." "We got a lot of publicity," Pon said later, "all of it bad."

And things had only gotten worse from there. Every dealer Pon encountered rejected it. Not a single American car dealership was willing to take it on. In one story he would tell, Pon drove from New York City to Massachusetts in a snowstorm to see a dealer, and the man wouldn't even come outside once he'd looked out the window and seen the car!

Pon had a limited budget on the trip, and since he'd made no sales, he eventually had to sell the car itself, and for well below market price. "I had a big bill at the Roosevelt Hotel," he said, "and I couldn't meet it. So, in desperation, I sold the car and all the spare parts I had brought with me to a New York imported-car dealer for eight hundred dollars, just to pay that hotel bill."

When he returned to Germany—where the car was already being seen in a very different light—Pon had a hard time convincing Nordhoff that things had gone so badly for him in the States. Nordhoff decided he had to see for himself, so he too had flown over to America in 1949. And he too had found it obvious that Americans did not want his car. One customs official had even laughed at the pictures Nordhoff showed him of the VW: "You want to sell that car here?" he'd asked. "Good luck."

As the world had entered the 1950s, the chances of selling the VW in America continued to look grim. Aside from the fact that it came from Germany, in American eyes, the car had another problem. As Ford historian Douglas Brinkley has written: "The VW didn't look anything like anything—animal, vegetable, or automobile—ever seen in America." People wanted big cars because the automobile had become a sign of upward mobility: the bigger, the better, the higher your class. Drivers wanted a big white Buick or a color-coordinated pink-and-ivory Olds. They wanted elongated roofs and tailfins and a wider trunk; they wanted a smooth ride, a big upper-class tent that shielded them from sound. They wanted names like Thunderbird, Corvette, and Starlite, cars that long-legged American cowboys could stretch out in. They wanted an automobile with a team of horses up front. Henry Ford had already given the people mobility. Now they wanted their mobility in a larger-than-life package.

Or did they?

Soon it would become obvious that there was a section of America that was hungry for something else. Once again, the little Volkswagen was on the verge of getting caught up in a larger cultural and economic wave of change. And yet again, it would become a symbol of that new world still waiting to emerge.

Part Four

o o

Like Pigeons from a Sleeve

". . . Because the only people for me are the mad ones, the ones who are mad to live, mad to talk, mad to be saved, desirous of everything at the same time, the ones who never yawn or say a commonplace thing, but burn, burn, burn . . . What did they call such people in Goethe's Germany?"

—Jack Kerouac, from *On the Road*

George Lois was hanging out a window with an advertisement for matzo in his hand. Goodman's Matzo, a brand of the crackerlike unleavened bread used for the Jewish Passover, was a new client of DDB's, and George was on the account. He loved the ad he'd come up with: a white sheet of paper with a giant matzo filling the page and the words "Kosher for Passover" hand-lettered in Hebrew underneath. Unfortunately, Mr. Goodman wasn't as thrilled about the ad as George was, and he rejected it at the account meeting. Undeterred, George went to Bill and asked if he could repitch the ad to Mr. Goodman on his own. Art directors didn't usually go to a client's office to pitch an ad to customers, especially not a client as tough as Mr. Goodman, but Bill decided to let George give it a try. His colleagues said it was a kamikaze move. But George was already off to Long Island City, beloved matzo ad in hand.

As George tells it, Mr. Goodman was "like a real rabbi rabbi, busy eyebrows, must have been ninety years old, and he had his whole family, his grandchildren and his grandchildren's grandchildren sitting there with him, ready to hear my pitch." The young guys were saying: "Hey, gee, Grandfather, I like that poster." But Mr. Goodman wouldn't budge: According to George, Mr. Goodman said "I don't like it" at least twenty times in a row. George knew that after the big deal he'd made of it at DDB, he couldn't possibly go back without this account. So George decided to jump out the window.

In his own words, it went like this: "We were on the third or fourth floor and there was a casement window there, see, so I go to the window and then I go *out* the window and I'm hanging there and I say 'Mr. Goodman, you make the matzos; I'll make the ads!'—that's a famous line now, by the way'—and he says 'Come back in! oh my God, oh my God, come back in! And then his grandkids start fanning him, and he looks like he's about to faint . . ." Suddenly alarmed, George pulled himself back inside and decided to leave from the door instead, thinking of the embarrassment he'd face after his impetuous stunt. But then, "the old guy recovers and stops me. He says 'Hey, wait, George, you know, if you ever quit advertising, I'll give you a job as a matzo salesman any day.' " In the end, George got his way: The matzo account ran, and it was a huge success. But was it worth hanging out that window? "I'd never do it again," George says.

Of course it wasn't a typical way of getting an account, outrageous even for DDB. And when word got out, some started to feel that DDB was more of a circus than an agency. But in truth, DDB was about as serious as any other agency. What most of Madison Avenue really had a problem with was not the creativity but the trust and risk such creativity required. "If you stand for something," Bill often said, "you will always find some people for you and some against you. If you stand for nothing, you will find nobody against you and nobody for you." In the 1950s, DDB was doing well, but it didn't look like a leader. It was still missing the three hallmarks of big-agency success: a big tobacco company, a Big Three carmaker (GM, Ford, or Chrysler), and a major "personal hygiene" company like Colgate-Palmolive or Procter and Gamble. What's more, it was still a *Mad Men* world. No other agencies were following DDB's example in terms of structure or style; by the end of the 1950s, DDB was still the only place in town that put the art director and the copywriter together in one room. So was the agency's approach revolutionary, or was their success just a fluke? New York City hadn't made up its mind yet.

In 1953, Dwight D. Eisenhower, a former general and hero from the Second World War, was elected president. Eisenhower, as a young army officer, had once had to cross America in a convoy, and he never forgot the experience: The cars had to crawl six miles per hour on average, and the majority of the roads the convoy took were unpaved, potholed, and dangerous. In the end, the cross-country journey had taken over two months to complete! Thus, one of Eisenhower's pet plans as president was to improve and upgrade the country's network of roads. A good interstate was necessary for travel and for commerce, he realized. And due in large part to Eisenhower's help, car companies would become the top profit-generators for the country; the 1950s was their heyday, a time when more than sixty million vehicles were sold. Many of the pre- and postwar kinks had been worked out; the unions were established and reputable now, and the automobile industry was taking better care of its workers. (In 1950, the famous "Treaty of Detroit" had been negotiated between the UAW [United Auto Workers] and General Motors, for example, in which the union agreed to a five-year contract that allowed for annual wage increases and steady improvements in technology.) Benefits like health care and pensions were becoming standard. And for the first time items like homes, cars, and appliances were attainable by a high percentage of the American population. The middle class had fully arrived.

By the end of the 1950s, there were three million cars coming out of Detroit every year. Individual states began to spend money on roads. New highways were built connecting big cities like New York, Boston, Chicago, Atlanta, and New Orleans. In the first half of the decade alone, more than 12,000 miles of state-funded roads were built. In addition, the National System of Interstate and Defense Highways Act (often referred to simply as The National Highway Act), a plan initiated long before he came to office but signed by President Eisenhower in the summer of 1956, used gasoline taxes to contribute $100 billion to building a network of national roads. Eventually, more than 40,000 miles of paved road would come out of the project, giving the United States a new geographical cohesion. It would also create a new class of suburban commuters, people who moved out of cities and started families. According to journalist Walter Cronkite, with the Highway Act, the American government "probably created the greatest change in our culture . . . When [Eisenhower] approved and pushed through Congress this great interstate highway network that we now have, he changed the entire face of America."

Aside from the growing desire for cars and streets, another factor that helped garner public support for the use of their tax dollars for road-buliding projects came from the perceived Soviet threat: The argument was made that a modern network of streets was necessary in case citizens had to flee during a nuclear strike. These were the years in America, after all, when atomic air raid drills became commonplace in schools all across the country.

With all the new freedom and mobility—alongside the underlying worry and suspicion that came wrapped in the Cold War—there was a feeling of *keeping up with the Joneses* that developed in the 1950s, an attitude that demanded a veneer of stability, a need to appear a certain way under any circumstances. That mood spread unconsciously through middle-class America and worked like a silent scale telling people when they were feeling too much emotion, or when they were not keeping up appearances as they should. The problem was that people nearly always felt "too much" emotion; and they nearly always felt like they were not appearing as well as they should.

In the fifties, people were supposed to live fairy-tale lives, like the Cleaver family in *Leave It to Beaver*. But it was Beaver himself who everyone loved; it was Beaver who was most American. He was the one questioning and contemplating. He represented curiosity, difference, *the idea.* As kids of that time approached their late teens and early twenties, some started asking hard questions, questions like: *Why are my parents pretending to be happy? Why do I have to grow up to be something I don't like? What's meaningful inside all this accumulation? Have I been tricked?* Thus while their parents experienced the prosperity of the 1950s in one way, many of their children were experiencing it in quite another: They were curious about what else was out there, and they were ready to break out.

In 1957, a book called *The Hidden Persuaders* was published. In it, author Vance Packard reevaluated all the focus groups and scientific tests that were being done in the name of understanding public tastes. In his view, all the methods, techniques, and research were actually covert agents of manipulation and abuse. The back cover of the first pocket edition of the book states:

In this book you'll discover a world of psychology professors turned merchandisers. You'll learn how they operate, what they know about you and your neighbors and how they are using that knowledge to sell you cake mixes, cigarettes, cars, soaps and even ideas.

The book would eventually sell millions of copies. And while Packard was right about the effect, he was wrong (at least in part) about the culprit. No one group was doing this consciously to anyone else; in truth, it was the whole country that was fooling itself.

By the end of the 1950s, a recession had set in, the first downturn since the Depression, and people were worried. At least the older generations were worried; the young people were ready to act. Mobility is as much about freedom and new vistas as it is about capitalism or the free market, and the young were taking up the former while the elder worried about the latter. Mobility in the 1950s meant prosperity, but it also meant the ability to communicate more widely, to be exposed to different lifestyles and different views, to get into a car or a bus and experience the country like Jack Kerouac's character in *On the Road*. Mobility brought adventure, both physical, emotional, and mental. By funding the building of national interstates, the American government was thus connecting the country in unexpected ways. And there would be consequences.

$$48$$

When Carl Hahn joined Volkswagen in 1954, he was twenty-seven years old. The tall, handsome economist had studied and worked in countries all over Europe, and had done his thesis on European economic unification. The potential in economic interaction between countries thrilled him, and he had a personal interest in European unity too. As a teenager, he'd been drafted into the Second World War by the NSDAP. A month after Germany had surrendered, he'd found himself in a U.S. prison camp. The Americans had treated him fairly, and he'd eventually been released. But those were early, formative years, and they instilled in him a deep desire to understand other cultures, to look deeply into the relationships and exchanges that structured the world. While he was living in Paris, he wrote to Nordhoff directly and presented him with an idea for how to export cars in a way he called "Europeanization," hoping Nordhoff might hire him. Volkswagen was his "dream job," he said. He saw it as the perfect place to further explore the economic ties and structures that were possible in a more internationally interdependent world.

Interest in automobiles ran in Hahn's family. His dad had worked for Auto Union (the same car company that Porsche had once built a famous race car for), and Hahn had grown up surrounded by automobiles. In reaching out to VW, he was looking to bridge his two passions: international economics and cars. But Nordhoff's response to Hahn's effusive letter had been curt; he didn't think Hahn's idea of "Europeanization" would work for VW. Still, Nordhoff also said that he liked Hahn's way of thinking, and if Hahn ever found himself in Wolfsburg, he should stop by. Hahn made sure to "find himself" in Wolfsburg shortly after.

Nordhoff and Hahn immediately hit it off, and Nordhoff eventually offered Hahn a job as his personal assistant. But Nordhoff was the type of man who did everything for himself, and soon

*Heinrich Nordhoff and Carl Hahn. It
was often said that Hahn was like a
son to Nordhoff.*

Hahn felt he was not being given enough of a challenge. He threatened to leave, and Nordhoff decided to make a change: Carl Hahn would work in the export department instead.

Hahn's new appointment at Volkswagen happened around the time that the United States was finally beginning to take a second look at the little car that it had rejected and ridiculed for so long. By the mid-1950s, while most adult Americans still identified the car with Hitler and the war, there was now a new generation that had come of driving age who had less connection to the car's turbulent history. Even so, the American market was generally not very open to foreign cars. The British had enjoyed some initial success in exporting to America, but that trend had quickly faded as Americans found it increasingly inconvenient to track down parts and get the right maintenance on the British cars. Nordhoff learned a lesson from those problems, and he combined it with another lesson he'd learned from Henry Ford. In the early days of the Model T, Ford had sent representatives to all the states to introduce the cars to people, and to cultivate a feeling of familiarity between the average American and this new growling machine. He'd shown farmers how they could use it in their daily work. He'd gone to all kinds of communities, regardless of class. And he'd also set up service shops, places that could sell and repair parts. It was the beginning of the modern dealership, and it was a strategy that worked. Now Nordhoff was ready to bring that same strategy back to America.

Service shops and easy access to parts had been a founding tenet of the Volkswagen company in Germany and in Europe, so it made sense to Nordhoff to proceed in that same way in America too. In that spirit, Nordhoff sent over a complex man named Will Van de Kamp, a man who reportedly had the temper of a preacher and the zeal of a missionary. It was Van de Kamp's job to bring the Volkswagen to the driveways of American homes. Van de Kamp was in love with both the little car and its company, and his eccentricity and intense energy were very useful. He found a team of people to do just what Henry Ford's team had once done, to travel through the states and introduce the car to people, to set up service centers and dealerships wherever they could. Van de Kamp was adamant that the new dealerships strictly adopt "the Volkswagen way"—a way focused on quality and service, putting customer service concerns above concerns with sales. Throughout the mid-1950s, he and his team drove in a special VW bus all through America, setting up shops and hanging that lollipop VW blue-and-white sign on the doors. The dealerships were all built to have the same look so they could be recognized immediately.

Van de Kamp's love for the car was contagious, and as he and his team traveled the country, they began converting people, especially young people. The car certainly had its advantages: It could get thirty-five miles to the gallon, and if something broke down, the design was so simple that people could usually repair it themselves. But a person had to have a thick skin to drive a VW in those days: The car got strange looks on the street, and it wasn't unusual for drivers to get ridiculed. Perhaps because of this, however, owners began to feel protective of their cars, to think of them as special and unique. And they really were: At the time, the VW was the smallest, oddest-shaped car on any American street, the very antithesis of the sleek, glamorous cars coming out of Detroit. It did not blend in.

One of the men Van de Kamp found himself working with in America was Max Hoffman. Hoffman had met Ferdinand Porsche at his last Paris Auto Show in 1950. Though it was the Porsche 356 Hoffman had fallen in love with, the connection between the two men turned out to be Ferdinand Porsche's last gift to his little Volkswagen as well. Through Hoffman, the Porsche brand would soon make its way into the States and start its own great journey there. But Ferry and Nordhoff's contract meant that they shared dealerships, and so, in 1950, as Hoffman began selling the Porsche, he had no choice but to let the little VW tag along too. The Bug's sexy sister got all the attention, but Hoffman pawned off some VWs on dealerships in the process; thus a very slight pickup in sales occurred for the VW in 1950: out of the nearly 7 million cars that were sold in America that year, 330 of them were Volkswagens. But as the years wore on, and as Van de Kamp and his team made their rounds and spread the word, some of the dealers that had gotten "stuck" with their VWs would come to find that the beetle-like car was selling even faster than the Porsche.

While most Americans might not have been comfortable with foreign cars yet, in the 1950s, thanks to new innovations in passenger planes, it became much easier and much more affordable to travel to Paris or London or Rome. Americans began thinking of themselves as cosmopolitan, and while West Germany wasn't really considered a part of that cosmopolitan world, perceptions of the country were much different than they'd been in 1946. With the Truman Doctrine, the Marshall Plan, and the Soviet threat, West Germany was being seen not as Germany (in the old sense), but as a friend. Events like the Berlin Airlift, which took place for nearly an entire year under Truman's presidency, made Americans feel connected to West Germans. At the time of the Berlin Blockade in the summer of 1948, General Clay cabled his superiors in D.C. and said ". . . the world is now facing the most vital issue that has developed since Hitler placed his political aggression . . . Only we have the strength to halt this aggressive policy here and now. It may be too late the next time." And the American government listened to him. American planes flew in food and raw materials, providing Berlin with everything from bread to electricity, when the Soviet Union cut off the city's basic supplies. One American who flew supplies to West Germany at this time—in a typical example of how events like the Airlift were changing American and German perceptions of one another—felt hostile about having to help the Germans, having ideas of the *Übermensch* of Nazi propaganda in his mind. But when his plane landed in the American Sector, that whole view he'd built up suddenly dissolved: A German man about his own age came running to his plane with tears in his eyes, unable to speak English but conveying his gratitude quite clearly. "I couldn't understand what he was saying," the American pilot said, "but I could understand the feeling."

This new understanding between Allied countries and West Germany would later have big effects in terms of exports for the Volkswagen plant. The change in relations was something men like Nordhoff and Hahn were conscious of; they knew what it could mean for VW sales. In the long term, both men believed that the United States would eventually be open to automotive exports from Europe. But that didn't mean that the Volkswagen was going to be any American's car of choice. In the past ten years, other European countries had succeeded in making People's Cars of their own. In France, there was now the rear-engine 4CV Renault. In Italy, there was the Fiat 500. And in Britain, there was the Morris Minor. All of these cars had some market resemblance to the Beetle, and all of them had their eye on becoming the first successful European "small car" in the American market.

In its attempt to become a player in the American market, it helped VW that both Nordhoff and Hahn spoke excellent English. They were also both charismatic and great with the press; both men had the kind of innate European charm that Americans found attractive. In 1954, *Reader's Digest* did a piece on Nordhoff and Wolfsburg, referring to Heinrich as "noble," and noting that he had nice blue eyes. The piece also called the city the "town that a little car had built." At the end of the 1940s, most American press about the car had focused on Hitler. In 1949, when Pon and Nordhoff had tried to bring the Bug to America, the car had been flatly rejected. Now, five years later, American citizens had warmed to West Germany, and the article was focused not on Hitler and the Nazis but rather on Nordhoff and the "miracle town." Wolfsburg was being rewritten as a success story of the West. In 1954, *Time* magazine decided to do a long article about Nordhoff and his town in their special issue called "Germany: the Fabulous Recovery." A hand-drawn picture of Nordhoff is on the cover of that issue, alongside a VW sign with sunbursts of Beetles streaming out of it. Inside, Nordhoff is described as being "like a diplomat."

This new way of thinking of Wolfsburg—as a model town of the West—had great benefit for Volkswagen. Sales of the car increased quickly. In 1955, the time when Americans first nicknamed Wolfsburg a "gold-rush town," Volkswagen suddenly found itself the single biggest exporter of foreign cars to the United States. In 1956, *Road & Track* did a road test of the car, writing of the Beetle:

> *[It] has gained an unmistakable wheel-hold in the garages and hearts of the American car-buying public. Of the 51,000 cars imported into this country in 1955, 34,000 were Volkswagens, and for this year the figure should be raised by 10 to 15 thousand . . . The only mystery is: how did it happen? Espe-*

cially with practically no national advertising? Of the various explanations, probably the simplest is that the Volkswagen fulfills a need which Detroit had forgotten existed—a need for a car that is cheap to buy and run, small and compact, light and maneuverable yet solidly constructed, and, perhaps above all, utterly dependable and trouble free.

It sounded good. And it was. But compared to America's Big Three that were selling millions of cars each year, VW's 34,000 was a small blip. All together, foreign car sales amounted to less than 1 percent of the U.S. market. Nevertheless, in the wave of VW's small success, Nordhoff decided to open his own U.S. branch and factory in 1955.

The idea of an American factory, however, very quickly proved to be a mistake. Just six months after the decision had been made and the land purchased, new studies came in that showed VW would never be able to sell enough cars in America to sustain the costs of having a factory there. There were also antitrust issues, and it became clear that the decision to buy land had been too rash. Nordhoff took full responsibility for the blunder, and they sold the factory and decided instead to have offices in the States (in Englewood Cliffs, New Jersey), but not to produce cars there for now. The new division of the company would be called Volkswagen of America.

Almost as soon as VW began to have some success in the United States, however, that success came under threat from the French automobile company Renault. In January 1958, *Time* magazine reported that "the car that has come up fastest in the U.S. market in the past year is Renault's Dauphine." The article goes on to say that Renault was "within striking distance" of overtaking Volkswagen as the number one exporter to the United States: "Dauphine is already outselling Volkswagen in eleven U.S. states, including Texas," the article noted. Such developments worried Nordhoff considerably. That same year, just before his fifty-ninth birthday, he fell ill and had to have surgery at the Mayo Clinic in the United States. From his hotel bed in New York City, where he spent most of January recuperating, Nordhoff wrote a desperate note to his colleagues back in Wolfsburg telling them about the Renault sales. By 1958, a total of 200,000 Volkswagens had been sold in the United States (over the past twelve years), but Volkswagen was slowly losing its edge, he feared. Volkswagen of America needed a man who could lead it in a new direction. As Nordhoff languished in the St. Regis hotel, he summoned Carl Hahn.

Hahn flew to New York City and met Nordhoff in his hotel room. The two discussed American exports for a while before Nordhoff finally disclosed the reason that he had called Hahn all the way from Germany: He wanted Hahn to take over Volkswagen of America, move to New York, and assume full control of U.S. operations. Hahn hesitated. He wasn't at all sure that he was ready to take on such a huge responsibility. But Nordhoff reassured him: He'd thought it through, he said, and he knew Hahn was ready for this. A few short months later, Carl Hahn was living in the United States.

It became clear very quickly that Nordhoff had been right: Carl Hahn and America got along well. Hahn modernized VW's offices with computers and hired people to train the staff in service and efficiency. He also standardized service facilities, giving the American Volkswagen dealership network a sense of cohesion and a way to communicate among themselves and help each other. Millions of dollars were set aside to get updated service centers up and running all over the country. It was essential that customers never lack parts for the cars they bought, and to make that happen, the system needed to work like a well-oiled machine. Still, there was an even bigger decision Carl Hahn made in his first year, something that had not been a concern of Volkswagen before that time. If Volkswagen was going to continue selling cars, he reasoned, if it wanted a future in the United States in the midst of all the competition that was setting in, then it was going to have to enter the deep waters of American capitalism: It was time to advertise.

$$49$$

The first time Julian Koenig saw a Volkswagen, he found it such a strange sight that he stopped in midstep and watched it scoot around the corner of the street he was about to cross. Other than that one memory, however, he didn't have any real impression of the car. In fact, in 1958, when DDB decided to take on a car dealership called Queensboro Motors—the only place in the New York tri-state area that sold Volkswagens—it was Helmut Krone who knew the most about Bugs: He'd actually bought one back in 1950, making him one of Volkswagen's first American customers.

Queensboro Motors was owned by Arthur Stanton and it was part of a larger importing company that Arthur, his brother Frank, and their partner, Victor Elmaleh, owned. That larger company was called Worldwide Automobiles and it was the sole Volkswagen distributor for all areas east of the Mississippi. The Queens section of Worldwide was a new building and its design was based on a Hamburg garage called "The House of Glass": the walls were transparent. While a VW had its oil checked or wheels rotated, the car's owner could watch. The first ad DDB did for the dealership shows an alienesque VW rising from the floor, as its owner drinks coffee nearby, observing his car through the sleek, clear walls.

Arthur and Frank Stanton, the owners of Worldwide, were also two of the earliest American fans of the Volkswagen. In the late 1940s, having left their big New York corporate jobs and moved overseas, importing American cars to Europe and Africa and generally having a grand time—these two brothers had discovered the little VW and fallen for it. Arthur had even traveled to Wolfsburg to meet with Nordhoff and ask him for his permission to sell the cars in a dealership they'd set up in Morocco. Nordhoff was happy to say yes. Later, once Arthur and his brother decided to move their business back to America—now bringing over all the foreign cars they'd discovered in Europe to sell in the States—the VW was at the top of their list. As early as 1951, they entered into contracts with Nordhoff, and World-wide became the main VW dealership on the East Coast. (Max Hoffman had brought the VW over too, but Hoffman was set up on the West Coast.)

The Stantons' staunch support of the VW seemed to have been an odd decision—sales in the States were terrible at first—but very soon, it became clear that they'd simply been ahead of the game. By the mid-1950s, being one of the only sup-pliers of the car, and with word slowly spreading about the VW, the Stantons were flooded with orders for the little car. And because delivery still took a long time, and wasn't always pre-dictable, they often had a long waiting list for the cars, and peo-ple who would show up immediately to claim the stock as soon as it arrived from Wolfsburg. All this attention the car was get-ting was simply by word of mouth. Just think what could hap-pen if there was a bit of advertising involved, the Stantons thought. And Arthur was also wanting to publicize his new Queens-based "House of Glass."

Luckily for everyone involved, Arthur Stanton happened to be friends with Richard Avedon, the same photographer who had taken Julian Koenig's wedding pictures in 1951. Avedon was on his way to being known as America's most unique and capti-vating photographer; his portraits of presidents and cultural fig-ures would eventually become legendary. But back in the fifties, Avedon's style, like DDB's, was still considered strange, at least in terms of America's norm; thus DDB and Avedon were, so to speak, part of the same crowd. When Avedon was at dinner one night with Arthur Stanton and his wife, Joan, Arthur mentioned they were looking for someone to do their advertising. Avedon naturally suggested DDB. He even called and set up Stanton's meeting with Bill Bernbach. The Stantons loved the ads that DDB did for them, so when, less than a year later, Carl Hahn hap-pened to mention to Arthur Stanton that he was looking for an advertising agency, Stanton (like Avedon) immediately suggested that Carl Hahn go and talk to Bill. Word of mouth is a powerful thing.

Still, even after hearing Arthur's warm recommendation, Hahn didn't expect much; he'd been all over Madison Avenue, met with thousands (literally) of ad men, and he hadn't liked what he'd found there. "People presented me with all kinds of fancy offices and spins, but there wasn't much behind it all." The ads all looked the same, the only difference was "the color of lipstick they'd put on," Hahn said. But as it turned out, all those poor experiences actually served Hahn well: On the day he went to DDB, it was clear he had found something unusual. The meeting was friendly and informal. "There was nothing offered but water to drink," Hahn said. "Bill sat on his desk." But Hahn liked Bill from the start. He said that when he first met Bill Bernbach, he had the feeling he'd met a man who was being real with him, a breath of fresh air. And Bill liked Hahn as well; he found him elegant and regal, but also down to earth. The men fell into an easy friendship. And Bill Bernbach was excited about the possibility of such an account. He finally would have a chance to say a thing or two to both Detroit and the big ad agencies, or so he hoped.

Admittedly, coming up with an ad for Volkswagen that could make any kind of impact on Madison Avenue, let alone Detroit, seemed like a pretty unrealistic dream. Helmut Krone, in his black glasses and freshly pressed button-down shirt and having recently (just months before any talk about a VW campaign had begun) purchased his second VW Bug, leaned his long frame against the wall and watched as Bill walked Hahn to the elevator after their meeting. Helmut was flabbergasted by Bill's enthusiasm: "I still don't, to this day, know what went on in his head when he accepted the account; in fact, he worked very hard getting it," he said. And he wasn't the only one confused about Bill's choice. As Bill would soon learn, getting his team to do a few ads for a local Queens foreign car distributor was one thing. Getting them to create ads for a German car company was quite a different story.

George flat-out refused to work on the account. "I don't have to tell *you* why," he said. Bill was Jewish, after all, so George assumed he would understand. As George tells it, there was no way he was going to go to Wolfsburg and meet with a bunch of Nazis. "Let me give you a little history lesson, Bill," he said, "about what the Germans did to the Greeks in the Second World War. See, it all started when Hitler diverted troops from the Soviet lines in order to help Mussolini—"

"I know, I know," Bill said, "but—"

"Greek resistance fighters," George went on, "were tortured and treated with the same malice and blindness as the Jews."

Bill nodded in earnest empathy: "But these are different times now, George. We've got to try and think of the situation a little differently now."

"No chance," George said, though he didn't like talking to "the maestro" this way. "No chance."

Nevertheless, Bill continued trying to get a team together from DDB to take the trip to Wolfsburg that Carl Hahn had arranged for them. The trip would include test-driving the cars and going on a personal tour of the plant. George had refused to go. Julian Koenig is clear about the fact that his being Jewish did not prevent him from wanting to work on the account. George, however, would like to believe that it did. In any case, when the Lufthansa plane took off from Idlewild Airport in New York, Bill and Helmut Krone were on it, and so was Bill's account man (and friend) Ed Russell. George and Julian were not.

Arriving in Berlin, I imagine Bill found himself more nervous than he'd expected to be. It was his first intimate encounter with Germany, a country whose recent history was somewhat difficult to come to terms with in regard to his past; after all, his parents had come to America because they were persecuted for being Jewish, and the Holocaust had been the ugliest example of that same persecution. But the sting of rejecting someone based on their religious beliefs was also a very personal matter to Bill, since his parents had cut him out of their lives because he'd fallen in love with a Catholic girl. Of course, no one at DDB would have had a clue about such things: Bill always kept his private life removed from his public one.

But aside from emotional issues, there were also his philosophies regarding the difference between manipulation and persuasion, and the extreme power that the media can hold, ideas that directly opposed Hitler's propaganda tactics and abuse of power. Carl Hahn, who was Bill's tour guide for that trip, might have sensed a bit of these mixed feelings in Bill, even if they never spoke of it directly. The way one nation perceived another, the dangers and the liberations inherent in crossing racial or religious or national lines—these were things both men had firsthand experience with and so they approached their interactions with delicacy.

By 1959, the time of Bernbach's trip, the Volkswagen factory and Wolfsburg, taken together, were an example of how precision and clarity in engineering could be achieved without denying such nuance, and without dismissing the artistic and the emotional side of life. Bill was quick to perceive this as Hahn showed him around the city, pointing out the new Stadthalle, the new Cultural Center, and even the new Volkswagen swimming pool that had been built in Wolfsburg for the workers' children.

But it was the factory that impressed Bill the most. There, he observed the dedication and extreme concern with detail, the extra effort and energy that went into getting things just right, the way no corners were cut to avoid spending a few extra cents. As he spoke with the engineers and workers, as he got to know the car, and as he listened and watched the way Nordhoff interacted with his employees, one simple word kept coming to Bill's mind: honesty. To his delight, and perhaps to his surprise, Bill found himself face-to-face with an honest company and a very honest car. The factory was geared toward clarity, toward seeing the car exactly as it was, and selling it based on that impression. It was impossible not to see the contrast this presented to 1950s Detroit and all its glossy, slick advertising. And so, at the end of a long day of tours, walking back to the Volkswagen guesthouse with Ed Russell, Bill said, "This is an honest car. We have to give it an honest campaign." It was as simple as that. That very day, after the factory tour, Russell wrote those thoughts up in a requisition. So many ideas were pouring out of him that the requisition was five pages long. "I definitely remember the first sentence," Russell later recalled: " 'The Volkswagen is an honest car.' That was Bill's summation at the end of the factory tour."

If the Volkswagen had been given commercial birth by Adolf Hitler in a cloud of lies and propaganda, it was those words by Bill that allowed it to transform into a new incarnation. It could finally move into the future carrying a new history, the culmination of the past ten years of Nordhoff's philosophy and work, by sending people the message Bill so badly wanted to say to both Detroit and New York. And the words of that message, coming from an American Jewish man, were much more powerful than they ever would have been if they'd come from Wolfsburg alone. In coming together, Volkswagen and DDB found they made each other's messages stronger, and that meant they had a lot to share with everyone, including American consumers. But the important question on both the company's and the agency's mind was: Could honesty really sell cars? It was a gamble. Bill was willing to make that bet.

In his own way, "honesty" was a word Helmut Krone was having to face on that same trip. He was now in his parents' homeland, near the very same village where his mother and father had grown up, the one they used to tell him stories about. As a teenager, Helmut had called himself Bud and thus tried to distance himself from his origins. But in Germany, Helmut couldn't deny his past. For more reasons than one, it was difficult for him. When he tried to speak German, a language he still knew well but hadn't spoken in years, his words came out at a strange pace: At first, some of the Wolfsburg staff even thought he was "a little slow." Additionally, as the only member of the DDB team who owned a VW, and who was fluent in both German and English, Helmut was under a lot of pressure to help "translate" the little automobile. He owned one of them after all, and Bill liked to make a big deal of that.

Taken together, Helmut, Carl, and Bill, the German American working for the Jewish agency in New York, the former Nazi youth and internationally trained economist heading the VW operation in the States, and the Jewish creative agency boss who had married a Catholic Italian girl, were a sort of amalgamation of the larger shifts taking place in the world, shifts that had come hard and slow.

Back in 1951, West Germany's newly elected leader, Konrad Adenauer, had reached out to Israel, making an unprecedented and controversial speech in the Bundestag. He said it was Germany's responsibility to compensate Israel for the Holocaust, because Israel was the geographic representation of the Jewish people. There had been a lot of debate about this statement in both countries, and across the globe. An attempt had even been made on Adenauer's life in March 1952, about a year after the speech. But six months later, a shaky agreement was reached between the two countries, and on March 27, 1953, the Reparations Agreement went into effect: Over time, West Germany would pay Israel reparations of 250 million DM. Some saw it as blood money, and through the 1950s, the argument continued to simmer. Adenauer had hoped the reparations would ease the tensions between Germany and Israel, but at first it seemed only to have raised them.

Not long after Bill and Helmut got back from their tour of the Wolfsburg plant, however, Israel announced that it would be purchasing 45 million DM worth of goods from West Germany *outside* of that 1953 reparations agreement. It was front-page news. Nearly seven years after the reparations bill had been signed, Israel and West Germany were finally engaging in something that could be considered "normal trade." In DDB's offices, it felt like a good omen. On March 12, 1959, the morning that Israel's decision was announced in the papers, George heard a thump against his door. When he looked up from his work, he saw that a page of the *New York Post* had been pressed to the door's frosted glass. The headline read "Germany Sells Israel 32 Jets." After a beat or two, Bernbach opened the door with a grin, and George agreed to go to Germany. "It was one of those moments with Bill where you just couldn't say no," he said.

After Bill left his office, George darted up to Julian Koenig's office:

"You know what he just did to me?" George asked.

Cool as a cucumber, Julian responded: "Yeah, he showed you that *Post* headline."

"So what'd'ya tell him?"

"I told him I'd go."

50

They were like two mischievous boys on a field trip, joking with the Lufthansa flight attendants and unable to sleep a wink. During the layover in Paris, Julian took George on a whirlwind tour through the Louvre. It was a place Julian remembered well from the time he'd lived in the city, and he knew exactly where to find the museum's treasures. The two young New Yorkers also visited Longchamps horseracing track. That was Julian's idea, of course, but George was hardly opposed!

"An extraordinary thing happened there," Julian recalled. He put his money on horse Number 4, and though it looked for a moment like his horse might actually win, Number 4 crossed the line in second place. Julian threw his ticket down in the walking room where it fell amid the hundreds of other scraps of paper, all the other losing numbers that littered the floor. But just as Julian and George turned to walk away, Julian heard "that magic word," *objection,* blaring through the grandstand. Julian raced back to where he'd just thrown his ticket, reached down randomly into the mess, and somehow—to this day he can't quite explain it—pulled up his exact discarded ticket. The winning horse had been disqualified. Number 4 now had first place, and Julian cashed in. "It was the high point of my life," he later joked. With extra money in their pockets and an omen of good luck to see them off, George and Julian boarded the plane to Berlin.

Compared to Paris, the Germany that greeted them was somber, to say the least. Their West Berlin hotel was near the Ku'damm (Kurfürstendamm), just across from Fasanenstrasse and the ruins of a giant Jewish synagogue that had burned down during Kristallnacht. "That brought up certain feelings," Julian said. Nevertheless, when the car picked them up the following morning to take them to Wolfsburg, it was George, not Julian, who seemed angry and ready for a fight. "I was pissed off," George later said. "I was ready to do anything that might piss people off. I even practiced goose-stepping like a Nazi." But George had fought in Korea; he'd seen the chaos and violence of war firsthand, and he'd known the pain that racism—be it Irish against Greeks, or Greeks against Irish—could bring. "Here I was meeting these guys, these Germans, these very same people who had been there and probably done who knows what else during the war, and now I was supposed to *work* for them?"

But once they were settled in Wolfsburg, George calmed down. Both of them had a good feeling about the quiet little town. George would remember that at first sight, he thought the city looked "like a toy town, like a Grant Wood painting in real life." Julian found it pleasant as well. "We had a bully time," he said. "They treated us well." And it's true, they were very much guests of honor while they were there. They were taken on extensive tours of the plant, allowed access to any area or equipment they wanted to see. They could easily understand why Bill had spoken endlessly about honesty; one couldn't help but notice the sense of respect the workers had for their work. Each car went through four layers of careful painting sessions and cars got rejected for the slightest imperfections: a missing dot of paint under a door panel, a slightly imbalanced windshield wiper, an improperly measured piece of fabric covering the bottom of a trunk. Sometimes it took over 100 inspectors just to "okay" a single car, and the head inspector reported not to a manager in his section of the plant, but to Heinrich Nordhoff himself.

Another thing that struck the men of DDB was Nordhoff's policy not to change the look of the car, to stay true to Porsche's original design. This was the very opposite of Detroit's need for constant change, for always wanting to have a new, stimulating product to give customers a reason to discard their old models and make another purchase, even if their old models still ran fine. It was remarkable, one couldn't help but realize, that in this whole town, every VW car was in effect the same car. Yet they all felt like individuals, automobiles with their own personalities.

When they were introduced to Nordhoff, George and Julian found him reserved and hard to read. He was friendly, but aloof, not nearly as approachable as Carl Hahn. George couldn't help but think: *Now here is a man who was, certainly, at some point in the presence of Hitler.* Or maybe Nordhoff was just aloof with them because George told Nordhoff that the steeple of one of Wolfsburg's churches—one that had scaffolding around it and was still being built at the time—looked a heck of a lot like a V2 missile launching pad.

One part of the factory tour was to what George remembers as a "secret, hidden basement" and what Julian remembers as "a kind of auto museum." It couldn't have been the Auto Museum that exists in Wolfsburg today, because that wouldn't get built for another seventeen years, but it could have been simply a room (like a museum) in the factory where they kept the unusual or valuable cars. For instance, it was here they were shown the millionth VW, a gold car with shimmering jewels. "It was studded with rhinestones," Julian recalled, "like a tart ready to walk the German streets." In the same secret room, or museum, or storage area, George discovered an old military model of the Volkswagen that was concealed with a tarp. According to him, he ripped the cover from the "Nazi jeep" and jumped into it, "shooting" at their tour guide from the machine-gun mount. Those jeep VWs do indeed exist. I saw versions of them myself at the present-day Auto Musuem. But George remembers a lot of mischief around their discovery of them, including Julian jumping into the car with him as he shouted "*Ach! Ach! Ach!*"

Julian, however, only remembers the little tart.

Toward the end of their stay, a dinner party was thrown for George and Julian. It was a fun night. Julian told the Germans all about American baseball, and he and George—perhaps after a drink or two—even demonstrated "the American baseball slide" for the gathered crowd. Julian was a good player, and his baseball slide was indeed something worthy of being watched. Julian got a running start as George covered the napkin that served as home plate. Nobody played umpire. Julian was safe.

On the trip back, George had to admit to Julian that now he actually kind of liked what he'd previously (before the trip) been referring to as "the little Nazi car." There was, at least to an American eye, something kind of sweet about the car that made it almost comical when seen as the center of all that earnest technical attention at the factory. Julian was also impressed. "Julian was already talking about it like it was a bug," George said, "calling it a little beetle, that sort of thing, something kind of schmaltzy." Still, George couldn't help feeling a little guilty about his quick change of opinion. Once he was back in the DDB offices, in "an act of atonement for succumbing to helping sell Hitler's People's Car," his old anger got one last comic vent; he spent hours creating a twenty-four-page flip book where the Volkswagen symbol ever so slowly morphed into a swastika. "Very interesting," Bill said when he saw the little flip book. "Now throw it out." As for Julian, his first "ad" of the campaign was a photo of Hitler behind a desk with a miniaturized Volkswagen sitting in front of him. The caption read: "The man behind Volkswagen." Years later, Julian would still laugh at the memory of it: "It was just a joke."

In any case, Bill now had his team, and it was the very team he'd originally wanted. Julian was to be the copywriter on all the ads. Helmut was going to be art director for the Beetle. And George would do the art for the VW Bus. In typical DDB-style, that meant Julian was to spend his weeks shuffling back and forth between George and Helmut's offices, brainstorming with the German perfectionist and then comparing notes with the rebellious Greek.

It was beginning to look like Carl Hahn had made the decision to advertise just in time. According to a *Time* magazine article from October 1959, "Not since Henry Ford put the nation on wheels with his model T has such a great and sweeping change hit the auto industry." And that big change was something now referred to as the "compact car." With the recession setting in, Detroit finally took notice of the fact that small cars like the Volkswagen were indeed selling. The Big Three came up with plans of their own. Chevrolet was the first to introduce their compact car, the Corvair: "This is just a prelude," *Time* magazine said upon the Corvair's release:

Next spring Ford will roll out a compact Edsel called Comet. In a year Buick, Oldsmobile and Pontiac will come in both compact and regular sizes. All told, Detroit is betting $700 million on these cars—about $150 million on the Corvair, $100 million each for Falcon and Valiant, $350 million for the "bigger" compacts. How well this huge gamble pays off will affect not only Detroit, but automakers and buyers round the world. Says West Germany's Heinz Nordhoff, president of Volkswagen, with some understatement: "1960 will be the most interesting year in the history of the U.S. automobile industry."

And indeed it would.

$$51$$

In the United States in 1959, one book seen in dentists' offices, on subways and buses, in homes all across the nation, was the best-selling self-help book of the day, *The Magic of Thinking Big*. It's not surprising that a book with that title would have become a hit in the 1950s, but the book's message was not quite what you'd expect. It's easy to look back and criticize the media or the car companies or capitalism itself for the deep societal problems beginning to surface at the time, but back then, it wasn't so obvious that Thinking Big was truly a problem. And, in truth, dreaming big, fantasizing, wishing for the best: None of those things alone *were* problems. One has to look just a little longer and a little deeper to see what was really going on. And to remember that for Americans it was the first decade after the United States had become a superpower, and that the country was experiencing prosperity unequal to anything seen in former times. Likewise, one has to remember that the United States was still a segregated country, a place where blacks and whites weren't supposed to mix, and where being a woman, or of a certain color or class, was enough cause for discrimination—problems that we are still trying to understand clearly even today.

In the 1950s in America, there was an exaggeraged emphasis on thinking big. Thinking big in those days was heavily equated with the commercial world: As more of the population now had more money to spend, as the middle class expanded dramatically after the Second World War, this emphasis on thinking big quite often got misinterpreted as "buying big," and this led many Americans (perhaps subconsciously or unconsciously) to feel a void in their lives that was hard to define. The dominant culture of the time urged consumers toward believing that the answer to life's ills was in acquiring more, and this resulted in the well-known inertia of trying to *keep up with the Joneses.*

But that was only one part of a very complex nation. In the

decades since that time, in recalling literature such as Betty Friedan's *The Feminine Mystique* or Vince Packard's *The Status Seekers,* or in films that have been made about the 1950s such as *Pleasantville* and *Far From Heaven,* the decade has sometimes been seen as a time of suppressed emotions and out-of-control consumer desires. And while there is truth in those notions, and certainly those books and movies express a legitimate reality, the 1950s was also a *good* moment in history, a time of abundance and enjoyment and progress. To put it another way: There is nothing wrong with thinking big; in fact, it can be very healthy, and the prosperity and well-being of many Americans in the 1950s is a testament to that fact. But that does not dismiss the other current that was running parallel to that progress: Many were coming to the sober realization that there is no end to the struggle to keep up, it is a race *no one* can win. Likewise, no matter how good life is, or how much prosperity one experiences, it never pays to turn a blind eye to the larger realities of other individuals, groups, and views. Mysteriously, in 1959, DDB was able to sense that conflicted moment, and reflect it in a way that would ultimately resonate beyond their intentions or control.

The first DDB Volkswagen ad to run in *Life* magazine appeared on August 3, 1959. It was in black-and-white, and it showed a picture of two VWs from above, one covered by a sheet, the other not. The headline read: "Is Volkswagen contemplating a change?" DDB's VW campaign got its first public plug on Madison Avenue because of this ad. In the issue of *Advertising Age* from October 5, 1959, in a piece titled "Didn't Need Research," that first ad is shown alongside the article. The article reads:

> *The illustration in this Volkswagen ad makes wonderful use of Detroit's technique of creating interest in a new, completely changed model by covering it with a piece of cloth. The suspicion, of course, is that Volkswagen is not contemplating a change. But then the first line of copy shatters the easy assumption. "The answer," it says quite simply and candidly, "is yes." How can you avoid reading further? When you do, of*

Is Volkswagen contemplating a change?

Is Volkswagen contemplating a change? *The early Time magazine ad that Julian and Helmut created for Volkswagen.*

course, you learn that Volkswagen is constantly making changes—little changes that improve the car without transforming it in appearance . . . [then it quotes the original ad again] *"The Volkswagen has changed completely over the past eleven years but not in its heart or face."*

The ad simply stated what Julian had noticed on his trip to Wolfsburg: the car never changed, but was constantly improving. He'd played on that knowledge but had given the writing, as the author above suggests, the feeling of a surprise or a mistake so that one had to read on and solve the puzzle. But he'd also given the plain honest truth. Nothing to boost the reader's ego, other than the fact that the ad assumed people were smart enough to get the twist. The article in *Advertising Age* goes on:

This copy is so simple, believable, straightforward. No excitement. Just sheer, honest communication. It didn't need research to make it that way. Just one human being interested in making himself clear to other human beings. Too bad most advertising can't be made as clear and direct. The answer lies in the human beings that write the ads—and pay for them.

The piece generated only the smallest of waves, but from it, one can see how different DDB's approach was, how Julian had absorbed the proceedings at Wolfsburg and used them to create a new voice and tone, one that had never been seen before, even at DDB. What he had done, in retrospect, looks so simple. He even says so himself: "We had conspicuous obsolescence going on in every other car model in the world and here was this thing that doesn't change." Now, the ad looks somewhat obvious. But Detroit's "conspicuous obsolescence" was hardly obvious at the time. In any case, this was the first ad to run in *Life,* but it wasn't the first ad they'd made. The first ad they'd made would be the ninth Volkswagen ad to appear in *Life* magazine, but it would go down in history as the DDB shot heard 'round the world.

It was late spring 1959 and George and Julian had just returned from their trip to Wolfsburg. Julian and Helmut sat down together in Helmut's office on the twenty-fifth floor of the DDB offices, cigarette smoke drifting out the door and down the halls. Observing New York after Europe, Julian could acutely feel the difference: The culture felt very aggressive. Part of the aggressive feeling came from the mentality of thinking big, a kind of mad and endless grasping for more. What if they stopped thinking the answer was always in more? What if they started noticing the details again, looking at the little things?

In the first ad, Koenig went against every rule in the DDB book (he evolved a style he'd admired and would later attribute to a rival of Bill's named David Ogilvy) and wrote some of the longest copy in the history of DDB. He did it in a childlike cadence that no other ad executive would have dared use. It was a simple, honest little story:

> *Ten years ago, the first Volkswagens were imported into the United States. These strange little cars with their beetle shapes were almost unknown. All they had to recommend them was 32 miles to the gallon (regular gas, regular driving), an aluminum air-cooled rear engine that would go 70 mph all day without strain, sensible size for a family and a sensible price tag too. Beetles multiply; so do Volkswagens . . . Volkswagens snub nose is now familiar in fifty states of the Union, as American as apple strudel. In fact, your VW may well be made with Pittsburgh steel stamped out on Chicago presses (even the power for the Volkswagen plant is supplied by coal from the U.S.A.) . . . As any VW owner will tell you, Volkswagen service is excellent and it is everywhere. Parts are plentiful, prices low . . . Today in the U.S.A. and 119 other countries, Volkswagens are sold faster than they can be made. Volkswagen has become the world's fifth largest automotive manufacturer by thinking small. More and more people are doing the same.*

That was the first copy of the first Volkswagen ad. It was a tone that would be used for decades of advertising to come.

Helmut cringed when he read it, shaking his head and saying, "I suppose that means you want me to make the image small, like a little beetle?" As far as Helmut was concerned, the last thing the American consumer was capable of in the 1950s was "thinking small." But Julian held firm. He knew Helmut well enough by then to know that his resistance to the idea was not what it seemed: Sometimes, the more Helmut liked copy, the more he'd criticize it. Helmut would later say that he always gave what was wanted, but never what was expected. Working on that account, Helmut explained, they all knew that the biggest sin would be to tell a lie, to say anything that was not true. And the car was small. And simple. These things were true.

Pontiac's spirit of creative design brings you fresh, crisp beauty for 1960

Pontiac again shuns the mediocre to create the Fresh Point of View for 1960. The prow is proud, pointedly tasteful and exciting. The horizontal bars of the grille suggest order. There's harmony in the profile, a new-found freedom and grace, no meaningless adornment. yet there's a warmth to this design, a personable warmth you rarely see in an automobile. The interiors are exquisite, coordinated, a sensation to touch and feel. Pontiac has designed this with visual honesty, not just to be different, but to give you a motorcar of lasting good looks. Consequently you can expect adherents of clean styling, people of exceptional taste, to be driving 1960 Pontiacs. Don't you belong among them?

PONTIAC   THE ONLY CAR WITH WIDE-TRACK WHEELS

A typical car and a typical ad from 1960. Cars were made as big and wide as possible, and the ads were full of beautiful people enjoying their leisure time.

So Helmut gave Julian his "dour, Buster Keaton face" and went to work on a graphic for Julian's idea, opening up the space on the paper so the whole ad was practically a blank space. He put a very small Volkswagen Beetle in the upper left side of a sea-sized white paper. He used the most basic sans serif typeface to fit Koenig's words. He made paragraphs out of single sentences. He used full stops. He left a lot of empty blocks and widows.

David Ogilvy had written thirteen rules of what an ad should be in terms of composition and layout. Helmut took those rules and did just the opposite. As he later said, "I [did] my damnedest to break as many of these rules as possible. When Ogilvy said that the text always should be put in an antique typography, I put it in a grotesque one. When he said that the logo always should

Think small, the ad that became DDB's "shot heard 'round the world."

be clearly exposed, I'd hidden it . . . I think I managed to break seven of his rules." Actually, it was nine. Helmut had just created a layout that would revolutionize advertising.

Later Helmut revealed that he'd wanted the ad to be "Gertrude Steiny," meaning he wanted it to resonate almost as an error would, going about it in a way that didn't make sense, just like Bill and Doyle and Dane had done by choosing their punctuationless name. When George saw the ad, he told Helmut he needed to fix the widows and get rid of all those jumbled visual stops and starts. *You're probably right,* Helmut said, *It's probably the worst thing I've ever done.* "He always told everyone in the office that he hated it," George said. But even so, Helmut didn't change a thing; though he did think that his whole career was going to be ruined once it came out. He was so miserable, in fact, that when he heard the ad was going to appear in *Life,* he departed for St. Thomas so that he would be far away from New York City when it hit.

But what about the headline? Julian had wanted it to be "Think Small," picking up on the two words from the copy. Helmut, however, could not be convinced of such a thing; it was too strange, too contrary to the climate of the culture, too much. Since the art director always had final say on the headline, Julian had to give in. The two finally decided on the rather snide *Wilkommen* (Welcome). There are some ideas, however, that seem to keep rising to the surface no matter how many times they get rejected: When the ad was taken into a meeting with the German reps from VW to get it approved, the German man working on the account read the text and honed in on those same two words: Think Small. "That's it," he said. "That's the header!" Helmut reluctantly admitted it to Julian: "Stick with me, Helmut, and you're going to be famous," Julian joked. Still, even in their wildest imaginations, they could not have predicted what would happen next.

When Think Small hit the pages of *Life* magazine in February 1960, it was as if Julian and Helmut had written a bestseller. The contrast between it and other automobile ads of the time was so striking that it left an indelible imprint. Some people carried the ad around with them, showed it to friends over lunch, passed it around like a good book, even cut the ad out and hung it on their walls. They bought that issue of *Life* just to see (and own) the one Volkswagen ad. For the first time in a long time, there was an ad that truly got people's attention, rousing their imaginations and their spirit. And it held their attention, day after day after day. It was as if the ad had been the switch to turn on a collective lightbulb in people's minds: *We don't have to think*

big, people realized. "We were describing a small car," Julian later said about the Think Small copy, "[In that context], the ad wasn't earth shattering . . ." But it was. It expressed a sentiment that many people were feeling but didn't know how to say.

The people who didn't hesitate were the young; it garnered a sort of cult following in the way an indie rock band does before it goes mainstream. It was the college kids who first understood the VW ad campaign, tacking the ads to their dorm walls. And their love for it makes sense. This was, after all, the generation that had grown up in the 1950s, watching their parents playing the "pretend everything is OK" game. It felt good to be spoken to clearly and honestly for a change.

The Think Small ad was a tangible symbol of a new spirit, but it was only the most revolutionary (and thus the most remembered) ad of what was in reality a very large campaign. Another of the more resonant ads of that campaign was one that Julian and Helmut created in April 1960, the Lemon ad. In it, with the help of another DDB copywriter named Rita Selden, Julian used another lesson he'd learned in Wolfsburg: No car made it out the door without having been inspected, and then inspected again. Wolfsburg inspectors were certainly interested in noticing the details. The Lemon ad showed a perfectly fine looking VW, polished and shiny, but the copy read: "This little car missed the boat. The chrome strip on the glove compartment is blemished and must be replaced. Chances are you wouldn't have noticed it. . . ." The ad goes on to say that there are more inspectors at Volkswagen than there are cars produced daily: It's all about that German Quality Work.

The VW campaign would eventually spread to television as well, with equally famous spots like "Funeral" and "Snowplough," all of which are now popular videos on YouTube. Every ad in the DDB Volkswagen campaign stuck to Julian's tone—bluntly honest and witty—and Helmut's simple, clean design. It was the first time an ad campaign had become a topic that everyone in the country was talking about.

DDB's Volkswagen campaign is considered to this day to be

the best ad campaign ever conceived. At the end of the 1990s, *Advertising Age* listed it as number one in the Century's Top 100 advertising campaigns. And as Jerry Della Femina, "the pundit of advertising," once said, "In the beginning, there was Volkswagen. That's the first campaign that everyone can trace back and say 'That is where the changeover began.' That was the day when the new advertising agency was really born."

The reaction on Madison Avenue was slightly different. The other advertisers noticed the campaign, to be sure, but they hesitated about it. They weren't sure about the design, the text, or the ads' simplicity. Think Small hit national magazines in 1960, but the ad itself had been created nearly a year before, just after George and Julian had come back from Wolfsburg. It had run in a small local paper at the time, but had received little professional notice. And when the 1959 annual advertising awards rolled around, it was another agency's advertising for Renault that won: that ad showed a car with balloons flying out of the open sunroof. "This was voted the best car advertising from my peers," says Julian. "So much for my peers." But at the Art Directors Club, DDB did win some awards. Much to Helmut Krone's dismay, George Lois won *three* of them: one for the Matzo ad that he'd hung out a Brooklyn window to get approved; another for a campaign for men's ties; and the third for, well, the Volkswagen bus.

George's Volkswagen ad, one of his first for the company, showed a large family sitting very comfortably on an all-white background, positioned as though in a car. On the next page, readers saw that same family, and the same layout, except, the viewer realized, the people were not floating in white space, but they were sitting inside the VW Bus.

It wasn't long before Madison Avenue took notice of Lemon and Think small. The public, led by the young, had embraced the VW campaign, so they had to embrace it too. The effect was profound at DDB. Their budget, and their reputation, grew extensively in a matter of months. Soon they were known as one of the best ad agencies in New York. After Think small, anyone who was spending money on advertising was begging whatever agency they were at to come up with the next Volkswagen campaign. DDB rose to the coveted top ten list of profitable advertising agencies, and would stay there for over a decade, dominating the awards for art and copy in that decade, and often voted Best Agency in the industry's polls.

The impact left everyone at DDB clinging to their desks, for fear they might float away in all the enthusiasm they were generating. This was before "Where's the beef?" and before "Got Milk?" No ad had caught the public's imagination in such a way.

Julian had been joking when he'd told Helmut, Stick with me and you'll be famous, but now it had come to pass. Those who knew Helmut would later remark that the success of that campaign—the risk he took with it, and the fact that it was a German car that he'd traveled "home" to meet—had a profound impact on him. He relaxed into himself a bit. "Bud" was fully Helmut now. And Julian? Well, Julian tried to shrug it all off. "I'm just a writer of short sentences," he later said.

With the success of the Volkswagen advertising, so too came a giant wave of success for the little car itself. When the big Detroit automotive companies began doing research about what it was about the VW that had made it so popular so fast, the words they came up with were the very same words Bill had used to prompt his team in making their ads: The car was "sophisticated, witty, truthful, and to the point."

The VW truly was the People's Car. According to Ford biographer Douglas Brinkley, the Volkswagen was a "modern version of the Model T" because it "helped to open car ownership to people who might not have been able to afford a new car otherwise," by giving them the opportunity of owning a new car for the same price that most American manufacturers sold used ones. It also made owning a new car an option for the young: Kids going away to college could work summer jobs and save up enough money to buy and maintain a Bug.

Volkswagen could now compete with the Big Three, selling as many as 500,000 cars *in a single season.* In the year the DDB

It's ugly, but it gets you there.

It's ugly but it gets you there—*DDB ads often took what seemed to be a product's weakness and turned it into a strength.*

ad ran, sales of the Volkswagen increased 37 percent while other European carmakers experienced a 27 percent *decrease* in export sales. One year later the small car represented 46 percent of all automobile imports to the United States and Volkswagen became the third largest automobile manufacturer *in the world.* By 1961, 5 million VWs had been produced, and Nordhoff and the factory in Wolfsburg were churning out as many as 1 million a year. At the height of production, Volkswagen would be producing one car every four seconds—a huge difference between the one car every 300 hours that had been the case when Nordhoff first came on board. By 1968 the Beetle had become the best-selling vehicle in *any* country anywhere. Five years later, it would also surpass Henry Ford's 15 million Model T sales record and be the first car to ever reach the 20 million mark.

Workers at the factory celebrate as the one millionth Volkswagen comes off the line. Nordhoff stands in front of the car, lit by the spotlight.

For Volkswagen and DDB, it was a mutual success. Bill was soon known as the "prophet of Madison Avenue." Young men and women flocked to join DDB and learn from him. In the world of advertising, the movement that formed around Bill became known as the "Creative Revolution," and in the rest of America, the sixties had truly arrived. The wave of "thinking strange" that Bill Bernbach and Jack Kerouac and Bob Dylan and others like them had felt building, and had helped to build, was finally breaking. As the tide of the 1960s washed over the country, both Bill and the Beetle became stars. Soon there wasn't an advertising party in the city that Helmut, George, and Julian could go to without being asked for their "Bernbach stories" or their artistic advice.

Bill never changed a word of Julian's Volkswagen copy; even when others in the agency objected to it, Bill stood by him. In an interview, Bill said: "What I try to do with a creative person is to take the talent that is his—his, not mine—and then help to sharpen and discipline that natural gift to make it as effective as possible." But what Bill didn't expect was that some of those creative people would eventually want to try to make it on their own, and in some cases, that would mean having to leave him. In many ways, however, it would be this very "desertion" that would solidify Bill's success.

In the course of the 1960s, the Volkswagen became a symbol of the counterculture. Flowers and peace signs were painted all over it. It was taken to concerts and demonstrations. Along with its little brother, the VW Bus, it was driven to California and back on hundreds of freewheeling road trips. The hippies thought of it as a child, a friend, looking as "alive" as it did with its big headlights, soft curves, and shy profile. As John Muir, a famous Volkswagen mechanic known for his ability to "heal" Beetles, wrote: "While the levels of logic of the human entity are many and varied, your car operates on one simple level and it's up to you to understand its trip. . . . The type of life your car contains differs from yours by time scale, logic level and conceptual anomalies but is 'Life' nonetheless." In that spirit, the garage had become the bedroom where the little car slept. By 1969, the time when Muir wrote those words, the Beetle was well established as an American icon, having grown up alongside its drivers.

The 1950s teens had been the first generation of kids to be wooed by companies and the media alike; the fifties represented the first time the young had real consumer power. This was the first generation in the United States to have the chance of owning a car *as young adults* and the first generation to drive those cars across the country to pursue their dreams—dreams of becoming a famous musician or poet, dreams of being the first in their family to go to college, or just dreams of starting over someplace new. The generation that came of age in the sixties was more physically mobile than any that had come before, and this newfound mobility and freedom automatically impacted their actions and decisions as well.

The incredible creativity that we now associate with the sixties (but which actually began with the mobility of the fifties) was a direct result of this expansion and movement. New forms of thought emerged through new interactions between races, classes, and nationalities, and this meant new forms of activism and politics. The change was also an aesthetic one—noticeable in the art, media, music, and writing that arose. As more ideas and people met and mixed, the result was often a new sound, or a new form—like the Miles Davis record *Kind of Blue,* the poems and novels of "the Beats," or, for that matter, the creative revolution in advertising. The specific change was hard to define cohesively, but whatever it was, it was all about asserting and exploring freedom, which no longer meant only physical freedom, but also freedom of the mind.

The Volkswagen ads were a kind of "emancipated advertising" in that they freed Madison Avenue from the rut in which it had (unconsciously) been stuck. But even more important, those VW ads asked people to be present, to pay attention to the details, to Think Small. Those ads spoke to people clearly, and in a tone of equality: They didn't "talk down," they just talked. And people responded because they were tired of being manipulated; they just wanted to be treated like intelligent, important members of society.

Thinking small—seeing clearly and perceiving differently—was liberating. But it was not always easy. In fact, it was often quite difficult. The sixties were a time of awakening, but those years were also full of protests, struggles over civil rights and the Vietnam War, unnecessary losses due to drugs, and heartache over the murders of some of America's most important (and controversial) leaders. Yet the overall effect—though it certainly came with a price—was one of an acceptance of greater diversity in the country, and a desire to discuss and reevaluate old norms.

Which is why, to some degree, the Volkswagen became even

more of a "People's Car" once it became the chosen car of the youth in the United States. Its very acceptance by them—the car's journey from being a product of Nazi Germany to becoming an icon of the Summer of Love—showed that this new generation, confused as it certainly still was about many things, had at least figured out that transformation *is* possible and that there *is* worth in finding new ways to see. Tied to that search for a new perception was the ability to handle difference, to allow old definitions and categories to interact and connect. In that sense, the Beetle could be the car that your professor drove, the car that you drove, or the car driven by your mom and dad. It could also be a Disney character, or show up in a Kubrick film. *Playboy* could do an article on it advising "If you are Jewish and somebody should ask you what kind of car you drive say: 'A VW, and I know, but it's a helluva solid little piece of machinery.' "

Psychologist and philosopher William James once wrote that true genius is the ability to see things in an unhabitual way. It's the greatest gift one human being can give another—the very essence of freedom—because in seeing things differently and sharing that new view, one opens up more space for communion, for confidence, and for love. Thinking small intensifies possibility, which in turn intensifies the experience and quality of one's life. The DDB ads for Volkswagen presented an unorthodox view both in the world of advertising, and in the world of the consumer. The habitual way of living in America at the time was to think big—to believe that more and bigger were the answers to life's ills—and the ads turned that accepted "fact" on its head and thus ushered in a whole new era. Thinking big *and* thinking small are powerful, and need to work in harmony to be whole.

The great German pianist Alfred Brendel has said something similar: He defines genius as the ability to combine things that have never been combined before. And what was the original Volkswagen if not a combination of things that had never been combined before? Both literally, in terms of Ferdinand Porsche's technical design, and also metaphorically, in the way it combined ideologies and nationalities and ultimately transcended them all. In the words of Julian Koenig, "This was a distinct car which demanded attention if only you let people focus on it, found a way for them to be aware that it was there." And while the campaign was indeed based on honesty and truth, it wasn't an informative but rather a creative act that, in the end, was necessary to reveal that truth. What DDB understood was that information and truth do not convince alone—people can have access to all the facts in the world, but it's only once they've connected with those facts on a human level, an emotional level, that the truth is finally obvious to them. Again, in Julian's words, "With this car, there was no reason to resist the truth. All we had to do was reveal its magic in a style that would strike a chord." In the same way that a musical note on key is obvious to the ear, so too is a warm expression of the truth: Such things can mysteriously open our hearts.

54

Bringing the art of Franz Marc to Wolfsburg in 1952 might truly have been one of the highlights of Heinrich Nordhoff's life. Marc's *Tower of Blue Horses* had moved Nordhoff as a child, and as an adult, he was still moved by it, even though now, thanks to the Nazi campaign against modern art, that very painting was lost. For those who knew Heinrich well, it was hard to think of a moment when he had ever been so innocently joyful or proud as he was on the day of the Franz Marc opening. He spent many hours at the show among Marc's paintings, and he invited everyone he knew to come.

Nordhoff had been on the job for nearly five years when he brought Franz Marc to the town. It was also the very first art exhibition ever held in Wolfsburg. In his following seventeen years as director of Volkswagen, he put a great deal of time, energy, and money into bringing as much art to Wolfsburg as he could. During the Nazi reign, all modern art had been banned. But Nordhoff—thanks to the success of the Volkswagen factory—found himself in a position to be a patron. Among the artists with exhibitions in Wolfsburg in the 1950s and 1960s were Caspar David Friedrich, Manet, Renoir, Cezanne, Matisse, Juan Gris, Marc Chagall, and van Gogh. These shows briefly made Wolfsburg a kind of cultural center in Germany, bringing thousands of Germans to the town at a time, sometimes so many that there were often not enough hotel rooms to house them all. In 1961, for Wolfsburg's sixth art show, a French Expressionist exhibition, Nordhoff wrote the introduction in the brochure. In it, he talks about how the town and the factory are an "indivisible unit" created by hardworking and attentive citizens:

These people come from many different places, but none of them comes from Wolfsburg. Of course their first and foremost urgent task is to provide the necessities of life. However, it remains an incontrovertible fact that man cannot live by bread alone and that—though I hardly dare say so in such a town—work cannot satisfy all an active man's longings. There

Heinrich Nordhoff adjusts a painting at his last art show, 1967.

*is a special need for the things of the mind amidst noisy work
and roaring machinery. By this I do not mean the seriousness
and grandeur of great thought, but also first-class artistic and
aesthetic treats of which this exhibition is a unique example,
held as it is in a town that by its own wish is, and will remain,
a workers' town.*

The Franz Marc show was clearly the one that meant the
most to Nordhoff, but of all the art shows Heinrich Nordhoff
brought to Wolfsburg, many in the town today feel that the
grandest was the show of 1967. It was an exhibit of the art of
Vincent van Gogh, and it was the first time van Gogh's work had
been displayed outside of Amsterdam. For Wolfsburg, and for
Germany, it was a momentous occasion. More than 100,000 people from all over Europe came to see the exhibit. At the opening,
as if coming full circle somehow, Nordhoff reminisced about
Wolfsburg's first art show, the "unforgettable" exhibition of
Franz Marc. Sadly, the van Gogh exhibit was the last exhibit that
Heinrich would attend.

By the time of the van Gogh exhibit, Volkswagen had become
a multinational corporation selling close to 900,000 vehicles a
year. In the past decade, the export ratio had climbed 57 percent,
meaning that every second car exported by Germany was a Volkswagen. Wolfsburg had truly become the VW town and now had a
population of 80,000. In fact, according to polls taken in the early
sixties, more than 90 percent of car owners in the town drove a
Beetle, and the primary worker in nearly three-fourths of the
city's households worked for the factory. It was still a place of immigrants and refugees to a large extent: in the 1960s, thousands of
Italians moved to Wolfsburg, and Volkswagen erected an "Italian
Village" for them. There were also Greeks, Spaniards, Dutch,
Austrians, Yugoslavs, and Turks. There were tensions, to be sure,
but the city, the factory, and the car together had become a testament to reinvention.

Ironically, Wolfsburg sat just miles away from the East German border, a place that was the epicenter of the new divisions

and tensions created by the Cold War. Because of the factory's position, because many workers at the plant were Germans who fled the Soviet Zone, and because Nordhoff had always been partial to the ideas and business models of the United States, he was not afraid to speak up about the tensions between these two worldviews. More than once in his speeches in the United States, he talked of the responsibility of auto companies to communicate more directly with one another over borders, and to be more open to trade. He spoke about the necessity of keeping tariffs low and finding ways for Western countries to join in further economic agreements, and "economically unite the Free World." The Marshall Plan, he reiterated, had been the first important step toward unification of Europe.

But Heinrich Nordhoff's views about unity were not always popular. Nor were his ideas about what was best for Volkswagen. For a decade he'd been one of the most trusted and sought-after voices in German business, but in the 1960s he found himself questioned and challenged, embroiled in conflicts about how much of the company should be owned by the government, how much should be owned by private stakeholders, and how much should go to the public in stocks. There was also heated debate about whether or not VW should expand its line, or buy other lines like Audi, for example. Nordhoff only wanted to continue making Beetles, even at a time when to many others it was obvious that Volkswagen needed more than just one kind of car. Up until that point, the Beetle and the VW Bus were their only two cars on the market, and as the sixties were coming to an end, many at Volkswagen felt they saw signs that the success of the original Beetle had reached a plateau. New technologies and new safety concerns had surfaced, and many of VW's board worried that other companies would soon pull far ahead of VW if they did not modernize their brand.

With the government, and with VW's council and board, Nordhoff now found himself on the losing end of the arguments at times. Simultaneously, the German automobile industry, after an unprecedented boom in the 1950s, was tipping into its first recession since the end of the war; indeed, its first recession since the German people had been motorized. Nordhoff took all of these problems and fights very personally, and his health began to suffer as a result.

Nordhoff firmly believed there was an "organic harmony" between the workers and the management, an idea he'd adapted from the writings of Franz Marc. Nordhoff put his workers on a pedestal just as surely as they put him on one: He gave them higher wages and dividends (for the course of Nordhoff's years of management, wages would be at least 5 percent higher than those at any other German automotive plant), he made them partners in the company, and he told them again and again that they were an example of the best Prussian traditions of good quality work, discipline, selflessness, and modesty.

But Nordhoff's philosophy was at times eerily close to the NSDAP's idea of "working toward the führer": He felt that he knew what was best for the company, that it should be he who made the final decisions, and above all, he demanded loyalty. Anyone who left the company, for example, was not allowed to return, and he was firmly against any unions or workers retaining any authority that could conflict with his own. Because he had taken over the factory at a time when workplaces were undergoing the slow transition from the authoritatively installed sense of obedience to the new democratic one of individuality and choice, Nordhoff's way worked through the 1950s and early 1960s. It also worked because he really did care about the workers and because he really did have their best interests at heart. But the balance in such matters can be precarious; by the late 1960s, many felt Nordhoff had too much power and that he was no longer using it to make the wisest decisions.

After Nordhoff turned sixty-five—the age when most German executives retired—more and more people began to ask him to choose a successor and step down. Nordhoff delayed that decision for as long as he could. His ultimate plan was to retire in 1969, just as he turned seventy years old. But many wondered if he would ever be able to actually leave. Here was a man who had given ten hours a day, six and sometimes seven days a week of his life—for nearly twenty years—to the same company. Naturally it was hard for him to imagine leaving, or to separate his job from his own sense of self. Nevertheless, the role he played was just that: a role. And the role of manager of Volkswagen had to be filled by someone else, it had to go on without Nordhoff, and certainly he knew that. But nevertheless, he could not seem to let go.

In 1968, Nordhoff was finally pressured into agreeing to name a successor. At about just that time, his heart began to fail. He spent months in the hospital but eventually recovered enough to return to work (albeit cutting his time to forty hours a week). But when news came that the VW board of directors had voted to push his January 1969 retirement date up to March 21, 1968, it was one of the hardest blows of his life. He took it absolutely personally, and he did not know how to cope. In his desperate moment, in an act of avoidance and panic, he zoomed off to Baden-Baden—the very same spa town where Ferdinand

At the peak of his popularity, and as Wolfsburg becomes a "gold rush town," Nordhoff stands for this iconic photo with the factory and its workers.

Porsche had once been arrested by the French—and tried to conduct his business meetings there as if nothing were wrong. It was the Ides of March.

On the flight back to Wolfsburg, however, he collapsed. He was given oxygen and taken to the hospital as soon as the plane landed. A few weeks later, on Good Friday of 1968, Heinrich Nordhoff lay in his hospital bed and asked Charlotte, his wife of thirty-eight years, his best friend for nearly fifty, if she wouldn't mind having a glass of champagne with him. He was feeling better, and he wanted to celebrate. She rushed home and got his favorite bottle of champagne, and together with their daughter, Barbara, they sat in the hospital room in Wolfsburg and enjoyed a toast. Heinrich wrote out a few Easter cards and arranged to have gifts delivered to old friends. Then, late that afternoon, just before sunset, he died. Charlotte was there with him.

A few days later, Nordhoff's funeral was held in one of Volkswagen's giant factory halls. The workers all came, standing in a line that stretched down the long straight road running parallel to the factory, waiting to say their goodbyes. When his body was transported to the gravesite (in a cut-off Volkswagen Bus), the citizens of Wolfsburg crowded the streets, honoring him as he passed, saying their own silent goodbyes. Today, more than forty years after his death, it's doubtful there is a person in Wolfsburg who has not heard of Heinrich Nordhoff.

Part Five

. o o

Still Going . . .

All difficult things have their origin in that which is easy,
and great things in that which is small.

—Lao Tzu

On August 15, 1969, cars full of hundreds of thousands of young people jammed the New York State Thruway, causing the entire road to completely shut down for a time. The traffic was so heavy that people began simply abandoning their cars and walking the final miles toward their destination: the large farm that would forever be known as Woodstock.

Those three days of music and communal life still live on in the nation's collective psyche, even for the many generations born long after Woodstock took place. Over the years, the festival has taken on a somewhat mythical aura; it has solidified in America's collective memory as one of the most definitive statements

A Beetle in the traffic jam on the way to Woodstock.

of the American counterculture, the zenith of the hippie movement, that iconic place where Jimi Hendrix's guitar half-sang and half-wept the national anthem, expressing the tumultuous experience of a country that was torn, having just experienced one of the worst years in American history, a year in which both Martin Luther King, Jr. and Bobby Kennedy had been shot.

Today, attending large concerts or festivals is something many of us have done, but such events were not a common occurrence in 1969. And even by today's standards, Woodstock remains an awesome mass event. Today, at capacity, Madison Square Garden in New York City can hold about 19,700 people. With around 500,000 attendees at its peak, Woodstock had approximately twenty times that amount of people coming together (and living together!) on the same plot of land for three days, one of the first times so many had come together to commune through music. At a time of great conflict and pain in America—alongside the murders of King and RFK, John F. Kennedy had been assassinated earlier in the decade, and the war in Vietnam raged and divided the American public to a degree that had not been seen since the Civil War—the youth came together in a spirit of celebration, love, and hope. And the country noticed: Woodstock was the moment when the people in America who had once been considered misfits began to transform into the very people whose voices would endure.

Woodstock could not have happened without the revolutions in transportation and communication that had taken place over the previous twenty years. The Woodstock festival was held on a piece of farmland that could be reached only by car. Pictures taken by people on their way to the festival show roads dotted with Volkswagen Bugs and Buses. True to the dream out of which it was created, the Volkswagen had become the first car to motorize the German population, but it had also become the first car for many young people in other countries, including America, as evidenced by the driving choices of the generation that created and attended Woodstock. But the car had also been embraced by Americans of all ages and all walks of life. In fact,

A flower-painted Beetle at Woodstock.

it was America that first named the car the Beetle: the *New York Times,* viewing the car in 1938, had called it a "beetle," and years later, once the car began to sell in the States, the name stuck. Later, it was even translated to German and officially adopted by Volkswagen; the car was called "*der Käfer*" (beetle) there, too. Ferdinand Porsche's design had not only endured; it had become the symbol for a whole new generation. And it still looked almost exactly the same as it had in those early sketches that had littered his workshop's floor.

But just as Woodstock was the climax of a revolutionary decade, 1969 was the year when the original Beetle design reached the climax of its tremendous popularity. That climax was both a kind of ending and a moment of new beginnings. Jimi Hendrix and Janis Joplin died in 1970, and Jim Morrison followed them in 1971. The war in Vietnam came to a close. The Civil Rights bill (passed in 1964 thanks to the support of President Lyndon Johnson) was coming into effect, and desegregation and a newfound respect for diversity slowly began to take root. The political youth movement dwindled, changing form. The country began to stabilize, to recover from the aftermath of the war and the deaths of many great political leaders and cultural icons, but the voices that had defined the sixties would persist. Over time, the memory of those influential men and women gave the country new strength and inspiration; their unnecessary deaths at such young ages motivated others to search for greater clarity. Many legends would emerge from the 1960s, and in its own small way, the Volkswagen Beetle would be among them.

Throughout the 1970s, the original Beetle design would become known as one of the most versatile pieces of technology (especially automotive technology) in the world, with its engine being used to power everything from the Zamboni ice resurfacer to the landmark rotating Mercedes-Benz sign that sits on top of the Europa Center in the heart of old West Berlin. That same design had also led to the creation of the beautiful Karmann Ghia, a coupe and convertible that was produced from 1955 to 1974 by VW, which used the basic mechanics and chassis of the Beetle.

In total, 21.5 million Beetles had been sold by 1979, having surpassed the Model T's sales record as early as 1973. But as the seventies came to a close, the new market of small and affordable cars that had sprung up in response to the Beetle's popularity—alongside new technology, new regulations in emissions and safety standards, and the switch to using unleaded gasoline—slowly eased the original VW out of production. Wolfsburg introduced a new staple car—the Volkswagen Golf. The generation that grew up in the 1980s in Germany is sometimes referred to as the "Generation Golf," because so many of them bought the car, which was modern and fresh with state-of-the-art technology. Thus the old Beetle vanished quickly from the German market. And although the Golf didn't sell well in the United States (where it was known as the Rabbit), as Germany slowed and eventually stopped production on the original Beetle, it soon disappeared from the American market as well. The last original Bug was sold in the United States in 1979.

The Beetle was born in Germany and became an American star, but it was in Mexico that it got its last and perhaps sweetest farewell. Though it was no longer sold in Europe or the States, the original design continued to be produced in Mexico and Brazil until 2003. But at 9:05 a.m., on July 30, 2003, the very last Volkswagen of the original Porsche design (number 21,529,464) rolled off the assembly line to the sound of a mariachi band. As the musicians played *"El Rey"* ("The King"), preparations were made for the car to be transferred to Wolfsburg where it would live the rest of its days in the Wolfsburg Auto Museum. The last original Beetle was painted a sweet Aquarius blue, and its headlights looked surprisingly large underneath all the flowers that were placed on its hood that day.

In many ways, the Beetle was Mexico's first People's Car too—its presence there was and is very strong. Because the people were so sad to see the original little Beetle go, a whole campaign was created to say goodbye to it. One of the television ads showed a very small parking space. Each big car that tried to fit into the space failed and had to leave. Finally, the words *Es increíble que un auto tan pequeño deje un vacío tan grande* (It is incredible that a car so small can leave such a large void) fill the screen. A memorable print ad showed a 1964 Beetle on one side of the page and a 2003 Mexican Beetle on the other. The 1964 Beetle was the very model that was made the year the factory had opened in Puebla, and the 2003 Beetle was the last original Beetle to be produced there. Underneath the first car were the words *Erase una vez . . .* (Once upon a time . . .) and underneath the second car *Fin* (The end).

But was it?

When Franz Marc (the young artist who had made such an impression on the adolescent Heinrich Nordhoff) was fighting in the First World War, he wrote in a letter home: "An observation

that has plagued me through my military life is the eternal return of the same types of people. I often feel that there exists
only a limited number of individual human types . . . In the
same sense, 'events' are repeated unbelievably often if one has a
somewhat somnambulistic feeling for this and 'sees' them . . . It
is not an idle thought, for it reaches deeply into the secret of
artistic creation; perhaps it is even its explanation . . . The True
has always been true. . . . "

Many economists, politicians, mathematicians, writers, philosophers, and artists have spoken of this idea of repeating
events and reincarnations; for example, Nietzsche's theory of
eternal recurrence, Jung's studies on archetypes, or Ernst Haeck-
el's biological analyses and drawings collected in *Art Forms in
Nature.* Indeed, when looking at many of the themes that rever-
berate through the VW story—the destruction caused by war,
the idea of "making the world safe for democracy," discussions
about the free market and capitalism, the balance between manipulation and persuasion, and struggles over human and civil
rights—it does seem that these motifs have recurred again and
again in different ways and at different times throughout the
history of civilization itself.

Toward the end of the 1990s (when I was a teenager), a lot of
the music we listened to, the clothes we wore, and even the
ideas we had about politics and peace and war were recurring
from the 1960s, a decade whose narrative we'd all somehow
absorbed. We were attracted to that narrative for reasons we
didn't really understand but that had to do with things teenagers instinctively hunger for—exploration, acceptance within a
group, something to take you outside of yourself and connect
you to a bigger picture—and our ideas of Woodstock, Jimi Hendrix, Dylan, The Doors, John Lennon, Miles Davis, Andy Warhol, and the reverberating legacies of men like John F. and
Robert Kennedy and Martin Luther King Jr., became ways for us
to connect to that bigger picture: They might've represented the
spirit of the 1960s, but that spirit was alive and potent for us.

As Thomas Frank writes in *The Conquest of Cool,* many

Americans who became teenagers in the 1990s "understand 'the sixties' almost instinctively as the decade of the big change, the birthplace of our own culture, the homeland of hip, an era of which the tastes and discoveries and passions, however obscure their origins, have somehow determined the world in which we are condemned to live." As 1990s teenagers, we were different from teens of the 1950s, and the notion that had changed us was what the 1960s had come to represent: As young people, we were more collectively aware of the power that *the people* can have, especially young people, and of the complex responsibility that such freedom entails.

With the 1990s being so linked to the 1960s in its recurring themes, it's no surprise (in retrospect) that the '90s were the decade that gave the Beetle new life. Just about anyone in the 1990s would have said the primary image—and often the *only* image—that came to mind when the word "Volkswagen" was heard was the Beetle. Yet the Beetle was no longer for sale, and hadn't been for over ten years. Two young designers, J Mays and Freeman Thomas, who were working for the Audi Volkswagen design studio started to ask: Why? *Why* wasn't there a Beetle? In the years since the original Beetle had gone off the market, the car's reputation had only grown; it seemed it could be possible to bring back the Bug or to make a whole *new* Bug. The very idea was thrilling, and Mays and Thomas worked earnestly on a new design for the car. The style they came up with was basic and geometric; in profile, it looks like just three semicircles: one big one (the body) placed on two smaller ones, which represent the wheels. The design carried all the simplicity and playfulness that people remembered and loved from the original Bug. Many comments were made about how soft and feminine it was; Ferdinand Porsche's grandson, Ferdinand Piëch (the man who would eventually succeed Carl Hahn as chairman of the board of management of Volkswagen), even described it as "womb-like."

The concept car for the New Beetle (called Concept One) was created in the early 1990s and first shown at the 1994 Detroit Auto Show, but with utmost secrecy, as Germany had not yet committed to producing it. Many doubted they would ever commit. But the response in the United States was huge. People were ecstatic over the car. There was clearly a desire for Concept One to become a reality; the American people wanted a New Beetle. Word about Concept One spread fast after the show, and car magazines went wild discussing it, speculating about whether it would ever be built. Major publications like the *Wall Street Journal* even put the car design on their front pages. For such a small car, the New Beetle was a very big deal.

However, Wolfsburg didn't want to make another Beetle. The Volkswagen managers felt it was "too emotional," and they weren't comfortable with the translation gap that existed in the way Americans and Germans saw the car; this would be a car built *just* for the American market, it seemed, and that was a risky venture. The Golf had remained the star of Wolfsburg, the European bestseller, and it was a very modern, very "rational" car. Those were the kinds of cars that the Volkswagen managers wanted to continue producing. They had no desire to harken back to a bygone era or design.

But popular desire for the car in the United States was so strong that the German executives eventually gave in. They said they would build Mays and Freeman's Concept One (it would be called the New Beetle), but they absolutely required it to be modern and up to the German VW standard of quality. Thus it would be built using the Golf platform. The original Porsche design with the engine in the back would no longer be part of the new design. One ad for the New Beetle said it best: "The engine's in the front, but its heart's in the same place."

It was a good thing the executives at Wolfsburg listened to J Mays and Thomas Freeman: The New Beetle literally saved Volkswagen of America. According to automotive writer David

Kiley, "by 1993, sales were so far in the toilet and the company was losing so much money that talk of leaving the U.S. was on the table in Germany." It was the New Beetle that put Volkswagen back on the map in the States. The discussion of Concept One marked the first time Volkswagen had really been back in the American public news sphere since the glory days of the original Beetle. Publicity built up alongside anticipation for the car. People were on tenterhooks wondering if a New Beetle would indeed come to be. And this anticipation alone made Volkswagen a brand Americans began to reconsider.

When the New Beetle was finally unveiled at its first public auto show in 1998, four years after Concept One had been developed, people cheered. The event had the feel of a class reunion or a sports match, not a corporate event. In celebration of the new model, VW had created a car covered in heat-sensitive paint that would change colors when touched. The car gave off a warm vibe that harkened back to its heyday in the sixties. In fact, when the car was first introduced to the press, the event was decorated with life-size posters of Jimi Hendrix, John Lennon, and Janis Joplin, and most of the guests came dressed in tie-dyed clothing. When it went on the market in March 1998, the car was a huge hit, with more than 55,000 sold in the United States by the end of the year. Mays and Freeman had done something that hadn't been done before *anywhere*: They had created a successful new design based on a well-known model from the past; they had kept the *soul* of a car intact, even as they changed its look.

The 1998 New Beetle remained on the U.S. market from 1998 until 2010. A total of 477,347 cars were sold during this time. Mays and Freeman were celebrities themselves after designing the New Bug. Funnily and fittingly enough, they went on to become head designers at Ford, the home of the Model T, the original "People's Car."

(57)

Maybe it was some of that same conflicted spirit from the 1960s, rekindled in the 1990s of my teenage years, that I sensed on that evening in 2007 when, three years after having graduated from college and moved to Germany, I was unexpectedly captivated by the glowing city of Wolfsburg. That night, riding back to Berlin from the countryside, I'd come upon the city by surprise, and from that moment on, for reasons I am still trying to understand, it was a place I could not forget. The glowing smokestacks, the huge glass buildings and doors and walls, the whole strange, electric feeling I'd had in passing through the town—all of that stuck like a bur in my mind, and soon I found myself on a train heading back to Wolfsburg.

It was all very confusing at first. In looking for the story of the Beetle, I was trying to reconcile my ideas of Nazi Germany with my ideas of the Summer of Love, and the city itself was an odd new reality for me. Having never even heard of Wolfsburg before that moment when I saw its lights, I had no idea of its history, and I had no idea what to expect. Traveling there was one of those trips you take when you sit and wonder the whole time, "why am I doing this again?" I had set off with little more than a printout from GoogleMaps containing directions from the Wolfsburg train station to the Wolfsburg Auto Museum; wanting to understand how the town was connected to the Bug, I'd thought the Auto Museum would be the right place to start.

Arriving on the train into Wolfsburg is an experience that still captivates me (and I've since been there many, many times). The small, almost bucolic train station does nothing to prepare you for what you see as soon as you pull into town. The towering brick presence of the VW factory seems to rise out of nowhere, then stays in your field of vision, regardless of where you move.

The factory takes up the entire opposing bank of the canal

that runs in a straight line parallel to the train station, so it is "standing right beside you" as soon as you disembark. The towering brick is a dirty industrial red, like something a Charles Dickens character might see walking down a grimy nineteenth-century London street. Simple, geometric, sturdy: one literal mile connected from start to end like a rusty paper that has been bent into long rectangular folds and then unfurled. Its dramatic length plays with the horizon: From the fat power station and its four brick smokestacks, a string of connected brick cubes push in and out as far as the eye can see, finally shooting upward again into the high-rise of executive quarters at the far end. Smack in the middle of the power station's main wall there glows a giant blue-and-white VW sign, like a cyclopean eye watching over the city. I was told that if this sign were flat on the ground, you could drive a People's Car in a perfect continuous U-turn all the way around it.

Henry Ford once said "The man who builds a factory builds a temple. The man who works there, worships there." And there is indeed a feeling of reverence that comes with seeing the old VW factory stretched out across the bank, separated from the canal by a singular, long lonely road, giving it an unobstructed imposition, like a benevolent giant. Its southern façade seems to have its chest puffed out, nestled up close to the water with a further angle of pooled river cut in front like a moat. I would get a strange feeling sometimes when I walked near the factory and thought of the flood of foreign and German workers who'd poured over the bridges and through the tunnels to take up jobs there, of the British soldiers who made it their home once the Nazi regime had been beaten, of the DDB team, or of Nordhoff, Ferry, and Porsche. Realizing that all those men have also walked the grounds, the heavy brick factory transforms into a testament to what the car has endured.

In Wolfsburg today, the tradition of art and creativity that was started and nurtured by Nordhoff has become a staple of the town. Carl Hahn, the young man whom Nordhoff sent to New York to head Volkswagen of America, eventually moved back to Wolfsburg with his wife and children in 1964, and continued the city's legacy of artistic patronage when he became the chairman of the board of management at Volkswagen. The old Castle Wolfsburg, for example, which was home to a group of artists in the 1950s known as the Schloss Strasse 8 (Castle Street 8), is now full of art organizations, including a museum dedicated to the castle's history (and the history of Wolfsburg), the esteemed City-Galerie Wolfsburg, and the lively Verein Junge Kunst (Young Art Association). And while the city is small, it is packed full of architectural gems, diverse works that have a kind of futuristic quality to them. There are two unique minimalist churches and one cultural center designed by the great Finnish architect Alvar Aalto; a long, modern theater built by another architectural great, Hans Scharoun, and, most recently, and perhaps most visually spectacular and strange, there is the Phaeno Science Center, a building shaped like a stretched rhombus that sits by the train station, just across the canal from the factory and Autostadt, designed by Iraqi-British architect Zaha Hadid.

The Zaha Hadid building, the Phaeno Science Center, in Wolfsburg. This building sits across the canal from the factory, and is one of the first sites seen upon arrival at the train station.

There is also the magnificent Kunstmuseum (the Wolfsburg Art Museum), one of Carl Hahn's pet projects, a looming bastion of metal created by renowned architect Peter Schweger, prominently located in the center of town, facing the Volkswagen factory from the far end of Porschestrasse.

The factory on one end of the city, the art museum on the other, both connected by one long, pedestrian walkway—it's hard to imagine a better testament to the legacy of Heinrich Nordhoff.

In addition to all these wonderful, unique structures, there is another attraction, one that draws around two million visitors to the city annually. Sitting to the north of the VW factory, this giant enclosed enclave of landscaped vistas and buildings wrapped up in luminescent glass and steel is called the *Autostadt*. At Wolfsburg's inception, rather than using the lugubrious name of The Town of the Strength through Joy Car, as Hitler christened it, most people (when they were not in Hitler's presence) called the city the Autostadt, the Auto City, and now this name refers to a cultural center and theme park. Today, if you arrive at the right moment in Wolfsburg, you'll get caught in a herd of tourists and visitors heading to the Autostadt. You are led toward it as soon as you exit the train station; moving sidewalks go over the bridge and deposit you in its mouth. When I first saw the signs for it, I thought it might be the Auto Museum that I was looking for, but as I soon found out, the Autostadt and the Auto Museum are two very different things.

The Autostadt is a miniature Epcot Center, or a modern, extended World's Fair, stretching across twenty-five acres. It was designed in large part by Gunter Henn, one of Germany's most famous architects, but hundreds of other architects have taken part in the conception of its structures and projects. Renowned international artists often "curate" the car pavilions and events. The result is that the entire place feels like an enclave of modern art and architectural development, and the strange ponds of water, mounds of earth, and vegetation between the various buildings and marquees creates an almost alien environment; everything is so carefully sculpted and unique. When I was there, I even found myself wondering if the ducks swimming in the Autostadt ponds were real (they are!) because they swim in such perfect fashion, as if designed to play their part.

The Autostadt is a cultural hub as much as it is a tourist attraction: Classes and events are common occurrences—everything from sold-out rock concerts (Sting was there during one of my stays) and dance festivals to yoga lessons and self-help groups. There are numerous restaurants and bars. There's a day care center. There are theaters that show 3-D films about mobility, a guided walk through the evolution of roads, and the longest printed line in the world. There are also all sorts of multimedia, interactive activities (some of which change regularly), everything from a program to calculate your carbon footprint, to areas where you can learn how to design a car. Visitors can also learn about various fuels and modes of engine propulsion, about the impact of automobiles on the environment, or about the stock market in relation to automotive business models. There's an obstacle course for adults, little baby electric Beetles for the kids to drive, and a posh Ritz-Carlton where people can spend the night and swim in a heated pool that looks up at the giant brick Volkswagen factory.

There are also seven pavilions dedicated to car manufactur-

A picture from inside the Autostadt.

ers at the Autostadt, one for Volkswagen itself, and one each for its "daughter" companies. Volkswagen is not only Volkswagen, after all: It also owns Audi, Bentley, Bugatti, Lamborghini, Seat, and Škoda—the VW parent company calls these brands its daughters, and each of these brands have their own building in the Autostadt.

But the centerpiece of Henn's Autostadt design is a huge glass-and-steel, five-floored building called the ZeitHaus (House of Time), where more than eighty vintage cars from various companies and designers are showcased. In the other pavilions of the Autostadt, you can see a Lamborghini, a Bugatti, and an Audi A2 circa 2001, but in the House of Time, you can see these brands aslongside classic Cadillacs and Jaguars, a 1922 Rolls-Royce Silver Ghost, one of Ford's Model Ts, and a replica of one of the first gasoline-powered Benz automobiles. And of course there are also remade models of Porsche's prototypes for the Bug, a replica of Porsche's NSU car, a replica of one of the original V3, a Porsche 356, and that millionth rhinestone-studded "German tart" that Julian and George saw on their Wolfsburg trip.

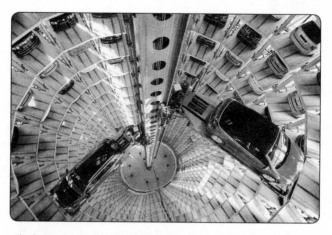

The large glass towers that hold the cars customers have purchased. A large robot picks the car up and brings it down to "greet" the customer in the Autostadt.

The Autostadt opened in May 2000. By then, VW had spent about 430 million euros on the project. Now the place sees two million visitors a year and has been the template—much like Ford's factory was the template for the VW factory all those years ago—for a host of new German museums that have sprung up in the past decade, all of them top tourist sites, and all of them worth the traveling time to see. The Autostadt is also the place where people from all over Germany (and the world) can come to pick up their new Volkswagens. They can order their cars from any local dealership in their hometown, specifying what features they'd like. Then the cars are made according to each purchaser's requirements and delivered to the Autostadt where the customers come to meet them. Volkswagen gives each customer free tickets to the Autostadt, free lunch, and a tour of the factory. Then, they can watch as their personal car is delivered from two giant, 200-foot-tall glass towers that hold the new cars like Cabbage Patch Kids waiting for their homes. The magnificent towers are connected through a tunnel to the factory, and you can see the cars moving along the assembly line. Volkswagen staff then introduces each individual to their car, showing off all the car's special details and parts. At the end of the day, customers can get into their new VW and drive away through giant doors.

In some way, the Autostadt is one giant advertisement, a public relations stunt on par with anything ever done by the likes of Edward Bernays. In another way, it is a piece of modern art, a way of using the corporate world to advance the creative one. Perhaps the Autostadt is the perfect symbol of Wolfsburg because it is a microcosm of all the worlds that Wolfsburg has always teetered between: that balance between the organic and the ersatz, between persuasion and manipulation, between the profit-oriented and the gift. Being so technical and modern, and yet also being a place totally devoted to the love of cars, it's certainly a place where emotion and reason are allowed to collide.

The cars in the Autostadt are beautiful, and the Autostadt itself is an incredible place, but I can understand why so many

Beetle lovers say that the Auto Museum is where they feel they are truly in the presence of the spirit of the Bug. The Auto Museum is not part of the Autostadt. The Auto Museum was built in the 1980s, and it doesn't look as if it's had any real renovations since that time. Architecturally and in terms of presentation, it's the total opposite of the modern, slick, alien-egg-like Autostadt. And it is also less visible. Whereas the Autostadt is directly beside the factory and impossible to miss, the unassuming Auto Museum is out of the way, at the outskirts of the main strip of town, and a place you have to know about to find. It looks like an abandoned elementary school from the 1950s, and there are tiny, childlike pictures of Beetles stenciled on its pale concrete one-story walls. Inside, the place feels a bit like a garage, and even smells of rubber and oil. Admission is six euros, and the front desk will give you a little pin of the blue-and-white VW "eye" to wear, a miniature version of the logo that hangs on the car factory's outer wall.

At the Auto Museum, once you've walked down a long hall lined with the German versions of the DDB ads for the car, the museum opens out into a warehouse filled with a rainbow of Volkswagen Bugs. Natural light streams in from the high thin windows, mixing with the soft light of overhead lamps. Herbie the Love Bug is here, and so is a Beetle that is made entirely from Legos. There is a Beetle that swam the Straits of Messina, a Beetle made from wicker, and another carved entirely from wood. But it's the real thing, the original cars made only to be cars, that draw the most attention—Beetles from the '40s, '50s, '60s, '70s, on and on to that last original Beetle that was produced in Mexico in the hot summer of 2003. From afar, they all look exactly the same; only their colors set them apart, and yet somehow, they appear to have wholly distinct personalities, perched there with their round faces and sweet eyes.

The first time I went, I felt as though I was at a petting zoo. There are signs everywhere begging customers not to touch the cars, and yet the Bugs are smudged with fingerprints. It's like everyone turns into a kid as soon as they go through the door.

And everyone stops to sign the guest book on their way out, thankful to have some way of expressing the happiness they feel. The book is splayed wide on a wooden table, and its pages are fat with exclamation marks and hearts and drawings of Beetles that visitors have done, most of them anthropomorphized (one entry shows the car wearing a New York Mets baseball cap). There are entries in Spanish, German, French, and Japanese. On my first trip, I saw an entry from a man from Wyoming that said: *Hello again wonderful place. This is my 3rd visit. There's nothing better than this!* Then, a couple wrote: *This is our favorite place in the world!* (And they were from *Hawaii*!) A young man from the United Kingdom used an entire page to describe how he'd just celebrated his thirtieth birthday at Wolfsburg: *That's one lifetime ambition fulfilled,* he wrote.

One of the first original Volkswagen Beetles that I saw during my initial visit to the Auto Museum was a baby blue 1960 edition, the last car Heinrich Nordhoff drove before his death, one that was built based on the 1949 model that Ben Pon first took over to the United States. When I first saw this car and read Nordhoff's name on the plaque beside it, I had yet to know who he was. Years later when I went back, after completing all my research, it was this car I wanted most to see. I liked knowing that I was in the presence of the same little blue car that Nordhoff had driven to work.

Does it seem too sentimental that people talk this way about the car and its birthplace? I might have thought so at first. But not anymore. Now when I am in the Auto Museum I am just like all the other fans. It's one of those places that allows you to remember when your parents handed you the keys to your first car, or the time you went on your first road trip, or that moment when you had your first kiss, or whatever other memories and emotions you might associate with a beloved car. No matter your age, it is one of those places that gives you permission to be young.

58

George Lois, at the age of eighty, is still a wildfire of words and energy. This is the man who came up with the slogan "I want my MTV," the man behind many infamous *Esquire* covers of the 1960s, the man who helped make Tommy Hilfiger a fashion star—and George will gladly tell you all about it himself. He's got no qualms about announcing his accomplishments. Julian Koenig—the man behind the Timex watch slogan "it takes a lickin' and keeps on tickin'," the man who worked on RFK's campaign (both JFK and RFK were impressed by "Think small"), and the man who named Earth Day (while working on Senator Gaylord Nelson's 1969 committee that first established Earth Day, Julian came up with the name, which just so happens to rhyme with "birthday" and fall on his birthday!)—is also extraordinary in person. But at ninety years old, Julian is quieter, calmer, less glamorous, more contemplative and philosophical than George. Julian has plenty of witty stories and jokes, but he only offers them when asked, and he's less concerned with listing his accomplishments than with being precise.

When I first asked Julian about some of the anecdotes I'd heard from George about their time together in Wolfsburg, Julian simply looked at me and said: "Do you know anything about George?" After a pensive pause, he went on: "I read what George wrote about our trip to Wolfsburg, and it's an inaccurate description. It stars George." And that's true: George has published books about the business of advertising, and the stories in them do undoubtedly tend to center around George. Even so, somehow he avoids coming off as an egomaniac; rather he appears as a man with maybe a bit too much energy, a man who finds it hard to stop. He exaggerates, but perhaps only because he is so caught up in the story that he wants it to have the same effect on others that it once had on him. Another thing about

George: talking with him, one gets the sense he has always looked up to Julian Koenig.

Julian has plenty of good things to say about George too. "We were buddies," he says, talking about those early days at DDB. "He and I got on very well. We did good work together. And it was always very swift. That's the thing with George. You get an ad instantly. With Helmut I can remember sitting there for two hours and he wouldn't put my headline down. He would just sit there and hesitate and stare at his board . . . George is the best art director I've ever worked with, in the sense of satisfaction. He would do something instantly, and with enthusiasm. With Helmut it was always relentless." But Helmut and Julian had a lot of genuine respect for each other too, and you can see it in Julian's eyes when he remembers him. "We were close," Julian says, "but it was never easy with Helmut, it was always uphill."

These days, however, with Helmut no longer around to take part, and regardless of the respect they obviously have for each other, it's George and Julian who have the heady disagreements, disagreements that go back to the Volkswagen campaign. The VW campaign was a moment in history that has followed them their entire lives, not only because it was such a success, but because of everything that came after. George had nothing to do directly with Think Small or Lemon or any of the other DDB Beetle ads. He was in the environment, "consulting" in a *very* broad sense, but the truth is, he didn't like Helmut's layout for Think Small at first, and he had no influence on Julian's copy at all. Over the years, however, George has sometimes been mistakenly credited for those ads, and he hasn't gone out of his way to speak up for Julian, or to set the record straight. Likewise, when reading George's books (the first of which was written over forty years ago) and interviews, as time passes some of the "good stories" that are attributed to Julian (and others) in the earlier accounts do indeed become attributed to George in the later stories, though it doesn't seem malicious so much as a trick of age and memory and ego.

DDB and VW tied George and Julian together, but that was

The founders of the second creative agency in the world: Fred Papert, Julian Koenig, and George Lois, 1962.

just the beginning of a long partnership and the first of many famous advertising campaigns. Not long after those first VW ads began sending their shock waves through the country, George and Julian were approached by another friend in the business named Fred Papert. Papert made a radical proposition: George and Julian should leave DDB and start their own creative agency.

"I knew there couldn't be only one creative agency," George later said. Papert's proposal struck a chord. It was 1960. The time seemed right. And there was the desire to see if they had the talent to succeed without Bill. In any case, they were not leaving because they had any problems with Bill. If anything, they were leaving because they wanted to be more like him. The three men even styled their name after Doyle Dane Bernbach: "Papert Koenig Lois," no commas. George insisted on being the third position in the title because he wanted his name to be in the same position that Bill's name was at DDB.

But even once they had put their plans into motion, they put off telling Bill the news. It wasn't until late December 1960 that they made their way to his office. They both wore dress coats, an unusual sight at Doyle Dane Bernbach. They met at the elevator at an appointed hour. The first time they had tried to go to

Bill's office to break the news, Julian had instead taken the elevator down to the lobby and gone home. But by the second attempt, they managed to make it through Bill's open door. As soon as he saw the two in their dress coats, he must have known something was up. "We go into the room and we don't have anything in our hands," George says. "No ads or anything to show him like usual, so Bill was cautious. He goes and sits behind the desk in the corner of the room—I'd never in my life seen Bill sit behind a desk before."

"I told him we were leaving," Julian recalls.

"Julian said we were leaving," George says. "But he said it just like that, 'Bill, we're leaving,' and so I had to jump in and try and smooth it out. I told him we were very excited about starting the second creative agency, thinking he'd be proud of that."

But Bill was hurt, not proud. "There can only be one creative agency in the world," he told them. It felt like a punch in the stomach to Julian and George. They stammered out something about how it could work "just so long as we model ourselves after you." That softened Bill a bit. "I don't want to lose ya," he said. "This is just something we feel in our gut, Bill," George replied. "It's just something we have to do." And what could Bill say? He had once done the same thing himself, hadn't he? "It's not about the money," George said. "We're not taking a single one of your accounts." That itself was quite an unusual move, a sign of how much Julian and George respected Bill. After all, when Bill had left Grey all those years before, he'd taken the Ohrbach's account with him. He probably wouldn't have been able to leave had he not. As Julian and George left his office for the last time, Bill gave them both long hugs. "Just know you've always got a home here," he said. And they knew he meant it.

Helmut Krone was not happy to hear what Julian and George had planned. Not only did he feel left out, and not only did it seem that Julian had "sided" with George, he also thought they were simply crazy: Even if they'd asked Helmut, there's no way he would have left DDB then. Like Bill, Helmut thought there could be only one creative agency, and that was Bill's agency. Like so many others, he just didn't think DDB's model would work anywhere else. When Helmut saw Julian and George walking together through Bryant Park just after they'd resigned, he called out a mocking "cuckoo-cuckoo." And he wasn't the only one: A lot of people at DDB saw them as traitors, or thought they were setting themselves up to fail.

As it turned out, however, there could indeed be more than one creative agency in town. In fact, all of Madison Avenue would eventually use the same arrangement Bill had pioneered. It is a transformation that has since been called the Creative Revolution of advertising. It happened in the late 1960s when the entire advertising establishment, mirroring the counterculture as it challenged the status quo, began a structural reorganization, eventually throwing out many of its old policies and ways.

It might seem like Bill's students were rejecting him by leaving, but in reality, it was the ultimate sign of his success. DDB didn't suffer; it actually benefited from their departure. In fact, it was perhaps Julian and George's move that truly solidified Bill Bernbach as a name everyone on Madison Avenue knew, the leader of a revolution, a man who transformed the structure of advertising and instigated a new norm on Madison Avenue. It was by leaving Bill that his "students" spread his philosophy and ideas, and DDB became a kind of "founding father." In 1965, *Advertising Age* wrote: "It is quite possible that the effect of DDB is as culturally significant as that of, let us say, writers such as Mickey Spillane, Kerouac, Ernest Hemingway, or artists such as Paul Klee, [or] Andy Warhol. . . . " By the 1980s, a whole new generation of advertising agencies such as Wieden+Kennedy (inventors of Nike's Just Do It ads), Goodby, Silverstein (Got Milk?), and Chiat\Day (creators of the Think Different ads for Apple, one of which featured Bill Bernbach himself)—all used the same structure of free association and teams that DDB had begun, to create beyond-the-box ideas born from the spirit and revolution that began with Bill.

Papert Koenig Lois was a huge success. The agency made millions of dollars and produced scores of legendary ads. Eventually others began to break off from Bill to start new agencies; Mary Wells Lawrence, a protégée of Bill's who became the first female CEO of a company listed on the New York Stock Exchange (Wells Rich Greene), was one of the more successful and famous ones. Helmut Krone would also leave for a while, and though he would be known as one of the most influential and brilliant art directors of his time, he would eventually go back to DDB and stay there for the rest of his career.

In the early years of DDB, Bill carried a card around in his pocket that said, "He might be right." He would pull that card out in meetings and hand it to the person he was meeting with: It was supposed to remind them both to keep open minds. And that would prove to be something Bill himself constantly struggled with. The more famous he became, the more difficult it was for Bill to remember that the other guy might be right. But even those who disagreed with him found it hard to stay angry at Bill for long. "We disagreed sometimes about how an ad should be

PKL and their staff in the lobby of the Seagram Building, NYC.

done," Helmut once said about his relationship with Bill. "And now and then we played this game of getting a little mutual antagonism out of the way before settling down to work. But he never squashed me . . . He could have so easily . . . But he always left me some breathing room. Yes, we argued, but all the while we did it with love . . . "

Bill Bernbach died in 1982 at the age of 71. One of the last things he talked to anyone about was Volkswagen (DDB was working on a new ad for them at the time). When the guys from DDB reluctantly left his hospital room the night he died, Bill reassured them: "I'll be back on Monday," he said, "and we'll do some great stuff."

"What a different life it would have been without Bill Bernbach," Helmut Krone later said. That was true in more ways than one. No one who ever worked with Bill was able to leave him behind because from that day forward, no matter where they went, their time at DDB would be one of the most important parts of their résumé. But a person's legend is often bigger than the actual woman or man. And "trying to live up to one's legend" is oftern a road to insecurity or hubris. Bill's reputation became so big that he was rarely capable of sharing the stage. Some felt that Bill disowned his "sons and daughters" when they left him; he never sent any business their way or praised or recommended them, but in truth, he was always aware of them, watching them from afar. In 1978, for instance, nearly eighteen years after George and Julian left DDB, tragedy struck George's family: He lost one of his beloved sons. That very next morning, Bill was waiting downstairs in the lobby of George's building, just standing there quietly, so that when George came down he could give him a hug.

In the end, who was most responsible for the VW ads, most claimant to the fame that followed? It's hard to say. And frankly, it doesn't matter. The magic was in the interaction. DDB was an environment that nurtured ideas, and it was that inexplicable chemistry that made every new ad at DDB seem unexpected but fated, or as George once put it, "like pulling pigeons from a sleeve."

$$\textbf{59}$$

In the years following the Second World War, the push and pull between Germany's banks, its businesses, its governments, and its people—especially in the form of labor movements and work councils—evolved into a new system that helped people get out of their own way, and for a while, the market was in a state of grace. No matter which way you slice it, postwar Germany was eventually a major triumph in the history of democracy, a time when the choice was made for a national economy based on freedom, rather than one based on governmental or corporate controls. As the next twenty years in Germany would show, Realpolitik in the country became a matter of economic rather than military might. In an interview from February 1975, in the Swiss journal *Finanz und Wirtschaft,* West German chancellor Helmut Schmidt summed it up well when he said, "For some years now our economic policy has simultaneously been our foreign policy." And one strong pumping organ of that economic policy has been Volkswagen.

People in America (and that included me, before spending so much time in Germany) rarely understand what a giant international company Volkswagen has evolved into in the decades since the Second World War. Most of us don't even know that the VW Group (which is a subset of Volkswagen AG) includes Audi, Bentley, Bugatti, Lamborghini, Seat, and Škoda or that today VW is Europe's largest carmaker and the second largest car company in the world. In 2009, VW's corporate earnings were 911 million euros (about $1.2 billion), and this in the midst of a worldwide recession.

The Volkswagen parent company became an *Aktiengesell-schaft* (Volkswagen AG) in 1960, when it first decided to open some of its shares to the public. In that new configuration, 20 percent of the company was retained by the state government, 20 percent was retained by the national government, and the other 60 percent was sold to stakeholders and shareholders. For clarity, to imagine this same configuration applied to an American car company like Ford, it would be as if the American national government controlled 20 percent of Ford, while the state of Michigan controlled another 20 percent, and the rest was owned by private investors and stockholders. This is not a comparison that would literally hold true, but it does highlight the very different ways the two companies started: VW as a national enterprise, and Ford as a private one.

While many car companies have had moments where they were at times publicly owned (in other words, owned and funded by the taxpayers and the government), that has been less a rule or founding principle of other car companies and more a temporary fix to save a company from going bankrupt, or to carry it through a changing political and social climate (after the Second World War, for example, many European car companies experienced some degree of public ownership until they could survive as private enterprises). But the reason why Volkswagen has been more *permanently* structured as a (partly) publicly owned company goes back to the way the VW company itself was formed.

Because the plant was built using funds of the German Labor Front—a national, governmental organization that had been formed by the Nazis from the workers' unions and required all workers to pay fees to it—it was built from the money provided by German workers. And because of that, German workers' unions (IG Metall, for example), which are economic powerhouses in Germany in their own right, still, to this day, have an agreement with VW that gives them an important stake in the management of the company (an agreement reached between VW and the unions after the Second World War) and a very big say in VW's decision-making process. Volkswagen's executives, for example, have to have the consent of labor representatives before they can do something like move the production of a car to a new plant.

And while the German national government relinquished its

20 percent of VW shares in 1988, the government of Lower Saxony still owns 20 percent. In fact, there is something called the "VW Law" that effectively gives the state government of Lower Saxony the ability to block any resolution that it does not agree with at Volkswagen. So even though it has only 20 percent of the company's shares, it could nevertheless exercise full control of the plant, but even more specifically, if another car company or person should have controlling shares of the stock, the state of Lower Saxony could prevent them from taking over the company as a whole. (The European Court of Justice, in 2007, ruled that this law was not constitutional, and thus the balance at VW is currently being reconfigured, as is the VW Law.)

In any case, as it now stands, the people (the workers) and the government (the state leaders) both have a heavy influence at Volkswagen, and the company thus spends a lot of time and energy balancing its management concerns, its unions, its shareholders, its stakeholders, its "daughter" car companies, and its authoritative figures. With such a large size and with so many differing voices, decisions do not always get made quickly or efficiently. The company that few thought would survive in 1945 has become an international economic powerhouse, but it has done so using a business model and a method of production that can appear inefficient and slow at times, operating in a far different manner from other German car companies—companies like Porsche.

Today, Porsche and Volkswagen are two of Germany's most famous carmakers. They both started with one man, Ferdinand Porsche, but as businesses, they have evolved very differently over the years. Volkswagen is a giant operation on all counts. Porsche has an incredible image and reputation, but remains more a boutique, luxury car company. (Volkswagen AG sold over 6 million vehicles in 2010, and Porsche sold less than 100,000, but Porsche made more money *per car*.) The differing sizes and products of these two companies has meant that, though they started in the same place, they have become very different business models. In fact, in Germany in 2007, it would have been very hard to find two companies as structurally different, and with such a differing *Weltanschauung* (philosophy or worldview) as Volkswagen and Porsche.

But the split between them goes beyond their structural style and business models, tied to a dynastic feud between two families that are really one family: the Porsches and the Piëchs. It's such a complex, soap-opera-like family division—one that includes affairs, deals with Arab investors, and every imaginable kind of familial problem, multiplied tenfold—that it's hard to remember it all started with one man. When Ferdinand Porsche died on January 30, 1951, he left behind a design firm in Stuttgart (the design firm that was in that very moment transforming into the Porsche car company of today) as well as a dealership in Salzburg, Austria (which would later become the biggest dealership in Europe). The financial backing that allowed these two Porsche firms to grow came in large part because of the new agreements that were made between Porsche and Volkswagen when Nordhoff, Ferry, and Anton met on September 17, 1948.

Porsche had two children, Louise and Ferry, and it was to them he left the Porsche businesses when he died. Louise and Ferry had a close relationship, but they were very different people: Ferry, as he described himself, was more of a mother's boy, and had a tender, spiritual side that Louise perhaps had as well, but that she was less apt to show. Louise always came off as very strong, sometimes rude or gruff, with a personality much more like her father's. Today, Ferry's sons carry the Porsche name, and Louise's children have the last name of the man she married, the man who was in prison with her father in France, Anton Piëch. As was always the case with Ferdinand Porsche himself, business and family remained deeply intertwined; thus the rivalries, miscommunications, and struggles within the family soon extended to the Porsche and Volkswagen firms, and have played out in the wider German arena of politics and economics since Ferdinand Porsche's death.

In Ferdinand Porsche's will, he gave Ferry control of the Stuttgart design firm, and Louise control of the Austrian dealership. Anton, Louise's husband, hardly outlived her father, dying very suddenly in 1952. Louise was thus left to raise her four children more or less alone and simultaneously hold down the Austrian side of the Porsche company. Ferry and his family were dealing with the German part of the Porsche business in Stuttgart, a town and country where "Porsche" was already a name that carried weight. The Porsche and Piëch children thus grew up in different countries, and in very different ways. The Piëch children were sent to Austrian boarding schools, for instance, schools that Louise's son, Ferdinand Piëch, the family member who would (much later) become the leader of Volkswagen, now describes as "elitist, Spartan, and strict." Ferry's boys, on the other hand, went to the Waldorf schools, German schools inspired by Rudolf Steiner. Steiner is the founder of Anthroposophy, a philosophical movement guided by "living through deeds of love, and allowing others to live with tolerance for their unique intentions." One oft-repeated motto of the Waldorf schools (which are still prominent in Germany today) is, "Receive the children in reverence, educate them with love and send them forth in freedom," a big difference from the Spartan, strict world that was known by Ferdinand Piëch! But the Porsche boys could be harsh too, often reminding Ferdinand Piëch, for instance, that he did not directly bear the Porsche name.

But even though he did not carry the Porsche name, there had rarely been a minute in Piëch's life when he could escape the ghosts of his father and grandfather. When he would begin his rise at Volkswagen, for example, there would be rumors about his father Anton's complicity in labor camps during the Second World War. Many tried to keep Piëch from rising to authority, saying that if the story got out about the role his father had played in the use of forced labor at VW, it would not bode well for the company's public image. With Ferry still around, the Porsche boys could lean on their father, a man who was able to be more accountable for himself, to discuss his activities during the Second World War with them and with the public, and to share or deflect the burden of that weight. Both Louise and Ferry gave their children a great deal of love and support, but growing into adulthood without a father certainly took its toll on Ferdinand Piëch.

In any case, these kinds of underlying tensions within the Porsche and Piëch families understandably carried over into the workplace. For example, in the 1960s, Ferdinand Piëch (who was working for the Porsche company at the time, and had not yet joined VW) created a race car known as the Porsche 917. But his method of building this car—using the best parts and the best research and engineering advisors, regardless of time and cost—caused a great deal of tension. The Porsches disagreed with his reasoning and approach, and this exploded into a huge family argument, though the 917 was a landmark race car, debuting in 1969 and going on to win Le Mans.

By 1970, it had become clear to Ferry and Louise that their children were not getting along and that the fighting was affecting the business. They ultimately made the decision that *none* of their children would be allowed to work at Porsche ever again. The children could own their shares in the company and be on the board, but they couldn't hold official management positions there. This is how Ferdinand Piëch ended up at Volkswagen. His response to this new rule was to start working at Audi, which eventually led him to VW.

As Ferdinand Piëch became the chairman of the board and guiding personality of Volkswagen, so too did the two companies take on the Porsche/Piëch feud. The Porsche brothers criticized the VW business model and their cousins' complicity in it (and they also contested the VW Law, which would have kept them from being able to own VW). But Piëch learned how to operate in the VW world, and it worked to his benefit *and* to the benefit of VW (Piëch saved VW from financial troubles and deflected yet another near buyout from Ford). The feud reached its boiling point in 2008, when Porsche nearly took over Volkswagen, after the ECJ ruled against the VW Law, thus making such a takeover possible. It might have been the most heated move for acquisition in all of German industry, made all the more spectacular because it almost worked: Porsche nearly took over VW, a company *fifteen times* its size. But it had been a speculative, hedge fund kind of move, heavily involving stocks, and when the market collapsed in 2008, the deal collapsed as well. The Porsche company was thus left vulnerable, with copious amounts of debt, very angry investors, and the possibility that they would have to file for bankruptcy. All this, and in the blink of an eye.

By the end of 2008, it was clear that Porsche now needed to be bailed out. And it wasn't long before Volkswagen owned 49.9 percent of Porsche, and Porsche, though no longer in fear of bankruptcy, lost its potential claim to VW. Ferdinand Piëch was the figurative head of VW as all this took place, though he had stepped down as CEO in 2002 to become chairman of the supervisory board; Wendelin Wiedeking, the CEO of Porsche, was forced (many believe by Piëch) to leave. To a large degree, Wiedeking (backed by the chairman of the Porsche board, Wolfgang Porsche) was behind the Porsche move to take over VW, mainly because Wiedeking believed that VW's business model was outdated and needed to be changed. Wiedeking became a sort of pawn in the battle between VW and Porsche; thus his final resignation was the sure sign that VW and Piëch had "won." But in truth, there was no clear winner or loser, just a monumental shift in the relationship between VW and Porsche.

Negotiations about how this new VW/Porsche relationship will be structured are still continuing as I write. If the current deal goes through, Porsche will receive billions of dollars from VW to pay off its debts. The Porsche and Piëch families will get 50 percent of the merged VW/Porsche company; thus, VW (which once had only Ferdinand Piëch as the family representative) will now be partly owned by the Porsches. In turn, the Porsches will have less direct control of the Porsche company itself. The German state of Lower Saxony would still keep 20 percent of VW, the Emirate of Qatar would get another chunk based on its dealings with Porsche, and the rest of the company will remain with the investors and stockholders. Porsche will become a "daughter" company of VW, and thus Porsche will be VW-owned.

What is certain in all this maneuvering is that the two companies are once again owned in part by the same family—and both the Piëchs and the Porsches have benefited from this. As Dietmar Hawranek wrote in *Der Spiegel* in 2009, "The assets of the Porsches and Piëchs have multiplied. Before the investment in Wolfsburg, they owned 100 percent of Porsche, a small sports-car maker. Now they own more than half of the world's second-largest automobile group. As dirty as it was, it was an extraordinarily profitable family feud. . . . The merger places the German-Austrian industrialist clan on a level with the world's biggest corporate dynasties: the Fords, the Agnellis, and the Peugeots."

So for the moment, it seems the VW business model will prevail, though this (like everything else in the story) is more complex than meets the eye, and is currently in the midst of change. Volkswagen AG is one big company made up of many individual, smaller ones, and so far, this setup has worked in large part because Volkswagen does not infringe on the other brands, but allows them their freedom in production and design methods, even as the companies share certain mind-sets and technologies. Hopefully, the same will hold true for Porsche. The challenge for Volkswagen AG is to find a way to continue growing, even as it champions basic German traditions and deeply rooted work methods like joint responsibility and participation (*Mitbestimmung* and *Mitverantworung*). Until now, the guiding force of VW has been sustainability rather than huge profits— even though the huge profits have come—so while they haven't made as much money as they might have made with a smaller cost base (in other words, had their business and manufacturing philosophy been predominantly based on the "lean model" as developed by Toyota, and as used by Porsche), they *have* made a profit, and that's been enough. At the same time, the management at Volkswagen AG seems to know it must be flexible, that they cannot restrict change as they continue to grow.

Already, Porsche and VW are intermixing in new ways: Michael Macht, an expert in lean production who was once the CEO of Porsche, has recently been named to head the Volkswagen Group's global network, for instance, and Volkswagen AG has named Matthias Mueller, previously VW's top car strategist, to be the new CEO of Porsche. But the true test of Volkswagen AG might be how it merges these differing structural models into a new strategy, one that remains true to the company's history and methodology while at the same time evolving certain aspects to reflect its new acquisitions. In one sense, the traditional Volkswagen business model has demanded a slowness that can be frustrating. But in another sense, this slowness has been the company's strength, keeping it from overreaching itself, guaranteeing good engineering and good quality work.

German-born economist Fritz Schumacher once wrote, "Character . . . is formed primarily by a man's work. And work, when properly conducted in conditions of human dignity and freedom, blesses those who do it and equally their products." Every big company is now trying to find the right balance in this sense—the balance between becoming big while at the same time attending to the details, because the details are what will ultimately make or break them—and VW is no different. In the global automotive market, VW is second only to Toyota when it comes to profits and units sold, and VW's chief executive has promised to surpass Toyota by 2018. Volkswagen now talks about becoming the biggest and most profitable car company in the world. In fact, this has become a kind of slogan of VW's, and lately, they say it often.

There is something rather puzzling about VW's constant voicing of such a desire; it strikes one as out of step with the overall VW approach from the past. On some level of course, every car company wants to be the top car company in the world. But if VW has to change its entire focus in order to do so, it's doubtful it will find much satisfaction in such a victory, or that such a victory will be long lived. If VW is able to continue with its system of checks and balances, to make good products and treat its workers well, then one can only wish them luck. "We always need both freedom and order," to quote Schumacher once more. "We need the freedom of lots and lots of small, autonomous units, and, at the same time, the orderliness of large-scale, possibly global, unity and coordination." If Volkswagen can keep its ego at bay, it could be a terrific example of how big companies can step into the future without losing the vital ability to think small.

The story of the Volkswagen is part of the human story, not just the story of any one country, time, family. In Germany, the Beetle was transformed from the pet of a dictator who unleashed extreme violence and destruction on his country and the world to an object that represented new economic and social potential. And that immigrant Bug that came to the United States only to be rejected eventually became a symbol of transformation and hope; it became *American* in a very real way. The Beetle is just a car, to be sure. But its story is not just a story, it's *our* story, the story of coming from humble and diverse beginnings, of standing strong in the face of adversity, of having faith. And that's where the magic is.

We are always trying to find what moves us, and to figure out the best way to move. And we're always thinking about where we want to go, without forgetting where we've come from. While it's clear we will find, and must find, new ways of mobility in the coming years, it's hard to say what changes will come with the next decade, or what mode of transportation and energy will be the best one for our planet and our health. We have to develop a new perspective about energy, and our new leap into the future requires a solid understanding of the details of our past. In that sense, it helps to know the story of how we have progressed so far, and to know that we *have* progressed. It took Lewis and Clark two and a half years to travel from one side of the United States to the other on their first cross-country journey. Later, with horse and carriage, it took a good six months to make the same trip. Trains cut that time down to just weeks. Then came cars, allowing for individual mobility from any point A to any point B.

At each one of these transitions in movement, there was a corresponding revolution in thought. The story of the Volkswagen exemplifies that sort of change. About a century ago, many people thought the idea of a "People's Car" was impossible: It seemed irrational to propose that the majority of the population in America or Germany or so many other countries across the world would actually want, and be able, to own their own cars, to have such power of mobility within their immediate control. But if there's one thing that the story of the Beetle shows us, it's that we should be prepared to be amazed. If our experiences with the mobility change as much in the next century as they have in the previous one, where will we end up? In that regard, the Beetle's story proves that anything is possible: The craziest ideas can be the ones that become the most valuable, and the best answers can be the ones we least expect.

The discussion today about the best way to move forward is urgent, but it is not new. Ferdinand Porsche created electric vehicles and hybrids over a hundred years ago. Today, very important innovations are being made as companies, scientists, and concerned citizens all over the planet explore new ways for us to power ourselves, experimenting with biofuels, biomass, wind and solar power, plug-in hybrids, electric vehicles, and hydrogen power. There are also strides being made toward developing new forms of public transportation and infrastructure, and more energy-efficient buildings and homes. And of course there is the exciting possibility of solutions we haven't discovered yet. One thing that does look likely, however, is that our future will consist of all of the above—that these new forms of mobility will coexist, and that it will not be any one new energy source that will save us, but rather a change in our mind-set and awareness, one that allows for numerous small solutions rather than one big fix. Because another thing the Beetle's story proves is that we *can* hold contradictory notions in our minds at once, indeed, we *must,* in order to grow. In other words, we have to learn how to do *big* things by noticing the details, by being clear and present. By thinking small.

. . . And Going . . .

There's a famous old Volkswagen television commercial from the sixties that shows an original Beetle driving off into the distance while a voice in the background says *"diese Wagen läuft und läuft und läuft und läuft und läuft . . .,"* "this car goes and goes and goes and goes and goes . . ." No one knew how true that statement would become. Twenty years after it had ceased being sold in Germany and America, the Beetle came back to life. And now, it's come to life *again.*

And the world has changed in the meantime. In 1998, we were just getting used to the Internet and email, but today, as the 2012 Beetle arrives, we have practically created a whole new virtual world. And the economic, political, and social structures of that world reflect our new connection and scope. The real world is the same size, but we are much more aware of each other, and information, images, and trends get transported at the speed of light. The car is growing up with us: The first time many people heard of the 2012 Beetle, after all, was in a Super Bowl advertisement in February 2011 that millions of people viewed on YouTube. Soon after, the car was unveiled in three countries at once with live webcasts in New York City, Shanghai, and Berlin. Those three locations alone, and the fact that such a PR event was even possible or profitable, shows how the world has changed, and also what markets are most important to VW now.

But the 2012 Beetle is also a testament to the fact that there are some things that never change. For one thing, the market still revolves in large part around the ways and means by which we move and communicate. But there is another thing

The animated black beetle from the 2011 Super Bowl ad that received millions of hits on YouTube.

too: When it came to creating the third generation of the Beetle, the designers went all the way back through history to Ferdinand and Ferry Porsche, and all the other engineers who worked on the first VW and the first Porsche in the Porsches' workshops and garages. The designers of the 2012 Beetle kept an original model of the Beetle close at hand, and if you place the old and the new next to each other, you will see the family resemblance, especially in the back of the car (what is called the C-pillar, the part behind the rear doors). The front of the car has been lowered and stretched, and the windshield has more of a mischievous tilt. The back of the car has been stretched too; the rear fender is fatter and more masculine, and the wheelbase is also bigger so the car has a bigger stance. The whole car looks energized, still playful, but ready to pounce. The rear headlights are no longer big circles, but rather curvy U-shapes, and the wheels are big 10-spokes, about 19 inches in diameter. The overall effect of these changes is that the 2012 Beetle looks a heck of a lot like the Porsche 356, the first sports car sold by Porsche, and one that Ferry built using his father's original Beetle design.

In designing the 2012, Volkswagen group design chief Walter de Silva and Volkswagen brand design chief Klaus Bischoff wanted to develop a car that returned to the VW roots. But the

2012 is no "small car"—it's 71.2 inches wide, 58.5 inches tall, and 168.4 inches long, which means it is 3.3 inches wider, half an inch lower, and 6 inches longer than the New Beetle from 1998. But the 2012 Beetles also come with built-in spoilers; the inner painted carbon–look dashboards remind one of the original Beetle as well, although they removed the classic flower vase that has been around since before the car became the hippie car of choice. Ambient lighting is available in a choice of red, white, or blue. The car offers three engines: a 2.5L gasoline five cylinder, a 2.0L TDI Clean Diesel (the most fuel-efficient Beetle ever, VW says), and a 2.0L TSI turbocharged gasoline engine. Maybe one day there will be a hybrid Beetle too, especially since Porsche created the world's first hybrid over 111 years ago. But for its size and comfort, the car gets good gas mileage, an average of 33 miles per gallon.

Themes recur. And just as it was for Nordhoff, Volkswagen's current desire to be a success in America is part of the 2012 push. Germany is still trying to understand America, and to have a presence in its market. During the unveiling of the 2012 model, the CEO of Volkswagen of America, Jonathan Browning, told reporters that "The U.S. is the most important market for

The twenty-first-century Beetle. The 2012 model has elements of the early Porsche design.

the Beetle, and it is a critical part of the new chapter we are trying to write for Volkswagen in the U.S. and worldwide." VW is
spending tons of money in the States now—including $5 billion
on a new car plant in Chattanooga, Tennessee, its first American
factory since the 1980s.

But this plan will work only if Americans buy the cars, and it's
a much more complicated kind of world now, a fact that is reflected in the closer ties between branding and design that have
come to exist. Today, because technology advances happen
quite rapidly, and are available to the masses much more
quickly, when it comes to selling a product, it's not only a matter of being on the cutting edge of technology; it's also a matter
of having a recognizable brand with a comprehensive design
(Apple is a very good example of this).

In a 2009 documentary about design called *Objectified,* German designer Dieter Rams names a few of the "rules" that go
into making a good design. The ones that struck me as particularly relating to the classic design of the Beetle are the following: Design is a matter of clarity, of being clear; design is
innovative; design makes a product understandable; good design is honest; design is long-lived; and finally, good design is
"as little design as possible." The design of the original encom-
passed all these rules, and perhaps the 2012 will prove to as
well.

But brand is also a matter of story. As Allen Adamson wrote
online for *Forbes* magazine on April 25, 2011, "While consumers do appreciate knowing how fast a car can go, and whether
they can fit two sets of golf clubs into the trunk . . . this isn't
what drives car-buying behavior. It never has been and never
will be. Instead, it's the whole brand story that steers people's
rides. That's why smart auto companies, smart auto branders,
make sure that they've got a genuinely distinctive and compelling story to tell about what makes their brand of car different in
a way people care about. The best of the best know how to

An early dealership in the United States, selling Porsches and Volkswagens.

weave the rational and emotional aspects of the story together in a way that really sets their brands apart. . . . "

In that sense, brand (and story) and design are linked. A design that is honest and long-lived and clear reflects a brand that has those same characteristics: The design is inspired by the product, after all, and so the two are intimately linked.

In that same documentary I mention above, one designer quotes Henry Ford as saying that "every object tells a story, if you know how to read it." Right now, our story is one of a global, increasingly connected, increasingly diverse world, a world in which no one country can really "own" its products, because those products take on a life and story of their own once exposed to the differing cultures that create the global market, a market that now must be accurately accessed by a car company for that company to succeed. And the Beetle is certainly a car that belongs to the world. Germany is the caretaker, but no longer does it really own the Beetle or its story. When the 2012 Beetle appeared to the public for the first time on April 18, 2011, it was called "the darling of the New York Auto Show": The car is still an object we want to love. Its story is still being written.

In that sense, the primary driving force of the Beetle's innovation and success is not just the profits, or competition, or the marketplace, it's how the car fits into the narrative of its customer's lives.

It could be telling that the twenty-first-century Beetle looks a lot like a Porsche. Perhaps when VW says it is "going back to its roots," that means it is ready to fully connect with its own story, the one that began with Ferdinand Porsche. And in a wider context, as citizens and consumers, perhaps we are likewise approaching a moment where we can reevaluate our history and mobility with a deeper clarity. Like that famous T. S. Eliot poem "Little Gidding," the car's story is coming back to where it started, but knowing that place for the first time. And perhaps we are too. After all, the truth has always been true. And as the story of the Beetle shows, the greatest moments happen—collectively and individually—when we find new ways of bringing that truth into view.

Acknowledgments

o o

Honestly, I have no idea how to properly express gratitude to everyone who has contributed to the creation of this book; there's no true beginning or end to the list of names deserving thanks—everyone I've learned from, everyone behind the scenes who have quietly done essential work, all the front desk attendants and mechanics and factory workers and writers and filmmakers, and all the people over the years who have shared the stories of their original Beetles with me—to try and name you all would need a space as long as my lifetime, but please accept my sincere appreciation. Your work matters.

Daunting as the task may be, there are also some people I would very much like to try and express gratitude to here directly for all I have learned from them, and for their enthusiasm and important contributions to this book. First, to Richard Morris of Janklow & Nesbit. From our very first phone call, I knew I was lucky enough to have found someone who felt a similar inspiration from this story. Still, I had no idea how much time, effort, and thought he would ultimately give. Not only did he help me advance a little further on that long road to finding one's voice as an author, but it is no stretch to say that his advice, support, and unwavering confidence in this project is a primary reason this book came to light. I am also sincerely grateful to Susanna Porter at The Random House Publishing Group, whose unparalleled editorial eye helped me to get to the essence of this story, and whose support, direction, and advice has helped me to find new clarity and responsibility as a writer. Also at Random House, I am indebted to Priyanka Krishnan for her editorial honesty and truly exceptional talent, and for her administrative patience and perseverance; this book would not have been the same had Richard, Susanna, and Priyanka not been on board. Respect and gratitude also go to the editorial and publishing staff, especially Libby McGuire, Jennifer Hershey, and Kim Hovey. I would also like to thank Benjamin Dreyer, Shona McCarthy, and the entire managing editorial group, for their amazing work, and for catching and alerting me to key points; this book is a much better read thanks to them. I am grateful to the publicity and marketing teams; these amazing people who are the conduits between this book and the wider world, especially Susan Corcoran, David Moench, Theresa Zoro, Kristin Fassler, Quinne Rogers, and Leah Johanson. Thanks also to the design and art departments, especially Beck Stvan and Evan Gaffney. And thank you Amelia Zalcman, Deborah Foley, Toby Ernst, and Caroline Teagle at Random House, and Zenya Prowell and Becky Sweren at Janklow & Nesbit for helping in numerous essential tasks.

Very big thanks also goes to the amazing staff at the archives of Volkswagen AG in Wolfsburg. So many days and months (indeed, years) full of discussions and questions to Dr. Ulrike Gutzmann on the archive staff have left me with a deep respect for her and for the work she does. I could not have asked to meet a better person. Likewise, the work and time of Dr. Manfred Grieger was essential to this book, as was the study *Das Volkswagenwerk und seine Arbeiter im Dritten Reich*, which he worked on with German historian Dr. Hans Mommsen. Thanks also to the archivists and staff for the tours of the Volkswagen factory and the Place of Remembrance, for all the meetings, the coffees and lunches and dinners and walks, the access, and for providing so many wonderful sources and photos for this book. I also have to thank former Volkswagen CEO, and a man who has done so much to expand the borders of corporate thinking, Carl Hahn, for discussing this book with me, and for providing insight into the character of both Bill Bernbach and Heinrich Nordhoff. Thanks also to his wonderful assistant, Ute Krause. I would like to have written more about Hahn in this book, and on that note, I recommend his autobiography (which is only available in German right now, but hopefully will come out in English soon). I would also like to thank Carl Hahn for his role in bringing the Kunstmuseum to Wolfsburg, and to the wonderful staff and curators there. The exhibit on James Turrell that I happened to see during one of my longer stays in Wolfsburg was a very moving moment for me, and one that fit well with the themes of this story.

With warm regards and sincere gratitude, I would also like to thank Porsche AG, especially the exceptional Dieter Landenberger, Porsche's head of archives, for the hours and hours of discussions and emails in which he not only helped me to get to know Ferdinand Porsche but also to understand Germany's history of automobiles and technology, not to mention helping me understand some basic technical and mechanical questions regarding the workings of the automobile. Mr. Landenberger's energy and knowledge have contributed greatly to this book. Thanks also to Porsche for opening their archives, for the wonderful tours of their magnificent museum and factory, and for being so kind and giving. A special thanks to Jens Torner of Porsche AG as well, for sitting with me and going through hundreds of photos until we found just the right ones. Thanks also to Dieter Gross for helping me to navigate the Porsche libraries.

Much gratitude also goes to the staff at the Autostadt in Wolfsburg. Again, I was very lucky to be introduced to Andrea Mueller on my first visit there. Her love for the Autostadt, for cars, and her vast knowledge of VW history helped me greatly, as did her generosity in giving me tours of the grounds, and answering any question I might ask of her through emails and in person throughout my visits. Also at the Autostadt, I am grateful for the discussions I had with Dr. Wolfgang Kaese, who is in charge of a wonderful bookshop, and who knows so much about cars and their history. Thanks also to the administrative staff at the Autostadt for helping me find resources and photos.

• • •

Time after time, I was astonished by the good nature and generosity of so many in Wolfsburg, and that is especially true of the staff of the Institut für Zeitgeschichte und Stadtpräsentation, especially Alexander Nedelkovski and Katje. Thank you for helping me navigate your archives and photo collections, and for always helping me to track down the right person, place, or date. In Wolfsburg, I am also very thankful to the beautiful and effervescent Renate Riemer for the tours and the talks, the lunches, and for giving me a look at the history of Wolfsburg from someone who had lived through much of it herself. Thanks also to Anna Krause and Axel Bosse, to Justin Hoffmann at the Kunstverein Wolfsburg, to Susanna Pflieger, Stadt Galerie Wolfsburg, to the staff of the Wolfsburg library, and to all those who work for the Volkswagen Auto Museum.

Special thanks also goes to journalist and photographer Klaus Gottschick for sharing his memories of Nordhoff with me, as well as his photos.

I would also like to thank Juliane Aswald and Brian Amelung of the Volkswagen factory in Dresden, for their hospitality, for the tour, and for answering all my questions not only about the Phaeton but also about car history in Germany. Thanks also to all the exceedingly professional and excellent staff members of the libraries in Germany, especially the Gedenkbibliothek in Berlin, and to the Arsenal in Berlin for the film series of old Volkswagen promotional films, to the Neuer Berliner Kunstverein for providing such an amazing video archive, and to Silke Wittig for helping me to navigate through those archives. I also appreciate the collection of the Deutsches Technikmuseum in Berlin, and the Technikmuseum in Munich, and I am also thankful to the very knowledgable and efficient staff at the British Library in London, and to the transportation museum and archives there as well. And thanks especially to so many friends in Europe, some of whom I must name here because of the role they played (whether they know it or not!) in my discovery of

Wolfsburg, and the good luck I had there: Anne Koenig, Jan Wenzel, Micz Flor, Kito Nedo, Tobias Zielony, Matthias Fischer, and Vera Tollmann. Thanks also to Adam Raymont and the Raymont family for so many gifts given in Berlin. And warmest thanks to Prague and London, for the unceasing exchange of emails and thoughts about so many topics and themes in this book. In case you doubt or have forgotten, I send you my sincere love.

Thank you also to everyone who is a part of Pulse, to the amazing staff and the flux of personalities of the past seven years of the project, especially Jin Love and Nicola Gerndt. Big thanks also to that initial start-up staff at ICD, especially Mark Donfried, Nora Circosta, Stefanie Averwald, and Anya Kinneavy, and to all the interns and flux of staff over the years who have contributed so much. Thanks also to so many in Berlin for inviting me to conferences, lunches, or dinners in which I got a glimpse into the political and economic complexity of international relations, and to everyone there who have allowed me to ask them questions and learn from them as I've worked on this book.

In the States, the staff at Volkswagen of America has been very helpful over the years, and I want to give warm thanks to Steve Keyes and Tom Wegehaupt, two former Volkswagen employees who have since moved on to other projects, but who helped me greatly when I was first starting out on this journey. More recently, I am greatly indebted to the wonderful energy and enthusiasm of Carsten Krebs and VW of A, and to many others on the Volkswagen staff, especially Sheriece Matias.

Many in New York City have already been mentioned, but there are many more! One of the most charming and important presences in this whole process for me was the great Julian Koenig, and I am forever grateful to him for sharing his time, stories, and jokes. It is a pleasure to know you. Thanks also to his daughter Sarah Koenig for her time and patience and help. I also had the opportunity to spend a few afternoons talking with George Lois, and as everyone who knows him will tell you, he is a whirlwind of energy that one can never forget. Thank you George for being generous and kind, and thanks to his son Luke for his help in finding photos. Thanks also goes to Fred Papert for talking with me about his two former business partners, and for just being an interesting and intelligent guy.

I was very nervous the first time I went to meet Bill Bernbach's son, John, and so I would like to thank him for making time in his schedule to answer my many questions, and for being kind and helpful in every way. Thanks also to his wonderful secretary at Engine, Debbie Brown, and to a fellow-southerner, Laura Hynes.

I am also very grateful to Alicia Brindak at DDB Worldwide for answering all my questions and putting me in touch with the people I needed to speak with, as well as helping me to find photos and permissions. Thanks also to Jeff Swystun at DDB for his support and help with this book. I also have to thank the original Doyle Dane Bernbach staff, and so many who helped build and create it. Much respect goes to the memory of Helmut Krone, and to his daughter Kathryn Krone. Thanks and respect must also be given to legends and legacies of Bill Charmatz, Bob Gage, Phyllis Robinson, Bob Levenson, Helmut Schmitz, David Oglivy and Paul Rand. Thanks to the wonderful staff and wonderful resources of the New York Public Library, to the Ad Club and the One Club in NYC, to Bob Contant and Terry McCoy, and the entire staff of St Marks Bookshop, past and present; to Greg Foley for sharing his creative spark and essential advice, to Marilyn Apelson for the dinners full of deep literary discussion, to Wade Lawrence at the Bethel Museum for his generosity, and to Marlon Stolzman, whose friendship and support has changed my life immeasurably: I'm so glad you noticed that hot pink folder at IMG! Your friendship is a rare gift.

This list seems to be ordered by cities, and on that note, I'd like to express gratitude to a few more. Much gratitude goes to Detroit and its automotive legacy, as well as to the staff at the archives and museums of Ford and GM. Thanks also for the awakenings I've had in D.C.; and to so many in Seattle, for the support, the faith, the endurance, and especially for the love that your presence in my life allows me to feel. Also to R., a rare and true intellectual soulmate, for the tender, mindful communication and love.

Very warm thanks to the Carolinas and all my family there, especially my grandmothers and great grandmother, who have taught me as much about story as anyone. Thanks also to my aunts and uncles in the north, to the many libraries all over the country that I've frequented in my research, to Savannah's School of Art and Design, and to the members of my family in my hometown of Atlanta, especially to my father for always encouraging me to follow my dreams, to my mother for always letting me know that I have a place to come back to, and my brother for showing me that true inner transformation is real. Thanks also to Allison, Emily, Colleen, and Dori, for all the years of friendship, support, patience and faith in this book.

I have to also thank all the German musicians, writers, and philosophers who inspired me from a very young age, and who are, as much as anything else, responsible for my pilgrimage to Germany, and thus for my eventual discovery of this story, a story which I am thankful for as well, as it has taught me a great deal, and given me an inspiring journey, as well as the chance to meet and work with many beautiful people. In writing this book, I was gifted access to the public and personal archives and memories of so many. It took a delicate balance on all our parts, and I was lucky enough to be able to find people who were willing to seek out the truth with me, though no doubt there is still more truth yet to be discovered.

One of the hardest things in writing this book was not being able to include every story, name, and moment that happened. And in that sense especially, please know that any and all mistakes in this book are my own. There were also times when one person's memory or take on an event differed from another. This is human nature, and it makes our lives rich and full of fruitful debate, but it is not easy to present such a vast web in linear and concise fashion. I've tried my best, and I am still learning, but I only hope that everyone who helped with this story can feel my deep admiration and respect for all their work and openness and talent. All their lives and contributions are rich and nuanced, and they matter much more than this book can tell.

Bibliography

o o

Unpublished Sources

Letters

From Ed Russell to Julian Koenig · Letters from Ed Russell to *Advertising Age*

Interviews

Volkswagen workers, Wolfsburg Museum Collection

Film

Auto-Kino: Unternehmensfilme von Volkswagen: *Silikose (1949/51); Sinfonie eines Autos (1949), und Sisu—Tiere im nordischen Urwald (1952).*
Guenter Riederer, Kino Arsenal: Eine Veranstaltungsreihe von CineGraph Babelsberg, Berlin-Brandenburgisches Centrum fuer Filmforschung und dem Aresenal, in Zusammenarbeit mit dem Bundesarchiv-Filmarchiv, der Deutschen Kinemathek und der Historischen Kommunikation der Volkswagen Aktiengesellschaft. Berlin, 19 April 2010.

Collections and Archives

Stadt Wolfsburg, Institut fuer Zeitgeschichte und Stadtpraesentation, Wolfsburg · Volkswagen Corporate Archive, Wolfsburg · Volkswagen of America Archive, Herndon, VA · New York Public Library, New York · British Library, London · Stadt Archive, Berlin · Zentral- und Landesbibliothek Berlin · Deutsches Technikmuseum, Berlin · Deutsches Historisches, Berlin · Porsche Archive, Stuttgart · Library and Media Center at Savannah School of Art and Design, Savannah · Stadtbibliothek Wolfsburg · Technical University, Berlin · The Henry Ford, Dearborn Michigan · General Motors, Online Archive · Opel, Media Archive

Dissertations

Nedelkovski, Aleksandar. *Kunst als identitätsstiftendes Medium untersucht am Beispiel der Ausstellung 'Heidersberger: Stadt-Werk, 1963.'*

Technische Universität Kaiserslautern: Master-Fernstudiengang "Management von Kultur- und Non-Profit-Organisationen." Abgabedatum: 30 April 2010.

Turner, Ian David. *British Occupation Policy and Its Effects on the Town of Wolfsburg and the Volkswagenwerk 1945–1949.* Department of European Studies and Modern Languages, University of Manchester Institute of Science and Technology, Submitted: 15 October 1984.

Author Interviews/Discussions

John Bernbach, NYC · Axel Bosse, Wolfsburg · BCN New York City · Manfred Grieger, Wolfsburg · Ulrike Gutzman, Wolfsburg · Carl Hahn, Wolfsburg · Justin Hoffman, Wolfsburg · Wolfgang Kaese, Wolfsburg · Julian Koenig, New York City · Dieter Landenberger, Stuttgart · Andrea Mueller, Wolfsburg · George Lois, New York City · Renate Riemer, Wolfsburg

Published Sources

Book of Nations, New York World's Fair, Volume 785 by William Bernbach, Herman Jaffe, Clarence Pearson Hornung. New York, Winkler & Kelmans, 1939.

Koehler, Volkmar. *Kulturpolitik in Wolfsburg—die Anfänge.* Stadt Wolfsburg, Institut fuer Zeitgeschichte und Stadtpraesentation, 2010.

Strauss, Werner. *Wolfsburg—Kleine Stadtgeschichte.* Wolfsburg, Texte zur Geschichte Wolfsburg, Stadt Wolfsburg, 2002.

Auto Museum Volkswagen: Schatzkammer der Marke. Wolfsburg, Stiftung Auto Museum Volkswagen.

Directive to Commander-in-Chief of United States Forces of Occupation Regarding the Military Government of Germany; April 1945 (JCS 1067): United States Government.

The Fireside Chats of Franklin Delano Roosevelt. Radio addresses to the American people broadcast between 1933 and 1944.

The Jewish Question: A Selection of Articles (1920–1922) published by Mr. Henry Ford's paper *The Dearborn Independent* and reprinted later under the general title of "The International Jew." 1936.

The German-American Relationship: The Importance of Vision: Speech by the Ambassador of the United States of America Richard R. Burt on the Occasion of Ceremonies Commemorating the Fortieth Anniversary of Secretary of State James F. Byrnes's "Rede der Hoffnung," Given at the Grosses Haus of the Wuerttembergisches Staatstheater Stuttgart, September 6, 1986. U.S. Diplomatic Mission to Germany.

Public Relations, Edward L. Bernays and the American Scene. Internet Source: F. W. Faxton Company: Annotated bibliography of, and reference guide to, writings by and about Edward Bernays from 1917 to 1951.

Top Secret-OSS-Psychological Analysis of Adolph Hitler. Walter Langer, M.O. Branch Office of Strategic Services, Washington, D.C. With the collaboration of Prof. Henry A. Murray of Harvard Psychological Clinic, Dr. Ernst Kris of the New School for Social Research, and Dr. Bertram D. Lawin of the New York Psychoanalytic Institute.

Typisch Wolfsburg! Von Werden einer neuen Stadt 1938–2008. Wolfsburg, Stadt Wolfsburg, 2008.

Volkswagen Writes History: A chronicle of facts and pictures—from the past to the present. Wolfsburg, Volkswagen AG. 1998.

Wortprotokoll der Uebertragung der Grundsteinlegung des Volkswagen Werkes bei Fallersleben am 26 Mai 1938. Erstellt vom Rolf Linnemann, März 1987. Eigentum der Stadt Wolfsburg, Stadtarchiv F264.

Selected Bibliography

Arendt, Hannah. *Eichmann in Jerusalem: A Report on the Banality of Evil.* New York, Penguin, 2006.

Baaske, Edwin. *Der VW Käefer: Bilder einer Legende.* Bielefeld, Delius Klasing Verlag, 1995 (Stadtarchiv 4047).

Barber, Chris. *Birth of the Beetle.* Haynes, 2003.

Baudrillard, Jean. *The System of Objects.* London, Verso, 1996.

Beier, Rosmarie. *Aufbau West Aufbau Ost: Die Planstadte Wolfsburg und Eisenhüttenstadt in der Nachkriegszeit.* Ostfildern-Ruit, Gerd Hatje, 1997.

Bernays, Edward. *Propaganda.* Brooklyn, IG Publishing, 2005 (original, 1928). Kindle Edition.

Bobbio, Norberto. *Liberalism and Democracy.* London, Verso, 2005.

Brinkley, Douglas. *Wheels for the World.* Penguin, 2003.

Brody, Kenneth. *The Avoidable War: Lord Cecil & the Policy of Principle.* Transaction Publishers, 1999.

Brokaw, Tom. *Boom! Voices of the Sixties.* New York, Random House, 2007.

Bullock, Alan. *Hitler: A Study on Tyranny.* New York, Harper Collins, 1991.

Canetti, Elias. *The Torch in My Ear.* London, Granta (in cooperation with Farrar, Straus and Giroux Inc.), 1999.

Challis, Clive. *Helmut Krone: The Book.* Cambridge Enchorial Press, 2005.

Clausewitz, Claus von. *On War. (Vom Kriege)*. Project Gutenberg. Original from 1832. English edition from Kindle Books, 2009.

Della Femina, Jerry. *From Those Wonderful Folks Who Gave You Pearl Harbor*. Simon & Schuster, 2010. Original: 1970.

DeLorenzo, Matt. *The New Beetle*. Osceola, WI, MBI Publishing Company, 1998.

Edelmann, Heidrun. *Heinz Nordhoff und Volkswagen*. Goettingen, Vandenhoeck und Ruprecht, 2003.

Eichstaedt, Ingrid. *Wolfsburg: Die 'goldenen' 50er Jahre*. Wartberg, Wartberg Verlag, 1995.

Ford, Henry. *My Life and Work*. New York, Doubleday, 1922.

Ford, Henry (with Ralph Waldo Trine). *The Power That Wins*. Bobbs-Merrill, 1929.

Fox, Stephen. *Mirror Makers: A History of American Advertising and Its Creators*. University of Illinois Press, 1997.

Frank, Thomas. *The Conquest of Cool*. University of Chicago Press, 1997.

Frankenberg, Richard von. *Porsche: The Man and His Cars*. 1969.

Gaddis, John Lewis. *The Cold War: A New History*. New York, Penguin, 2006.

Galbraith, John Kenneth. *The Great Crash 1929*. New York, Avon, 1979.

Gordon, Lois and Alan. *American Chronicle*. Yale University Press, 1999.

Gregor, Neil. *Daimler-Benz in the Third Reich*. Yale University Press, 1998.

Griffin, Susan. *A Chorus of Stones: The Private Life of War*. New York, Doubleday, 1992.

Hahn, Carl Horst. *Meine Jahre mit Volkswagen*. Munich, Signum, 2005.

Harth, Annette and Scheller, Gitta and Herlyn, Ulfert and Tessin, Wulf. *Wolfsburg: Stadt am Wendepunkt*. Opladen, Leske & Budrich, 2000.

Hartrich, Edwin. *The Fourth and Richest Reich*. New York, Macmillan, 1980.

Harvey, Chris. *Porsche*. Gallery Books, 1985.

Heidersberger, Heinrich. *Wolfsburg: Bilder Einer Jungen Stadt*. Berlin, Nicolaische Verlagsbuchhandlung, 2008.

Helfand, Jessica. *Paul Rand: American Modernist*. New York, William Drentell, 1998.

Herlyn, Ulfert and Tessin, Wulf. *Faszination Wolfsburg 1938–2000*. Opladen, Leske & Budrich, 2000.

Hitler, Adolf. *Mein Kampf*, reprint, Munich, 1943.

Hitler, Adolf. *My Struggle*. 1992.

Hitler, Adolf. Edited by Max Domarus. *Speeches and Proclamations 1932–1945: The Years 1932–1938*. Bolchazy-Carducci Publishers, 1992.

Hochschild, Adam. *To End All Wars*. London, Houghton Mifflin Harcourt, 2011. Kindle Edition.

Hodemacher, Juergen. *Wolfsburg.* Duesseldorf, Droste, 1983.

Hopfinger, K. B., *Beyond Expectation.* Foulis, 1956.

Jackall, Robert. *Image Makers.* University of Chicago Press, 2000.

Junge, Gertrude (Traudl). *Until the Final Hour.* Arcade Publishing, 2003.

Kaplan, Frank. *1959: The Year Everything Changed.* New Jersey, John Wiley & Sons, 2009.

Kempe, Frederick. *Father/Land.* Indiana University Press, 1999.

Kempka, Erich. *Ich habe Adolf Hitler verbrannt.* Grenz Verlag, 1951.

Kershaw, Ian. *Hitler.* W.W. Norton and Company, 2010. Kindle Edition.

————*Hitler 1889–1936 Hubris.* 2000.

————*Hitler 1936–1945 Nemesis.* 2001.

Keynes, John Maynard. *The Economic Consequences of the Peace.* New York, Harcourt Brace and Howe, 1920.

Kiley, David. *Getting the Bugs Out.* New York, John Wiley and Sons, 2002.

Koslowski, Peter. *The Truth of Capitalism in the German Economic Tradition: Historicism, ordo-Liberalism, critical theory, solidarism.* Heidelberg, Springer Verlag, 2000.

Kuby, Erich. *Alarm im Werk.* Munich, Franz Schneider, 1955.

Lears, T. Jackson. *Fables of Abundance: A Culture History of Advertising in America.* Basic Books, 1995.

Levenson, Bill. *Bill Bernbach's Book.* Villard, New York, 1987.

Lewandowski, Juergen. *New Beetle.* Wolfsburg, 1998.

Lewis, David. *The Automobile and American Culture.* University of Michigan, 1983.

Linge, Heinz. *Bis zum Untergang.* Herbig Verlag, 1980.

Lippmann, Walter. *Public Opinion.* Harcourt, Brace, and Company, 1922.

Loewenstein, Hubertus. *A Basic History of Germany.* Inter Nationes, 1965.

Lois, George. *George, Be Careful. Saturday Review,* 1972.

————*The Art of Advertising.* H. N. Abrams, 1977.

————*Covering the '60s.* Monacelli Press, 1996.

————*George Lois on His Creation of the Big Idea.* Assouline, 2008.

Lorin, Phillippe. *Five Giants of Advertising.* Paris, Assouline, 2001.

Ludvigsen, Karl. *Porsche: Excellence Was Expected.* Bentley Publishers, 2008.

————*Battle for the Beetle.* Bentley, 2000.

Marc, Franz. *Correspondence with August and Elisabeth Macke.* 1964.

————*Letters from the War.* 1992.

Marcantonio, Alfredo. *Remember Those Great Volkswagen Ads?* 2000.

Marx, Karl. *Das Kapital.*

McCullough, David. *Truman.* Simon & Schuster, 1992.

McLeod, Kate. *Beetlemania.* Smithmark, New York, 1999.

McLuhan, Marshall. *Understanding Media, the Extensions of Man.* Edited by Terrence Gordon. Gingko Press, 2003.

Moennich, Horst. *Die Autostadt.* Munich, Wilhelm Andermann, 1951.

Mommsen, Hans and Manfred Grieger. *Das Volkswagenwerk und seine Arbeiter im Dritten Reich.* Duesseldorf, 1996.

Morgenthau Jr., Henry. *Germany Is Our Problem.* New York, Harper & Brothers, 1945.

Müller, Fabian. *Ferdinand Porsche.* Berlin, Ullstein, 1990.

Müller, Peter. *Ferdinand Porsche: Der Vater des Volkswagens.* Stuttgart, Leopold Stocker, 1998.

Muir, John. *How to Keep Your Volkswagen Alive,* 1969.

Nelson, Walter Henry. *Small Wonder.* Boston, Little, Brown & Co., 1965.

Nitske, W. Robert. *The Amazing Porsche and Volkswagen Story.* New York, Comet Press Books, 1958.

Nordhoff, Heinrich. *Reden und Aufsaetze.* ECON Verlag, 1992.

Odih, Pamela. *Advertising in Modern and Postmodern Times.* Sage Publications, 2007.

Ogilvy, David. *Ogilvy on Advertising.* New York, Vintage Books, 1985.

Othmer, James P. *Adland: Searching for the Meaning of Life on a Branded Planet.* New York, Doubleday, 2009.

Overy, Richard. *The Twilight Years.* New York, Viking, 2009.

Packard, Vance. *The Hidden Persuaders.* New York, Cardinal Pocket Books, 1957.

Parkinson, Simon. *Volkswagen Beetle: The Rise from the Ashes of War.* Veloce Publishing. (Stadtarchiv 4002).

Patton, Phil. *Bug.* Massachusetts, Da Capo Press, 2002.

Perel, Sally. *Ich war Hitlerjunge Solomon.* Munich, Wilhelm Heyne, 2007.

Pogue, Forrest C. *George C. Marshall: Ordeal and Hope, 1939–1945.* New York: Viking, 1966.

————*George Marshall: Statesman, 1945–1959.* New York, Viking, 1987.

Pohl, Hans and Hebeth, Stephanie and Brueninghaus, Beate. *Die Daimler-Benz AG in Jahren 1933 bis 1945.* Stuttgart, Zeitschrift fuer Unternehmensgeschichte, Beiheft 47, 1986.

Porsche, Ferry. *We at Porsche.* Foulis, 1977.

Railton, Arthur. *Der Kaefer: Der ungewöhnliche Weg eines ungewöhnlichen Automobils.* Zurich, Eurotax, 1985.

Rasmussen Mikkel. *The West, Civil Society, and the Construction of Peace.* Palgrave Macmillian, 2003.

Reich, Simon. *The Fruits of Fascism: Postwar Prosperity in Historical Context.* Cornell University, 1990.

Reich-Ranicki, Marcel. *The Author of Himself.* London, Orion, 2001.

Reuss, Eberhard. *Hitler's Motor Racing Battles*. Haynes Publishing, 2008.

Riechert, Udo. *Neubeginn im Schatten*. Wolfsburg, Steinweg, 1987.

Rosenbaum, Jean. *Is Your Volkswagen a Sex Symbol?* Hawthorne Books, 1972.

Rosenfeld, Gavriel and Paul Jaskot (editors). *Beyond Berlin*. University of Michigan, 2008.

Russell, Bertrand. *Political Ideals*. 1917.

——*The Problems of Philosophy*. 1912.

Sachs, Wolfgang. *For Love of the Automobile: Looking Back into the History of Our Desires*. Berkeley, University of California Press, 1992.

——*Die Liebe Zum Automobil: ein Rückblick in die Geschichte unserer Wünsche*. Hamburg, Rowohlt, 1984.

Schenzinger, K. A., H. Simon, and A. Zischka. *Nordhoff*. William Andermann, 1969.

Schneider, Christian. *Stadtgründung im Dritten Reich*. Wolfsburg and Salzgitter, 1978.

Schumacher, Fritz. *Small Is Beautiful, Economics as if People Mattered*. Reissued by Harper Collins, 2010.

Schwartz, David. *The Magic of Thinking Big*. Wilshire Book Company, 1959.

Shuler, Terry. *The Origin and Evolution of the Volkswagen*. Princeton, N.J., 1984.

Sloan, Alfred. P. Jr., *Adventures of a White Collar Worker*. 1970.

Speer, Albert. *Inside the Third Reich*. New York, Simon & Schuster, 1997.

——. *Spandau, The Secret Diaries*. Macmillan, 1976.

Steinberg, Jonathan. *Bismark: A Life*. Oxford University Press, 2011. Kindle Edition.

Stoelzl, Christoph. *Die Wolfsburg Saga*. Stuttgart, Konrad Theiss Verlag GmbH, 2008.

Strache, Wolf. *100 Years of Porsche*. Stuttgart, Porsche, A.G., 19

Taylor, A. J. P. *The Habsburg Monarchy, 1809–1918*. University of Chicago Press, 1976.

Taylor, Blaine. *Volkswagen Military Vehicles of the Third Reich*. Da Capo Press, 2004.

Terkel, Studs. *The Good War. An Oral History of World War Two*. New York: Pantheon, 1984.

Tresidder, Jack. *The Complete Dictionary of Symbols*. Duncan Baird Publishers, 2004.

Turner, Henry Ashby. *General Motors and the Nazis*. Yale University Press, 2005.

Vaitheeswaran, Vijay. *Zoom: The Global Race to Fuel the Car of the Future*. New York, 2007. (Kindle Edition.)

Wells, Mary. *A Big Life in Advertising*. New York, Knopf, 2002.

Willens, Doris. *Nobody's Perfect: Bill Bernbach and the Golden Age of Advertisng*. Self-published, CreateSpace, 2009.

Womack, James (with Daniel Jones and Daniel Roos). *The Machine That Changed the World: Based on the Massachusetts Institute of Technology 5-Million-Dollar 5-Year Study on the Future of the Automobile*. New York, Simon & Schuster, 1990.

Wood, Andrew. *New York's 1939–1940 World's Fair*. Arcadia Publishing, 2004.

Wood, Jon. *Great Marquees of Germany*. Viscount Books, 1985.

Zentner, Christian. *Adolf Hitler Chronik 1889–1945, Aufstieg und Untergang*. St. Gallen, Otus, 2005.

Catalogs

Place of Remembrance of the History of Forced Labor for the Volkswagen Factory. Volkswagen AG, Wolfsburg.

"50 Jahre Volkswagen Werbung." Stern magazine spezial, 2002. (Eigentum der Stadt Wolfsburg Stadtarchiv 4654.)

Käfer: der Erfolkswagen. Prestel. Museum fär Kunst und Gewerbe Hamburg, 29 August bis 30, November 1997.

Französische Malerei: von Delacroix bis Picasso. Organized by Volkswagenwerk, 8 April–31, May 1961. Stadthalle Wolfsburg.

Historical Notes: A Series of Publications from the Volkswagen, AG Corporate Archives, Wolfsburg

The British and Their Works: The Volkswagenwerk and the Occupying Power 1945–1949. Editors: Bernd Graef, Manfred Grieger, Dirk Schlinkert. Wolfsburg, 1999.

Henk 't Hoen: Zwei Jahre Volkswagenwerk, Als niederländischer Student im 'Arbeitseinsatz' im Volkswagenwerk von Mai 1943 bis zum Mai 1945. Editors: Manfred Grieger, Ulrike Gutzmann, Dirk Schlinkert. Wolfsburg, 2005.

Richter, Ralf. *Ivan Hirst*. VW Publication. Wolfsburg.

Überleben in Angst: Vier Juden berichten über ihre Zeit im Volkswagenwerk in den Jahren 1943 bis 1945. Editors: Manfred Grieger, Ulrike Gutzmann, Dirk Schlinkert. Wolfsburg, 2007.

Abfahrt ins Ungewisse: Drei Polen berichten über ihre Zeit als Zwangsarbeiter im Volkswagenwerk von Herbst 1942 bis Sommer 1945. Editors: Manfred Grieger, Ulrike Gutzmann, Dirk Schlinkert. Wolfsburg, 2009.

Olga un Piet: Eine Liebe in zwei Diktaturen. Editors: Manfred Grieger, Ulrike Gutzmann, Dirk Schlinkert. Wolfsburg, 2009.

Towards Mobility: Varieties of Automobilism East and West. Editors: Manfred Grieger, Ulrike Gutzmann, Dirk Schlinkert. Wolfsburg, Volkswagen AG, 2009.

Volkswagen Chronicle: Becoming a Global Player. Editors: Manfred Grieger, Ulrike Gutzmann, Dirk Schlinkert. Wolfsburg, Volkswagen AG, 2008.

Work Exhibition 1. Editors: Manfred Grieger and Dirk Schlinkert. Wolfsburg, Volkswagen AG, 2006.

Porsche Museum and Porsche Archive Publications
Porsche Chronicle, 1931–2008. Munich, Piper Verlag, 2008.
Die Autos. Stuttgart, Porsche Museum, 2009.
Ferdinand Porsche und der Volkswagen. Stuttgart, Porsche Museum, 2009.
Ferry Porsche. Stuttgart, Porsche Museum, 2009.
Pionier des Hybridantriebs. Stuttgart, Porsche Museum, 2010.

Speeches
Robert Gage at Art Director's Club of Montreal. 1963.
Julian Koenig at The Advertising Writer's Club. 9 November 1961.
Lore Parker, Vice President of DDB. 15 October 1966.

DDB News Interviews
Phyllis Robinson: from *Great American Copywriter Vol. 2,* published 10 March 1971 · Bill Bernbach Interview from 1974 · Bill Bernbach from June issue *DDB News,* 1969 · Helmut Krone Interview, September 1968 · Online reprints of other interviews/clippings by Tadahisa Nishio

Letters
Bill Bernbach to Bill Moyers. 17 August 1964 · Bill Bernbach's letter to Grey. 15 May 1947 · "Toynbee v. Bernbach"

Magazines, Journals, and Newspapers
Advertising Age · *Autogramm: Die Zeitung fuer Mitarbeiterinnen und Mitarbeiter der Marke Volkswagen* · *Bug Power* · *Business History Review* · *Dearborn Independent* · *Die Strasse* · *The Economist* · *Esquire* magazine · *The Financial Times* (London) · *Forbes* · *Foreign Affairs* · *Harper's Magazine* · *International Spiegel Online* · *ID* magazine (Bugs Issue) · *Journal of Commerce* · *Le Monde* · *Life* magazine · *Motor* · *New York Times* · *The New Yorker* · *The New Republic* · *Reader's Digest* · *Road & Track* · *Rolling Stone* · *Der Spiegel* · *Der Tagesspiegel* · *Time* magazine · *The Villager* · *Die Welt*

Articles
Adamson, Allen. "Volkswagen, BMW Understand What It Takes to Stand Out." *Forbes,* 25 April 2011.

Bedford, Paul. "He Tried Harder." *Creative Review,* vol. 42, February, 2001.

Clark, Blake. "The Car That Built a City." *Reader's Digest,* February 1954.

DeJesus, Erin. "Mad Women." *Bust Magazine,* December/January 2009.

Friedmann, Jan. "Adolf Hitler's Time in Jail." *Der Spiegel Online,* 23 June 2010.

Goerl, Stephen. "German Challenge." *New York Times,* 25 October 1953.

Hawranek, Dietmar. "The Porsche Story: A Fierce Family Feud." *Der Spiegel,* 21 July 2009.

———"Designing Cars for Hitler: Porsche and Volkswagen's Nazi Roots." *Der Spiegel Online,* 21 July 2009.

Henderson, David: "Germany Economic Miracle." *Library of Economics and Liberty, The Concise Encyclopedia of Economics.* 2008.

Kiley, David. "The Volkswagen Beetle Rides Again." *AOL Autos,* 18 April 2011.

Lasky, Melvin. "The Volkswagen: A Success Story." *New York Times,* 2 October 1955.

Michener, James. "A Tough Man for a Tough Job." *Life,* 12 May 1952.

Piper, Ernst. "Allein gegen Hitler." *Der Tagesspiegel,* 1 November 2009.

Schaefer, Daniel. "VW Chairman Adds Scalp to List of Victims." *Financial Times,* London. 25/26 July 2009.

———"Protective Layers." *Financial Times, London* 17 June 2010.

Schütz, Erhard. *Der Volkswagen,* 2000.

Tallmer, Jerry. "Notebook: Salinger as Touchstone in My Life, in all Our Lives." *The Villager,* Volume 79, Number 35, 3–9 February 2009.

Tolliday, Steven. "From 'Beetle Monoculture' to the 'German Model': the Transformation of Volkswagen, 1967–1991." *Business and Economic History,* Volume 24, no. 2, 1995.

———"Enterprise and State in the West German Wirtschaftswunder: Volkswagen and the Automobile Industry, 1939–1962." *Business History Review,* 22 September 1995.

Walker, Lester. "Secrets by the Thousands." *Harper's Magazine,* October 1946.

Weissenborn, Stefan Robert. "Benz war's nicht: Ein Schweizer Historiker ist überzeugt: Das erste Auto der Geschichte baute ein anderer. Und zwar viel früher." *Die Welt.* 28 November 2009.

Wilcke, Gerd. "Rise of a New German City: Roads and Cars Dominate in Shiny Volkswagen Town." *New York Times.* 14 May 1961.

Articles with no Stated Author

Autocar. "Production Is Their Wealth." 3 February 1950.

Communication Arts. "Helmut Krone." September 2005, pages 61–62.

The Economist. "Inside the Miracle: How Germany Weathered the Recession." 11 March 2010.

———"GM Auctions Opel: A Disputed Bid." 25 July 2009.

———"A Special Report on Germany: Inside the Miracle." 11 March 2010.

The Independent. "Sell of the Century." 25 January 2010.

Motor. "Hitler's Volkswagen." 31 December 1935.

———"The Volkswagen Revealed." 27 December 1938.

———"KdF Volkswagen: Neither Myth nor Menace." 28 February 1939.

———"The Truth Behind the KdF." 12 March 1941.

———"The 1947 Volkswagen Saloon." 7 May 1947.

———"The Volkswagen DeLuxe Saloon." 18 April 1956.

———"Round Australia." 13 November 1958.

New York Times: "German Car for Masses." 3 July 1938, page 112.

———"Volkswagen Gives Up Plans to Produce Here for the American Market." 25 January 1956.

———"Deliveries of Volkswagens Here Keep a Fleet of 60 Vessels Busy." 27 June 1964.

———"Policy Defended by Volkswagen: Importer, 14 Distributors of Car Deny U.S. Charges in Antitrust Action." 15 March 1958.

———"Nazi Automobile Plant Started 25 Years Ago." 26 May 1963.

Der Spiegel. "In Koenig Nordhoff's Reich." 1955.

Time magazine. "Pas de Pagaille." 28 July 1947.

———"Business and Finance: Germany's Flivver." 25 August 1952.

———"Business Abroad: Comeback in the West. 15 February 1954.

———"Retail Trade: High Fashion at Low Prices." 6 September 1954.

———"Business Abroad: Renault on the Go." 6 January 1958.

———"Autos: The New Generation." 5 October 1959.

———"Tariffs: Think Big." 2 November 1962.

Rheinischen Merkur. No. 36, 3 September 2005.

Road & Track. "1956 Volkswagen Sedan Road Test." October 1956.

———"1961 Road Test." December 1960.

Wheels Magazine. "Volkswagen and the Herald." December 1959.

Internet

www.life.com · Online Presidential Speech Archives · Online Libraries · George Lois: www.georgelois.com · DDB: www.ddb.com · Volkswagen AG: www.volkswagenag.com · Truman Library: www.trumanlibrary.com · Ford: http://www.ford.com/ · Volkswagen Auto Museum Wolfsburg: http://automuseum.volkswagen.de/ · Bill Bernbach interview on YouTube: http://www.youtube.com/results?search_query=Bill+Bernbach&aq=f · Julian Koenig on YouTube: http://www.youtube.com/results?search_query=Julian

+Koenig&aq=f · George Lois on YouTube: http://www.youtube.com/
results?search_query=George+Lois&aq=f · German Libraries: www.voebb
.de · Library of Economics and Liberty: http://www.econlib.org/library/
Enc

Radio
This American Life · KCRW's Bookworm with Michael Silverblatt

I Tunes U
Stanford Lectures · Open University · CUNY, City University, New York ·
Masterworks of International Relations

Films and Documentaries
Alfred Brendel: Man and Mask. Mark Kidel, 2000.
Annie Hall. Woody Allen, 1977.
American Experience: The Crash of 1929. PBS, 2009.
Art & Copy. Doug Prey, 2009.
Aus eigener Kraft. Volkswagen, 1954.
Berkeley in the Sixties. Mark Kitchell. Liberation Entertainment, 2007.
Blind Spot: Hitler's Secretary. Heller, Andre, 2002.
Brutalität in Stein: die Bauten der Nazis gestern und heute. Michael Kloft.
    Spiegel TV, Hamburg, 2002.
Bunker: Die Letzten Tage. Martina Reuter und Gavin Hodge. 2004.
Century of the Self. Adam Curtis: BBC television, 2002.
Der Chroniken des Adolf Hitler. Erwin Leiser. Germany, 2006.
Deutschland im Kalten Krieg. vor 60 Jahren begann der Konflikt der Super-
    mächte; Cassian von Salomon [Ltg.]; Bernd Jacobs [Red.]; Spiegel TV,
    2008.
Dwight D. Eisenhower: Commander in Chief. Biography Series, A&E, 2005.
FDR: Years of Crisis. Biography Series, A&E, 1994.
Fuel. Joshua Tickell, 2008.
George Marshall and the American Century.
Die Gläserne Manufaktur von Volkswagen in Dresden. VW Dresden promo.
Hitler: eine Bilanz. Guido Knopp. BMG, 1995.
————*Der Diktator.*
————*Der Kriegsherr.*
————*Der Verbrecher.*
————*Die Luftbrücke.*
Hitler: ein Karriere. Joachim Fest, 1977.
Landslide: A Portrait of President Herbert Hoover. PBS, 2009.
Life in the Thirties. NBC News Special, 1995.

Mister Volkswagen. Hans Castrop. Stuttgart: Süddeutscher Rundfunk, 1997.

Mythos für Millionen: die witzigsten, besten und schönsten Highlights aus der Geschichte des VW-Käfer! [DVD Video] / *ein Film von Manfred Breuersbrock und Gandulf Hennig.* Potsdam, 2003.

No Direction Home. Bob Dylan. Scorsese, 2005.

Der Nürnberger Prozess. Spiegel TV: Hamburg, 2003.

Passageways: James Turrell. France, 2006.

Die perfekte Stadt für zeitgenössische Kunst. Ein Film von Axel Bosse und Frank Woesthoff, 2009.

Porsche Way: Der Porsche Weg. Stuttgart, Porsche Museum, 2010.

Die Stunde Null: Berlin, Sommer, 1945. Spiegel TV, Hamburg, 2009.

Unser Krieg: Amateurfilme aus dem II Welt. Michael Kuball, 2007.

Volkswagen Story. Published by Volkswagen of America.

Die Vossstrasse: ein virtueller Stadtrundgang. Christoph Neubauer, 2008.

Der VW-Komplex. Hartmut Bitomsky, 1990.

Who Killed the Electric Car? Chris Paine. Sony Pictures, 2006.

Wilhelm II. Der letzte Kaiser. Hamburg, Spiegel TV, 2009.

Audio CD's

Der Käfer im Wunderland: Volkswagen in den langen fünfziger Jahren. Wolfsburg, Volkswagen AG, 2010.

Mit dem Käfer zum Golf: Eine Reise durch 10 Jahre Volkswagen Geschichte. Wolfsburg, Volkswagen AG, 2009.

Niemand Wusste was Morgen sein würde. Wolfsburg, Volkswagen AG, 2008.

World War II: A Military and Social History. Childers, Thomas: "The Origins of the Second World War" lecture, and "Hitler's Challenge to the International System": From The Teaching Company, Course 810.

Notes

o o

Chapter 1

5 *Ethnic ad agency:* Sometimes people also referred to DDB as a "Seventh Avenue" agency as well.

5 "unabashedly recognizably": Fox, 275.

5 "No one in America knows": Kaplan, 26.

6 "Baby Hitler": *New York Times,* July 3, 1938.

Chapter 2

7 "bright blue—bordering on the violet": OSS, 22–23.

8 *Strength through Joy Car:* In German, this is *der Kraft durch Freude Wagen,* which is also widely known as the Kdf-Wagen.

8 "Until now the automobile has": Sachs, 61. From *Das Automobil erobert die Welt. Biographie des Draftwagens,* Berlin, 1938, 356.

8 "model German workers city" and ideas behind city planning: *Wortprotokoll der Uebertragung der Grundsteinlegung des Volkswagen Werkes bei Fallersleben am 26. Mai 1938,* compiled by Rolf Linnemann, March 1987 (Stadtarchiv Wolfsburg), 6–7.

10 *He certainly wasn't himself:* According to one city planner, Titus Taescher: "Hitler hatte damals offenbr ganz andere Dinge im Kopf. Es war whol die planerische Vorbereitung fuer einen Einmarsch in die Txchechoslovakei, und er fand nicht Zeit und Interesse, sich anzusehen, was vir vorbereitet hatten." 3 November 1970: Wolfsburg Musuem Austellung. Stadtarchiv 21.

11 *It was well known that Hitler's preferred place in any car:* Linge, 13. Hitler's valet, Heinz Linge, tells about a time when shots were fired in an assassination attempt and hit Himmler's car instead, in the area of the front seat, at which time Hitler told Linge, "That was certainly intended for me because Himmler does not usually drive ahead. It is also well known that I always sit at the side of the driver. . . ."

Chapter 3

13 "Freedom has been sacrificed": Otto Julius Bierbaum. Sachs, 7–8.

Chapter 4

17 "It now costs the average American": Wood, 90.

18 "the audience had never even considered": *Wired,* Issue 15.12,
11–27, 2007.

20 "The eyes of the Fair are on the future": World's Fair pamphlet.

21 "It is Germany's great good fortune to have found a leader":
Kempe, 17.

Chapter 5

23 *Ginzkey:* In 1924, Ginzkey's carpet factory provided the world's largest carpet to the Waldorf-Astoria hotel in New York City.

24 *Bela Egger:* the company Porsche first got a job for, through Ginzkey's
contacts.

25 *Tires and Wheels:* The first air-filled tires were invented in 1888 and
were later used for bicycles. In 1895, André Michelin used one on a
car for the first time, though it did not quite work. It was not until
1911 that the first successful tires were made by Philip Strauss.
Around this same time, the Goodyear car company began to add carbon to rubber to give the tires a longer life. Charles Goodyear had invented vulcanized rubber in 1844. Vulcanized rubber is rubber with
added chemicals so that it will not melt in hot weather or break in
cold weather, as the original rubber (gum from tree sap) did.

26 *Energy and its relation to mobility:* France deserves a word here, to
be sure, having developed the *systeme panhard,* "the basic fore-to-aft
formation of radiator, engine, clutch, gearbox, prop shaft, and rear
axle. This was far removed from the German Daimler-Benz horseless
carriage, which had a gasoline engine turning a belt drive to the
wheels." Vaitheeswaren, Location 363.

Chapter 6

28 "I never witnessed": Kershaw, Kindle Location 565.

30 "He is very young": Frankenberg, 5.

30 Porsche was also a very good driver, and he liked to race, so he also
built a racing version of the Lohner-Porsche. Around the same time
as that first Paris show, Porsche took to the streets of Vienna and set a
record with it.

33 "grant to human beings their conquest": *Allgemeine
Automobil-Zeitung,* 1906, no. 17, 33. From Sachs, 9.

33 "at odds with himself": Hitler, 19.

34 "prostrate with grief": Kershaw, Location 750.

34 Aloisia also worked at Bela Egger.

36 "a wonderful car—one, single, wonderful car": Brinkley, 106.

36 ——"At the time, Ford himself wondered aloud whether his company would ever build even a tenth Model T."

Chapter 7

38 Bill Bernbach finished his studies in 1932, but the graduation ceremony was not until 1933.

40 "Now Bill, what you do is": Jackall, 69.

41 I could not find this first ad that Bill always later claimed he did for Lord & Thomas.

Chapter 8

42 "Hitler: Our Last Hope": Zentner, 38.

44 *Deutsche Qualitätsarbeit:* According to an essay called "German Quality Work" by Alf Luedtke in *Towards Mobility,* VW AG, 175— "The notion and claims of 'German Quality Work' had their social and cultural bases in artisanal trades. In due time, not merely artisanal but industrial masters and engineers and, even more, skilled industrial workers took 'German quality work' as a notion of reference. To all of them it would connect perfectly with self-assessment and aspiration. . . . Thus in the 1920s as in the 1930s young semi-skilled male workers who had been trained on the job to operate, for instance, universal machine tools were a case in point. They themselves but likewise company superiors, union functionaries and external observers regarded them as producers of 'quality work.' "

44 *Connection between German Quality Work and a mistrust of free trade:* As Jonathan Steinberg points out in his book *Bismarck: A Life,* artisans and craftsmen historically developed an attitude against the new idea of capitalistic free trade, and beginning in the late 1800s, this sentiment was often tied to anti-Semitism. Thus in a very real sense, the ideas that Hitler took to the extreme were not new ideas in the history of Germany but rather familiar ones, which helped Hitler use those ideas toward his own ends.

45 *Communism:* It was Bolshevism in the early 1900s in Russia (Lenin, Trotsky). The word Bolshevism and Menshevism was ultimately dropped and it became Communism instead. Hitler often talked of the Bolsheviks as the enemy. I used Communist here because it is less confusing.

46 Historian and professor Thomas Childers talks about the shock of the country after World War One in the audio learning series: "The Origins of the Second World War" lecture, and "Hitler's challenge to the International System" lecture.

48 "Paris was a nightmare": Keynes, Location 34.

48 ——"by the very persons who": Location 1848.

48 ——"deeply and inextricably": Location 31.

48 ——"the perils of": Location 1274.

49 "I do not change my nationality": Frankenberg, 22.

51 "very positive attraction . . .": Frankenberg, 24.

Chapter 9

53 It is contested how often or how seriously Adolf Hitler considered his own suicide.

54 "The obituaries were, as it turned out": Overy, 50.

54 ——"willfully ruined a fine genetic inheritance": 98–99.

54 ——"The power of the popular biological argument was evident in its most extreme form": 106.

55 Hitler was the 55th member of the NSDAP. He was given number 555 though, because they were numbering bigger to look bigger.

56 "The art of propaganda": *Hitler*, 1992, 165.

57 "I'm finished. If I had a revolver": Kershaw, Location 2906.

57 "Crisis was Hitler's": Kershaw, 2738.

58 "The man who is born to be": Brody, 70; Bullock, 117.

58 "Landsberg was a university": Kershaw, *Hubris*, 240.

59 "I've brought a new customer for you": Reuss, 48–49.

60 "making his hair stand": Spiegel, Friedmann, 2010.

60 *Henry Ford's People's Car:* In 1925, Henry Ford's *My Life and Work* was a bestseller in Berlin. In America, the Model T had debuted in 1908 with a purchase price of $825.00. Over ten thousand were sold in its first year, a record in any country. Four years later the price was lowered to $575.00 and sales again soared. By 1914, Ford's company had a 48 percent share of the automobile market, and because of Ford's assembly line, one car could be made every 93 minutes. By 1918, half of all cars in America were Model T's.

61 "No sooner did production start up than the company's executives began prowling the factory floors": Brinkley, 141.

62 "Things will develop": *Automobil Revue* Volume 7, 126.

62 "right of way in the literal sense": Sachs, 45.

62 *Fuhrer without a Fuhrerschein:* The term Fuhrer was used as a military title in Germany during the 18th century. Hitler brought this term into politics and christened himself "the Fuhrer" when he was head of the NSDAP. The term means to drive, guide, or steer and is used in combination with other words in German such as "Fuhrerschein," which means "driver's license" in English and is used in the same way in Germany today.

Chapter 10

64 Daimler-Benz was actually still called Daimler Motor in 1923. It merged with Benz in 1926. Daimler is creator of the Mercedes. Thus "Mercedes-Benz."

68 "in recognition of his outstanding merit": Frankenberg, 34.

68 *thirty test samples:* None of these early Daimler cars exist today. None have been found, so it's hard to say what the car looked like. Most agree it was an evolved idea of the Sascha but with a 1,000 cc engine. It could also have been like the 8/38.

Chapter 11

72 *Turm der blauen Pferde* (Tower of the Blue Horses): This Franz Marc painting was at the Nationalgalerie in Berlin. Marc, alongside other artists such as Wassily Kandinsky, was part of an art group called "Blaue Reiter" that formed before the First World War.

72 "not halfway, not dishonest, not unfinished": Nordhoff's letter to Charlotte Fassunge. 9 December 1923. Barbara Graefin Cantacuzino's private archive. Edelmann, 2003. 27.

72 "No one should pride himself": Marc, LfW, 56.

77 "The automobile changed our dress, manners, social customs": Brinkley, 333.

80 "acquire companies in individual countries and build upon their existing reputations.": Brinkley, 369.

Chapter 12

82 Paul Rand's work and ads can be found at paul-rand.com.

84 "Just as warfare": Hochschild, Location 2624–29.

85 "with the high responsibility": Coolidge—Address Before the American Association of Advertising Agencies, Washington, D.C. October 27, 1926, Library of Congress. Speech online at: http://www.presidency.ucsb.edu/ws/index.php?pid=412

86 "There is no one self": Lippmann, 173.

86 "high excitement in the booming field": Mark Crispin Miller in introduction to Bernay's Propaganda, Kindle Location, 40–42.

86 "When I came back from the war": Bernays interview, YouTube.

90 "We are going into the Reichstag": Kershaw, Location 3950.

90 "I just snuck": Scorsese, *No Way Home.*

Chapter 13

93 "Tree Frog": in German, *Laubfrosch.*

93 "The one will be too heavy": L. Betz, *Das Volksauto.* Rettung oder

Untergang der deutschen Automobile-industrie (The People's Car: Salvation or decline of the German auto industry). Stuttgart, 1931, 45, 73. Sachs, 43–44.

94 *gathering some of the best:* Porsche would have some of the best engineers in the world working with him: Karl Rabe, Josef Kales, Erwin Komenda, Karl Froehlich, Josef Mickl, Josef Zahrednik, and Franz Xaver Reimspiess. All of these men deserve books written about them, and all of them are the true creators of the People's Car, for Porsche relied on them and they worked as a team. It was Reimspiess that made the logo, the same VW still uses today.

96 *Adolf Rosenberger, investor and account for Porsche:* Adolf Rosenberger was Jewish and would resign when Adolf Hitler was elected to office in 1933. Rosenberger left Germany, though Porsche still employed him for some time as their "foreign representative" in the United States and in France. The Porsches and Rosenberger would continue to argue over finances. Rosenberger would claim that the Porsches had not paid him what he was owed. The Porsches would claim to have helped him flee and to have been giving him money even when he was no longer working for them. After the war, Rosenberger wanted the firm to give him money under the table; they would not. In the end, the Porsches gave him a new Volkswagen, and legally paid him a smaller sum of money than what he'd asked. Rosenberger moved to California and stayed there the rest of his life.

96 The first projects of the Porsche design firm went toward a midsize, two-liter car called the Wanderer.

97 The design of the car's body came in large part from Erwin Komenda.

98 *Tatra:* Much later, long after Porsche and all his designers were gone and after the torsion bar had proven to be an asset in the Volkswagen, Tatra would sue VW over this issue, and win. Hans Ledwinka and Tatra played a big role here. Once one starts looking deeply, however, there are examples of "Beetle-like" cars all over the place from around this time. So many people were experimenting with so many of the same ideas, options, and tools. Porsche and his engineers most certainly used a lot of what they saw around them, especially the very advanced Czech companies like Tatra. In the end though, for whatever mysterious reason, there was only one car that became the Bug.

Chapter 14

101 "The motor vehicle": Sachs, 47. From Hitler's speech on 11 February 1933.

103 Goering would later oppose the idea of the Volkswagen, claiming it would nationalize private industry and hurt the country in the end.

104 "No symbolic groundbreaking": Sachs, 48.

104 "Just as horse-drawn vehicles": *Die Strasse,* 1939, no. 20, 242.

105 "The erasure of stubborn differences": Sachs, 53.

105 *widespread construction of the first modern highway:* The first bit of autobahn did not come from Hitler but from the Weimar Republic, but Hitler was the first to make it into a program and to actually build the plans that had been made. Mussolini had also attempted to build highways.

105 "Nothing to cramp or delay you": Sachs, 52. From W. Bade, *Das Auto erobert die Welt. Biographie des Krafwagens,* Berlin, 1938, 316f.

106 "German car makers have made": *Motor,* 1935.

109 "It should look like a Beetle": This is attributed to Hitler in various books about the Beetle, but with no references, only word of mouth. "Wie ein Maiekaefer soll er aussehen. Man braucht nur die Natur zu betrachten, um zu wissen, wie sie mit der Stromlinie fertig wird."

Chapter 15

111 *Mercedes:* Created by Daimler, this was always Hitler's favorite car, the one he was sure to be seen in around town. The car had been named after Mercedes Jellineck, the daughter of Emil Jellineck, a former patron of the company and a wealthy and influential Jew.

111 *Auto Union race car:* Giving them race-car funds was one of the best moves Hitler could have made. Porsche's Auto Union Type C race car would become one of the most famous race cars in German history. The government's annual funding would also lead to the famous Silver Arrows, the racing cars that dominated the European races from 1934 until the outbreak of war. In those years, Germany was clearly emerging as a dominant automotive power again. An issue of the magazine *Der Nürburgring* filled its front cover with a photo of him: "Adolf Hitler, the patron of the German motor car," it read.

113 *Kaiserhof Hotel:* Very famous Prussian hotel. It used to be close to the Reichskanzlei and was a sign of power and prestige.

113 For the hardcore VW fans: I have used slightly different dates here than Chris Barber does in his very excellent book on the Beetle. There is no definite date (the month, we know, but we don't know which came first), and in my research, the way I have presented these meetings is the way that made sense with the documents I found. Barber puts Werlin's visit after the Exposé was mailed.

115 "In my opinion, a people's car does": Porsche Musuem, FP and the VW, 15.

Chapter 16
116 "chess match for power": Kershaw, Location 4899.

Chapter 17
121 "Well, I suppose there's nothing": Porsche gets different phrases like this attributed to him in his biographies. They are all paraphrases. See Nelson, 40–41.
122 "Who is a Jew": Goering is often quoted with this phrase, though it was a popular one at the time and probably did not originate with him. Many Germans had Jewish friends or acquaintances who didn't count for them as "real Jews." Karl Lueger, the mayor of Vienna who Hitler so liked when he lived there, once said something quite similar when the press asked him why he talked so badly of Jews but then still had friends or dinner partners who were Jewish businessmen.
124 "There can be only one Volkswagen": Hitler/Domarus, 880.
127 "the most significant public monument in America": Brinkley, 291.
130 *The Porsche plant:* Hawranek, *Der Spiegel Online,* 21 July 2009.

Chapter 18
131 "a psychologocial balance": *Hitler* documentary, Fest.
131 ———"We will not lie and we will not cheat"
131 "Germany needs and desires peace": Arendt, 37.
133 "Let there be no doubt": Hitler speech from 1937 Auto Show.
135 *extended learning trip to the United States:* A member of the DAF, Bodo Lafferentz, was sent with them as well to watch over things and a man from Porsche's workshop, Dr. Feuereisen, a man who would later work for VW and be an engine of the service department, was also with the group.
135 "without having to be supervised": Ferry Porsche, 107.
136 *German banker unaware of war:* "Little of this sentiment was really understood on the German side. A German banker visiting the City of London in May 1939 was mystified by the endless talk of war and the evident preparations for its imminent arrival." Overy, 356.
139 "There are 75,000": Ghislaine Kaes's "Lecture on the Trip to North America by Dr. Ing.h.c. Ferdinand Porsche in 1936," given 29 January 1937. Recorded in VW's *Place of Remembrance.*
139 "Automated operations require": Otto Dyckoff, *Place of Remembrance,* 26.

Chapter 19
140 "an unscrupulous criminal": Hitler, speech from 1939 Auto Show.
141 "sense of spaciousness almost unmarred by interior columns." "The

building drew attention as a harbinger of a new era in industrial design. Factories would no longer be doomed to the look of 'old prison workshops' . . . ," Brinkley, 136.

142 "visually with the center of town": Rosenfeld, 89–115.

142 ———"considered this axis"

145 "Chianti bottle and dagger ruled": Nelson, 78.

145 *to help Germans save their money:* The car was being advertised for 990 marks. In reality, the car would have cost each person closer to 1200 marks due to hidden added costs such as a "delivery fees," which made little sense as customers were expected to travel to Wolfsburg and pick up the cars themselves.

146 "nothing would induce him to pull the trigger": Ferry Porsche, 7–8.

Chapter 20

153 *Hoover:* He did not allow direct and obvious intervention in the domestic market, but he did set up some potential solutions that FDR would later capitalize on. Hoover's real mistake, however, was to allow direct intervention in the *international* market by greatly restricting international trade, a move that had devastating economic consequences.

154 "After all,": Fireside Chat, 12 March 1933.

155 "Politics was the first big business": Bernays, *Propaganda,* Location 889.

156 *German government became openly totalitarian:* There was also a slide toward paranoia, which added a new level of violence and horror to industrial relations. Hitler was afraid of leaks about the People's Car, for instance, and jailed one Opel exec after his trip to America because he thought the man had given away the secrets of the car. Porsche and his team would eventually be told to smash all the original VW prototypes to keep them out of enemy hands.

Chapter 21

158 "One stated: After what has happened there . . ." All Ranicki quotes here are from *The Author of Himself,* 39, 40. Phoenix Books, London, 1999.

161 This conversation between Porsche and Hitler is reported in various books, though of course none of us knows the exact words, it was something to this effect.

Chapter 22

161 "Through night and blood": Clausewitz, Location 14.

162 "Until four-thirty this morning": Roosevelt, Radio Address, Location 3413.

162 "That Hitler came into political existence": McLuhan, *Understanding Media*, 1964, p. 262.

165 "You, the people of this country": Roosevelt, Fireside chat, 3 September 1939.

165 The National Association of Manufacturers, NAM, had formed in a previous cycle of recession at the end of the 19th century as a way of supporting foreign export.

166 "Even a neutral": Roosevelt, Fireside chat, 1939.

166 "Tonight over the once peaceful roads": FDR, Fireside Chat, 1940.

166 *Bertrand Russell:* In an open letter to Russell at the time he was removed from his position in NYC, Albert Einstein wrote his often quoted phrase: "Great spirits have always encountered violent opposition from mediocre minds."

167 "We are now in this war" FDR, Fireside chat, 1941.

167 "Private industry will continue to be the source": FDR, Gearing up for the war in 1940 chat.

Chapter 23

169 *Chauffeurska:* Hitler's close inner daily circle was in large part comprised of his drivers. Hanfstaengl called this "sycophantic entourage" his Chauffeurska. Kershaw, Location 5801.

169 "I belonged to a circle": Speer's testimony, Nuremberg, Germany, 7–19 June 1946.

170 "With the success of a sleepwalker": Reuss, page 215, translation of Mommsen.

170 "I think you have a rather good idea there": Ferry Porsche, 145.

171 Speer was right about the organization having a lack of standards or efficient rules. Only in 1944, for example, would the Volkswagen factory be officially designated as the prime car manufacturer for the Nazis.

172–173 *Porsche also courted by Stalin:* Porsche knew Russia firsthand because he had been invited there by Stalin. He accepted the offer, was given a tour of their country and industry, and was even offered a job as the director of the development of the Soviet auto industry, a job which he had considered taking but eventually declined, saying he did not want to leave his home, or live in a country where he could not understand the language.

173 "working towards the Fuhrer": Kershaw explains this beautifully in his books on Hitler, but basically it was the idea that anyone in the country always had the feeling that in their everyday acts they were doing what was best for the country and since Hitler was the symbol

of the country, he embodied that country and one did everything that would please him.

173 *Nordhoff at Opel's Brandenburg plant:* It was here that the air-cooled engine of Porsche's VW also made it into Nordhoff's life once more: It had once been thought that Hitler did not like this particular engine, but now the Nazis had decided air-cooled engines were best for war, and thus the truck factory was encouraged to design a truck that could use one. An air-cooled engine for a heavy-duty truck was impractical so Opel engineers developed one that used both air and oil to keep itself cool: Oil absorbed heat from the cylinder barrels, but the heads were cooled by air. This truck never made it into mass production, however, but its design gave Nordhoff quite a headache.

173 "The future looks dark": Heinrich to Charlotte: 12 August 1943, Privatarchiv Barbara Cantacuzino. Edelmann, 61.

174 "He is a real genius": Taylor, 26.

174 "Hitler drove around the country": Trudl Junge, 71.

175 "At most a half-dozen men": Ferry Porsche, 141.

177 *Mein Kampf* from loudspeaker: *Niemand Wusste was Morgen sein würde.* Wolfsburg, Volkswagen AG, CD 1, Title 3.

177 *Women workers at VW:* Some women arrived pregnant. Many others got pregnant while working there. In one of the more horrific crimes of the time, 365 children would eventually die, most before the age of one, in connection to camps such as these within the town. The doctor overseeing the factory nursery would later be sentenced to death.

178 *Burned his foot by holding it to a hot stove:* "Under no circumstances could I continue living this way. Since I was rejected each time I reported myself sick because (as the ineterpreter told me) neither blood nor any injuries were visible, I thought out a plan. In the middle of the night while everyone was asleep, I went to the red-hot stove in the hut and pressed my left foot against the back of it utterly fearlessly . . . The next morning I reported myself sick and was certified unfit to work on the huts . . . Since I was working in the kitchen, I began to regain some of my strength." Cesare Pilesi, *Place of Remembrance,* 72.

Chapter 24

184 "anguish and disbelief and bewilderment": Ferry Porsche, xi–xiv.

184 *Ferry and Hitler:* Ferry, though he at times cooperated with the Nazi government to a great extent, was leery of Hitler, but he would later write in *We at Porsche* that he'd always been impressed with Hitler's automotive skills: ". . . here, I thought, was a man who had taken the

trouble to study and understand this particular problem of the Volkswagen. He asked a surprising number of technical questions, all of
which made good sense." Porsche, 91.

185 *Indiscriminate bombing:* The Japanese bombed Shanghai civilians in
1937, before Hitler began ordering bombs dropped on civilian targets.

187 "The German people celebrate the Führer's birthday": Goebbels
speech on Hitler's birthday, 1943.

187 ———"Confidence is"

Chapter 25

189 "If the war is lost, the nation will also perish": Hitler to Speer, Hartrich, 31.

189 ———"all industrial plants, all important electrical facilities, water-
works, gasworks, all stocks of food and clothing, all bridges, all railways and communications installations." 31.

Chapter 26

197 *Images of destroyed Germany:* from Spiegel documentary films and
archival footage, especially *Die Stunde Null.*

198 "England would be chained": Rasmussen, 88.

200 "a certain American aircraft company": Walker, *Harper's,* 1946.

201 "with a few modifications": Turner, 165.

Chapter 27

202 *Hirst:* The thoughts I give to Hirst here are taken from his own recol-
lections that can be read in full in the Volkswagen publication *Ivan
Hirst.*

204 "constructive pragmatism": This term is borrowed from *Changing
Lanes,* a publication from the archive of VW that they have made
available in English as well as German.

207 *The Works Council:* An important part of German history, and of the
Volkswagen factory. In Germany, trade unions have a partner or counterpart called the Works Council. A Works Council, or *Betriebsrat,* is
made of elected workers from a company and functions as a representative body for the workforce and meets with trade unions as well
as with the executives of the company to negotiate and discuss whatever issues (economic or social) might arise. They are elected for
four-year terms, and they can come from any trade union affiliation
or political party, and no outside labor group affiliations are necessary for them to be elected. Works Councils were first legally recognized in Germany after the First World War in 1918. With the Works

Councils Act of 1920, the name became official as a law was passed
requiring all business enterprises with more than 20 employees to
set up a Works Council. 1n 1930, Germany had more than 150,000
different Works Councils registered. In 1933, when Hitler became
Chancellor, all those Works Councils were thought to give too much
control to the workers, a threat to the greater authority, and all of
them were subordinated to a new arm of the Nazi Party called the
German Labor Front, or DAF. The German workers were not happy
about this, and some of the Works Councils continued "under the
table" and at their own risk. Works Councils resumed again after
the war.

207 *It was all the workers could do:* According to Volkswagen records,
938 cars were created in February and 1,052 in May. *The British and
Their Works,* 24.

210 ———"Ten thousand cars and an empty stomach": The original
reads: Mehr und schmackhafteres Essen, sonst können wir vieles
nicht vegessen! 10,000 Wagen, nichts im Magen, wer kann das vertra-
gen?"

211 "There was one genuine currency": from documentary *George Marshall and the American Century.*

Chapter 28

217 "almost no free exchange of commodities, persons and ideas": Hartrich, 110.

218 "Here was a situation that was not ever going to": *George Marshall
and the American Century.*

218 ———"We needed everything"

219 *Dictators of democracy:* Hartrich explains it like this: " Demokratur, a
postwar addition to the German language, expressed the cynical reaction of the Germans to the political contradiction they perceived between what the Americans preached and what they practiced.
Formed from Demokratie and Diktatur, it focused on America's di-
lemma of 'dictatorship by democracy' ": 95–96.

219 "unless we exterminate or move twenty-five million": Loewenstein,
168.

220 "The American people want to help": U.S. Embassy: online at http://
usa.usembassy.de/etexts/burtstutt5688e.htm.

220–221 "did not coincide with what the German encountered in his
daily existence under Allied military-government rule": Hartrich, 91.

221 ———"democracy will only be acceptable to the Germans when": 98.

223 ———"Napoleon sought to impose democracy": 98.

Chapter 29

225 *Motivational Research:* Ernest Dichter and the Institute for Motivational Research started inviting the customers to something like group therapy sessions where they talked about the products and said what they liked and disliked. This was the first "focus group." It was a mix of "mining the unconscious" and also "active consumer input." Dichter, a prominent student of psychoanalysis who emigrated to the United States in 1937, began to connect the dots between basic drives in the human psyche to wider behavioral trends and decisions of the market as a whole. Universities such as Columbia in NYC and the University of Michigan developed their Social Research departments around this time too. Men like Rensis Likert, Robert Merton, and Paul Lazarsfeld studied ways of understanding sociological issues through things like focus groups and questionnaires. In 1941, the National Opinion Research Center was established, a social research organization that would go on to conduct national polls in everything from economics to mental health. And by the time Bill was writing his letter at Grey in 1947, the American Association of Public Opinion Research would have been created too.

226 "Our agency is getting big": All following quotes from Bill in this chapter are from Bill Bernbach's letter to Grey. 15 May 1947.

Chapter 30

232 *It's better if they can:* The words of Porsche and Ferry in this chapter come from stories told by Ferry himself in *We at Porsche* as well as from stories told in other books from the 1950s and 1960s such as *Small Wonder* and *The Amazing Volkswagen Story,* and also from other conversations and archival digging. These stories often get repeated, and the paraphrasing changes. I've tried to present the cumulative effect of these differing stories.

Chapter 31

234 Phyllis Robinson would later write Clairol's famous "It lets me be me" ad. She was also the first woman copy chief on Madison Avenue.

235 "a nice little guy, very creative": Willens quoting Ned Doyle, 19.

236 "agency bean counter": interview with Lois, Hiott.

237 "having with me partners who do what I don't do well": Bill interview, *DDB News.*

Chapter 32

239 "One way of life is based upon the will of the majority": Truman speech, 1947.

240 These quotes are often attributed to Stalin and have been for many years. I have no idea how to trace them back to where or when he said them.

241 *The argument for export:* Another line of reasoning that was made at the time was that exporting Volkswagens, if only for a limited time, would help prevent the market from being overtaken by American models. The claim was made that people needed cars, and giving Volkswagen a two-year window, under British control, to export cars to Switzerland and Sweden, could ultimately be a good thing for the British motor industry as well, as it would give them time to evaluate the needs of the European market and to adjust their own production ability.

Chapter 33

244 *Nordhoff's first day:* The contract is dated for January 1st, but the 5th was officially his first day after the Christmas break.

248 "Hold on a minute now": VW: *Ivan Hirst,* 89.

249 "warmth of contact" and "close but cold": *Ivan Hirst,* 90.

Chapter 34

251 Nuremberg Trials and the role of Henry L. Stimson: One very strong voice in opposing the Morgenthau Plan was lawyer and statesman Henry L. Stimson. In opposition to the punitive measures of the Morgenthau Plan, Stimson fought hard for proper judicial proceedings. His plans for how to hold German war criminals accountable eventually led to the Nuremberg Trials.

252 "Who else is to be held responsible": Speer, ITR, 516.

Chapter 35

260 "industrial feudalism": Mommsen and Grieger, Volkswagenwerk, 976; minutes of discussion concerning employment of the Director of Human Resources of 18 December 1947 (VWCA 98, no. 11); quoted in *The British and Their Works.*

262 "cradle to grave paternalism": London's *The Times.*

262 "work comrades": Edelmann, 161.

263 "I am firmly convinced": Notes from company meeting on October 1, 1949; *The British and their Works,* 51.

Chapter 36

264 These quotes by Bill are in many of his speeches in various forms, and also have simply been passed down by word of mouth in advertising for decades. A list of the most popular of them can be found

here on DDB Worldwide's website as a pdf: http://www.rm116.com/adcenter/files/bb_quotes.pdf

265   "There was a spirit of high adventure": Willens, 13.

265   "We did it to see Bill's eyes light up": Willens, 28.

269   "Two people who respect each other": Fox, 253.

Chapter 37

270   *The Cisitalia:* This car became so expensive to create that it was not finished until the 1950s, and only after a long, complicated journey. It was never raced.

272   "If I'd created it myself": according to Ferry Porsche.

Chapter 38

278   *Social Market Economy:* This form of economics was often called Ordoliberalism because the first ideas of it were published in the journal *Ordo,* the economic journal associated with the Freiburg School.

281   "like economic heresy": Hartrich, 141.

Chapter 39

282   "competition for the soul of Germany": *Economist* quoted by Hartrich, 117.

283   "The truth of the matter": George Marshall's speech, 5 June 1947.

284–285   *Possible buyout of VW plant:* The company was still up for bids, in a sense. The British did not want to own it; they wanted it to go to Germany again, they did not want it to be broken up and used for its designs and parts. For that reason, when France expressed interest in owning the factory, the British resisted and deferred. The Australians were an option, but as the Cold War progressed, they realized it would be too distant and too much of a gamble for them. The Russians and the Americans were both taking serious looks. The Cold War was already coming to life, and thus going to the Russians was avoided too. The most serious negotiations were with Ford. B.I.O.S. Final Report No. 768.

285   "What we're being offered here": Brinkley, 545.

Chapter 40

287   Oberst and Erhard dialogue: Hartrich, 4.

290   "It doesn't go; it flies": Nordhoff speech, from audio CD Der Kaefer in Wunderland.

Chapter 41

291   "transformed the German scene from one day to the next": Hartrich,132.

292   ———*Where were those eggs:* "The reaction of the public was mixed: pleasure at being able to once again find something to buy, and anger at those who had withheld their food from the market places. One hapless farmer's wife sampled the accumulated wrath of the hungry city dwellers when she arrived in the Frankfurt main station with two baskets of fresh eggs on the second day of currency reform. She was immediately surrounded by a crowd of hostile women . . . pelted by eggs": 132.

293   "was to instill pyschologically": Vernon Walters, *George Marshall and the American Century.*

295   *VW Bus:* At the time in Germany, there had been growing need of a delivery-type vehicle, one that could carry large loads. With all the reconstruction and hauling of people and parts in Europe, it was an obvious need, but not one that had been attempted in such a version before. Ben Pon himself had come up with a plan for such a vehicle, a truck based on designs of the Volkswagen that could carry a load of up to 750 kg. Pon's ideas were just sketches, but he had presented them to Colonel Radclyffe in 1947 and the idea had been buzzing around the factory since then. Detailed designs and sketches for such a vehicle came into existence once Nordhoff was at the helm. The same ideas of streamlining that Porsche had used with the original Volkswagen were incorporated into these new designs. The scooped-out nose gave the vehicle a low drag coefficient (0.44 compared to the Volkswagen's 0.39, which was quite good for the larger design) while at the same time providing more room for the driver and the passenger. Such a Beetle-based streamlined design also meant the car would need less fuel and have twice the acceleration value of any similar-sized truck. The first models of Type 2, the transporter or VW Bus as it's now known, were ready and unveiled in November of 1949.

295   "brocaded felt slippers": Nelson, 269.

296   "nonfunctioning blinkers": VW archive, *Changing Lanes.*

297   ———"I would like to request with all possible urgency"

Chapter 42

299   "really burning issues": *Changing Lanes.*

301   "master of equivocation" and wording of British decision: Turner thesis, Institut für Zeitgeschichte, Wolfsburg, 22248.

301   Nordhoff letters to Hirst and Radclyffe: *Ivan Hirst,* 95–97.

Chapter 43

302   "In Manhattan last week": *Time.* September 1954.

304   "Say something meaningful": Lore Parks, vice president and copy su-

pervisor at DDB in the 1960s said this in a speech she gave on 15 October 1966.

304 *Take Helmut Krone:* In his own words, "I'd like to propose a new idea for our age: until you've got a better idea, you copy. I copied Bob Gage for 5 years. I even copied the leading between his lines of type." From the September 1968 edition of *DDB News.*

304 "He had the capacity for infinite pain.": Challis, 239.

305 "A German Son": Challis.

306 *About Bauhaus spirit:* The Bauhaus was the defining European movement of the 1920s, alongside the Dutch de Stijl school in Holland (Piet Mondrian). This led him to discover the work of the Turkish and Russian Constructivists of the 1930s, the work of men like Fehmy Agha, who soon became the art director of *Vanity Fair* and *Vogue,* then toward the art and design of men like Lester Beall and the infamous Alexey Brodovitch. Brodovitch had started his career in Diaghilev's Ballet Russe and eventually come to the United States to teach a whole new kind of education in design, not to mention transforming the look and feel of *Harper's Bazaar,* pulling in artists from all over Europe, Russia, and Ukraine, men such as A. M. Cassandre, Irving Penn, Cartier-Bresson, and a man who would later play a role at DDB, Richard Avedon.

Chapter 44

309 "There some 9,000": *Autocar,* 3 February 1950.

311 *Bielefeld market research institute:* from *Changing Lanes,* 140.

313 "Only now do I have the feeling": Edelmann, 100.

Chapter 45

314 "What's wrong with that kid?" Lois.

314 "He's nasty": George Lois interview, and all following George Lois quotes from NYC interviews unless otherwise stated.

316 *More about Krone:* In 1957, he had begun work on a then relatively unknown new instant photograph camera company called Polaroid, and alongside Robert Gage, it would be DDB's ads that made Polaroid into a household name.

319 Julian Koenig's brother, a talented filmmaker, was blackballed during the McCarthy era on claims that his art took too communist an approach.

320 "splendid way to build a society": the remaining quotes attributed to Julian are from my interviews with him.

321   "It's a disaster working with Julian": Challis, 59.

322   "and it happens just like that": Bill interview, nurturing talent.

Chapter 46

323   "I think it's very Catholic": Patti Smith to Michael Silverblatt, KCRW, 5 March 2010.

324   *80 percent were refugees: New York Times,* 1955.

324   "That was a blessing for us": Hartrich, 219.

325   The Swiss registration figures . . . From 18 April 1956 issue of *Motor* magazine, in the article titled "The Volkswagen DeLuxe Salon: Road Test"

325   *More on Ivan Hirst:* With the dissolving of the Allied High Commission, all the army officers who had been stationed and working there were now out of jobs and expected to go home. This was very hard on many of them, after being here for ten years or more, with no real roots. Hirst found it difficult too, and he was not yet 40 years old. He'd been well taken care of by the British with a good job in Hamburg and a nice home. He wasn't sure what to do now, and again he thought about the Volkswagen plant. He wrote to Heinrich, perhaps hoping Nordhoff might offer him a job. Hirst was always welcome to visit, Nordhoff said. Hirst found Nordhoff frustrating, and even as he respected him, his anger toward him would grow throughout his life. They exchanged Christmas cards each year, but not much else. As Nordhoff rose and rose, and as Wolfsburg began to be thought of as "his city," as he brought it to life, he also talked less and less of the British and men like Hirst who had helped so much. The press made him the new father of the company, and it was only to Porsche that he ever gave credit; he rarely mentioned Ivan Hirst. Hirst and his wife, Marjorie, ultimately moved back to his parents' home in Manchester and started over again in the country of their birth. But great men always get their due. Years later, Volkswagen lovers would seek him out and he'd get the thanks he deserved.

326   "Today, everywhere in Germany": BBC *On This Day,* May 9.

326   *Der Spiegel* calls Nordhoff the king: Nelson, 133.

327   "social capitalism": Edelmann, 166.

329   "We got a lot of publicity": *Small Wonder,* 174.

329   ———"I had a big bill at the Roosevelt Hotel": Nelson, 174.

330   "No, this is no automobile," the man said, as Nordhoff would later tell it, "I've never seen one like this." Nelson, 175.

330   "The VW didn't look anything like anything—animal, vegetable, or automobile": Brinkley, 587.

Chapter 47

332 *General Motors, Chrysler, Ford:* Walter Chrysler formed his company in 1925. Buick, Cadillac, and Chevrolet were brought together to form GM.

333 George's dialogue here from interview. Hiott, 3 December 2009.

336 "He probably created": Walter Cronkite on Eisenhower, from documentary *Dwight D. Eisenhower: Commander in Chief.* At 1:15:30.

337 "In this book you'll discover": Vance Packard, *The Hidden Persuaders.*

Chapter 48

338 "dream job": These thoughts taken from interview with Carl Hahn in 2010.

338 Carl Hahn: Curiously, it would be Hahn's idea of "Europeanization" that would later mature into the global reach of what is today the Volkswagen Group.

342 ". . . the world is now facing" : Hartrich, 56.

342 "I couldn't understand what he was saying": Luftbruecke, documentary.

343 Nordhoff description: *Reader's Digest,* 1954.

343 Nordhoff article: "Comeback in the West": *Time* magazine, 1954.

343 "It has gained an unmistakable": *Road & Track,* 1956.

344 "the car that has come up fastest": *Time* magazine; "Renault on the Go," 6 January 1958.

Chapter 49

348 "People presented me": Carl Hahn interview Hiott. All following CH dialogue unless otherwise noted.

348 Hahn and VW had tried another, bigger agency before DDB, and it hadn't worked out.

348 "I still don't, to this day, know": Krone interview, *DDB News.*

348 "I was wondering what was going on in Bernbach's head because it really had Nazi connotations to it, the car, and I didn't think it was something we should do" Krone, Challis, 61.

349 "I don't have to tell *you* why": George Lois interview, Hiott. All following GL dialogue comes from these interviews.

350 *Helmut Schmitz* is another important name in this story, as he became the German counterpart at DDB, helping to revolutionize German advertising. Schmitz was there in Wolfsburg when Krone and Bill went too, and his relationship with them would last for years and years.

351 "This is an honest car": Railton, 172.

351 "I definitely remember" Challis, 61.

351 Bob Gage, rather than taking over art direction for the VW, assigned it to Krone. In Gage's words: "He was right for it." Gage also admits he thought the car was ugly and Krone "thought it was beautiful." Challis, 60.

352 *Some saw it as blood money:* At the time of negotiations between Israel and West Germany, a bomb was sent to Adenauer—a man gave it to two children on the street and asked them to deliver it to Adenauer's office, but they took it to the police instead. It blew up at Munich's police headquarters, killing one police officer. Adenauer chose not to make a big deal out of it, and to a large degree the whole event stayed out of the press. David Ben-Gurion, Israel's prime minister at the time, appreciated Adenauer's response and it deepened the relationship between the two states.

353 "You know what he just": from GL interviews and GL's books.

Chapter 50

354 "That brought up certain feelings": Julian Koenig interviews, Hiott, NYC, 2009. All Julian quotes from author interviews, unless otherwise stated.

354 DDB, because of the unique ethnic mix of the partners (Doyle, Dare, and Bernbach), was often referred to as "two Jews and an Irishman" (Della Femina). Now George, who was Greek and had been picked on by the Irish kids in his neighborhood, was working for two Jews and an Irishman on a German campaign for a car that still had Nazi connotations.

355 "secret, hidden basement": Version of George Lois's story as recounted here comes from author interviews with Lois. He has also recounted similar versions of this story in his own books and interviews over the years.

357 "This is just a prelude": *Time* magazine. "AUTOS: The New Generation" Monday, 5 October 1959.

Chapter 51

358 In *The Magic of Thinking Big,* Schwartz actually encourages people to scrutinize their thoughts and overcome self-doubt and worry: In essence, it's not the material objects or the accumulation of material objects that is the problem here. And Schwartz's book was not the problem: It was popular because people were so caught up in trying to keep up with the rat race that they were very unhappy and thus needed books to help them, as Schwartz's book did, to refocus on

what was meaningful. It seems like a paradox, but thinking big and thinking small can be exactly the same thing. The title caught people's minds because of the consumer culture, but what they were looking for was a cure to that kind of Bigness and an entry into real Bigness: meaning, connection, confidence, love.

359 "The illustration in this Volkswagen ad": *Advertising Age,* 5 October 1959.

361 ——"This copy is so . . . believable" The first ad would appear in the *Journal of Commerce,* which is now apparently owned by *The Economist.*

361 "We had conspicuous": Julian Koenig interview, 2009.

362 "Ten years ago": Koenig's first Think Small copy in *Life,* 22 February 1960.

362 *How did the VW become known as the Beetle?* The earliest time the car was referred to as a beetle is in a *New York Times* article from June 1938. Hitler, too, apparently said it should "look like a beetle," and at the time of the car's creation, it was a popular idea to look to insects for ideas of streamlining. Here, Julian uses the word too. He'd thought it looked very beetle-like when he saw it in Wolfsburg. It would eventually become the way Americans saw it, though the original VW was not officially named the Beetle for decades.

362 "I suppose that means you want me to make the image small": Lorin, 15.

365 "That's the header!": Story of Schmidt comes from Julian Koenig.

Chapter 52

366 "This little car missed the boat": copy from Lemon ad in *Life,* 11 April 1960.

367 "In the beginning": Della Femina, p. 28.

368 *Bud became Helmut:* pointed out in *Helmut Krone. The book* by Clive Challis.

368 "a writer of short sentences": Julian Koenig on *This American Life.*

368 "modern version of the Model T" because it "helped to open car ownership to people who might not have been able to afford a new car otherwise" Brinkley, 587.

370 "What I try to do with a creative person": Bill interview, DDB News.

Chapter 53

371 "While the levels of logic": Muir, 3.

373 "If you are Jewish": *Playboy,* "Snobs Guide to Cars," July 1964.

373 Quote from Alfred Brendel documentary *Man and Mask.*

374 "This was a distinct": Julian Koenig interview, Hiott.

Chapter 54

374 Franz Marc's "Tower of Blue Horses," created in 1913 and formerly owned by the Nationalgalerie in Berlin, was seized in 1937 and shown at the Munich "Degenerate Art" exhibition. The Nazis removed it from this exhibition when German officers from WWI, the same war in which Marc had fought in and died on the side of Germany, protested that the Nazis were defaming a fallen hero. In 1940, Herman Göring confiscated the painting for his private collection. Since the end of WWII, numerous rumors have been told about its possible whereabouts, but it has not been found.

374 Carl Hahn later told me that it was actually DDB that did the brochures for each of these exhibitions: Hahn, alongside Helmut Schmitz, and his partnership with DDB would ultimately bring the Creative Revolution in advertising to Germany too. Years later, on VW's fiftieth birthday, Carl Hahn was given a book by DDB about the VW ads. Think Small was the first ad in the book. And in that book, the creative credits read: Art: Helmut Krone. Text: Julian Koenig/Helmut Schmitz. Hahn's office is actually located inside the Wolfsburg Art Museum building, next door to the main exhibition space.

375 "These people come from many different": Nordhoff, brochure.

376 *Eighty thousand people living in Wolfsburg: New York Times,* 1963.

377 "economically unite the free world": Nordhoff's *Reden und Aufsaetze.*

Chapter 55

384 *one of the worst years in American history:* Among other things, 1968 had seen the assassinations of Martin Luther King and Bobby Kennedy, the TET offensive, and the disastrous riots and beatings at the Democratic National Convention in Chicago.

384 The first stadium concert was in 1965. It was in Shea Stadium, and the band was the Beatles.

Chapter 56

387–388 "An observation that has": Franz Marc, Sunday, 28 March 1915, 36.

389 "understand the sixties": Frank, 1.

391 "by 1993 sales were so far in the toilet": Kiley, AOL, 2011.

Chapter 57

400 *Hello again.* All these entries I copied from the guestbook into my notebook, then I mixed the geographies and a few words because

there's no way for me to get anyone's permission to use their words, and I didn't want to invade their privacy.

Chapter 58

401 "Do you know anything": Julian Koenig, Hiott.

403 "I knew there couldn't be only one": George Lois, Hiott.

405 The story of Helmut calling out "cuckoo" comes from author interview with George Lois.

405 "It is quite possible that the effect of DDB is": *Advertising Age,* Baker, 1 November 1965.

406 ". . . we disagreed sometimes about how an ad should be done": Challis, 218.

407 "I'll be back on Monday": Levenson, 3.

407 ———"What a different life it would have been": Challis, 217.

407 *More on Bernbach:* One of Bill's biggest sources of creativity was always reading and the arts. He became a chairman of the Municipal Arts Society. He was on the board of the Salk Institute. He was on the National Book Committee. He taught at NYU. He was vice chairman of Lincoln Center's film committee for a time. Julian would later work with Bobby Kennedy. Later, he worked with Bill Moyers on the Johnson campaign. He had the chance to have worked for Goldwater but he said though Goldwater had good ideas, he was an angry man and "anger begets anger and triggers conflict." DDB did one of the most memorable political TV ad campaigns of all time about the atomic bomb: the little girl picking the petals of a flower as a man counts down.

407 "like pigeons from a sleeve": Lois, *George Be Careful.*

Chapter 59

408 "For some years now our economic policy has": Original: Unsere oekonomische Politik ist schon seit Jahren zugleich Aussenpolitik gewesen.": Hartrich, 5.

415 "The assets of": Hawranek, *Der Spiegel,* 2009.

416 "Character . . . is formed primarily by a man's work." Schumacher, 59.

417 ———"We always need both freedom and order:" Schumacher, 69.

...And Going...

420 *diese Wagen läuft und läuft und läuft . . .* VW commercial: http://www.youtube.com/watch?v=ljPB0DanK74

422 "The U.S. is the most important market for the Beetle": Kiley, AOL, 2011.

423 Volkswagen opened the Westmoreland Assembly Plant in Pennsylvania in 1978. It was not profitable and closed in 1988.

423 In Tennessee there is another big work in progress.

423 Quotes from designers are in *Objectified,* 2009.

423 "While consumers do appreciate knowing": Adamson, *Forbes,* 2011.

425 Little Gidding: "Four Quartets" by T. S. Eliot: *We shall not cease from exploration /And the end of all our exploring /Will be to arrive where we started /And know the place for the first time.*

Index

o o

About the Author

o o

ANDREA HIOTT was born in South Carolina and
graduated with a degree in philosophy from the
University of Georgia in Athens. She then went
to Berlin to study German and neuroscience,
and ended up staying and working as a freelance
journalist. In 2005, alongside a group of
international artists and writers, she co-founded
an interdisciplinary journal called *Pulse,* now
created in partnership with the Institute for Cultural
Diplomacy. She serves as editor in chief.